52 WEEKS of PURSUIT

Volume 1

Mark G. Trotter

LIVING
FAITH
BOOKS

Dedication

To Jim White (Boss-Man),
my youth pastor and mentor
in those crucial first years after my salvation;
whose wisdom has influenced and shaped my ministry;
and whose godly example as a husband and father
was used of God to change the course and destiny of my life.

First published in 2019 by Living Faith Books.

Living Faith Books
3953 Walnut St
Kansas City, MO 64111

Cover Design: Brandon Briscoe

Formatting: Joel Springer

ISBN: 978-1-950004-01-0
Printed in the United States of America

TABLE OF CONTENTS

WEEK 1 / Genesis 1-15   17

WEEK 2 / Genesis 16-31   28

WEEK 3 / Genesis 32-50, Exodus 1-4   37

WEEK 4 / Exodus 5-24   45

WEEK 5 / Exodus 25-40, Leviticus 1-5   55

WEEK 6 / Leviticus 6-24   66

WEEK 7 / Leviticus 25-27, Numbers 1-12   76

WEEK 8 / Numbers 13-32   85

WEEK 9 / Numbers 33-36, Deuteronomy 1-17   94

WEEK 10 / Deuteronomy 18-34, Joshua 1-5   106

WEEK 11 / Joshua 6-24   116

WEEK 12 / Judges 1-21   126

WEEK 13 / Ruth 1-4, 1 Samuel 1-17   136

WEEK 14 / 1 Samuel 18-31, 2 Samuel 1-8   145

WEEK 15 / 2 Samuel 9-24, 1 Kings 1-3   155

WEEK 16 / 1 Kings 4-19   165

WEEK 17 / 1 Kings 20-22, 2 Kings 1-16   174

WEEK 18 / 2 Kings 17-25, 1 Chronicles 1-9   182

WEEK 19 / 1 Chronicles 10-29   189

WEEK 20 / 2 Chronicles 1-21   196

WEEK 21 / 2 Chronicles 22-36, Ezra 1-10   203

WEEK 22 / Nehemiah 1-13, Esther 1-7   212

WEEK 23 / Esther 8-10, Job 1-21   220

WEEK 24 / Job 22-42, Pslam 1-11   229

WEEK 25 / Psalm 12-53   236

WEEK 26 / Psalm 54-89   246

FOREWORD

Coming from an unchurched background in Miami, Florida, I was radically saved my sophomore year of high school in 1972. For the next several decades, alongside my formal Bible College education, I became the beneficiary of godly men who took a vested interest in my growth and personally invested their lives and their teaching into me. Other men made significant investments in me without ever knowing my name through the access I had to their teaching resources.

Through the investment of these men—and through the outworkings of their influence over the course of several decades—I fell in love with the word of God and made my life about consuming its truth. In addition to reading and studying the Bible, I read commentaries, listened to sermons, attended conferences and took extensive notes on every sermon I heard. I am mentioning all of this to say that, though I wrote the material in the following pages, it reflects an approach to the Bible that I learned from other men. And the accumulation and conglomeration of their teaching is, no doubt, so woven into my understanding, my vocabulary, and my presentation of the word of God that footnoting the enclosed material to give proper credit was simply an impossible task. Obviously, all direct quotes have been footnoted.

In the name of giving credit where credit is due, however, some of the people who have been major influences in shaping my thinking from a biblical standpoint in the early years were men like Warren Wiersbe, John Phillips, David D. Allen, Clarence Larkin, Harold Wilmington, A.W. Tozer, Andrew Murray, John MacArthur, and Jeff Adams. Though I have probably landed in a different place theologically than each of the men listed, this is my official recognition of their investment, along with my sincerest thanks.

I also give special thanks to my editor, Shannah Hogue; my graphic design artist, Brandon Briscoe; and to my precious wife, Sherry, for the countless hours invested in literally every aspect of this project.

Mark G. Trotter
WordStrong Ministries

INTRODUCTION

One of the most impactful passages of scripture in my life is Colossians 3:1-2. The reason it has proved to be so impactful to me is because of the tremendous depth I have found in its simplicity (2 Cor. 11:3). In Colossians 3:1-2, the Holy Spirit inspires Paul to make clear the wholesale change that is to be evidenced in the life of every person who has experienced God's transforming power in salvation. Paul writes, "If ye then be risen with Christ, seek those things which are above, where Christ sitteth on the right hand of God. Set your affection on things above, not on things on the earth."

The phrase "if ye then be risen with Christ" takes us back to Paul's explanation of salvation in Colossians 2:12. He explained that when we called on the name of Christ for salvation, from a spiritual standpoint we were (1) placed into Christ's death and died with Him, (2) placed into Christ's burial and buried with Him, and (3) we were placed into His resurrection — and the power of God which raised Christ from the dead is the same exact power He put into operation to raise us to new life in Him! Wow! That is some unbelievable power!

So, when Paul says in Colossians 3:1, "if ye then be risen with Christ" again, his point is since we have experienced such glorious transforming power, we are now to live the remainder of our lives in constant pursuit of the spiritual realities that are above our heads in the unseen world — not the things we can see down here on the earth, things that are part of the system of evil Satan used to hold us captive, and almost landed us in an eternity forever separated from God in the lake of fire! He's letting us know that the resurrection power of Christ has not only raised us out of the world's system, but above it, and, therefore, the pursuit of our life, for the rest of our life, should be to seek Christ and the things that are part of His everlasting kingdom. And, of course, both the Old and New Testaments are clear that the way God has chosen to reveal Himself to us is through His holy, inspired, infallible, inerrant and preserved word (Psa. 18:1-2; Heb. 4:12). That is actually what is behind the title of this devotional study: *52 Weeks of Pursuit: Pursuing God Through the Pages of His Word*. And that is why the theme verse for this study is Jeremiah 29:13: "And ye shall seek me, and find me, when ye shall search for me with all your heart."

52 Weeks of Pursuit is designed to provide a structure for reading through the Bible in a year, while also providing enough commentary to keep the reader focused on the big picture, as well as some of the more pertinent events that are key to comprehending God's purposes, plan and will in His unfolding revelation of scripture. Most of the 52 weeks reading assignments are based on a five-day reading schedule, though there are several weeks where it became necessary to include a sixth day. Though this book is laid out according to a 52-week format, the pace may certainly be increased or decreased according to the preference and learning style of each individual.

To receive the maximum benefit from this study, however, it is important to be aware of some of the basic biblical presuppositions that have framed its content.

1. THE BIBLE IS A SUPERNATURAL BOOK.

52 Weeks of Pursuit was written with a firm, overarching belief that the Bible is a supernatural book. By that I mean that the Bible is a book that was not only supernaturally **inspired** as *"holy men of God spake as they were moved by Holy Ghost"* (2 Pet. 1:21), but a book that has also been supernaturally **preserved** by God (Psa. 12:7; Mat. 5:18).

Because of the Bible's supernatural quality, the Apostle Paul let us know in 1 Corinthians 2:9–13 that our natural human *eyes* can't *see* its wisdom… our natural human *ears* can't *hear* it… and our natural human *hearts* can't *comprehend* it (1 Cor. 2:9). Its wisdom must, therefore, be *"revealed"* to us — a work the Holy Ghost is more than willing to do (1 Cor. 2:10) — as we employ the biblical principle of *"comparing spiritual things with spiritual"* (1 Cor. 2:13); or, comparing scripture with scripture. It is both the design and intent of *52 Weeks of Pursuit* to direct the reader into this God-ordained method which the Spirit uses to reveal His supernatural truth. That is why the **HIGHLIGHTS & INSIGHTS** section in each day's commentary is laden with numerous cross references.

2. THE BIBLE HAS THREE TREMENDOUSLY SIGNIFICANT LAYERS OF APPLICATION.

One of the key ways we are able to clearly see the supernatural quality of the Bible is by identifying its three layers of application.

1) The HISTORICAL Application.

This layer of application is simply understanding that the Bible always details for us a record of history that is 100% accurate. The events recorded in scripture really happened to real people, exactly as they have been recorded.

2) The DOCTRINAL (or PROPHETIC) Application.

This is the layer of application of which many believers are unaware, and yet this is the layer of application that actually brings the Bible to life! It is based on the belief that as God was inspiring the human authors of the Old Testament to record the events of history, He did it in such a fashion that they perfectly and graphically picture New Testament principles and truths that are sometimes hard to conceptualize.

3) The INSPIRATIONAL (or DEVOTIONAL) Application.

Because of the timeless quality of the Bible, the historical events we find in Scripture, along with their doctrinal (or prophetic) counterparts, have a very practical and powerful inspirational, or devotional, application to believers throughout history (1 Cor. 10:6,11; Rom. 15:4).

Perhaps an illustration can help to clarify these three layers of application.

In the Old Testament, God's people were in bondage in Egypt. Egypt at that time in history was the world power and was under the domination of a wicked king, who was called Pharaoh. Day in and day out, God's people labored under the taskmasters' whip, longing for a deliverer so they could be released from their bondage. Finally, God delivered them... and He did so through the blood of the Passover Lamb. That biblical account details exactly how the events unfolded, and reflects the HISTORICAL Application.

But what's interesting about that story is that more column inches are given to the record of that historical event than any other event in the entire Bible! The story of God's deliverance of Israel encompasses the books of Exodus, Leviticus, Numbers, Deuteronomy — and even on into the book of Joshua! Understanding the amount of biblical space given to this event causes us to have to step back and ask the obvious question: *WHY?* Why devote *one chapter* to something as monumental as the record of creation (Gen. 1), for example, and almost *five entire books* of the Bible to the account of God delivering the children of Israel out of their bondage in Egypt? The reason is simply this:

> The "exodus" is not just a **portion** of Israel's history.
> It is a **portrait** of the Christian life!

Because the fact is…

We, too, were in bondage in "Egypt." Egypt in the Bible is always a picture of sin and the world. And the Bible teaches us that this world's system is under the domination of a wicked "king," who is called Satan. And in our bondage, day in and day out, we labored under the taskmasters of sin, self and Satan, longing for a deliverer. And finally, God brought us out (which is what the word *"exodus"* means!) through the blood of the "Passover Lamb" (1 Cor. 5:7 says that Christ is our Passover!). Understanding that New Testament connection to Old Testament history reveals to us the DOCTRINAL or PROPHETIC Application.

Making that biblical connection, we are then able to see that this entire Old Testament section of scripture chronicling Israel's exodus, their wilderness wanderings and their ultimate entrance into the place of abundance in Canaan (Exodus–Joshua) is illustrating our journey as New Testament believers. We ought to allow God, by His Spirit and word, to help us navigate through the "wilderness" that lies between our exodus out of the kingdom of darkness and our entrance into the new type of existence God intended us to experience in this life – what Jesus referred to as the *"abundant"* life (Joh. 10:10b). And this, of course, reveals to us the INSPIRATIONAL or DEVOTIONAL Application.

God even helps us to make this devotional and inspirational application to our lives through Israel's exodus by specifically saying to us in 1 Corinthians 10:6, *"Now these things were our examples, to the intent we should not lust after evil things, as they also lusted"* And lest we still fail to make the connection that Israel's exodus was a picture of ours and that it has tremendous practical application to our individual lives, God repeats Himself five verses later, saying: *"Now all these things happened unto them for ensamples: and they are written for our admonition..."*

Throughout *52 Weeks of Pursuit*, the reader will find many references to these three layers of application.

3. THE BIBLE IS REALLY ALL ABOUT JESUS!

Perhaps the clearest and most beautiful explanation of what the Bible actually is is how the word "Bible" is expressed by our deaf friends through sign language. In this vehicle of communication, the word for "Bible" is conveyed by a combination of signs for two separate words: first, the sign for the word "Jesus" followed by the sign for the word "book." Quite simply, our deaf brothers and sisters refer to the Bible as the Jesus Book! And from a biblical standpoint, there could not be a more *precise* and *concise* explanation of the Bible! The Bible is God's book that is literally all about Jesus! And throughout His ministry, Jesus Himself repeatedly made that abundantly clear. For example…

In John 5:39, Jesus is in the midst of a discourse with the religious leaders of His day, the Pharisees, about the fact that He healed a man on the Sabbath. Recognize, of course, that Jesus is actually the Lord of the Sabbath (Mar. 2:28)! Jesus wants them to face the reality of who He is! So, He says to them, *"Search the Scriptures; for in them ye think ye have eternal life: and they are they which testify of <u>me</u>."* What Jesus is actually saying to them is, "Look: you pride yourself in knowing the Old Testament because you think you'll obtain eternal life because of what you know. But," he says, "you're actually missing the point! Because the entire Old Testament is really all about ME! And eternal life isn't about *what* you know — it's about *who* you know!" Jesus is revealing that the Old Testament is actually about *Him!*

In this same discourse with the Pharisees in John 5, Jesus says in verse 46, *"For had ye believed Moses, ye would have believed me; for he* (that is, Moses) *wrote of ME (Jesus!)."* By *"Moses"*, Jesus is referring to the Old Testament books written by Moses — Genesis, Exodus, Leviticus, Numbers, and Deuteronomy. Wow! Is that actually to say that these first five books are all about Jesus? Really? Where?

In another passage, at the beginning of Jesus' public ministry, John records the account of Jesus calling His twelve disciples. He says in John 1:45, *"Philip findeth Nathanael, and saith unto him, We have found him, of whom Moses in the law, and the prophets, did write, <u>Jesus of Nazareth</u>, the son of Joseph."* And once again, here is a very clear New Testament reference revealing to us that the entire Old Testament (the law and the prophets) is really all about Jesus!

In Luke 24, we read of the 40 day period after Christ's resurrection when He was teaching His disciples about the kingdom of God (Acts 1:3). Luke says of Jesus in Luke 24:27, *"And beginning at Moses and all the prophets, he expounded unto them in all the scriptures the things concerning <u>himself</u>."* And here is that same truth yet again! The New Testament quite clearly and repeatedly reveals that the Old Testament is really all about Jesus!

But again, if it really is all about Him, we would have to ask the obvious and glaring question: *where?* Or maybe the question is: *how?* How is it all about Him?

One of the key purposes of the Old Testament section of *52 Weeks of Pursuit* is to show exactly *where* and *how* Christ is revealed in the Old Testament. It is for this purpose that, in each day's reading assignment, after providing an **OVERVIEW** of the chapters, and **HIGHLIGHTS & INSIGHTS** concerning their content, there is a section entitled **CHRIST IS REVEALED.** In it, you will find *how* and *where* Christ actually is in the chapters in that day's reading with corresponding New Testament cross references.

As you make this incredible journey through the word of God, may *"the God of our Lord Jesus Christ, the Father of glory… give unto you the spirit of wisdom and revelation in the knowledge of him: the eyes of your understanding being enlightened; that ye may know what is the hope of his calling, and what the riches of the glory of his inheritance in the saints, and what is the exceeding greatness of his power to us-ward who believe, according to the working of his mighty power."* (Eph. 1:17–19)

Volume 1

WEEK 1, DAY 1: **TODAY'S READING: GENESIS 1–3**

OVERVIEW:

Creation of all things; creation of Adam and his bride; their commissioning; temptation by Satan; Adam and his bride rebel against God, forfeiting the Garden of Eden, their relationship with God, and the ability to fulfill their commission.

HIGHLIGHTS & INSIGHTS:

Genesis means "beginnings." The book of Genesis records the beginning of the universe, man, woman, marriage, the family, sin, judgment, death, sacrifice, salvation, worship, civilization, false religion and war.

In the first ten words of the Bible (Gen. 1:1), God sums up the five elements of science: *time* ("beginning"); *space* ("heavens"); *motion* ("created"); *matter* ("the earth"); and *energy* ("created"). In this simple verse, God destroys atheism ("*God* created"), denies polytheism ("God [*singular*] created"), and dispels evolution ("God *created*").

Man is the crown of creation. God formed the first man in His own image and likeness (1:26) and gave him the place of dominion (1:28) over the whole earth from the garden of Eden (2:8). Lucifer once held the position as the crown of creation (Ezek. 28:11–17; Isa. 14:12–14) and held dominion over the whole earth from Eden, the Garden of God (Ezek. 28:13). Since Lucifer couldn't have the place of God in the universe, he sought to have the place of God in the life of man. Sadly, he was successful (Gen. 3:6).

Some interesting things to note in today's reading…

God clearly defines marriage in the first two chapters of the Bible!

Sure, the world can invent its own scandalous definition of marriage, but the Creator of human life made His definition extremely simple and clear from the very beginning: Marriage = One man. One woman. One lifetime. (Gen. 1:27–28; 2:24)

Adam's Bible only has two verses!

God's instruction to Adam boils down to this:

1) Enjoy the intimacy of the physical relationship designed for marriage partners of the opposite sex until the whole earth has been replenished! (Gen. 1:28)

2) Eat as much as you want, from any tree you want—except one! (Gen. 2:16–17)

Wow! How hard could those two things possibly be? Well, evidently—pretty hard! (See Gen. 3:6)

Man's choice is represented in a tree.

Before the foundation of the world, God made an incredible choice. He didn't have to do it this way, but the glorious reality is—He did! He chose to create man in a relationship with Himself (3:8a). Through "the tree of the knowledge of good and evil" (2:17), God beautifully offered man the opportunity to exercise his will by making his own choice concerning this relationship. He could choose to *continue* his relationship with God by *not* eating of the tree, or he could choose to eat of the forbidden tree, suffering the consequence of spiritual death (2:16–17) and, thus, severing his relationship with the holy and loving God who created him.

In today's reading, man made the fateful choice to sever his relationship with God (choosing his own way) by partaking of that tree, and as a result, every person born from Adam's corrupted seed enters this world spiritually dead (Rom. 5:12; Gen. 5:3) and, thereby, separated from our perfectly holy God (Heb. 7:26; Isa. 59:2). Isaiah 53:6 is clear that all of us have made the same fateful choice Adam made: "All we like sheep have gone astray; we have turned every one to *his own way*." We aren't three chapters into the Bible before the entire human race has completely run amok!

And yet, there's good news! In the New Testament, we find that the holy and loving God of the Bible is still offering man a *choice* concerning his relationship with Him! God became a man in the person of Jesus Christ and, in His own body, bore the penalty of the curse of our sin through His death on the cross. And consider the words the Holy Spirit inspired the Apostle Peter to use to describe Christ's incredible sacrifice for us in 1 Peter 2:24, "who his own self [Christ] bare our sins in His own body [watch this now] on the *tree!*" The Holy Spirit inspired the Apostle Paul in Galatians 3:13 to use the same phrase, "Christ hath redeemed us from the curse of the law, being made a curse for us: for it is written, Cursed is everyone that hangs [here it is again] on a *tree!*" Man's relationship with God comes down to a decision we make—represented in the choice of a tree! To state it succinctly...

- The first man *chose* to partake of the fruit of a *tree* in the garden, choosing to *sever* his relationship with God.

- All of us have the opportunity to *choose* to partake of the fruit of the *tree* of Calvary (the forgiveness of sin!), choosing to *enter* a relationship with God!

Have you ever exercised your will in making that choice? (Acts 4:12; Rom. 10:9)

The first recorded words of Satan in the Bible.

The first recorded words of Satan (3:1) come in the form of a question, a question about what God said ("Yea, hath God said?"), about the *Word of God!* Questioning the Word of God will become Satan's M.O. throughout the remainder of the Bible—not to mention the remainder of human history (Matt. 4:3, 6; 2 Thes. 2:2).

The first temptation.

Genesis 3:6 tells us that Satan tempted the woman on three points: through the lust of the flesh ("the tree was good for food"), the lust of the eyes ("it was pleasant to the eyes"), and the pride of life ("a tree to be desired to make one wise"). And in 1 John 2:16 we learn that those are the only three plays in Satan's playbook. He continues to run those three plays simply because they keep working! In Matthew 4:1–11, however, when Satan tempted the Lord Jesus Christ the same way he tempted the woman, Jesus resisted the temptation by quoting Scripture that applied to each of Satan's specific attacks (Ps. 119:11). As James 4:7 says, "Resist the devil and he will flee from you."

The Author of the Bible (God) establishes its theme by the second chapter.

As we make our way through the *52 Weeks of Pursuit* we'll discover that the God of the Bible is extremely ordered, patterned, and structured. So one way He calls our attention to something that He doesn't want us to miss in the Bible is by breaking His pattern! It's His way of saying, "You may want to slow down here and see what's really going on!" Such is the case in Genesis 2:1–3. In chapter 1, God concluded each successive "day" of creation with the phrase, "And the evening and the morning were …" (1:5, 8, 13, 19, 23, 31). But something strange happens on the seventh day! The ultra-patterned God suddenly breaks His pattern! As He gives us the details concerning the seventh day, He does **not** say, "And the evening and the morning were the seventh day." Interesting.

And even more interesting is what He does include in His description of this seventh day! We find that, first of all, this is a day that God *blessed*. What was so special about this particular day that God chose to bless it? Secondly, we find that this is a day that God *sanctified*. The word *sanctified* means "to set apart." God set this particular day apart to Himself! He said, "This day is Mine." Or, "This is My day!" Again, it makes you wonder why He would do something like that? I mean, since He was the one who created every day, weren't they all His anyway? Did He really need to set a particular day apart in order for it to be His? And then, thirdly, we find that this is a day in which God *rested*. Wow! Rested? Really? Are we to assume that the omnipotent God of the Bible got Himself just plum tuckered out from the exhausting work of speaking things into existence on the previous six days? Did He really need a day to refresh Himself? Somehow, I don't think so!

What God is doing in 2:1–3 is giving us a glimpse into how He thinks and, thus, how He reveals truth in His supernatural Book. Because when we take the details of this seventh day and compare them (1 Cor. 2:10, 13) with what God reveals throughout the remainder of the Bible in terms of the unfolding of human history—it gets very exciting!

Because God finds another very interesting way to get our attention in 2 Peter 3:8 where He inspires Peter to write, "But beloved, be not ignorant of this one thing..." In other words, you may have missed some things in this book, but make sure this one doesn't get added to the list!" Oh, okay, Peter, so what's this "one thing" we better be sure not to miss? Here it is! Peter continues, "that one day is with the Lord as a thousand years, and a thousand years as one day." And obviously, God is letting us know here that, as God, He doesn't count time the way we do. That's an important truth, but somehow it doesn't seem to merit the fanfare of being "one thing" we better be sure not to miss!

However, if we were to take that little equation in verse 8 (one day = one thousand years) and plug it into Genesis 1 and 2, the first time "days" are mentioned in the Bible, what it would say to us is that after 6000 years (each of the first 6 days X 1000), the next 1000 years (represented in the seventh day) would be a period of 1000 years on this planet that would have *no evening or morning*, it would be the most *blessed* thousand-year period in the history of the world, it would be a time when God would be at *rest*, and it would be a period of time known as His Day—"the Lord's Day," or "the Day of the Lord."

From this point in the Bible, everything in it will be wrapped around that very *theme* and pointing to that very *day*! What day? The seventh Day! And it just happens to be...

- A thousand-year "day" that has no "evening or morning." (Rev. 20:1–5; 21:23)

- It is a thousand-year "day" that, throughout the Bible, is called"the Day of the Lord" or, simply, "that day" because He *sanctified* it as such.

- It is a thousand-year "day" when God will be *blessed* like no other time in human history because His Son is receiving the glory that is due His name. (Ps. 29:2: Phil. 2:9–11; Ps. 66:4)

- It is a thousand-year "day" when sin has been vanquished and God is finally at *rest*. (Heb. 4:3–5; Acts 3:19–21—"times of *refreshing*" and"times of *restitution*")

May "*that day*" be our pursuit through the Bible and through our lives (2 Tim. 4:8)!

CHRIST IS REVEALED:

As *Creator* – Genesis 1:1 (John 1:1–4; Heb. 11:3; Col. 1:16–17)

As the *Seed of the woman* – Genesis 3:15 (Isa. 7:14; 9:6–7; Gal. 4:4)

In *Adam* – Genesis 2:21–24 (John 19:34; Eph. 5:28–32)

> Note: God caused a sleep to fall upon Adam, and from the substance that came from his side, God formed for him a bride. God caused a "sleep" to fall upon the second Adam, Christ (1 Cor. 15:45–47), and from the substance that came from His side, God formed for Him a bride.

As the *Sacrificial Lamb* – Genesis 3:21 (Prov. 27:26)

WEEK 1, DAY 2: **TODAY'S READING: GENESIS 4–6**

OVERVIEW:

The sacrifices of Cain and Abel; Cain murders Abel; genealogy from Adam to Noah; the days of Noah; Noah's ark.

HIGHLIGHTS & INSIGHTS:

The entrance of sin into the perfect environment into which man was placed caused unbelievably devastating physical and spiritual ramifications. The curse of sin given in chapter 3 is already clearly manifest in chapter 4 as Cain murders his own brother.

Cain's is the religion of *human works*. Sadly, billions of people follow "Cain's religion" to this very day! Cain offers to God the fruit of his own labor. His offering recognized God as Creator, but it did not recognize Cain as a sinner. Abel's religion, however, is that of *faith*. His offering not only recognized God as Creator, but also his own sinfulness. He recognized that the blood sacrifice of a lamb was necessary to atone for his sin. (See Heb. 9:22; 11:4; Pro. 27:26.)

God asks Cain a question in Genesis 4:9, giving him the opportunity to confess his sin. Rather than own his sin in repentance before God, however, Cain goes "out from the presence of the Lord and dwelt in the land of Nod, on the east of Eden" (4:16). From this point in the Bible, virtually every positive move will be from *east to west*—while virtually every negative move will be from *west to east*. Note, also, that the word *Nod* means "to stray" or "to wander." Even the land in which Cain chose to dwell speaks of his willful choice to refuse to confess his sin, to trust the blood of the lamb, or to move toward God.

Where did Cain get his wife? It's the age-old question. Obviously, Cain married one of his sisters. By the time he takes a wife, Adam and Eve have many descendants, and there is no Divine prohibition against taking one of them to be his wife. The very idea of marrying a relative sounds strange and even repulsive to us, until we realize that, though in a much larger sense, all of us are descendants of Noah, and all of us who are married have likewise married another descendant of Noah.

Like Genesis 2:1–3, chapter 5 is another passage where God reveals to us how He thinks—and just how supernatural His Book actually is! Between the account of Cain and Abel in chapter 4 and the account of the days of Noah in chapter 6, God dedicates all of chapter 5 to provide us a genealogy. For many people who are seeking to read through the Bible in a year, genealogies can seem somewhat "boring" (if we're allowed to say that!), but they do at least provide an opportunity to do some speed-reading! Remember, however, that Proverbs 30:5 says, "Every word of God is pure!" Don't ever forget—everything in the Word of God is important, and there is nothing in God's Book that is random.

First of all, the genealogy is important because it provides for us a very significant timeline. It lets us know that there is actually a 1,653-year period between Genesis 4 and 6! Sure, that's important—but why not just provide a verse, or maybe a footnote at the end of chapter 4, that says something like, "And, oh, by the way, there's a 1,653-year gap between what just happened here with Cain and Abel and what happened next with Noah." Why 32 verses? That's more verses than God spent talking about the entire first six "days" in Genesis 1!

Here's the reason: through the meaning of the names of the 10 men who are listed in the genealogy in Genesis 5, God is going to do something to literally blow our doors off! Check this out...

> #1 is ADAM – and his name simply means "man."
>
> #2 is SETH – his name means "appointed."
>
> #3 is ENOS – his name means "desperately wicked."
>
> #4 is CAINAN – and his name means "possession."
>
> #5 is MAHALALEEL – meaning "praise of God."

#6 is JARED – which means "descent."

#7 is ENOCH – and his name means "dedicated" or "train up."

#8 is METHUSELAH – which means "man of the sword."

#9 is LAMECH – meaning "powerful." And,

#10 is NOAH – and his name means "rest."

And when we compare the meaning of these names to what God reveals throughout the remainder of the Bible, we see that, more than simply providing us a timeline through the listing of these ten men, God is actually using the meaning of their names to provide for us, not just an outline of the Bible, but an outline of the entire course of man's 7,000-year history on this planet! Let me explain…

The first man, Adam, meaning "man," represents *creation*—and specifically, the creation of man. And God did that in Genesis 1:26a. God said, "Let us make man in our image after our likeness."

Then, Seth, meaning "appointed," represents the *commission* God gave to the "man." After God created the man in Genesis 1:26, God *appoints* man to have dominion over everything in the earth and sea (v. 26b) and *appoints* him, or *commissions* him (along with his bride), to "be fruitful, and multiply, and replenish the earth" (v. 28). That's was his commission, or what he was appointed by God to do.

And then, there's Enos. After man was appointed to carry out the commission, something happened to his heart: it became "*desperately wicked*" (Jer. 17:9)! And so, Enos represents the *fall of man*—where man loses the "image of God" and, thus, the ability to reproduce "sons of God." He now only has the ability to reproduce "sons of Adam." After his fall, Genesis 5:3 says that Adam "begat a son in his own likeness, after his image," which, of course, was *fallen*. And that's a problem! It certainly looks as if the plan of God through man has been forever thwarted!

But through the next name, Cainan, meaning "possession," God shows us the direction the plan is going to go and how He will fulfill it. In Genesis 17, God enters into an unconditional covenant with a man by the name of Abram, or Abraham—along with "his seed" after him. That seed, of course, was the Nation of Israel! And listen to what God said to Abraham in Genesis 17:8, "And I will give unto thee, and to thy seed after thee, the *land* wherein thou art a stranger, all the land of Canaan, for an everlasting [listen to this next word] *possession*! God also told Abraham in 17:6, that "kings shall come out of thee." And we begin to see that the Nation of Israel would produce the King who would rule over the whole earth—and all of the Gentile nations of the world would come to Jerusalem to "praise the God" of Israel!

Interestingly enough, the next name in the genealogy is Mahalaleel, meaning "praise of God." And in 1 Kings 10, during the reign of Solomon, the Nation of Israel is the "praise of God," and the kings and queens of the Gentile nations are coming to bow before the king of Israel—the "son of David" (hello?)—and present him gifts. It is the glory days of the Nation of Israel as they are, indeed, the "praise of God."

But then, no sooner are we out of 1 Kings 10 before in 1 Kings 11, the Nation of Israel begins their "descent." And again, interestingly enough, the next man in the genealogy "just happens" to be Jared, meaning "descent." This "descent" ultimately leads them to be taken into Babylonian *captivity*, and there's no more king in Israel. And once again, it looks like the plan of God will not be fulfilled.

But then, all of a sudden, a very *dedicated* man comes on the scene. In fact, Jesus said of this man in Matthew 11:11, "Among them that are born of women there hath not risen a greater than John the Baptist." And he has some *instruction* for the Nation of Israel, doesn't he? He has some *training up* to do, as it were!

And just what is it that he's *training up*, or *preparing* the people for? Obviously, the *First Coming of Christ*—the coming of "the man of the sword!" (See Eph. 6:17; Jn. 1:1,14.) And the "man of the sword" (the meaning of the next name in the genealogy, Methuselah!) was here on this planet "full of grace and truth" (Jn. 1:14).

But when He comes the next time at the *Second Coming of Christ*, it won't be like that at all! Revelation 19:15 says that the "man of the sword" will use that sharp sword that goes out of his mouth to smite the nations! Mark 13:26 says He'll come, not with grace and truth, but with "great power and glory"! And the meaning of the name of the next man in the genealogy is Lamech, which means "powerful"!

And at the Second Coming of Christ, when He comes in power and smites the nations, putting his enemies under his feet, He will bring in that period of rest on the earth that we call the millenium—which, as we saw yesterday from Genesis 2:1–3, is the theme of the entire Bible and that to which all of human history is moving!

Wow! How about a God that can take the names of ten men and not only preach the message of the entire Bible, but completely unfold the entire history of mankind on the earth?! Note, then, that the ten-point outline of history revealed in Genesis 5 is as follows: 1) Creation. 2) Commission. 3) Fall. 4) Nation of Israel. 5) Reign of Solomon. 6) Captivity. 7) John the Baptist. 8) First Coming of Christ. 9) Second Coming of Christ. 10) Millennium.

Finally, notice in chapter 6, as God describes the sinful days of Noah, that there is not much difference between Noah's time and ours! He describes it as wicked (v. 5), violent (v. 11), corrupt (v. 12), and "every imagination of the thoughts of [man's] heart was only evil continually." Keep in mind that Jesus said in Matthew 24:37, "But as the days of Noe [Noah] were, so shall also the coming of the Son of man be." Even so, come, Lord Jesus!

CHRIST IS REVEALED:

Through Abel's *blood sacrifice* – Gen. 4:4 (Heb. 9:19–22)

Through Abel's *sacrificial lamb* – Gen. 4:4 (John 1:29; Heb. 11:4)

In *Methuselah* (meaning "the man of the sword") – Gen. 5:27 (John 1:1,14; Eph 6:17; Heb. 4:12; Rev. 19:15)

WEEK 1, DAY 3: **TODAY'S READING: GENESIS 7–9**

OVERVIEW:

Noah, his family, seven pairs of every clean living creature and one pair of every unclean living creature enter the ark as God had commanded; the great flood; the rainbow covenant; the new beginning; the curse upon the descendants of Ham (the Canaanites).

HIGHLIGHTS & INSIGHTS:

"The Lord said unto Noah, Come thou and all thy house into the ark" (Gen. 7:1). It is the first invitation extended by God in the Bible. Hallelujah, it certainly isn't His last! In Matthew 11:28, Jesus said, "Come unto me … and I will give you rest." In Acts 16:31, Paul said, "Believe on the Lord Jesus Christ, and thou shalt be saved, and thy house." The Bible ends with God extending a similar invitation: "Come. And let him that is athirst come. And whosoever will, let him take the water of life freely" (Rev. 22:17).

People constantly want to call Noah's world-wide flood into question. The fact of the flood is proven by God's record of it here in Genesis through Moses (Gen. 7:1–8:22), as well as by the Lord Jesus Christ (Matt. 24:37-39; Luke 17:26), the prophets (Isa. 54:9), and the apostles (1 Peter 3:20)—along with the ancient historical records of virtually every civilization on the earth!

More importantly, the flood teaches us at least two key practical principles that we will see repeated throughout the entire Bible:

1. God will punish sin!

In Genesis 7, the ark was God's secure refuge from the judgment that was to come. Just as Noah was saved from the wrath to come and found rest within the ark, Colossians 3:3 says to those of us who have called upon the name of the Lord Jesus Christ, "your life is hid with Christ in God."

2. There must be death to the old before He will establish the new.

Notice that after the death of all mankind, God begins again with eight souls (Noah, his three sons, and each of their wives). From this point in the Bible, we will discover that eight is the number of new beginnings. In 8:15, God speaks to Noah and tells him to take his family out of the ark along with all of the animals—which, no doubt, brought a jubilant "praise the Lord!" from everyone! Taking a 7-day and 7-night cruise might be nice, but 370 days is a little much! And my idea of a cruise is not exactly a floating zoo! Though in Noah's case—it sure beat staying home!

But recognize, God is starting over. Just as He had given King Adam I dominion over the earth and had given him the commission to "be fruitful, and multiply, and replenish the earth" (Gen. 1:28), God starts over with King Noah I, likewise giving him dominion over the earth and commissioning him to "be fruitful, and multiply, and replenish the earth" (9:1–2). And one of the principles we need to learn early on in our journey through the Bible is that anytime God moves in a significant way—we need to be looking for Satan to counter! Especially when man's commission is involved!

Noah is no sooner off of the boat before Genesis 9:20–21 says, "And Noah began to be an husbandman, and he planted a vineyard: And he drank of the wine, and was drunken; and he was uncovered within his tent"—which is usually what happens when people get drunk! They usually end up taking their clothes off—which usually leads to some kind of sexual sin. Which, in this case, it did! Though God thankfully spares us the gory details, Noah's son, Ham, commits an act of sexual perversion with his father. We discern that from the fact that, in Genesis 10:19, Ham's children settle in a place that becomes known for homosexual activity—a place called Sodom and Gomorrah!

So here is the man to whom God had extended grace and had chosen to give the earth a new beginning—and he's lying drunk, naked on his bed, in a perverted, sinful, and unnatural sexual relationship! And from here, the whole earth begins to be filled with corruption once again, as we will see demonstrated in Genesis 11.

From an extremely practical standpoint, may we all learn that just as Satan sought to come against Adam because of his commission, and came against Noah because of his commission, Satan will likewise come against us because of our commission! (See Matt. 28:19–20; 2 Tim. 2:2) May God help us!

Finally, notice two things. In 9:8-17, God enters with Noah what verse 16 describes as an "everlasting covenant." This is the first of five covenants in the Bible that God refers to as "everlasting."

- The Noahic Covenant (Gen. 9:16)
- The Abrahamic Covenant (Gen. 17:7)
- The Priestly Covenant (Num. 25:10–13)
- The Davidic Covenant (2 Sam. 23:5)
- The New Covenant (Jer. 32:40).

And as God replenishes the earth through Noah's three sons (9:18-19), note that through Shem come the Asians, through Ham come the Africans, and through Japheth come the Europeans.

CHRIST IS REVEALED:

Through the *Ark* – Gen. 7:1, 7 (Acts 4:12; 2 Cor. 5:17)

> Remember: To be delivered from the wrath of God to come (1 Thess. 1:10), you must be "in Christ," the only ark of safety (Col. 3:3).

WEEK 1, DAY 4: **TODAY'S READING: GENESIS 10-12**

OVERVIEW:

The descendants of Noah; Babel: the origin of races and languages; God's call and covenant with Abram; Abram's journey to Canaan and Egypt.

HIGHLIGHTS & INSIGHTS:

The genealogy in chapter 10 lists one name after the other—until we get to Nimrod (vs. 8–10). All of a sudden God interrupts the list to provide us His commentary concerning this guy. This is another way God draws our attention to something extremely significant He wants us to see! In fact, God does the same thing in the genealogy in 1 Chronicles 1:10 when He gets to the name Nimrod!

Nimrod is the grandson of Ham, who, as we've already seen, is associated with a curse. His name means "rebel," and his epithet is that "he was a mighty hunter before [or, against] the Lord" (Gen. 10:9). He was obviously a keen hunter of animals in the land of Shinar, but the context lets us know that he was also hunting something else—men! Men to become a part of a kingdom (v. 10). Nimrod wanted to set himself up as king over a kingdom of rebellion against God!

Nimrod and his kingdom are significant because the theme of the Bible is a *kingdom* in which our Lord Jesus Christ will rule and reign over all the earth from His throne in Jerusalem for a period of 1000 years. (See Gen. 2:3; 2 Peter 3:8; Rev. 20:1–5.) As we've seen, the history of mankind and God's record of it in the Bible is nothing more than God moving to put His Son on that throne—and Satan doing everything he can, not only to stop Him, but to put himself there! (See Isa. 14:12–14; 2 Thess. 2:4.)

Note that the first mention of *kingdom* in the Bible is in reference to a king, whose name means "rebellion," who is seeking to establish a world empire. If you are unfamiliar with the Law of First Mention in terms of Bible study, it is simply this: God has so orchestrated the revelation of His Word that the first time a key biblical word or principle is mentioned in the Bible, the usage of the word foreshadows its future scope. For example, the first time love is mentioned in the Bible is in Genesis 22:2. The context is that of a loving father offering his only begotten son as a sacrifice. The future scope is obvious (Jn. 3:16)! And the future scope of the first mention of kingdom is that during the Tribulation Period there will be a king of rebellion, referred to biblically as the Antichrist, or the Beast (1 Jn. 2:18; Rev. 6:1; 13:1–18), who will come on the scene seeking men and women to be a part of a world empire that is set in opposition to all that Christ and His kingdom is and shall be.

Note that the first mention of *Babel* is also in Genesis 10:10 and is likewise connected to the reign of the Antichrist. From this point in the Bible, Babel or Babylon (Hebrew = Babel, Greek = Babylon) will always stand for that which is in opposition to God and His people, and its ultimate demise is not recorded until Revelation 17 and 18, near the end of the Tribulation Period!

Nimrod recognized in Genesis 11:1–4 that, to establish a world empire, he would need to unify the people, both governmentally and religiously—and thus, the statement in verse 4, "Let *us* build *us* a city and a tower." The city is the symbol of government, and the tower symbolizes religion. Practically speaking, the city and tower of Babel were Satan's attempt to unite the people of the earth in a one-world government, with a one-world religion, under one king. Obviously, Nimrod is a forerunner and type of the Antichrist, a king of rebellion who seeks to establish a world empire by unifying the people of the earth in a one-world government and religion. This is the principle of Ecclesiastes 3:15: "That which hath been is now; and that which is to be hath already been." In other words, if you want to understand the things that are happening in the present and the things that will be happening in the future, you must understand the things in the past. Or, as the old saying goes, "History repeats itself!"

In striking contrast to rebellious Nimrod, chapter 12 introduces us to faithful Abram—a man who symbolizes submission to God. God's call to Abram was: "Get thee out of thy country…unto a land that I will show thee…and in thee shall all families of the earth be blessed. So Abram departed, as the Lord had spoken unto him" (12:1, 3–4). Without hesitation, consideration, or deliberation, in faith, Abram left his homeland and all that he knew and loved for an unidentified and an unspecified land (12:1). For his unwavering faith, God holds up Abram as a shining example (Heb. 11:8).

Even though Abram exercised such great faith in God on one hand, when famine struck (Gen. 12:10), rather than exercise that same faith and trust in God, it says that "Abram went down into Egypt." This is the first mention of Egypt in the Bible. Note that Egypt is always a downward move in Scripture and will always be associated biblically with the world and sin. The point of 12:10 is that, rather than trust God, Abram looked to the world to meet his needs.

Abram exemplifies the fine line between walking by *faith* and walking by *sight* and between walking in the *Spirit* and walking in the *flesh* (Gal. 5:16-17).

CHRIST IS REVEALED:

As the *promised seed of Abraham* – Gen. 12:3 (See Gen. 18:18: Matt. 1:1; Acts 3:25–26; Gal. 3:16.)

In *Abraham* – (Abraham is a type of Christ in that he leads the way to a better land of promise. See Heb. 11:8–11, 13–16.)

WEEK 1, DAY 5: **TODAY'S READING: GENESIS 13–15**

OVERVIEW:

Abram and Lot separate; Abram moves to Hebron, builds an altar; Melchizedek's blessing upon Abram; God's covenant with Abram.

HIGHLIGHTS & INSIGHTS:

After the downward move into the world's system of evil and its web of sinfulness in chapter 12, "Abram went up out of Egypt" (13:1), back to the place of blessing and intimacy with God that he had at the first (13:3–4). It's the same solution our Lord Jesus Christ identified for those times we find ourselves in the world's snare, having "left our first love." Jesus said, "Remember therefore from whence thou art fallen, and repent, and do the first works" (Rev. 2:4–5). Do you need to follow Jesus's admonition and Abram's example? Note the simplicity of Jesus's counsel in Revelation 2:5: Remember. Repent. Repeat.

We might call the situation between Abram and his nephew, Lot, in Genesis 13:5–9, "the curse of God's blessing!" Sometimes even the blessing of God in our lives forces us to make tough decisions. As we observe these two men navigating through this much-needed, but volatile separation, Lot illustrates a *carnal* believer—walking in the flesh—while Abram illustrates a *surrendered* believer—walking in the Spirit.

Notice that Lot chooses the lust of the eyes and the lust of the flesh (13:10–11). He chooses Sodom, thinking it is a place of peace, protection and prosperity, when in reality, it was the exact opposite. It was actually a place of conflict, danger, and cursing! Lot illustrates how important it is that we look through *spiritual* eyes rather than *physical* eyes in order to live the victorious Christian life. Paul said, "While we look not at the things which are seen, but at the things which are not seen: for the things which are seen are temporal; but the things which are not seen are eternal" (2 Cor. 4:18).

Chapter 14 illustrates that the Spirit-filled life is a life that is blessed by the Lord Jesus Christ, as Melchizedek blesses faithful Abram. Note that Melchizedek, whose name means "Righteous King," is the King of Salem (Hebrew, "shalom" or peace) and is a priest of the most high God. Note, also, that this mysterious king-priest of Jerusalem, who is given no human biographical or genealogical background, blesses Abram and receives tithes from him. Sound familiar? Melchizedek is, obviously, a picture and type of our Lord Jesus Christ. Like Melchizedek, the Lord Jesus Christ, our Righteous King, is not of human descent. He is the Prince of Peace, the God and Lord of peace, and will soon take up His throne in Jerusalem to rule as King over all the world. He blesses those who are surrendered to Him, and He alone is worthy of tithes of all that we possess.

Those, like Abram, who are surrendered to Christ's Lordship, hear the word of the Lord in their hearts saying, "Fear not...I am thy shield, and thy exceeding great reward" (Gen. 15:1).

CHRIST IS REVEALED:

In *Melchizedek, the King of Salem* (Jerusalem), *The King of Peace, The Priest of the Most High God* – Gen. 14:18–20 (Ps. 110:4; Heb. 7:1–6, 17, 21; Isa. 9:6; Rom. 15:33; 2 Thess. 3:16)

WEEK 2, DAY 1: **TODAY'S READING: GENESIS 16–18**

OVERVIEW:

Birth of Ishmael of Hagar; Abram's name changed; the covenant of circumcision; Sarai's name changed; Isaac promised to Abraham and Sarah; Abraham's prayer for Sodom.

HIGHLIGHTS & INSIGHTS:

God had already promised Abram a son (Gen. 15:4), but after ten long years, Abram and Sarai were still childless—and neither of them were spring chickens at this point! Abram was 85, and Sarai was 76!

Rather than trust the Word of God by faith, Sarai turned to the world for help and sought to fulfill God's will in the power of the flesh. (Sound familiar?) Sarai offered Abram her Egyptian maid, Hagar, to be assured of a seed for Abraham. (Note: The Hurrian laws from that period describe this as a custom of the day. If a son was born of that union, he would legally be regarded as the wife's.) At the age of 86, Abram did receive a son, Ishmael, by Hagar.

Sarai's dreadful decision (and Abram's willful compliance) points to one of the most difficult lessons of the Christian life—learning to wait upon the Lord (Isa. 28:16)! Sometimes God places us in a position of testing our faith, and we may have to wait two weeks, two years, or as in Abram's case, twenty-five years for our prayer to be answered—or for God's promise to be fulfilled.

The result of Abram and Sarai's decision to run ahead of God—attempting to carry out God's will through carnal means—should remind us of the painful consequences of trusting the power of the flesh. To this day, Ishmael (the Arabs) and Isaac (the Jews) are in conflict (and, many times, at war) with each other—and their conflict will continue until the Second Coming of Christ. The situation illustrates perfectly the principle of Galatians 5:17: "The flesh lusteth against the Spirit, and the Spirit against the flesh: and these are contrary the one to the other." We would do well to ask ourselves: "What prayer am I trusting God to answer, or what promise am I trusting God to fulfill, where I might be tempted to get ahead of God and try to bring it about in the power of the flesh?"

By the time we come to chapter 17, recognize that Abram was 99 years old and Sarah was 90. Obviously, it is humanly impossible for Sarah to give birth to a child. But God revealed something tremendously significant to Abraham in 17:1—"I am the Almighty God!" In 18:14, God appears to him again, and asks, "Is any thing too hard for the Lord?" Oh, may we remember this reality today with the prayer we're trusting God to answer or the promise we're trusting God to fulfill. Jesus said in Luke 18:27, "The things which are impossible with men are possible with God!"

Note that through Ishmael and Isaac, God is already teaching us the most important truth in all of Scripture! He rejects the first birth (that which is born of the flesh) and accepts the second birth (that which is impossible with men but is possible only with God)—the spiritual birth! (See John 3:3–6.)

Some other interesting things to note…

In the same way that God gave Abram a seal of His covenant with him in Genesis 17:10–14 (circumcision), God gives to those of us who are children of Abraham by faith in Christ (Rom. 4:11–13; Gal. 3:7) a seal of His covenant with us—the Holy Spirit! (See Eph. 1:13; 4:30.)

God changed the name of Abram and Sarai. Abram, which means "high father," is changed to Abraham, meaning "father of many nations," reflecting his new relationship with God and his new identity based on God's promise of seed. Sarai, which means "my princess," is changed to Sarah, which simply means "princess." The limiting personal pronoun *my* is dropped from the meaning of her name since she would become the ancestress of the promised nations and kings. Note, also, that in the same way God changed their names, as the seed of Abraham (Gal. 3:16), God changed our name the moment we placed our faith in Christ, reflecting our new relationship with Him and our new identity in Him! (See Acts 11:26; Rev. 3:12.)

God enters into an everlasting, unconditional covenant with Abraham (Gen. 17:7–8). The promise of God to Abraham wasn't dependent upon Abraham's faithfulness to God, but on the faithfulness of God to His own name and to the promise of His Word to Abraham. Once again, in that same way, as Abraham's children (Gal. 3:6–7), God likewise entered into an everlasting, unconditional covenant with us! (See John 3:16; Rom. 8:37–39.) God's promise of salvation to us is not dependent upon our faithfulness to God (or we'd all lose it!), but is based upon God's faithfulness to His own name and to the promise of His Word to us. Praise the Lord!

CHRIST IS REVEALED:

As the *Angel of the Lord* – Gen. 16:7

> Note: The Angel of the Lord is a pre-incarnate appearance of the Lord Jesus Christ. Those, like Hagar in this passage, who had an encounter with the Angel of the Lord recognized that in seeing this Angel, they had seen God. (See Gen. 22:11–18; 31:11–13; Exod. 3:2–5; Num. 22:22–35; Judg. 6:11–23; 13:2–5; 1 Kings 19:5–7.)

As the *Seed of Isaac* – Gen. 17:19 (See Luke 2:23–24; Heb. 11:18.)

WEEK 2, DAY 2: **TODAY'S READING: GENESIS 19–21**

OVERVIEW:

The visit of the two angels to Lot; Sodom destroyed; Lot's wife; Lot and his daughters; Abraham and Sarah sojourn in Gerar; the conflict between Abraham and Abimelech over Sarah; the birth of Isaac; Hagar and Ishmael; the covenant between Abraham and Abimelech.

HIGHLIGHTS & INSIGHTS:

There's *a lot* to learn from the life of Lot!

It's easy to read over the simple phrase in Genesis 19:1, "and Lot sat in the gate of Sodom," and miss the incredible significance. In the Old Testament, "sitting in the gate" meant that you were somebody. I mean, when you spent your afternoons hanging out with the fellas down at the gate, you had achieved some pretty major status in the community. But let me assure you, being a bigwig in a city as morally corrupt and whacked out as Sodom is not the position any God-follower should ever want to attain! In the words of James, I think that might be called "friendship of the world" (Jam. 4:4). And this wasn't a position Lot attained overnight! It was actually the culmination of Lot's gradual downward spiral into a life of carnality, worldliness and ungodliness. God carefully details Lot's downward spiral into a life of sin in a seven-chapter span in the book of Genesis. Check out the progression…

- Lot "lifted up his eyes" toward Sodom. (13:10)
- Lot "pitched his tent" toward Sodom. (13:13)
- Lot "dwelt" in Sodom. (14:12)
- Lot "sat in the gate" of Sodom. (19:1)
- And even after God confirmed its destruction, Lot "lingered" in Sodom. (19:15-16)

And we must not miss that this pattern is repeated over and over in the lives of many in Scripture—as well as the lives of many believers right up to the present day! Seldom, if ever, are Christians suddenly overtaken by the world. As in the case of Lot, it begins with *friendship* with the world (Jam. 4:4); then becomes *loving* the things of the world (1 John 2:15); until finally, the ways of the world have become such a part of the fabric of who we are, we become completely *engulfed* by Satan's diabolical system of evil (Eph. 2:2)—much like we were before God delivered us out of it at salvation. (See 2 Tim. 2:26; 2 Pet. 1:9.)

Satan makes this world's system look attractive, promising, alluring and enticing, but it's designed to chew us up and spit us out! When Abraham gave Lot the choice of the land he wanted (13:8–11), Sodom appeared to Lot to be a place of peace, prosperity, and protection. In the end, it turned out to be a place of conflict, compromise, and casualty. Lot went into Sodom with his communion with God, his wife, his testimony, his character, and his wealth, and came out with none of them! None!!! Oh, may God help us to see this present evil world for what it is!

Lot, who in this passage lost everything to the fire of God's judgment (19:15–29), pictures for us the life of a worldly believer who loses everything to the fire of God's judgment at the Judgment Seat of Christ (1 Cor. 3:11–15). God affirms through Peter (2 Pet. 2:7–8) that Lot (like many believers today) was saved—"yet so as by fire" (1 Cor. 3:15).

And just a brief note to husbands and fathers—Lot's life screams out the urgent warning of how the decisions we make effect our wives and children. (Gen. 19:26, 30–38).

The story of Lot's wife is a sermon in itself. Jesus said it very succinctly, "Remember Lot's wife" (Luke 17:32). What a power-packed three-word sermon! The Lord Jesus Christ holds her up as an example and warning to all who reject His offer of salvation.

The atrocity that was schemed and carried out by Lot's daughters (Gen. 19:30–38) began the Moabites and Ammonites. These two nations were consistently a thorn in Israel's side (Num. 25:1–3; 1 Kings 11:33), teaching us, once again, that there are always painful consequences to sin.

It seems unthinkable that Abraham would try to pass off Sarah as his sister (Gen. 19) within twenty years of making the same mistake with Pharaoh, until we realize that God spends a great deal of time and extends a great deal of mercy teaching us the same lessons over and over again.

In chapter 21, God proves His faithfulness to His Word. Isaac, the miracle child of promise, is born to Abraham and Sarah.

CHRIST IS REVEALED:

In *Isaac* – Genesis 21:12 (Gen. 17:19; Gal. 3:16)

WEEK 2, DAY 3: **TODAY'S READING: GENESIS 22–24**

OVERVIEW:
Abraham's willingness to offer his only son, Isaac; God's reaffirmation of His covenant with Abraham; Sarah's death; Isaac's marriage to Rebekah.

HIGHLIGHTS & INSIGHTS:
Genesis 22 is one of the greatest chapters of the entire Bible. It lifts the curtain for the dress rehearsal of Calvary. In this chapter, God takes out His divine brush and paints an unbelievably beautiful picture of the offering of His only begotten Son.

Note the incredible similarities…

- Isaac's birth was prophesied in Genesis 18:10: "<u>Sarah</u> thy wife shall <u>have a son</u>."
  Christ's birth was prophesied in Isaiah 7:14: "Behold a <u>virgin</u> shall conceive, and <u>bear a son</u>."

- Isaac's birthday was preset. Genesis 21:2 says that Isaac was born "at the <u>set time</u> of which God had spoken to [Abraham]."
  Christ's birthday was preset. Galatians 4:4 says, "But when the <u>fulness of the time</u> was come, God sent forth His Son, made of a woman."

- Isaac received his name before his birth. Genesis 17:19 says that God told Abraham, "Sarah thy wife shall bear thee a son … and <u>thou shalt call his name</u> Isaac."
  Jesus received His name before His birth. Matthew 1:21 says that God told Joseph, "And she [Mary] shall bring forth a son, and <u>thou shalt call his name</u> Jesus."

- Isaac was <u>conceived by a miracle</u>. (Gen. 18:11–14)
  Christ was <u>conceived by a miracle</u>. (Luke 1:34–37)

- Isaac was the <u>only begotten son of his father</u>. (Gen. 22:2; Heb. 11:17)
  Jesus was the <u>only begotten Son of His Father</u>. (John 3:16)

- God had in mind a particular place for Abraham to offer his son, on one of the mountains in the land of Moriah (Gen. 22:2). Moriah means "chosen by Jehovah," and while the passage doesn't tell us which mountain, but we've already seen enough of the picture to know which mountain in particular Jehovah had chosen! Genesis 22:3 says, "And Abraham … and Isaac his son … went unto <u>the place</u> of which God had told him."
  God also had in mind a particular place to offer His own Son. Luke 23:33 says, "And when they were come to <u>the place</u>, which is called Calvary, <u>there</u> they crucified him (Christ)."

- Both Isaac and Jesus rose from the dead. Isaac <u>rose from the dead</u> figuratively after three days (Gen. 22:3–4; Heb. 11:19). Jesus, of course, <u>rose from the dead</u> literally after three days! (1 Cor. 15:3–4).

- Isaac walks to the place of sacrifice the Lord had shown his father, <u>carrying the wood that was to be used for his own execution</u>. (Gen. 22:5–6)
  Jesus walked to the place of sacrifice shown Him of His Father, <u>carrying the wood that was to be used for His own execution</u>. John 19:17 says, "And he [Jesus] bearing his cross went forth into a place … which is called … Golgotha."

The instrument of sacrifice didn't fall upon Isaac in Genesis 22:9–14 because he was just the picture! One day, 1900 years later, it would fall on the Lord Jesus Christ. And when Isaac asks his father about where the lamb was that would be offered as the sacrifice for sin, check out the answer Abraham gives: "Abraham said, My son, God will provide himself a lamb" (22:8)! Of course, there was the immediate fulfillment (v. 13) in the ram caught in the thicket (i.e., a male lamb wearing a crown of thorns!). But there is a prophetic fulfillment as well! Abraham did not say, "God will provide a *lamb for himself*." He distinctly said, "God will *provide himself* a lamb!" Obviously, Jesus was the fulfillment of the picture.

John said, "Behold the Lamb of God, which taketh away the sin of the world" (John 1:29).

As we stand in awe of God and His incredible, supernatural Word today, may we keep this in mind: If ever there was a promise that God might have reneged on—which is obviously impossible!—but if ever there was a promise that God might have changed His mind about, it would have been the promise of offering His beloved Son! And we can rest assured that if He kept that promise, He's going to keep all of the other ones! Paul put it this way in Romans 8:32: "He that spared not his own Son, but delivered him up for us all, how shall he not with him also freely give us all things?"

CHRIST IS REVEALED:

In *Isaac's willingness to be offered* – Genesis 22:1–14 (John 3:16; Luke 23:33: Heb. 11:19; John 1:29)

In *Isaac's relationship to his bride* – Genesis 24

> Note: In Genesis 24, Abraham (a picture of God the Father) sends out his unnamed servant (who is a picture of the Holy Spirit, who is not come to glorify his own name—John 16:13–14) to find a bride for his only begotten son. The servant returns, coincidentally enough, with a Gentile bride (a picture of the church) who comes into the tent of Sarah (a picture of the nation of Israel—John 1:11–12) after she died.

WEEK 2, DAY 4: **TODAY'S READING: GENESIS 25–27**

OVERVIEW:

The death of Abraham; the birth of Jacob and Esau; Esau sells his birthright; Isaac sojourns in Gerar; Isaac blesses Jacob with the Abrahamic Covenant.

HIGHLIGHTS & INSIGHTS:

After the death of Abraham, Isaac finds himself in the same predicament his father was in some fifty years before. He is the recipient of God's promise of seed, but his wife of twenty years remains barren. The fulfillment of God's covenant promise demanded that Isaac and Rebekah have sons. Rather than follow the sin of his father, however, Isaac learns to "intreat the Lord" (25:21) for the very thing his father had looked to the world and the flesh to provide. (Praise the Lord, the Scripture says that the iniquities of the fathers—Exodus 34:7; Numbers 14:18—are *visited* upon the children unto the third and fourth generation. When a *visitor* comes to our door, we don't have to let them in!) Do note, however, that when the iniquity of his father *visits* in Genesis 26:7, Isaac responds just as his father, Abraham, had done! He lies about his wife being his sister. We would do well to learn the biblical principle that we must always be on guard against the sins to which our father was susceptible! (Exod. 34:7; Num. 14:18)

As a result of Isaac's faithful prayers, God grants Isaac and Rebekah conception. Rebekah sensed a struggle within her womb and enquired of the Lord as to the meaning. The Lord explained in 25:23, "Two nations are in thy womb [Israel and Edom], and two manner of people shall be separated from thy bowels; and the one people shall be stronger than the other people; and the elder shall serve the younger."

God continuously finds ways in the Old Testament to remind us that He rejects the first birth ("that which is born of the flesh"—John 3:6a) and accepts the second birth ("that which is born of the Spirit"—John 3:6b). As in the story of Ishmael and Isaac, God points us to that fact through His record of the lives of Jacob and Esau.

There is another incredible picture that God paints through the bizarre story in Genesis 27 of the firstborn blessing coming to Jacob, the younger, instead of Esau, the older. Christ, our older brother (Heb. 2:11), the one to whom belonged the firstborn blessing (Col. 1:15; Rom. 8:29), was cursed (2 Cor. 5:21) and rejected of His Father (Matt. 27:46)—that the firstborn blessing might come upon us! Needless to say, God is quite an artist! He paints pictures of New Testament principles, concepts, and truths through the Old Testament record of actual historic events!

CHRIST IS REVEALED:

The *Seed through whom the nations of the world would be blessed* – Genesis 26:4 (Gal. 3:16)

In *Esau* – Genesis 25:23 (Mal. 1:2–3; Gal. 3:13)

WEEK 2, DAY 5: **TODAY'S READING: GENESIS 28–31**

OVERVIEW:

Isaac confers the Abrahamic covenant upon Jacob; the vision of Jacob's ladder; Jacob's journey to Haran; Jacob's marriages to Leah and Rachel; Laban's jealousy; Jacob flees.

HIGHLIGHTS & INSIGHTS:

The remainder of the book of Genesis focuses primarily on Jacob. Joseph will most certainly be spotlighted, but his story is actually contained within the context of the account of Jacob's life.

The name Jacob means "supplanter"—as in deceiver, schemer, or conniver. As we have already seen in chapters 25 and 27, he more than lived up to his name. Jacob is a graphic picture of the worldly or carnal believer who trusts the arm of the flesh to provide what God is more than willing and fully intending to provide by His own hand. For example, the plan to obtain the firstborn blessing for Jacob that Rebekah (Jacob's mother) deviously schemed and Jacob deceitfully carried out was totally unnecessary. God had already revealed to Rebekah that the firstborn blessing was to be Jacob's when Jacob and Esau were yet in her womb! (See 25:20–23.) We don't know how God would have accomplished bestowing the blessing upon Jacob since it appears that Isaac was intending to be willfully disobedient to God's Word by giving the blessing to Esau, but God most certainly could and would have been able to pull it off without Rebekah and Jacob's deception and dishonesty. As Bob Jones, Sr., used to say, "It is never right to do wrong in order to do something right."

As we have already seen through the first half of the book of Genesis—and will continue to see in the the remainder of our journey through the Word of God—there are always painful consequences to sin. Although Jacob received the *blessing* from Isaac in chapter 27, his deception in obtaining it brought *cursing* (conflict) upon him. For example:

- Esau planned to kill him—causing Jacob to run in fear for the next twenty years. (Gen. 27:41–45)

- Once Jacob left home to escape Esau (chapter 28), he never saw his beloved mother again.

- He was deceived by his uncle Laban. The "supplanter" was supplanted—the "conniver" was connived. It's the biblical principle of Galatians 6:7–8: "Be not deceived; God is not mocked: for whatsoever a man soweth, that shall he also reap. For he that soweth to his flesh shall of the flesh reap corruption."

- His family life was riddled with conflict. And this is the biblical principle of Proverbs 11:29: "He that troubleth his own house shall inherit the wind." (In other words, everything becomes difficult—like riding a bicycle against the wind.) May we all beware!

Jacob leaves his home in chapter 28 to go to Haran, and he stops at Bethel. As he lays down to rest from the long journey, he uses a stone as a pillow and has a very unusual—but significant—dream: Jacob's ladder. The dream verified that God was going to give Jacob, by the power of His Spirit, what he was striving so tenaciously to gain in the power of his own flesh! Jacob was the one with whom God intended to continue the Abrahamic Covenant all along. Oh, that we would learn to trust our perfect heavenly Father!

In chapter 29, the deceiver becomes the deceived as Jacob is outsmarted by his own father-in-law, Laban. Thus, the statement, "What goes around, comes around!" By the end of chapter 29, Jacob has two wives, and in chapter 30, he falls prey to the principle of the iniquity of the fathers being visited upon the children's children (Exod. 34:6–7). In great Abrahamic fashion, he takes the handmaid of each of his wives through whom to have children. The result, as one would expect, is great conflict. And yet, it is through Jacob's relationship with these four women that his 12 sons were born—sons through whom God established the 12 tribes of Israel.

CHRIST IS REVEALED:

In *Jacob's Ladder* – Genesis 28:11–12

> Note: Genesis 28:11–12 foreshadows that the promises would culminate in something that would bridge heaven and earth. In John 1:43–51, Jesus identifies Himself as the Ladder. He is the one who opens heaven for us and brings heaven's blessing to our lives—and He alone is the onewho can bring us to the Father.

In the *Birth of Joseph* – Genesis 30:23–24 (Gen. 50:20; Matt. 1:21; 1 Tim 1:15; John 3:16)

> Note: Joseph was born into the world to save and preserve his people.

As the *Angel of God* – Genesis 31:11

WEEK 3, DAY 1: **TODAY'S READING: GENESIS 32–36**

OVERVIEW:

Jacob gets word that Esau is coming; Jacob wrestles with the Angel of God; Jacob's name is changed to Israel; the peaceful reunion between Jacob and Esau; Dinah, Jacob and Leah's daughter is raped; the revenge carried out by Simeon and Levi; Jacob's return to Bethel; God reaffirms the Abrahamic Covenant with Jacob.

HIGHLIGHTS & INSIGHTS:

When we left Jacob in chapter 31 in yesterday's reading, he had finally rid himself of his adversary, Laban. As chapter 32 begins, he has to concern himself with an even greater adversary—his own brother, Esau, who had threatened to take his life twenty years earlier.

Before Jacob can be reconciled with his brother, however, he first needed to be reconciled with his God. Notice that 32:24 says that "Jacob was left alone." Many times God is most at work in our lives when we feel most alone. That night Jacob wrestled all night with the "man" who is the "angel" of Jehovah in the Old Testament, the Lord Jesus Christ. God brought Jacob to this place of aloneness because He wanted to break him. God wanted Jacob to cry uncle, as it were, or in the words of Galatians 2:20, "Not I, but Christ." The key was getting Jacob to face who and what he really was.

God asked Jacob his name in Genesis 32:27 (obviously knowing it full well!), so that he would have to say, "I am Jacob." Or, in other words, so he would have to admit, "I am a schemer. I am a deceiver. I am a liar." Once Jacob admits his name, God graciously changes it! Jacob ("supplanter") becomes Israel ("God prevails") signifying one who has "power with God and men" (32:28). Verse 31 indicates that by the time this significant night was over, God had given Jacob the dawn of a new day. He not only had a new name, but a new walk. For the rest of Jacob's life, he would walk with a limp.

Interestingly though, as chapter 33 begins, he is not living up to his new name and his new position with God. He is called Jacob, not Israel, and it says that he "lifted up his eyes," indicating that he is not walking by faith, but by sight. He becomes a classic illustration of believers in Christ who are given a new name (Acts 11:26; Rev. 3:12) and a new position (Phil. 3:15; Eph. 1:4), yet don't live up to who they are "in Christ." Chapter 33 finds Jacob, despite his tremendous calling, continuing his scheming, his lying, and his patterns of disobedience. Though he has the mark of God on his life, he is walking like the man he used to be before his life-changing encounter with God. That's why Ephesians 4:22–24 tells us, "That ye put off concerning the former conversation the old man, which is corrupt according to the deceitful lusts; And be renewed in the spirit of your mind; And that ye put on the new man, which after God is created in righteousness and true holiness."

Keep in mind as we are reading of Jacob's journeys that back in Genesis 31:13 God had called Jacob to return to Bethel. As he journeyed toward Bethel, the place of his vision and his vow, he discovered the beautiful valleys and opportunities for financial gain near Shechem (33:18). Jacob ended up staying there for 10 entire years—until his precious 14-year-old daughter was raped by the king of Shechem's son. As the old saying goes...

> Sin will take you farther than you want to go,
>
> Slowly, but wholly, taking control.
>
> Sin will leave you longer than you want to stay.
>
> Sin will cost you far more than you want to pay.

Unbelievably, even after the atrocity meted out upon his daughter, and the atrocity meted out by his two sons who murdered in cold blood every single Shechemite male in revenge for their sister, Jacob's only concern still seems to be only himself! Notice in 34:30 that Jacob's response includes eight first-person pronouns in one sentence (me, me, I, me, me, I, I, my)!

In Genesis 35:1, God again reminds Jacob of his previous instruction to return to Bethel (31:11–13). Sadly, Jacob had been living in Shechem for ten years—when Bethel was only *thirty* miles away! It serves as a great reminder to us that it is easy to be moving in the right direction spiritually, and yet fall far short of full surrender (Heb. 4:1, 9, 11).

In chapter 35, Jacob leads his family back to Bethel, where God reaffirms to him the Abrahamic Covenant and the fact that He had changed his name. Praise God for His unbelievable patience, mercy and grace toward people like Jacob, or, shall we say—people like us!

CHRIST IS REVEALED:

In *Benjamin* – Genesis 35:16-19

> Note: In this first mention of "Bethlehem" in the Bible, that a mother is told, "Fear not; thou shalt have this son also" (v. 17). She then gives birth in the city of Bethlehem to one to whom the father calls "the son of my right hand." Centuries later, another mother is told, "Fear not … thou shalt … bring forth a son" (Luke 1:30–31). And she gives birth in the city of Bethlehem (Luke 2:4, 7) to the one God the Father calls "the Son of My right hand." (See Eph. 1:20; Heb. 1:3, 13; 8:1; 10:12; 12:2)

WEEK 3, DAY 2: **TODAY'S READING: GENESIS 37–41**

OVERVIEW:

Joseph's dreams; Joseph sold into slavery; the enticement and lies of Potiphar's wife; the imprisonment of Joseph; Joseph interprets Pharoah's dreams; Joseph is made a ruler of Egypt.

HIGHLIGHTS & INSIGHTS:

The narrative in this section dealing with the life of Joseph is very interesting reading, completely self-explanatory, and the applications to the believer's life are abundantly clear.

By "comparing spiritual things with spiritual" (1 Cor. 2:13), however, this section reveals that Joseph is the most comprehensive type of Christ in the entire Bible! Consider this list of amazing "coincidences" (similarities) in the life of Joseph and Jesus.

1. Both were the beloved of their fathers. (Gen. 37:3; Matt. 3:17)
2. Both regarded themselves as shepherds. (Gen. 37:2; John 10:11–14)
3. Both were sent to their brethren by their fathers. (Gen. 37:13–14; Luke 20:13; John 3:17; Heb. 10:7)
4. Both were hated by their brethren without cause. (37:4–5; John 1:11; 7:5; 15:25)
5. Both were plotted against by their brethren. (Gen. 37:20; John 11:53)
6. Both were severely tempted. (Gen. 39:7; Matt. 4:1)
7. Both were taken to Egypt. (Gen. 37:36; Matt. 2:14–15)
8. Both were stripped of their robes. (Gen. 37:23; John 19:23–24)
9. Both were sold for the price of a slave. (Gen. 37:28; Matt. 26:15)
10. Both were bound. (Gen. 39:20; Matt. 27:2)
11. Both remained silent and offered no defense. (Gen. 39:20; Isa. 53:7)
12. Both were falsely accused. (Gen. 39:16-18; Matt. 26:59–60)
13. Both experienced God's presence through everything. (Gen. 39:2, 21, 23; John 16:32)
14. Both were respected by their jailers. (Gen. 39:21; Luke 23:47)
15. Both were placed with two prisoners, one of which was later lost and the other saved. (Gen. 40:2–3, 21–22; Luke 23:32, 39–43)
16. Both were around thirty when their ministry began. (Gen. 41:46; Luke 3:23)
17. Both were highly exalted after their sufferings. (Gen. 41:41; Phil. 2:9–11)
18. Both took Gentile brides. (Gen. 41:45; Eph. 2:11–13)
19. Both were lost to their brothers for awhile. (Gen. 42:7–8; Rom. 10:1–3; 11:7–8)
20. Both forgave and restored their repentant brothers. (Gen. 45:1-15; Micah 7:18–19; Zech. 12:10–12; Rev. 1:7)
21. Both were visited and honored by all earthly nations. (Gen. 41:57; Isa. 2:2–3; 49:6)

CHRIST IS REVEALED:

In *Joseph* – (see connections above)

By the *Wisdom of Joseph* – Genesis 41:39 (Col. 2:2–3)

WEEK 3, DAY 3: **TODAY'S READING: GENESIS 42–45**

OVERVIEW:

Joseph's brothers buy corn and bow down to him; Simeon is detained and Benjamin is summoned; Joseph's brothers return to Egypt for food; Judah offers to take the place of Benjamin; Joseph reveals himself to his brothers.

HIGHLIGHTS & INSIGHTS:

Throughout the second half of the book of Genesis, God reminds us of the life principle that "what goes around, comes around" or, in biblical terms, "Be not deceived; God is not mocked; for whatsoever a man soweth, that shall he also reap" (Gal. 6:7). Jacob willfully deceived his father by "the skins of the kids of the goats" (Gen. 27:16) and was deceived by his sons in a similar manner in chapter 37:31–33.

This principle is observed throughout Scripture. Pharoah, intent on destroying God's people by the waters of the Red Sea, saw his own people drowned there instead (Ex. 14:28). Korah caused a division among God's people and was swallowed alive by a division in the ground (Num. 16). Haman, who built the gallows to hang Mordecai (Esther 5:14), was hanged on those very gallows (Est. 7:10).

Because of this biblical principle, as adverse situations unfold in our lives, it is always a good practice to step back and ask ourselves, "Is this happening in my life because I am reaping according to what I've sown?" God may be trying to reveal to us how it is that we need to "cleanse ourselves from all filthiness of the flesh and spirit, perfecting holiness in the fear of God" (2 Cor. 7:1).

The whole story of Joseph's dealings with his brothers in this section foreshadows that coming day in another time of tribulation (Rev. 6:5–8) when the remnant of Israel will confess its guilt in connection with the death of the Messiah and will mourn for Him as one mourns for an only son (Zech. 12:10).

As the brothers make their second trip back to Joseph, you can begin to detect a change of heart:

- Judah, who so ruthlessly sold Joseph for profit with no concern for his father's heartbreak in chapter 37, pours out his heart in intercession before Joseph in chapter 44, offering himself as a slave to spare his father the doubly-painful sorrow of losing Benjamin. Judah moved from selling his brother into slavery to being willing to become a slave on his brother's behalf.

- The brothers' willingness to return the money.

- The confession of the truth to Joseph's steward.

These were positive signs of their change of heart, but they were still making some horrendous mistakes. They took Joseph a present and confessed their sins to Joseph's servant rather than to Joseph himself. This mistake has been made by lost sinners throughout the history of the church. God works in the life of the sinner to bring him to the end of himself, and to God Himself, but many seek to win their salvation on their own. They bring something to God or confess their sin to a man rather than to God Himself. Or, like Judah, they want to make some sort of sacrifice. Salvation would be graciously offered to Joseph's brothers upon simple confession and repentance. Likewise, salvation in Christ is graciously offered to sinful men upon simple confession and repentance. (See Rom. 10:9–13; Acts 17:30.)

In Genesis 45:13, Joseph, the incredible type of Christ, tells his brothers, "tell my father of all my glory." John 13:31 teaches those of us who are Christ's brothers (Heb. 2:11) that God is glorified as we glorify His Son! Oh, may we tell the Father of all of Christ's glory today! Philippians 2:9–11 says, "Wherefore God also hath highly exalted him, and given him a name which is above every name: That at the name of Jesus every knee should bow, of things in heaven, and things in earth, and things under the earth; And that every tongue should confess that Jesus Christ is Lord, to the glory of God the Father."

CHRIST IS REVEALED:

Through *Joseph's Dealings with his Brothers* – Genesis 45:4–15 (Heb. 2:11; Rom. 5:8)

Through *Joseph's Sovereignty over the Affairs of Life* – Genesis 45:5–8 (Eph. 1:17, 20–22)

WEEK 3, DAY 4: **TODAY'S READING: GENESIS 46–50**

OVERVIEW:

Jacob's vision at Beersheba; the journey to Egypt; Joseph and the famine; the best land given to Jacob; Jacob blesses Joseph's sons; Jacob's prophecies upon his sons; the deaths of Jacob and Joseph.

HIGHLIGHTS & INSIGHTS:

In today's reading, Jacob begins the journey toward Egypt to be reunited with his beloved son, Joseph. At Beersheba, God spoke to Jacob in a vision of the night, assuring him that it was His will that he go to Egypt and that, though he would die there, God would eventually return His people to the Promised Land. As has been already noted, God is consistently hammering the point that Egypt is a *downward* move—and one must be brought *up* out of Egypt (Gen. 46:4). Egypt is a picture of sin and the world.

When Jacob is reunited with Joseph, it has been twenty-two long years, and an incredible amount of water has passed under the proverbial bridge. Joseph is now 39, and Jacob is 130. Joseph introduces his father to the Pharoah, and he grants Jacob the best part of Egypt for his family to settle in—an area called Goshen. After seventeen years in Egypt, Jacob realizes that he is close to death. He has one major thing that he makes Joseph promise him: "Bury me not, I pray thee, in Egypt." (47:29–31)

Chapter 48 records Jacob's (Israel's) last blessing. Joseph brings his two sons before his father, and he adopts them as his own sons and assures them of an equal inheritance. A strange thing happens as Israel bestows the blessing upon his sons, however. As Joseph brings his two sons before his father, Manasseh is brought toward Jacob's right hand, and Ephraim is brought toward his left hand. As Jacob reaches out to impart the blessing, he crosses his hands, giving the firstborn blessing of his right hand to Ephraim, the younger son. Though Joseph objected, Israel explained that God was once again going to bestow the firstborn blessing upon the younger son.

What is the meaning of this bizarre story? It is all an incredible picture! The Bible refers to Christ as the "firstborn among many brethren" (Rom. 8:29) who is "seated at the Father's right hand" (Col. 3:1). When we came before the Father and asked Him to bestow the blessing of eternal life upon us, in effect, God the Father crossed His hands. Since He only has one gift of eternal life, and that life is in His Son (1 John 5:11–12), God took His right hand and placed it on us and took His left hand and placed it on His Son. Christ gets our sin; we get His righteousness (2 Cor. 5:21). Christ dies our death—we get His life (Rom. 5:10). Christ gets our curse—we get the firstborn blessing (Gal. 3:13–14).

The scene in chapter 49 as the dying Jacob calls his sons into his bedroom is incredibly prophetic (Gen. 49:1 – "Gather yourselves together, that I may tell you that which shall befall you *in the last days*"). It is an extremely graphic and detailed picture of the Judgment Seat of Christ (2 Cor. 5:10–11)!

As Joseph comes to the end of his life in Genesis 50, he has the same passion as his father before him: He did not want his bones to remain in Egypt! Like his father, he wanted to be buried in Canaan. Why? Because Canaan was the land of Promise. Jacob and Joseph both realized that though they were *in* Egypt (the world), they were not *of* Egypt (the world)! (See John 17:11–16.) Joseph's request was not forgotten. Four hundred years later, as the children of Israel set out for Canaan, Exodus 13:19 says that they took Joseph's bones with them. Don't miss the incredible picture being painted here, because we also have the promise of God that He will not allow our bones to remain in Egypt (1 Thess 4:13–17)!

The book of Genesis begins with a man in a Garden and ends with a man in a coffin. It begins with life and ends with death. God says, "The wages of sin is death" (Rom. 6:23) and "sin, when it is finished, bringeth forth death" (James 1:15).

As we conclude the book of Genesis today, here is a simple way to remember the content of this vitally important Book. The book of Genesis is comprised of:

- ✦ FOUR KEY EVENTS. (Gen. 1–11)
    1. Creation (1–2)
    2. The Fall (3–5)
    3. The Flood (6–9)
    4. The Tower of Babel (10–11)
- ✦ FOUR KEY MEN. (Gen. 12–50)
    1. Abraham (12:1–25:8)
    2. Isaac (21:1–35:29)
    3. Jacob (25:21–50:14)
    4. Joseph (30:22–50:26)

CHRIST IS REVEALED:

Through *Joseph, who Sustained Life and Offered Provision from his Position on the Throne* - Genesis 47:15-17 (John 6:33)

As *Shiloh, the one who Holds the Scepter from the Tribe of Judah* - Genesis 49:10 (Luke 3:23-33)

WEEK 3, DAY 5: **TODAY'S READING: EXODUS 1–4**

OVERVIEW:

The bondage of the Jews in Egypt; Moses' birth and early life in Egypt; Moses' flight into Midian; the burning bush; God commissions Moses and Aaron to deliver Israel; Moses' return to Egypt.

HIGHLIGHTS & INSIGHTS:

Exodus means "the way out." The book of Exodus is the story of Israel's deliverance from bondage in Egypt. As we begin this portion of the Bible, notice that more column inches are given to the record of Israel's exodus than any other thing in the entire Bible! It is the subject matter, not only of the book of Exodus, but of Leviticus, Numbers, Deuteronomy and even part of the book of Joshua! Why so much detail about one event? 1 Corinthians 10:1–11 tells us why: the Exodus is not just a *portion* of Israel's history—it is a *portrait* of the Christian life! God tells us that we're given this incredible record of Israel's history, so that the same thing that happened to them—doesn't happen to us! The sad reality is that for most believers, it does!

To help you to "develop the pictures" as we make our way through Israel's Exodus, keep in mind that:

- *Egypt* is a picture of the world and sin. It will consistently stand for that which is in opposition to God and God's people. Just as Egypt held God's people in bondage in the Old Testament—it pictures the world's system that seeks to hold us in bondage in the New Testament (Eph. 2:2).

- *Pharaoh*, the wicked king of Egypt, is a picture of Satan, the wicked king of the world's system, who exercises his will in taking God's people captive (2 Tim. 2:26).

- *Israel* is a picture of the individual believer. Please note that Israel is not a picture of the church! In Exodus 4:22–23, God plainly declares that "Israel is my son" and commands Moses to tell Pharaoh to "let my son go, that he may serve me." In the New Testament, God reveals that as individual believers in Christ we now posses the title "son of God" (1 John 3:2; John 1:12; Rom. 8:14). Making the proper connection between Israel and the individual believer will keep us from wrongly "dividing the word of truth" (2 Tim. 2:15) and misapplying God's Word to our lives.

- *Moses* is a picture of the Lord Jesus Christ, the deliverer of God's people.

- *Amalek* is a picture of the flesh, which constantly wars with our spirits as we seek to walk with Christ (Gal. 5:16–17).

Keep in mind as you read about Israel's affliction in today's reading, that the Jews had gone down to Egypt and lived off the best of the land (Gen. 47:6). That luxury has now turned into sorrow and suffering. It is an inescapable principle of life: sin promises freedom and happiness, but in the end, it only leads to bondage and sorrow. Be constantly on guard against the "deceitfulness of sin" (Heb. 3:13; Rom. 7:11; Eph. 4:22)!

As the Hebrews remained in bondage for 400 years(!), it seemed as if God was either unaware or unconcerned of their situation. No doubt, they felt forsaken and wondered why God had not provided their deliverance. Had they only remembered what God said in Genesis 15:13–16, they would have known that God had already prophesied that the duration of their bondage would be 400 years. During these years when it seemed as if God was doing nothing, He was actually preparing His people (Exodus chapter 1), preparing the deliverer (chapters 2–4), and extending incredible mercy by giving the wicked nations of Canaan time to repent (Gen. 15:16). When we feel that God is either unaware or unconcerned with our circumstances, we must remember that God is constantly at work in our lives for our good and His glory (Rom. 8:28–29), even when we can't see it with our physical eyes!

At 40 years of age, Moses determined that it was time to accomplish the mission for which He had been called—to deliver Israel! There was only one problem, however. It wasn't *God's* time! Exodus 2:12 says that Moses "looked this way and that." Moses wanted to fulfill God's calling on his life—but he was walking by sight and not by faith (2 Cor. 5:7). God had 40 years of training planned for Moses in the land of Midian—serving as a shepherd for his father-in-law's flock before he would be prepared for the difficult task of shepherding God's flock.

CHRIST IS REVEALED:

Through *Moses* as *Shepherd* and *Deliverer* – Exodus 3:1, 11 (John 10:11–14; Heb. 13:20; 1 Pet. 5:4; Rom. 11:26; Titus 2:14)

> Note: Moses is one of the most perfect types of Christ in the entire Bible. Moses himself makes this declaration in Deuteronomy 18:15.

As the *Great I AM* – Exodus 3:13–14 (John 8:58; Heb. 13:8)

WEEK 4, DAY 1: **TODAY'S READING: EXODUS 5–9**

OVERVIEW:

Moses and Aaron go before Pharaoh; the first seven of the ten plagues.

HIGHLIGHTS & INSIGHTS:

Seven times God says to Pharaoh, "Let my people go, that they may serve me" (Ex. 5:1; 7:16; 8:1, 20; 9:1,13; 10:3). Notice that though the children of Israel would most certainly be the beneficiaries of God's delivering power, the actual purpose in delivering them out of the bondage of Egypt wasn't first and foremost for them—it was for Him! It was so the children of Israel could serve Him—not Pharaoh, and not Egypt! In recounting His purpose in Israel's Exodus in Ezekiel 20:9, God said, "But I wrought for my name's sake, that it should not be polluted before the heathen, among whom they were, in whose sight I made myself known unto them, in bringing them forth out of the land of Egypt."

The same is true for us. God's purpose in delivering us out of the bondage of Egypt (sin/world) was not simply so we could live comfortable, happy lives and go to heaven when we die. He saved us for His purposes and pleasure (Eph. 2:10; Rev. 4:11; John 17:3). He saved us so we would cease polluting His holy name! He saved us so we would cease serving our own selfish and worldly interests—so we could serve Him (2 Cor. 5:15)!

The ten plagues of Egypt had a fourfold purpose:

1. They were signs to Israel, assuring them of God's power and care. (Ex. 7:3; 1 Cor. 1:22)

2. They were judgments upon Egypt and its ruler Pharaoh for persecuting Israel.

3. They were prophecies of judgments that will come upon this world and Satan when Moses reappears on this planet during the tribulation period. (Rev. 16)

4. They were to show God's superiority over the gods of Egypt.

    *   The 1st plague of bloody waters was directed against the Egyptian god Osiris, the god of the Nile. (Ex. 7:20)

    *   The 2nd plague of the frogs was directed against Hekt, the Egyptian frog goddess. (Ex. 8:6)

    *   The 3rd plague of lice was directed against the Egyptian god Seb, the earth god. (Ex. 8:17)

    *   The 4th plague of flies was directed against the Egyptian goddess Hatkok, the wife of Osiris. (Ex. 8:24)

    *   The 5th plague of cattle disease was directed against the Egyptian god Apis, the sacred bull god. (Ex. 9:6)

    *   The 6th plague of boils was directed against the Egyptian god Typhon. (Ex. 9:10)

    *   The 7th plague, hail with fire, was directed against the Egyptian god Shu, the god of the atmosphere. (Ex. 9:23)

    *   The 8th plague of locusts was directed against Serapia, the god who supposedly protected Egypt against locusts. (Ex. 10:13)

    *   The 9th plague, darkness, was directed against the Egyptian god Ra, the sun god. (Ex. 10:22)

    *   The 10th plague, the death of the firstborn, was directed against all gods. (Ex. 12:29)

Notice Pharaoh's (Satan's) response to God's command to let his people go: "Pharaoh said, who is the Lord, that I should obey His voice?" (Ex. 5:2). Keep in mind that the world and Satan have no respect for God's Word—it is "vain" to them (5:9). Sinners will either yield to God's Word or resist it and become hardened (Ex. 7:14; Heb. 3:13).

Notice also that God says that His purpose in allowing Pharaoh to oppress Israel was so that His power and glory might be known to the world (Ex. 6:7; 7:5, 17; 8:10, 22). Today, God is fulfilling His purposes through His church (Eph. 3:10). That's why God sometimes allows us to be oppressed ("suffer persecution," 2 Tim. 3:12)—to reveal His power and glory to the world! Our response to persecution and suffering will determine whether or not we will fulfill God's purposes through us (1 Pet. 2:19–23; Phil. 1:28–29).

CHRIST IS REVEALED:

As the *Redeemer* from the bondage of sin – Exodus 6:6 (Rom. 6:14; Gal. 3:13; 1Pet. 1:18–25)

WEEK 4, DAY 2: **TODAY'S READING: EXODUS 10–13**

OVERVIEW:

The last three of the ten plagues—including the death of the firstborn; the Passover and Feast of Unleavened Bread instituted by God as a memorial feast.

HIGHLIGHTS & INSIGHTS:

God's desire in delivering Israel out of the bondage of Egypt was to totally separate them as a people unto Himself. He intended not only to bring them *out* of Egypt—but to bring them *into* Canaan (Ex. 3:8; Deut. 6:23; Lev. 25:38)! Canaan was the place of abundance. It was the place God had promised them; the place that signified victory over their enemies; and the place where they could experience a brand new kind of existence because of the intimacy of their relationship with God (Lev. 25:38b).

Although all of those things were gloriously true of God's desire for Israel, God also uses the historical account of their Exodus to teach us about our own exodus (1 Cor. 10:6, 11). Because God's desire in delivering us out of our bondage to sin, self, and Satan was to likewise separate us as a people unto Himself. Now that God has delivered us out of the clutches of Satan and the world's system of evil, He wants us to make absolutely no compromises with the world or the devil (2 Cor. 6:14–18). He wants to bring us into a brand new type of existence because of the intimacy of our relationship with Him, where we are experiencing the abundant life that Jesus talked about (John 10:10) and where we live in victory over our enemies—the world, the flesh and the devil!

With God's intentions for Israel in mind, it's interesting to note the four compromises Pharaoh (a picture of Satan) offered to Moses and the people of Israel (the individual believer in Christ) in the midst of the ten plagues. These are the same compromises Satan seeks to use to keep God's purposes from being fulfilled in and through us!

1. **Worship God, but stay in Egypt. (Ex. 8:25–27)**
   In other words, go to church, get involved, serve, tithe, even witness—just don't separate yourself from the world. Allow the world to still be your friend. It doesn't bother Satan one bit for us to be double-minded, to have a double allegiance. He welcomes it! God, however, despises it (James 1:8; 4:8). He demands complete separation from the world because friendship with the world is enmity with Him (James 4:4; 2 Cor. 6:14–18).

2. **Leave, but don't go too far away. (Ex. 8:28)**
   Satan says, "Sure, do the 'God thing,' but you don't have to be a fanatic about it! Give God a place in your heart, but don't go overboard with it!" God says, "If I'm God, follow me alone! If anything else is god, then follow it! But don't think that you can do both" (1 Kings 18:21). We can't be close to God and close to the world at the same time. Jesus said it is impossible (Matt. 6:24). He also said it makes Him sick (Rev. 3:15–16)!

3. **Leave, but allow your children to remain in Egypt. (Ex. 10:7–11)**
   Satan will let men think they're doing well spiritually, if in so doing, he can take captive the next generation. Men have been called, however, to bring their children up in "the nurture and admonition of the Lord" (Eph. 6:4) and to lead their families to worship God and God alone (1 Tim. 3:4–5; Titus 1:6).

4. **Leave, but keep your possessions in Egypt. (Ex. 10:24–26)**
   Satan wants us to think that our relationship with God and our relationship with our money and possessions are two different things. The simple biblical fact is—they aren't! Jesus said, "You cannot serve God and mammon" (Matt. 6:24)—and "Where your treasure is, there will your heart be also" (Matt. 6:21). If we've somehow convinced ourselves that we're walking in the perfect will of God for our life, but our treasure is in Egypt (the world)—we have been duped!

In order to avoid the death of the firstborn, the people of Israel had to kill a spotless lamb and apply its blood to the doorposts of their house. When God saw the blood, He "passed over" that house, and the judgment upon the firstborn was averted. Once again, God is painting an Old Testament picture to teach us the New Testament truth that we can only be delivered from the curse of death upon our first birth by applying the blood of the true, spotless Passover Lamb, the Lord Jesus Christ! (See 1 Cor. 5:7; 1 Pet. 1:18–19; John 3:3.)

Note the progression concerning the lamb in Exodus 12:3–5. It is "*a lamb*," then "*the* lamb," then "*your* lamb." The practical implications to each individual are powerful: in order for your sin to be removed, you need "*a lamb*" (Luke 2:11). But not just any lamb will do. It must be "*the* Lamb" (John 4:42)! But in order for your sin to actually be removed, "*the* Lamb" must become "*your* Lamb" (John 20:28)!

CHRIST IS REVEALED:

As the *Light to His People* – Exodus 10:22–23 (John 8:12)

The sacrifice of an *Unblemished Lamb with no Broken Bones* – Exodus 12:5, 46 (1 Pet. 1:19; Ps. 34:20; John 19:36)

As the *Passover Lamb* – Exodus 12:3–5 (1 Cor. 5:7b; 1 Peter 1:19; John 1:29)

WEEK 4, DAY 3: **TODAY'S READING: EXODUS 14–16**

OVERVIEW:
Israel's exodus out of Egypt and the crossing of the Red Sea; the song of Moses and Israel; manna from heaven.

HIGHLIGHTS & INSIGHTS:
As the Passover illustrates the Christian's salvation through the blood of the Lamb, so the journey of Israel from Egypt to Canaan is a picture of the battles and blessings of the Christian life. Like Israel, many Christians, after being delivered out of the bondage of Egypt, get lost in the wilderness of unbelief. That's not to say they lose their salvation—they just never receive all the inheritance that God intends for them. (Note: For those who are part of the body of Christ, losing your salvation is not taught in precept in the New Testament, nor is it pictured in the Old Testament. In the picture painted through the Nation of Israel in Exodus 14:13, they never returned to Egypt!)

The crossing of the Red Sea is a picture of the believer's identification with Christ. Israel was "baptized unto Moses" (1 Cor. 10:1–2); in other words, they followed their deliverer, Moses (a picture of Christ), identifying themselves with him as they went through the Red Sea. When they came up on the other side and the parted waters closed behind them, it symbolized that they had left the old life in Egypt behind. We make our public identification with Christ at our water baptism, which symbolizes the spiritual identification with Christ's death, burial and resurrection that was made when we called upon His name to save us—and symbolizes that we, too, are leaving the old life in Epypt (sin) behind!

Just as there is a law of gravity to which all are subjected, there is also a law of sowing and reaping to which all are subjected (Gal. 6:7–8)! Pharaoh reaped exactly what he had sown. In Exodus 1:22, he had been responsible for drowning many Jewish males—now the males in his army were drowned (Ex. 14:26–28). Our God will not be mocked (Gal. 6:7)!

Notice also that just as Moses and Israel sang a song praising God for their deliverance from their bondage in Egypt (Ex. 15), as believers in Christ, we too sing a song of deliverance praising God for our deliverance from Egypt (sin)! (See Col. 3:16; Eph. 5:19; Ps. 40:1–3.)

As the children of Israel begin their journey through the wilderness in chapter 16, God feeds them with bread from heaven that is called manna. In John 6:31–35, Jesus let us know that the manna was actually a picture of Him! Note at least eight ways the manna in Exodus 16 is a picture of Christ.

1. **It was a mystery.**

Verse 15 says, "And when the children of Israel saw it, they said one to another, it is manna: for they wist not what it was." In fact, the word *manna* actually means "What is it?" And they called it that because they couldn't explain it. It was a mystery to them. And this is exactly what Paul, in 1 Timothy 3:16, called "the mystery of godliness." And what was the mystery? That "God was manifest in the flesh." Manna is a picture of who Christ is—that incredible mystery that He is God manifest in the flesh—God in a human body.

2. **It was small.**

Verse 14 says it was "as small as the hoar [or white] frost on the ground." And, of course, "small" speaks of Christ's humility. Though He was the omnipotent, omniscient, omnipresent, Shekinah glory of the Godhead, He humbled Himself to be born into the world that He, Himself, had created, and He did so, as a *small* baby. Philippians 2:6–7 says that though Christ was equal with God, He made Himself of no reputation (He humbled Himself) by allowing Himself to be made in the likeness of men.

3. **It was round.**

The middle of verse 14 says that it was "a small round thing" which speaks of Christ's eternality. In John 8:58, Jesus said, "Verily, verily I say unto you, Before Abraham was, I am." Notice that He didn't say, "Before Abraham was, I *was!*" He clearly said, "Before Abraham was, I *am!*" In other words, like something that is round, He had no beginning and has no end. In Revelation 1:8, Jesus said to the Apostle John, "I am Alpha and Omega, the beginning and the ending, saith the Lord, which is, and which was, and which is to come, the Almighty." Listen, God could have made the manna any shape He wanted to make it, but because it was a picture of Christ, He made it *round*—having no beginning and no ending.

4. It was a gift.

The middle of verse 15 says "And Moses said unto them, This is the bread which the Lord hath given you to eat." John 3:16 says, "For God so loved the world, that he gave his only begotten Son." Romans 6:23 says, "The wages of sin is death, but the gift of God is eternal life through Jesus Christ our Lord."

5. It was white.

Verse 31 says, "And the house of Israel called the name thereof Manna: and it was like coriander seed, *white.*" White, of course, speaks of His purity and righteousness. It speaks of the fact that He came into this world without sin and without a sin nature—because He came by way of a virgin birth (Matt. 1:20).

   *Note that Romans 5:12 says that the curse of sin is passed through the man.

6. It was sweet.

The end of verse 31 says, "the taste of it was like wafers made with honey." Psalm 34:8 says, "O taste and see that the Lord is good." Psalm 119:103 says, "How sweet are thy words unto my taste! yea, sweeter than honey to my mouth." Of course, if you're ever really going to know His sweetness, you must taste of the Lord—you must take Him in! It wasn't enough for the children of Israel to admire the manna, or to respect it, or even to acknowledge that it was a gift from God—they had to eat it for themselves!

7. It was on the ground.

Do you know what they had to do to get the manna? They had to bow … bend … stoop. In other words, they had to humble themselves to get it. God could have put the manna anywhere He wanted. He could have suspended it in midair. He could have put it on the branches of the trees. He could have put it on the mountain tops. But you know what He did? He made it accessible to everyone! It came to where they were—but to get it, they had to stoop. And you know who could reach it best? Children! Because they don't have as far to bend. Jesus said in Matthew 18:3, "Except ye be converted, and become as little children, ye shall not enter into the kingdom of heaven." Jesus came to where we are, but to receive Him, we must humble ourselves.

8. It had to be received early.

Verse 21 says, "And they gathered it every morning, every man according to his eating: and when the sun waxed hot, it melted." There was an urgency concerning the manna, because once the sun rose on the earth, the manna melted. The opportunity to receive it was gone! Interestingly enough, the Bible says that, in the very near future, the "Sun of righteousness" (the Lord Jesus Christ) is going to arise on this planet (Malachi 4:1–2), and He will burn up all His enemies (Ps. 97:3). In 2 Thessalonians 1:7–9, Paul tells us that the day is coming "when the Lord Jesus shall be revealed from heaven with his mighty angels, In flaming fire [like the sun!] taking vengeance on them that know not God, and that obey not the gospel of our Lord Jesus Christ: who shall be punished with everlasting destruction from the presence of the Lord, and from the glory of his power." God's message concerning the manna was to be sure to receive it before the sun came up! And likewise, God's message to the people in these last days is to be sure to receive Christ before He rises in the eastern sky as the "Sun of righteousness" upon this planet! Isaiah 55:6 warns us, "Seek ye the Lord while he may be found, call ye upon him while he is near."

CHRIST IS REVEALED:

As *Manna* from heaven – Exodus 16 (John 6:31–35)

WEEK 4, DAY 4: **TODAY'S READING: EXODUS 17–21**

OVERVIEW:

Water from the rock in Horeb; Joshua leads Israel in defeating Amalek in battle at the Lord's command; Jethro brings Moses's wife and two sons to Moses in the wilderness; God appears to Moses on Mount Sinai; God gives to Moses the 10 Commandments; the civil law for the Nation of Israel and the consequences for disobedience.

HIGHLIGHTS & INSIGHTS:

As we move into Exodus 17 in today's reading, Moses illustrates what a trusting Christian does in times of testing—he turns to the Lord and asks for guidance! (See Ex. 17:4; Jas. 1:5.) In response, the Lord orders Moses to smite the rock at Horeb and out would flow water for the murmuring people of Israel. The picture is obvious: Christ, who is our Rock (1 Cor. 10:4), was smitten on the cross to provide living water to quench the souls of all who are thirsty (Jn. 7:37–38)!

At the end of chapter 17, Moses orders Joshua to lead the people of Israel in battle against Amalek (a picture of the flesh). Notice that God makes a point in 17:16 to let us know that the battle with Amalek is a battle that will continue from generation to generation. In Galatians 5:17, God makes a point to let us know that the battle between the Spirit and the flesh is a battle that we will face until we receive a glorified body (Rom. 8:23). As pictured in Exodus 17, our only hope in winning this battle is to allow our Joshua (the Lord Jesus Christ) to lead us to daily victory (17:10,13). Note that this battle was won only after Israel had received water from the rock! Water in the Bible is a picture of the Word of God—which is the weapon (the Sword) the Spirit of God who lives in us uses against the flesh! (See Eph. 5:26; 6:17; Ps. 119:9–11.)

Jethro, Moses's father-in-law, comes to the wilderness in chapter 18 and offers Moses some advice about how to delegate responsibility so that he and the people of Israel wouldn't get worn out (vs. 16–18, 21–22). Moses takes his advice (vs. 24–26), and it certainly lifted some of the burden and responsibility off of his shoulders. Whether or not this is what God intended, however, is unclear. Even Jethro didn't know if his plan would be pleasing to God (v. 23). Though Jethro's counsel makes a lot of sense from a human perspective ("the wisdom of men," 1 Cor. 2:5), we must always be careful when getting "wisdom from this world" (1 Cor. 2:6) because God says in Isaiah 55:8–9: "For my thoughts are not your thoughts, neither are your ways my ways, saith the Lord. For as the heavens are higher than the earth, so are my ways higher than your ways, and my thoughts than your thoughts."

In chapter 19, Moses meets with God on Mount Sinai. It is here that God reveals to Moses His plan for the people of Israel and the rest of the world (vs. 5–6). God desired Israel to be "a kingdom of priests and an holy nation." His intention was that Israel would be so different from the rest of the world that the people of the world would want what Israel had—namely, their God! And God's plan is still the same! 1 Peter 2:9 says, "But ye are a chosen generation, a royal priesthood, an holy nation, a peculiar people; that ye should show forth the praises of him who hath called you out of darkness into his marvelous light." God wants us to be so different from the rest of the world that they will want what we have—a personal relationship with the God of the universe!

In Exodus 19:11, God paints a prophetic picture of the Second Coming of Christ. God says, "Be ready against the third day: for the third day the Lord will come down in the sight of all the people upon Mount Sinai." Peter explains in 2 Peter 3:8 that a thousand years is as one day to God. Using that equation, it has been about 2000 years (or two days on God's time table) since Christ died on the cross. The third day is fast approaching, when the Lord will come down in the sight of the whole world (Phil. 2:10–11)!

Chapters 20 and 21 deal with the Law of Moses, or the Ten Commandments as we most often refer to them. We know that the Law is good (1 Tim. 1:8–9) because it embodies the character and nature of God's holiness, but we must be sure it is used for the right reasons! The Law was never intended to *provide our salvation* though it does have a very important purpose in bringing us to salvation! The Law was given to reveal to us our sin (Rom. 7:7) so that, in humility and contrition, we would cry out to God for the salvation He offers through His Son (Gal. 3:19–24)!

CHRIST IS REVEALED:

As the *Rock* from which water flows – Exodus 17:1–6 (1 Cor. 10:4; John 4:14)

Through *Joshua* – Exodus 17:9–16

  Note: Joshua is the Hebrew name for Jesus, the one who fights our battles and enemies for us.

Through the *Law* – Exodus 20:1–17 (Matt. 5:17; Heb. 4:15; Rom. 10:4)

WEEK 4, DAY 5: **TODAY'S READING: EXODUS 22–24**

OVERVIEW:

God gives examples of His judgments by which to judge right from wrong; Israel agrees to obey God's commands; Moses goes up again to meet with God on Mount Sinai.

HIGHLIGHTS & INSIGHTS:

Starting in Exodus 21 in yesterday's reading, God began giving Israel judgments by which to judge right from wrong. He lays down specific commands for how the Nation of Israel was to function in their relationship with Him and, thus, with one another. It is important to recognize that in this nation that God was forming in Israel the blueprint for their governmental structure would be different than any nation in the world. This nation would not be a democracy, a dictatorship, or a republic—Israel was the first and only theocracy: God Himself would serve as their King, Chief Executive, Ruler, Legislator and Judge. The plan was simple: They were to obey God, and the result would be protection and blessing. As God recounts the establishment of this theocracy in Jeremiah 11:4, notice that the key to their society wasn't how man related to his fellow man—but how man related to God. God, of course, knows that when men are rightly related to Him, they will be rightly related to one another. The opposite is also true—if men are *not* rightly related to God, no amount of laws can keep a society functioning properly. Romans 1:16–32 explains the inevitability of the moral decay of society when sinful human beings disregard the God who created them.

It is interesting to note that the very first thing God emphasizes after giving the Nation of Israel the Ten Commandments was the admonition to treat their servants properly (21:2–6). Keep in mind that this instruction comes immediately after they had been delivered from 400 years of abusive servitude at the hands of the Egyptians! The fact was, Israel's mindset concerning the treatment of servants needed serious renovation—or in the words of Romans 12:2, the people of Israel needed to be "transformed by the renewing" of their minds! Having been delivered from the bondage of our own backgrounds, each of us would do well to consider what areas of our life God intends for us to be "transformed by the renewing of [our] mind," areas where sinful behavior might be the result of old patterns of thinking.

The various laws in this section in the book of Exodus appear to be random, yet God was calculatingly laying down each one—not only because they were essential examples the people of Israel needed in order to understand God's holy character and values, but also because they were essential for how God wanted to put His holiness on display to the watching world through this unique nation! And keep in mind that, though God will ultimately fulfill His promises to the Nation of Israel during the Tribulation Period, right now, we are that "holy nation" through which God wants to put His glory on display to a watching world through our holiness (1 Peter 2:9)!

In this section God also begins to reveal his concern for the fatherless and widows, as well as for the poor. In 22:22–24, He warns against "afflicting" the fatherless and widows, and He takes up the cause of the poor in 22:25. God reveals His heart for these three groups of people throughout the Old Testament and continues His revelation into the New Testament. He tells us in James 1:27 that "pure religion and undefiled before God and the Father is this, To visit the fatherless and the widows in their affliction," and in Galatians 2:10, He tells us that as believers in Christ, we are to "remember the poor."

In 23:20–23, we are introduced to "the Angel of the Lord." He is none other than a pre-incarnate appearance of our Lord Jesus Christ (Gal. 4:14). Note in verses 20 and 21 that this Angel is:

1. "Before [us]," just as our Lord Jesus Christ is the "Author of our faith" as we run the "race that is set before us." (23:20a; Heb. 12:1–2)

2. The one who will "keep [us] in the way." (23:20b; Heb.13:5–6)

3. The one who will "bring [us] into the place which [He has] prepared." (23:20c; John 14:1–3)

4. The one of whom we must "beware." (23:21a; Gal. 6:7a)

5. The one whose "voice" we must "obey." (23:21b; John 14:15)

6. The one we must not "provoke." (23:21c; 1 Cor. 10:1–11)

7. The one who is an "enemy unto [our] enemies, and an adversary unto [our] adversaries" (23:21d). Note in Ephesians 6:10–18 that, in our battle with Satan and his network of demonic forces, we have not been called to fight but to "stand"! Jesus has already fought our enemies/adversary—and won!

The three feasts mentioned in 23:14–17, held at three different times in the year (23:14), obviously fulfilled an *Historic* purpose—and also a *Prophetic* purpose.

1. The Feast of Unleavened Bread (23:15) is the Passover feast held in the spring and is representative of the grace and forgiveness found in the offering of Christ as the true Passover Lamb. (1 Cor. 5:7)

2. The Feast of Harvest (23:16a), also known as the Feast of Firstfruits (v. 16b) or the Feast of Weeks (Deut. 16:16), represents Christ's resurrection and the subsequent coming of the Holy Spirit on the Day of Pentecost, 50 days after Passover. (Note: the word "pentecost" means "fiftieth day" and was held the day *after* seven weeks—or the day *after* 49 days had passed from Passover.

3. The Feast of Ingathering (23:16b), also known as the Feast of Tabernacles (Deut. 16:16), pictures the crowning of our glorious King, the Lord Jesus Christ, at His second coming when He will *tabernacle* ("dwell," John 1:14) on this planet with His "gathered" saints for a period of 1000 years.

What an incredible response the people have to "the words of the Lord"! With complete unity ("one voice") they declare to Moses, "All the words which the Lord hath said will we do" (24:3). Moses then wrote the words the Lord had spoken to him up on the mountain and read them to the children of Israel, and once again the people declare, "All that the Lord hath said will we do, and be obedient" (24:7). Wow! That, my friend, is the simple essence of the Christian life! It should be not only the declaration from the mouth of every believer in Christ—but also the determination in each of our hearts. You see, it's easy to *believe* every word of the Bible, and it's easy to *say* we will obey every word of the Bible, but it's quite another thing to actually *do* it! And that's exactly the case with the children of Israel here in Exodus 24. Just forty days after making this incredible declaration, Exodus 32:1 says, "And when the people saw that Moses delayed to come down out of the mount, the people gathered themselves together unto Aaron, and said unto him, Up, make us gods, which shall go before us; for as for this Moses, the man that brought us up out of the land of Egypt, we wot not what is become of him." As the old saying goes, "Talk is cheap."

One of the most simple, yet profound (and blessed!) verses in this entire section is found in 24:12. God is inviting Moses to come up to Mount Sinai to receive the infamous "tables of stone." It is obviously a very significant piece of the entire puzzle concerning God's dealing with man. The wording of verse 12, however, not only screams out the heart of the passage, but the very heart of God! Notice that God does not say to Moses, "Come up into the mount, and I will give thee tables of stone." What God says to Moses is, "Come up **to me** into the mount, and **be there**: and I will give thee tables of stone!" Even more than giving Moses the incredibly significant tables of stone, what God wanted was for Moses to come into His *presence*, just to *be with Him*! So often we relegate the Christian life to *doing*. God wants us to know that, though there are certainly many important things that we need to do, what is vitally important to His heart is that we simply desire to *be* with Him, like He desires to *be* with us!

As we continue our journey through the Word of God, remember that what is in God's heart is not simply that we *do* our assigned daily readings, but that every day we come up into His *presence* through the pages of His glorious Book—to *be with Him*!

CHRIST IS REVEALED:

Through *Moses* who delivers God's commands, consummates a blood sacrifice, and communes with God for 40 days – Exodus 24:2–3, 8, 18 (Heb. 10:12; Mark 1:13)

WEEK 5, DAY 1: **TODAY'S READING: EXODUS 25–28**

OVERVIEW:

God details His plans for the tabernacle; God details His plans for the High Priest's coverings.

HIGHLIGHTS & INSIGHTS:

In John 4, Jesus lets us know that our Father in heaven is seeking *worship*! But He is not just seeking any kind of worship—He is seeking the worship that only comes from "true worshippers" (John 4:23). Obviously, if there are "true worshippers," there must also be false worshippers and worship that God recognizes as unacceptable! We can conclude then that not everything that goes on in the name of "worship" is actually recognized by God and received of God as "true" worship.

Beginning in today's reading, our God is providing a detailed description and prescription for the "true worship" He desired from the Nation of Israel in the days following their Exodus from Egypt. It centers on what was basically a tent that was approximately 45 feet long, 15 feet wide, and 15 feet high, with an outer court measuring approximately 150 feet by 75 feet. The complete structure is most commonly referred to as the tabernacle, and it served the Nation of Israel as a sort of "mobile worship center."

The tabernacle was actually comprised of three sections: the Outer Court—into which the common people could come; the Holy Place—into which only the priests could come; and the Holy of Holies, or the Holiest of All—into which only the high priest could come (and that, only once a year on the Day of Atonement). This "mobile worship center" represented God's presence with His people Israel for over 400 years—from the Exodus to the building of the permanent temple under Solomon.

As we begin to discuss some of the details of the tabernacle, it is important to note that the Divine Architect (the Designer and Builder of the universe!) is now taking on His second "building project" through man. The first, of course, was Noah's Ark, which was a vessel by which God *saved* man—carrying him through the flood. The second, the tabernacle, (and specifically the Ark of the Covenant in the Holy of Holies in the tabernacle) was a vessel through which God *met* with man—as man carried God through the wilderness. In both building projects, the instructions for the construction of the *Ark* were very detailed and specific and were given to man by supernatural revelation. God left nothing to man's imagination or invention.

Other "tidbits" concerning the tabernacle:

- The tabernacle is referred to in Scripture by such names as the tent, the tent of testimony, the tent of the congregation, the tabernacle of witness, the tabernacle of testimony, the tabernacle of the congregation, and the place of dwelling.

- In Exodus 25–39, God provides for us a verbal diagram of the tabernacle, specifying the materials that were to be used in its construction, the furniture to be placed in it, the utensils to be used in it, as well as a description of those who were to minister in it.

- Exodus 25–27, where the prominent vessel of the tabernacle that is detailed is the Ark of the Covenant, reveals to us *God's* approach to *man*.

- Exodus 28–30, where the prominent "vessel" of the tabernacle that is detailed is the high priest, reveals to us *man's* approach to *God*.

- Historically, God designed this tabernacle because He wanted to dwell and commune with His people, the *Jews* (Ex. 25:8, 22). Practically, God designed the record of it so that all people through the annals of history would likewise know that through Christ (who is actually being pictured throughout the tabernacle) the same God wants to dwell in and commune with us—His *church*! (See 2 Cor. 6:14–16; 1 John 4:12–13; Hebrews 9:1–14.)

- Entire books have been written about the numerous pictures and types drawn by God in the layout, design, and contents of the tabernacle. Like any great work of art, the more you look at it, the more you see!

CHRIST IS REVEALED:

In the *Ark of the Covenant,* wood overlaid by pure gold (wood representing His humanity and gold representing His deity) – Exodus 25:10–11 (Phil. 2:6–8)

In the *Mercy Seat* – Exodus 25:17 (Rom. 3:24–25 – The word *propitiation* in Romans 3:25 is translated "mercy seat" in Hebrews 9:5, and 1 John 2:2 says that Christ "is the propitiation for our sins.")

In the *Table of Shewbread* – Exodus 25:23–30 (Jesus is the Bread of Life – John 6:33, 35, 48, 51)

In the *Candlestick* – Exodus 25:31 (Jesus is the Light – John 1:4–9; 8:12; 9:5; 12:35–36, 46)

In the *Veil* – Exodus 26:30–37 (Representing the physical body of Christ which was "torn" to bring us to God – Mark 15:38; Heb. 10:20)

Through the *High Priest* and all of his *Clothing* – Exodus 28:1–43 (Jesus is our High Priest – Heb. 2:17; 3:1)

WEEK 5, DAY 2: **TODAY'S READING: EXODUS 29–32**

OVERVIEW:

God gives instruction on the consecration of the priests; God explains how the tabernacle is to operate; God appoints specific men to oversee the building of the tabernacle; God emphasizes the Sabbath day; Israel sins against God; Moses intercedes for Israel.

HIGHLIGHTS & INSIGHTS:

For 40 days (since the end of Exodus 24), Moses has been back up on Mount Sinai receiving specific instruction from God. And do you remember the incredible initial response the people had to "the words of the Lord" when Moses came down from the mountain the first time? With complete unity ("one voice") they had declared to Moses with their mouth, "All the words which the Lord hath said will we do" (24:3)! Moses then wrote the words the Lord had spoken to him up on the mountain and read them to the children of Israel, and once again, the people declared with their mouths, "All that the Lord hath said will we do, and be obedient" (Ex. 24:7)!

But, as we've mentioned before, talk is cheap. God had called Moses to come back up to the mountain, and just 40 days after making these incredible declarations, Exodus 32:1 says, "And when the people saw that Moses delayed to come down out of the mount, the people gathered themselves together unto Aaron, and said unto him, Up, make us gods, which shall go before us; for as for this Moses, the man that brought us up out of the land of Egypt, we wot not what is become of him."

God has just spent four chapters giving Moses detailed instructions about Aaron (even referring to Aaron by name thirty-nine times in chapters 28–31) because Aaron would picture our High Priest, the Lord Jesus Christ. And here we find Aaron, the high priest, bowing to the pressure of the people, making a false god and leading Israel in the worship of it (Exodus 32:1–6). They actually dance about it naked—praising *it* for delivering them from Egypt! Absolutely unbelievable! How in the world could they be so fickle … so weak … and so downright sinful? Especially in light of God's words to Moses in chapter 29:44–45. "And I will sanctify the tabernacle of the congregation, and the altar: I will sanctify also both Aaron and his sons, to minister to me in the priest's office. And I will dwell among the children of Israel, and will be their God." Oh, had they only known the incredible future God had designed for them!

And yet, don't forget, the children of Israel in the Old Testament are a picture of the individual believer in the New Testament! We might do well to consider how many times, like Israel, we have exercised our sinful flesh despite God's supernatural working in our lives. And when God hasn't worked according to our timetable, how often we have redirected the glory for victories God had wrought to someone or something other than the one to whom it was due!

And then, notice Aaron's lame cover-up when confronted with his sin (Ex. 32:24). Aaron actually has the audacity to say to Moses (with a straight face, mind you!), that he simply threw the gold into the fire and out popped a golden calf! That "miracle" having taken place, the only natural thing to do, according to Aaron's whacked out rationalization, was to set it in front of the people so they could dance around it and party the day away in sensual lust! Though Aaron's explanation sounds totally absurd to us, I wonder how absurd the justifications we sometimes use to explain away our carnal behavior sound to God!

Sadly, the wonderful things that God had planned for His people, which He was detailing to Moses up on the mountain, were at that very moment being polluted by Aaron and the children of Israel down at the base of the mountain. (Make note that this great sin committed by the children of Israel in Exodus 32 became a sinful marker or milestone in Israel's history that Stephen even referenced when recounting Israel's history to their leaders in Acts 7:41–43!) The tragic fact is that, while God was painting a beautiful picture to Moses of how His people could exemplify His holiness and mercy, Israel was simultaneously painting the dreadful portrait of how God's people so often misrepresent and adulterate His love and His Word (1 Cor. 10:1–11).

CHRIST IS REVEALED:

Through God's plan for *Aaron the High Priest* – Exodus 29 (Heb. 7:26–8:1)

Through the *Sacrifice for Atonement* – Exodus 30:10 (Rom. 6:10; Heb. 7:27; 9:7, 12; 10:10)

WEEK 5, DAY 3: **TODAY'S READING: EXODUS 33–36**

OVERVIEW:
God commands the people to go to Canaan; Moses asks God to reestablish His presence with Israel; God rewrites the tables of stone that Moses had broken; God reaffirms His special relationship with Israel; Moses reveals the tabernacle plans and the people respond obediently.

HIGHLIGHTS & INSIGHTS:
As we begin today's reading, God has very simply had "Enough!" He reiterates His promise to give the land of Canaan to the children of Israel—but lets them know they'd be making the journey to get there without Him. Though His personal presence would not be with them, however, He would "send an angel" before them (33:2). This angel would provide the strength and guidance He knew they would need to overcome the enemies that would attempt to keep them from taking the land. Notice though that the angel that is promised here ("*an angel*") is different than the angel ("*mine Angel*") mentioned in Exodus 23:23 and 32:34—which was the *"Angel of the Lord."* (See the Highlights & Insights section of Week 4, Day 5.) God also informs them that His decision not to go with them was actually for their own good, "lest I consume thee in the way" (33:3). God tells them, "for thou art a *stiffnecked* people." Wow! What an indictment!

The word *stiffnecked* appears six times in the Old Testament and once in the New Testament. It is used to refer to the children of Israel all seven times. But by observing my own spiritual journey, as well as the journey of others, I'm quite certain God didn't stop dealing with "stiffnecked people" with the children of Israel in the wilderness! When God's plan for our lives doesn't line up with our own plans or when God is trying to use the circumstances of our lives (trials) to conform us into the image of His Son (Rom. 8:29), our reaction is often much like that of our spiritual forefathers in the book of Exodus—we tend to resist, to become stubborn and obstinate, or to "stiffen" our "neck."

There is an interesting contrast in today's reading, however, between those God describes as being *"stiffnecked"* (33:3, 5; 34:9) and those who have a *"willing"* heart (35:5, 21, 29), a *"stirred"* heart (35:21, 26; 36:2), and a *"spirit made willing"* (35:21). Based on your spiritual walk in the last six months, which term do you think God would use to describe you? Very simply, have you had a *"stirred"* and *"willing heart/spirit"*—or have you had a *"stiffened neck"*? Obviously, the two are mutually exclusive.

And even though the children of Israel were a "stiffnecked people," the thought of not having the Lord's presence with them was extremely disturbing to them. Exodus 33:4 says that when they heard that the Lord wouldn't be going with them, "they *mourned*." Their reaction made me wonder how we would react if the Lord were to tell us that He would still take us to heaven when we die, but rather than having His presence in and on our lives, "an angel" would be guiding us in the remainder of our journey. Would we be content or satisfied with the angel—simply being in proximity to the things of God, or would we mourn because we are passionate for *God Himself* and having *His Holy presence* with us? Would our reaction be like Moses's in 33:15, "If thy presence go not with me, carry us not up hence"?

Other practical gleanings to note in today's reading...

- Let us rejoice in the fact that, like Moses, the Lord knows each of us by name—and that we have found grace in His sight! (33:12, 17)

- Notice that Moses's passion quickly takes him from begging God to "show me thy *way*" (33:13) to begging God for Him to "show me thy *glory*" (33:18). May the passion that guides our hearts be a passion for God Himself—that He would receive "the glory due unto His name" (Ps. 29:2; 96:8).

- May the testimony of Moses's relationship with God be ours: "And the Lord spoke unto Moses face to face, as a man speaketh unto his friend" (33:11).

- Exodus 33:20 teaches us a vital and far-reaching lesson: No living flesh can see God! If we will truly see God in the fullness of His majesty, splendor and glory—it requires *death*! Very simply, we must *die* to ourselves; our *flesh* must be *crucified*! (See Gal. 5:24; Col. 3:5.)

- We would do well to follow the admonition God gave to Moses in 34:2–3: "And be ready in the morning, and come up in the morning unto mount Sinai, and present thyself there to me in the top of the mount. And no man shall come up with thee, neither let any man be seen throughout all the mount; neither let the flocks nor herds feed before that mount." Practically speaking, may we "ready" ourselves for each day by reserving the first part of it ("the morning") to get alone with God before we are distracted by our daily responsibilities (34:3) and to "come up" into the mountain of the Lord's presence (Psa. 24:3) to "present" ourselves to the Lord "a living sacrifice" (Rom. 12:1).

- "The name of the Lord" is a key phrase in the Bible. Exodus 34:5–7 defines "the name of the Lord" as the sum total of all of His attributes. Notice, that He is *God* and, as such, is merciful, gracious, longsuffering, abundantly good and abundantly truth!

- Check out Moses's prayer in 34:9: "If now I have found grace in thy sight, O Lord, let my Lord, I pray thee, go among us; for it is a stiffnecked people; and pardon our iniquity and our sin, and take us for thine inheritance." Notice that it is a prayer for:

  ‣ The Lord's *presence*.
  ‣ The Lord's *pardon*.
  ‣ The Lord's *possession*.

- Notice in 34:28 that it was said of Moses, "And he was there with the Lord forty days and forty nights." This "forty day" thing shows up quite a bit throughout the Bible, and it seems to be connected to a time of testing and/or trial.

  1. Noah's flood lasted 40 days and 40 nights. (Gen. 7:12)
  2. Noah waited another 40 days after the rain stopped before opening the window in the Ark. (Gen. 8:6)
  3. Moses was on Mt. Sinai with God 40 days and 40 nights—twice! (Ex. 24:18; 34:28–29)
  4. Twelve spies searched out the Promised land for 40 days. (Num. 13:25)
  5. Goliath defied God and His armies for 40 days before being defeated by David. (1 Sam. 17:16)
  6. Elijah fasted for 40 days on Mt. Horeb. (1 Kings 19:8)
  7. Ezekiel laid on his right side for 40 days to bear the iniquity of Judah. (Ezek. 4:6)
  8. Jonah warned that Ninevah would be overthrown in 40 days. (Jonah 3:4)
  9. Jesus fasted for 40 days in the wilderness. (Matt. 4:1–2; Mark 1:13; Luke 4:2)
  10. Jesus was on the earth 40 days after His resurrection. (Acts 1:3)

Finally, in chapter 35, God begins His second building project by instructing Moses to take up an offering from the people for the construction of the tabernacle. Obviously, God could have simply spoken the tabernacle into existence just as He did the entire universe, so it begs the question, why didn't He? While there are certainly other reasons, there are at least two very simple, and significant ones:

1. A Practical Reason.

This tent would serve as the place where God would "dwell" with man (Ex. 25:8), His "meeting place" with man (25:22), the place where He would "inhabit the praises of His people" (Ps. 22:3). In light of that purpose, God chose to allow the people to enjoy a sense of ownership in the project by encouraging them to provide both the funding and the craftsmanship (sewing, carving, goldsmithing, baking, dying, etc.) for its completion. As has been noted through the centuries, people regard that which cost them nothing as having little or no value. Obviously, God wanted to be sure that never happened with the tabernacle; He wanted to insure that the people of Israel always maintained a keen appreciation for this special meeting place with God which would be used to house the Ark of the covenant after the exodus and until the construction of the Temple (approximately 400 years!). Note also that the offering God specified was not in any way to be connected to law, but to grace! Exodus 25:2 says that the offering was to be given "willingly" and with their "heart."

2. **An Instructional Reason.**

God gave very specific details concerning the tabernacle's construction for a very monumental reason: This was no ordinary tent! This tent was the *earthly* representation of a *heavenly* tabernacle that Hebrews 8:2 refers to as "the true tabernacle, which the Lord pitched and not man." God's instructions for the tabernacle's construction revealed to Moses and the children of Israel specific details concerning His *earthly* dwelling place which follow the pattern of the *heavenly* tabernacle (Ex. 25:9; Heb. 8:5). One day we will understand that Exodus 25–30 and Exodus 35–39 actually reveal more about the universe than the most powerful and sophisticated twenty-first-century telescope—and more about the universe than all that God included in Genesis 1 and Job 38! But for now, comprehending exactly how the *earthly tabernacle* mirrored the *heavenly tabernacle* will take someone much more spiritually and biblically astute than I am—not to mention someone way more intelligent!

But one thing I do understand: Just as there were three parts of the tabernacle on the earth, there are three heavens (2 Cor. 12:2; Ps. 148). And just as God's presence was beyond the veil in the third part of the tabernacle (the Holy of Holies)—God's actual presence in the universe is beyond the veil identified as the frozen waters of "the deep" northward in the third heaven. (See Job 38:30; Isa. 14:13; Psa. 48:2.) And perhaps most importantly, the instructions concerning the tabernacle were so explicit because it was also a picture of Christ.

CHRIST IS REVEALED:

In the *Tabernacle* – Exodus 35 (Heb. 9:1–14)

The *Single Door* into the tabernacle– Exodus 35:15 (John 10:1–2, 7, 9)

The *Holy of Holies* into which only the High Priest could enter – Exodus 35:19 (Heb. 9:12)

WEEK 5, DAY 4: **TODAY'S READING: EXODUS 37–40**

OVERVIEW:

The tabernacle is completed and an inventory is taken; God commands Moses to set up the tabernacle; God's presence fills the tabernacle.

HIGHLIGHTS & INSIGHTS:

In chapters 37 and 38, the Spirit of God inspires Moses to once again list and describe the seven pieces of furniture to be placed in the tabernacle. These pieces were placed in a specific order in the physical tabernacle, from the courtyard to the Holy Place and into the Holy of Holies.

1. The Brazen Altar

2. The Brazen Laver

3. The Table of Shewbread

4. The Candlestick

5. The Altar of Incense

6. The Ark

7. The Mercy Seat

What's interesting is that, when the Apostle John refers to the Lord Jesus Christ becoming a human being and living among us, he says, "And the Word was made flesh and dwelt [literally, *tabernacled*] among us" (John 1:14). Jesus Christ is directly connected to the tabernacle. And what's more, the Holy Spirit of God inspired John to lay out the contents of his Gospel so that the order of the furniture found in the tabernacle in Exodus 37 and 38 is the exact order of what unfolds in the ministry of Jesus throughout John's Gospel!

He begins by leading us to the Brazen Altar of sacrifice, as twice in the first chapter He urges us to "Behold the Lamb of God, which taketh away the sin of the world" (John 1:29, 36).

We are then taken to the Laver in John 3:5, where the Spirit of God records, "Except a man be born of water and of the Spirit, he cannot enter into the kingdom of God."

Moving further into the Gospel of John (and into the tabernacle), the Spirit presents Christ as Living Water (ch. 4) and Living Bread (ch. 6), which pictures the food and drink of the Table of Shewbread. (And keep in mind, the tabernacle and its furniture in the book of Exodus is the *picture*, while Christ and the tabernacle in Heaven is the *reality*! It's easy to get those reversed!)

In John 8, we come to the Golden Candlestick and John records our Lord Jesus Christ as He proclaims, "I am the light of the world: he that followeth me shall not walk in darkness, but shall have the light of life" (John 8:12).

In John 14–16, the Spirit of God brings us, as it were, to the Altar of Incense, as Jesus teaches us to pray in His name—the name of the onethat is to the Father "a sweetsmelling savor" (Eph. 5:2).

Then in John 17, we are taken beyond the veil into the Holy of Holies to behold our Great High Priest, the Lord Jesus Christ, making intercession for us in the presence of God. Here Christ is seen not only as our High Priest, but as the Ark and the Mercy Seat through whom we have found access and acceptance with His Father and God. Jesus said in John 20:17, "I ascend unto *my* Father, and *your* Father; and to *my* God, and *your* God."

We now return to Exodus 39–40. The tabernacle had been made according to the divine *pattern*, and it was then ready to be filled with the divine *glory*. And in perfect fulfillment of the Old Testament picture, the Gospel of John closes with Jesus breathing on His disciples saying, "Receive ye the Holy Ghost" (John 20:22).

Wow! What a supernatural Book God has entrusted to our stewardship!

CHRIST IS REVEALED:

In the *high priest*, who on his *breastplate* bears the names of God's people before the presence of God – Exodus 39:8–21 (Heb. 9:11; 10:19–22)

In the *four colors* that represent the *four gospels* – Exodus 38:18, 23; 39:2–3, 5, 8, 24, 29

WEEK 5, DAY 5: **TODAY'S READING: LEVITICUS 1–5**

OVERVIEW:

The burnt offering; the meat (meal, grain) offering; the peace offering; the sin offering; the trespass offering.

HIGHLIGHTS & INSIGHTS:

Today's reading begins what is for many people one of the most challenging sections of the entire Bible. It is not challenging because the language is difficult to understand or the information is difficult to process, but because all of the intricate details regarding the sacrifices and feasts seem to be irrelevant to most church age believers. So reading chapter after chapter of them inevitably becomes boring and monotonous. However, these folks have mistakenly assumed that Leviticus has no application to us. Obviously, because of Christ's once-for-all offering of Himself, we no longer offer animal sacrifices or celebrate the Jewish feasts. But God tells us in 2 Timothy 3:16 that "All scripture … is profitable for doctrine, for reproof, for correction, for instruction in righteousness," and Romans 15:4 tells us that the things written in the Old Testament "were written for our learning"!

So just what do the teachings in the book of Leviticus have to do with our lives today? Well, consider the following:

- Leviticus contains more words spoken directly by God Himself than any other book in the Bible. (Lev. 1:1)

- Leviticus is quoted more than 40 times in the New Testament. Apparently, there is something very important that God wants to communicate to us in the book of Leviticus!

- Without Leviticus we could never understand the book of Hebrews or much of the terminology used in other New Testament books. Leviticus foreshadows and pictures many New Testament truths regarding the person and work of Jesus Christ.

- David continuously and emphatically declared that he delighted in God's statutes (Psa. 119:16, 54, 80). Many of God's statutes are recorded in the book of Leviticus (Lev. 3:17). Apparently then, David, the man after God's own heart, actually *delighted* in the book of Leviticus!

- The book of Leviticus reveals that God, through Jesus Christ, has prepared three things for us:

  1. A *Sacrifice*. (Jesus Christ, the Lamb of God—John 1:29)

  2. A *Priest*. (Jesus Christ, the great High Priest—Heb. 3:1)

  3. A *Place*. (Heaven, where Jesus Christ is enthroned—1 Pet. 3:22)

- But not only has God prepared these three things for us, He has also made each of us who are "in Christ"...

  1. A *Sacrifice*. (Rom. 12:1–2)

  2. A *Priest*. (1 Pet. 2:5)

  3. A *Place*. (Eph. 2:22)

The purpose of the book of Leviticus is twofold: first, to show us that we must worship the Lord in holiness (the word *holy* or some form of it appears 94 times in Leviticus!); and second, to show us that worship is the only pathway to peace, rest, and fruitfulness. God will not give us peace, rest, or fruitfulness until we are worshiping Him in holiness.

Historically, the events recorded in Leviticus occur at the door of the tabernacle over a period of one month (Lev. 1:1; Ex. 40:17; Num. 1:1). Having delivered His children by the blood of the lamb (the book of Exodus), God plans to take them to a place of peace, rest, and fruitfulness. But before they embark on their journey, they must first establish worship. The book of Leviticus is Israel's instruction book on worship. The word *Leviticus* means "that which pertains to the Levites" and is so called because the tribe of Levi was chosen by God to be Israel's worship leaders. The word *Levi* means "joined to God," and because the Levites were "joined to God," they had no inheritance in the promised land—God was their inheritance.

Prophetically, Leviticus 1–5 describes five types of sacrifices, each of which is an incredible picture, both of the Lord Jesus Christ and of New Testament believers.

Chapter 1 – The Burnt Offering

This offering represents the substitutionary sacrifice of Jesus Christ. As believers, this offering points us to the New Testament reality that we are to offer our bodies as "living sacrifice[s], holy, acceptable unto God" (Rom. 12:1). Note that the head and fat of the animal is laid upon the wood (Lev. 1:8), a picture of how we must lay our plans, our wills, our treasures and all that we are upon the cross of Christ (Luke 9:23). Also, the "inwards and the legs" were to be washed in water (Lev. 1:9,13), representing our "inner man" (Eph. 3:16) and our "walk" (Col. 1:10) being washed with the water of the word of God (Eph. 5:26–27).

Chapter 2 – The Meat (or, the Meal or Grain) Offering

This is the only bloodless sacrifice. It represents the sinless life of Jesus Christ. The remnant of this offering was given to Aaron's sons (Lev. 2:10), picturing Christ's righteousness given to believers (2 Cor. 5:21).

Chapter 3 – The Peace Offering

This offering represents the peace Jesus Christ purchased for us with His own precious blood (Col. 1:20; Eph. 2:14). Note that the kidney, caul, and liver—the organs used to filter out poisonous toxins—were taken away. Through this sacrifice, God teaches us that we have permanent, genuine peace with Him through our Savior Jesus Christ, who has taken away the poison of our sin.

Chapter 4 – The Sin Offering

This offering reveals how Jesus Christ has given believers victory over our sinful nature—the flesh. The sin talked about in this chapter is "ignorant sin," referring to sin that mysteriously permeates our flesh—sin that is so deeply rooted in us that we are sometimes even unaware of it. (See Ps. 19:12; 90:8; 139:23–24; Jer. 17:9; Rom. 7.) Note that the whole body of the bullock (an ox or horned cow) was to be taken outside the camp and burned, picturing the fact that our flesh is of no value or use to God and must therefore be "mortified" and "put off" (Col. 3:5–17; Rom. 6).

Chapter 5 – The Trespass Offering

This offering represents Christ's victory over specific individual sins, also called trespasses. This is the only sacrifice associated with money (5:15). Truly, "the wages of sin is death" (Rom. 6:23). Thanks be to God, Jesus Christ has paid the price for our sins with His own precious blood (Acts 20:28)!

In today's reading it will become obvious that the book of Leviticus is a book of violence and blood. In fact, the word *offering* occurs 387 times, and the word *blood* appears 88 times. Why would a loving God require such horrible violence? For several reasons:

1. "Without shedding of blood is no remission" for sin. (Heb. 9:22)
2. God never wants us to forget the horrific consequences of sin. (Jas. 1:15)
3. God wants us to know that He loved us so much that He voluntarily subjected His Son to the bloody violence of the cross to pay the price of our sin. (Lev. 1:3; Rom. 5:8)
4. We are in a violent war with our flesh. (Rom. 7:23)
5. God desires to have every part of us, severally and wholly, and that can be very excruciating! (Col. 3:5; Rom. 8:13)

CHRIST IS REVEALED:

As our *Voluntary Substitutionary Sacrifice* – Leviticus 1 (The Burnt Offering)...

who lived a *Sinless Life* – Leviticus 2 (The Meat Offering)...

and purchased *Peace with God* – Leviticus 3 (The Peace Offering)...

by *Paying* the *Price* for our *Sins* – Leviticus 4 (The Sin Offering)...

and giving us *Victory* over our *Flesh* – Leviticus 5 (The Trespass Offering).

WEEK 6, DAY 1: **TODAY'S READING: LEVITICUS 6–9**

OVERVIEW:

Restating of the sacrifices in a new order and with an additional offering; Aaron and his sons consecrated for and instituted in service to God.

HIGHLIGHTS & INSIGHTS:

We can be certain that our omniscient God doesn't suffer from short-term memory loss! When God repeats Himself, start digging because you're standing on buried treasure! In chapters 6 and 7, God repeats the discussion concerning the sacrifices and offerings in chapters 1–5. But by changing the order, He reveals to us something important!

In chapters 1–5, the order of the offerings (burnt, meat, peace, sin and trespass) shows God's transcendence toward man through the person of Jesus Christ because Jesus voluntarily offered (burnt offering) His sinless life (meat offering) to reconcile God and man (peace offering) by atoning for man's sin (sin and trespass offerings). In chapters 6 and 7, however, there is an additional sacrifice and a new order: burnt, meat, *priest's*, sin, trespass and peace. This new order reveals that man's ascension toward God is only through Jesus Christ, the great High Priest. It's no accident that the priest's offering is a bridge between the burnt and meat offerings and the sin and trespass offerings because the Bible teaches us that "there is one God, and one mediator between God and men, the man Christ Jesus; who gave himself a ransom for all" (1 Tim. 2:5–6a). Our Lord Jesus Christ is the only bridge to God!

Notice also that the peace offering is listed last in this new order, teaching us that peace is the result of our Lord Jesus Christ standing in the gap between God and man. Romans 5:1 teaches us that "we have peace with God through our Lord Jesus Christ," and Ephesians 2:14 says, "For he [Christ] is our peace, who hath made both one, and hath broken down the middle wall of partition [sin!] between us."

Notice also that the fire of the altar was forbidden to go out. Leviticus 6:13 says: "The fire shall ever be burning upon the altar; it shall never go out." This signifies that because of Christ's sacrifice for us, our God is always ready, willing, and waiting for us to enter into His presence. Psalm 86:5 declares, "For thou, Lord, art good, and ready to forgive; and plenteous in mercy unto all them that call upon thee." I join Paul in 2 Corinthians 9:15 in declaring, "Thanks be unto God for his unspeakable gift"!

Once the path to God has been established and clearly marked (chapters 1–7), God prepares His children for consecration to His service and to experience His glorious presence. Chapters 8 and 9 show us the consecration of the priests in preparation for God's glorious presence.

Be aware of several other key things we glean from the book of Leviticus.

First, note that all priests are Levites—but not all Levites are priests. You may need to read that again to get your head wrapped around it! But only Aaron's sons could become priests. In other words, you had to be born a priest. This pictures the New Testament truth that only those who have been born again into the family of the great High Priest, our Lord Jesus Christ, can serve and worship God as priests. (See 1 Pet. 2:5; Rev. 1:6.)

Secondly, notice that only the High Priest wears the "holy crown" (Lev. 8:9)—teaching us that there is only one High Priest who is also a King, our Lord Jesus Christ, and only He holds the place of preeminence, both in the universe and in our lives (Col. 1:18).

Thirdly, notice that when Aaron and his sons were consecrated for service to God, blood was placed upon their right ear lobes, right thumbs and right toes—symbolizing that all of their strength (denoted by the right side) was devoted to hearing and obeying God's *holy Word*, carrying out God's *holy work* and continuing in a *holy walk*. That threefold devotion is what our Lord also desires of us as New Testament priests (Col. 1:10)!

And finally, notice in Leviticus 9:6–7 that Aaron makes atonement for himself and the people as a prerequisite to God's glory descending upon the tabernacle—picturing the fact that atonement necessarily precedes God's presence. Unless we are in a right relationship with God, completely consecrated to Him, we will never experience the glory of His presence in our lives (Lev. 9:24).

CHRIST IS REVEALED:

As our *Mediator* and *High Priest* who intercedes before God on our behalf – Leviticus 9:7–24 (1 Tim. 2:5; Heb. 7:22–26)

WEEK 6, DAY 2: **TODAY'S READING: LEVITICUS 10–13**

OVERVIEW:

Nadab and Abihu are judged by God; the first kosher menu is created; instruction regarding postpartum purification; leprosy is identified and addressed.

HIGHLIGHTS & INSIGHTS:

In our reading today in Leviticus 10, we learn something tremendously significant about our holy, loving, gracious, merciful, tenderhearted, compassionate, forbearing and forgiving God—*He takes His Word very seriously!*

Though all of the qualities I just listed are wonderfully true of our God, when our sincere hearts, good intentions and pure motives don't align themselves to God's will and purposes as they are *revealed* in His *Word*—watch out! Just ask Nadab and Abihu! These men (Aaron's sons) allowed themselves to be so caught up in the emotional excitement of experiencing God's presence at the end of chapter 9 (vs. 23–24), they invented, as it were, their own self-styled way to worship God in chapter 10, verse 1.

Now, without understanding the God of the Bible, someone might think, "Well, isn't that admirable! These two men didn't want the expression of their worship to God to be limited by only what they learned in a Book. They wanted to be free to express themselves from their hearts and minds in a way that reflected their own ideas and personality!" And as "cool" and "organic" as that might sound to our modern way of thinking—God was not impressed! Not in the slightest! Out of the sincerity and goodness of their heart, Nadab and Abihu did what they thought was right in their own eyes by offering fire of their own creativity and invention to the Lord. God immediately let Nadab and Abihu, the children of Israel, and us know exactly how He felt about it by answering with fire out of heaven that "zap-fried" them right on the spot! Leviticus 10:2 says, "And there went out fire from the Lord, and devoured them, and they died before the Lord." And again, don't miss *why* God responded the way He did! Verse 1 says, "And Nadab and Abihu … offered strange fire before the Lord, which he commanded them not"!

The fire of God's judgment devoured them because they refused to worship God in accordance with His Word! This is such an important lesson for us! Jesus reiterated this principle in John 4:23 when He said, "But the hour cometh, and now is, when the true worshippers shall worship the Father in spirit and in truth: for the Father seeketh such to worship him."

Yes, God is certainly seeking *worship*—but not just any kind of worship! He is only interested in "true worship" that arises out of the spirit of a "true worshipper." And biblically, worship will always be not only in spirit, but will also always be in truth! That is—it will always be *generated* and *governed* by the truth of His Word. In response to the Word of God, true worship arises from deep within our innermost being (our spirits) and runs straight through our hearts, our minds, our emotions, and ultimately out of our mouths in honor, praise, and worship of God!

The practical lesson we must learn from Nadab and Abihu is that, with any activity we are witnessing or being influenced to participate in, we must train our brain to constantly be asking: What is the biblical precedence for this? Does the Bible give an example of this? Does the Bible specifically command me to do this? And if there is a biblical example and/or command, does it actually apply to me, as one who is living in the dispensation of the church age?

In the 21st century, though God may not be "zap-frying" people who violate His truth in worship, we must make certain we understand that "strange fire" is being offered to the Lord at literally every turn in "Christianity" and in almost every "Christian" denomination.

Nadab and Abihu are a graphic illustration of the principle God laid out in Proverbs 14:12: "There is a way which seemeth right unto a man, but the end thereof are the ways of death." Oh, my brothers and sisters, we must *learn* the truth of the Word of God—and respond and worship accordingly—and not *lean* upon our own understanding or our own natural instincts or inclinations!

After laying down Israel's dietary laws in chapter 11 and instruction regarding postpartum purification in chapter 12, God paints an incredible picture of the working and consequences of sin—through His teaching concerning leprosy in chapter 13. Throughout the remainder of the Bible, leprosy will always be a picture of sin. Just like leprosy, sin …

- Is a disease that spreads throughout the body.

- Often remains undetected by others.

- Defiles everyone it's near.

- Isolates the one(s) infected.

- Is fit only for destruction by fire.

However, we can choose to separate ourselves from sin: putting off the garment of the flesh (Col. 3:5–9) and allowing our High Priest, the Lord Jesus Christ, to apply the blood of the sacrifice (1 John 1:7) and to anoint us with "oil" (a type of the Holy Spirit) through the picture of Leviticus 13. When we do that, God lets us know that through Christ, our faithful High Priest, we can be restored to the joy of our fellowship with God—and man.

CHRIST IS REVEALED:

As our *High Priest* who identifies and cleanses the disease of our sin – Leviticus 13 (Heb. 4:14–15).

WEEK 6, DAY 3: **TODAY'S READING: LEVITICUS 14–16**

OVERVIEW:

The purification of lepers; purification of those with unclean issues; instructions regarding the Day of Atonement.

HIGHLIGHTS & INSIGHTS:

God is invisible and many of His truths relate to the unseen realm—and thus, the need for faith! As Hebrews 11:1 tells us, "faith is … the evidence of things not seen." Though the spiritual realm is invisible, God is an expert at teaching spiritual truths through physical realities. Leviticus 15 is a perfect example.

One of the beautiful things about this section of Scripture is the fact that God recognizes that we all have issues. God provides instructions here regarding "unclean issues" for the obvious reason of preventing the spread of infectious illnesses among the Israelites. However, God's stringent physical rules regarding "unclean issues" also teach us spiritual truths about "unclean" thoughts, attitudes and words that "issue" out of our hearts. Jesus reminded us that "those things which proceed out of the mouth come forth from the heart; and they defile the man. For out of the heart proceed evil thoughts, murders, adulteries, fornications, thefts, false witness, blasphemies: These are the things which defile a man" (Matt. 15:18–20). No wonder David prayed, "Set a watch, O LORD, before my mouth; keep the door of my lips" (Ps. 141:3).

In Leviticus 16, God introduces a special holiday into the Jewish calendar: the Day of Atonement. On this day, both the sin nature and the individual sins of the entire nation of Israel were atoned for, or covered. A simple way to remember the significance of this holy day is by breaking the word *atonement* into three hyphenated words: "at–one–ment." This is the day when Israel's sin was covered, making them "at one" with God. The Day of Atonement detailed in Leviticus 16 is a very descriptive picture of the person and work of our High Priest, the Lord Jesus Christ. In this chapter, the high priest enters the Holy of Holies with the blood of a sin offering—picturing the fact that our High Priest, Jesus Christ, would one day pour out His own blood as the ultimate atonement for sin upon the true altar in the third heaven! Hebrews 9:24 states it like this: "For Christ is not entered into the holy places made with hands, which are the figures of the true; but into heaven itself, now to appear in the presence of God for us."

Once the high priest in the Old Testament had completed this offering, he laid his hands upon the head of the scapegoat and confessed the sins of the children of Israel (16:21)—symbolizing that the scapegoat had carried away their iniquities. Isaiah prophetically described this portion of Christ's work saying, "the LORD hath laid on him the iniquity of us all" (Isa. 53:6). Praise God, our Lord Jesus Christ has carried our sins to a place that is as far as the east is from the west (Ps. 103:12). In other words, Jesus permanently eliminated the record of our sins—God remembers them no more!

Through the record of the Day of Atonement, God is teaching us that our Lord Jesus Christ has effectually dealt with both our sinful *nature* and our sinful *actions*. Praise the Lord!

Though there are many parallels between the high priest of the Old Testament and the person and work of our High Priest, the Lord Jesus Christ, two monumental differences must be recognized. First, the Old Testament high priest had to provide a sin offering for himself because he was as guilty of sin as the rest of the children of Israel. Jesus Christ, our High Priest, however, never offered a sin sacrifice for Himself because He was completely free and void of sin (Heb. 9:14; 7:22–28)! Secondly, the Day of Atonement was celebrated every year because "it is not possible that the blood of bulls and of goats should take away sins. And every priest standeth daily ministering and offering oftentimes the same sacrifices, which can never take away sins: But this man [Jesus Christ], after he had offered one sacrifice for sins for ever, sat down on the right hand of God; From henceforth expecting till his enemies be made his footstool" (Heb 10:4,11–13). Because of Christ's offering for sin, no other sacrifice will ever be necessary!

For those of us who have a personal relationship with Jesus Christ, we can glory today in the fact that our Savior offered Himself *one time* to *permanently* and *forever* pay the price for our sin—and sins! Hallelujah!

CHRIST IS REVEALED:

As our *Sin Offering* which effectually crucified our sin nature – Leviticus 14:19–32 (Rom. 5:8)

As our *Scapegoat* which carried away our sins – Leviticus 16:5–34 (2 Cor. 5:21)

As our eternal *High Priest* who intercedes for us – Leviticus 14:20 (Heb. 7:24–25)

WEEK 6, DAY 4: **TODAY'S READING: LEVITICUS 17–20**

OVERVIEW:

God forbids Israel from worshipping other gods and eating blood; laws protecting the sanctity of sex; the declaration of civil laws.

HIGHLIGHTS & INSIGHTS:

The first thing God made clear to Moses in Leviticus 17 was the *acceptable place* the sacrifice was to be offered. That place was "the door of the tabernacle of the congregation" (17:4). Notice that not bringing the sacrifice to the *acceptable place* was a crime worthy of *death* (17:9)! The next thing God emphasized to Moses in Leviticus 17 was the *acceptable price* that was to be offered in the sacrifice. That price was *blood*!

These two key things picture perfectly what God likewise emphasizes to us in the New Testament. There is only one *acceptable price* that can be paid for sin—"nothing but the *blood* of Jesus."[1] (See 1 John 1:7; Heb. 9:22; Eph. 1:7; Col. 1:14.) And that blood was shed from the one *acceptable place*: the cross of Calvary (Gal. 3:13). Anyone who offers any other *price* than what was paid through the *blood* of Christ or who goes to any *place* other than the *cross* of Christ for forgiveness of sin will receive *eternal death*! And in perfect fulfillment of the type, just as the *blood* was to be offered at the "*door* of the tabernacle," Jesus said, "I am the door" (John 10:9), and "He that entereth not by the door into the sheepfold, but climbeth up some other way, the same is a thief and a robber" (John 10:1).

As we make our way further into Leviticus 17, God continues to teach the children of Israel and us about the sanctity of *blood*. For hundreds of years, people thought that one of the ways a sick person could be healed was by draining out a good portion of their blood. Had they simply read and believed Leviticus 17:11, they would have known what science had not yet discovered—"the life of the flesh is in the blood"! That is a principle science now knows is true *physically* (sick people today are often given blood transfusions), but this is also a principle believers in Christ know is true *spiritually*. The only way we can have spiritual life inside of our fleshly bodies is through the shed blood of our Lord Jesus Christ! The life of the flesh is truly—*in the blood*!

Because of the sanctity of blood, God forbids the eating or drinking of it; that, too, was an offense worthy of death (17:10)! Note also that this restriction is repeated in the New Testament in an epistle addressed to those of us in the church age (Acts 15:20). Apparently, God wanted us to never lose sight of what a special substance blood actually is and wanted to be sure that we kept ourselves distanced from anything even remotely connected to devil worship (17:7) or the way the Egyptians worshipped their pagan gods (18:3). May this admonition serve as a reminder to us today to distance ourselves from any of the idolatry (Col. 3:5) we may have been involved in when we were slaves in the bondage of Egypt (Egypt picturing our bondage to sin, satan, and self)!

Over and over in today's reading, God calls us to holiness against the backdrop of a tremendously powerful spiritual reality:

- 18:2 — "I am the Lord your God."
- 18:4 — "I am the Lord your God."
- 18:30 — "I am the Lord your God."
- 19:3 — "I am the Lord your God."
- 19:4 — "I am the Lord your God."
- 19:10 — "I am the Lord your God."
- 19:25 — "I am the Lord your God."

- 19:31 — "I am the Lord your God."

- 19:34 — "I am the Lord your God."

- 19:36 — "I am the Lord your God."

- 20:7 — "I am the Lord your God."

- 20:24 — "I am the Lord your God."

May we realize today that there was a time when we were separated from the one true God—the God of the Bible. We walked instead according to "the god of this world" (2 Cor. 4:4). But the light of the glorious gospel shined past the blinders Satan sought to use to keep us bound to him and his worldly domain, and God now says to us: "I am the Lord your God"!

Against the backdrop of that glorious reality, may we heed what "The Lord our God" says to us today from 2 Corinthians 6:14-18:

> Be ye not unequally yoked together with unbelievers: for what fellowship hath righteousness with unrighteousness? and what communion hath light with darkness? And what concord hath Christ with Belial? or what part hath he that believeth with an infidel? And what agreement hath the temple of God with idols? for ye are the temple of the living God; as God hath said, I will dwell in them, and walk in them; and I will be their God, and they shall be my people. Wherefore come out from among them, and be ye separate, saith the Lord, and touch not the unclean thing; and I will receive you. And will be a Father unto you, and ye shall be my sons and daughters, saith the Lord Almighty.

CHRIST IS REVEALED:

As the *Holy Word of God* that protects our private and public lives from rampant wickedness – Leviticus 20:8 (John 1:1–2,14; Rev. 19:13)

---

[1]Robert Lowry, "Nothing but the Blood," 1876, public domain.

WEEK 6, DAY 5: **TODAY'S READING: LEVITICUS 21–24**

OVERVIEW:

The qualifications of priests; God sets the dates of the Jewish feasts; the death penalty instituted and carried out.

HIGHLIGHTS & INSIGHTS:

As we mentioned when we began reading the book of Leviticus, most Christians have a hard time getting through this book because they don't see how it applies to those of us living in the church age. But, as we've seen, Leviticus is the book of the *priesthood*. That alone should perk up our spiritual eyes, ears, and minds because God tells us in 1 Peter 2:5 that He has set you and me apart as "an holy priesthood, to offer up spiritual sacrifices, acceptable to God by Jesus Christ." The connection is obvious! The priesthood of the Old Testament provides us graphic pictures of our New Testament priesthood.

Every born-again believer is a priest (Rev. 1:6). Not in the same sense as an Old Testament priest, and certainly not in a Roman Catholic sense, but in a very *biblical* sense! As New Testament priests, we have been entrusted with the responsibility of teaching unbelievers to worship God properly: we call that teaching "evangelism." We have been commissioned to "go... and teach all nations" (Matt. 28:19). But, as New Testament priests, we have also been entrusted with the responsibility of offering up "spiritual sacrifices" that are pleasing to God. Biblically, we are to offer to God our *faith* (Phil. 2:17), our *finances* (Phil. 4:18), our *praise* (Heb. 13:15–16), our *witness* (Rom. 15:16) and most importantly—obviously, our *lives* (Rom. 12:1–2; 2 Cor. 2:15)! And all of these "spiritual sacrifices" are symbolically represented by the physical offerings presented by the Old Testament priests.

As we acquaint ourselves with this spiritual and biblical concept, keep in mind that as priests, we are ambassadors or representatives of God and, as such, have been called by God to represent Him on the earth in *holiness*! Peter said, "But as he which hath called you is holy, so be ye holy in all manner of conversation; Because it is written, Be ye holy; for I am holy" (1 Pet. 1:15-16).

In Leviticus 21, God presents a list of physical blemishes that prevented a potential priest in the Old Testament from offering "the bread of God" (21:16–17). These "physical blemishes" that were certainly binding upon the Old Testament priesthood are simply representative of the "spiritual blemishes" that limit our ability to function in our New Testament priesthood. Paul tells us in Ephesians 5:27 that we "should be holy and without blemish"! When our holiness is "blemished" by sinful attitudes and actions, we are hindered in our effectiveness to offer the Word of God (the bread of God) to the lost world and are unable to offer up acceptable spiritual sacrifices! Let's briefly examine some of the "blemishes" that are pictured for us in Leviticus 21.

1. BLINDNESS (21:18)
   In the New Testament, a blind man is one who is not adding to his faith the seven things God specifically intended for our spiritual growth and development (2 Pet. 1:5–9). It is someone who is not *spiritually mature*.

2. A BLEMISHED EYE (21:20)
   An Old Testament priest with a blemished eye was unable to see his reflection in the bronze laver where he was to wash/cleanse himself in preparation for service (Ex. 30:18). In the New Testament, we allow our eyes to be blemished when we hear the Word of God and choose not to obey it (James 1:22-25).

3. A FLAT NOSE (21:18)
   A flat-nosed Old Testament priest would not be able to smell the incense on the golden altar, picturing prayer, of course. A flat-nosed New Testament priest is a believer who neglects prayer and, therefore, experiences no power in his walk with God.

4. LAMENESS (21:18)
   Obviously, a lame Old Testament priest was very simply one who could not *walk*. It is a picture of New Testament priests who, because of spiritual blemishes in their lives, are no longer walking in obedience to the Word of God, and no longer walking in the Spirit (Gal. 5:16–17, 22–23).

5. A SUPERFLUOUS (or extra) BODY PART (21:18)
   An extra body part has no feeling, no place, no function and interferes with the service to be offered by the priest. New Testament priests can allow superfluous things to be attached to us, things that were never intended to be a part of our lives, namely bitterness, wrath, anger, clamor, evil speaking and malice (Eph. 4:31–32). These superfluous things have no place in the life of a believer and will make us unable to function properly in our responsibility to offer up spiritual sacrifices.

6. A BROKEN FOOT or BROKEN HAND (21:19)
   An Old Testament priest with a broken foot would not be able to keep his balance, walk, or run. A New Testament priest with a broken foot would likewise be unable to balance his spiritual responsibilities (Col. 3:1-17), "walk in the Spirit" (Gal. 5:16) or "run with patience the race that is set before us" (Heb. 12:1; Gal. 5:7).

7. BROKEN "STONES" (21:20)
   Obviously, "broken stones" would have caused an Old Testament priest to be unable to reproduce. It is a picture of New Testament believers (priests) who have broken God's revealed will through His Word, causing them to be unable to reproduce spiritual offspring (2 Pet. 1:8).

Some of us may find ourselves "blemished" in one of these areas pictured in Leviticus 21. May I remind you today that our Lord Jesus Christ has proven through His earthly ministry that He has the power to open the eyes of the blind, cause the lame to walk, and heal any deformity or abnormality in our lives. May we humble ourself before Him today that we might receive His spiritual healing.

CHRIST IS REVEALED:

As our *Perfectly Spotless High Priest* – Leviticus 21:16–23 (Heb. 8:1)

As the *Unrevealed Reality* of the eternal feasts of Israel – Leviticus 23:2, 21, 41 (Col. 2:16–17)

WEEK 7, DAY 1: **TODAY'S READING: LEVITICUS 25–27**

OVERVIEW:

Laws concerning personal property; the sevens of rest and liberty; the blessing of obedience and the cursing of disobedience; vows and tithes explained.

HIGHLIGHTS & INSIGHTS:

From a strictly practical standpoint, the weekly sabbath (the seventh day of the week) was intended by God to give "rest" to both man and beast. Also from a strictly practical standpoint, the sabbatical year (the seventh year in a week of years) was intended by God to give "rest" to the land (Lev. 25:1–7). From a Prophetic (futuristic) standpoint, God's system of working according to a pattern of seven—seven *days*, seven *weeks*, seven *months*, seven *years*, seven *weeks of years*, or seven *decades*—points to the fact that after six millenniums (6000 years) the seventh *millennium* will be one thousand years of "rest" on this planet (Rev. 20:1–6) when our Lord Jesus Christ rules and reigns on the earth, finally receiving "the glory due unto his name." (1 Chr. 16:29; Ps. 29:2; 96:8)

The Year of Jubilee, the 50th year at the end of seven weeks of years (7×7=49; Lev. 25:8), was intended by God to allow any of the children of Israel who, because of their debts, had been forced to sell their land or sell themselves into servanthood, to *return* to their family and *regain the possession* of their property. Note that this *jubilant release* and *proclamation of liberty* just happened to be enacted by the sounding of a trumpet on, of all days, the Day of Atonement (Lev. 25:9)!

In 1 Corinthians 15:52, Paul describes the moment when the trumpet will sound, when because of the atoning death of our Lord Jesus Christ (obviously pictured in the Day of Atonement) we will be released from our corruptible bodies and finally "delivered from the bondage of corruption into the glorious liberty of the children of God" (Rom. 8:21)! Paul likewise tells us in Ephesians 1:14 that we're given the indwelling of the Holy Spirit (in our mortal bodies) as the down payment guaranteeing "our inheritance until the redemption of the purchased possession," when we will receive, as he tells us in Philippians 3:21, a body "like unto his [Christ's] glorious body"! This is the "Jubilee" for which every child of God is presently groaning (Rom. 8:23), the "Jubilee" being pictured in Leviticus 25.

Chapter 26 is very clear and direct: Obeying God's Word brings *blessing* and disobeying God's Word brings *cursing* (conflict). The New Testament equivalent is Galatians 6:7–8: "Be not deceived; God is not mocked: for whatsoever a man soweth, that shall he also reap. For he that soweth to his flesh shall of the flesh reap corruption; but he that soweth to the Spirit shall of the Spirit reap life everlasting." Not understanding this inviolable biblical principle, many believers in the twenty-first century don't seem to connect the circumstances of their lives to the choices they have made in terms of the Word of God. For God's glory's sake, may we always choose *obedience*!

Looking back through the book of Leviticus we can see two clear divisions:

1) Chapters 1–10 describe our *Positional Standing* before God. (*Salvation*)

2) Chapters 11-27 describe our *Practical Standing* before God. (*Sanctification*)

As we close today, let's remind ourselves of the high points of Leviticus...

First, *remember* that the path to peace and fruitfulness starts with *worship*. Next, *rejoice* that through Jesus Christ's finished work, God has made us a *Sacrifice* (Rom. 12:1–2), a *Priest* (1 Pet. 2:5) and a *Place* (Eph. 2:22). Finally, *realize* that God's calling on our lives is that we be holy, for He is holy (Lev. 11:45; 1 Pet. 1:15–16).

CHRIST IS REVEALED:

As the *Redeemer* of the kingdom of heaven – Leviticus 25 (Acts 3:20–21; Rev 11:15)

WEEK 7, DAY 2: **TODAY'S READING: NUMBERS 1–4**

OVERVIEW:

The first numbering (census) of the Israelites; the encampment location of each tribe in relation to the tabernacle; the census and duties of the Levites: the Kohathites, the Gersonites, and the Merarites.

HIGHLIGHTS & INSIGHTS:

The book of Numbers was written by Moses in approximately 1445 to 1405 B.C. (Num. 33:2; 36:13) The book gets its name from the ancient Greek title of this book, *Arithmoi*, from which we obviously get our English word *arithmetic*. Later, Latin translators of the Old Testament gave the book the title *Numeri*, from which we get our English word *Numbers*. Interestingly, the word *numbers* (or some form of it) is found 127 times in this book, but it actually gets its name from the two "numberings" (censuses) of the men of war in chapters 1–4 and chapters 26–27. The first census took place the second year after the Jews' exodus from Egypt, and the second was made 38 years later, just as the nation of Israel was about to enter Canaan.

The book of Numbers actually picks up the history of the Israelites where the book of Exodus left off. Just one month had passed between the completion of the tabernacle in Exodus 40:17 and God's command to number the people in Numbers 1:1–2. During that one-month period, the instruction in the book of Leviticus was given. Whereas the book of Leviticus deals primarily with the believer's *worship*, the book of Numbers deals primarily with the believer's *walk*. Whereas *purity* is the central theme of Leviticus, *pilgrimage* is the central theme of Numbers.

The book of Numbers has incredible implications and applications for believers today. God makes that abundantly clear in 1 Corinthians 10:1–12 and Hebrews 3 and 4. In this book, we will see the nation of Israel, after they were gloriously delivered from the bondage of Egypt by the blood of the lamb, failing to take God at His Word and, as a result, wandering in the wilderness of unbelief rather than entering into their inheritance in Canaan.

As has been mentioned repeatedly in the *52 Weeks of Pursuit*, Israel in the Old Testament is a picture of the individual believer in the New Testament. Just like Israel, after being gloriously delivered out of the bondage of Egypt (sin, Satan, self, and the world!) by the blood of the Lamb, we too fail to take God at His Word and wander in the wilderness of unbelief rather than entering into the fullness of our inheritance in Christ (Eph. 1:18; Col. 1:12). The lessons to be learned in Numbers are numerous!

The census that God commanded Israel to make in today's reading was not of the entire nation, but only the men age 20 and above who were able to go to war. The total was 603,550 (Num. 1:46). One of the saddest realities in the entire Bible is that of these 603,550 men, 603,548 of them would die in the wilderness, having never experienced God's purpose for their exodus! As God made abundantly clear from the beginning, the purpose for the exodus wasn't just to bring them *out of Egypt*—it was to bring them *in to Canaan* (Ex. 3:8; Deut. 6:23)! As God warns us to learn from Israel's failure in the wilderness in 1 Corinthians 10:5–6, we should wonder whether it would be different for us. Out of every 603,550 believers today, would there be more than two who actually fulfill God's purposes for their exodus by allowing God to bring them into their "Canaan," the fullness of life in Christ? What an incredibly sobering thought! If those statistics are right, will you be one of the two? Will you trust God, not only to save you from the *penalty* of sin, but from the *power* of sin? Will you rise above the spiritual discouragement, disillusionment, defeat, and death of the wilderness and live in the spiritual peace, productivity, and power of Canaan?

As a sidenote, if there were 603,550 men at the time of the census, it would strongly suggest that Israel's total population would have been 2–2.5 million people! It has been estimated that it would have required nearly 50 railroad box cars full of manna per day just to feed the people! The land mass needed to accommodate this multitude when they camped at night would have exceeded 100 square miles!

The first four chapters of Numbers make very apparent that God always does things "decently and in order" (1 Cor. 14:40). God gave specific instruction for Israel to arrange itself into an orderly camp with its "mobile worship center" (the tabernacle) at the very center. God did not want Israel to be a chaotic mob as they journeyed, but intended Israel's orderliness, organization, and structure to be one of the key ways His people stood out from the rest of the world, so they would have the opportunity to tell them of their God. (See Num. 1:52; 24:2, 5.)

As we journey through the midst of the chaotic world of the twenty-first century with the lives of its people in such disarray, God wants the orderliness of the lives of His people—arranged according to the instruction of His Word with worship at the very center—to be one of the key ways our lives stand out from the rest of the world, so we have the opportunity to tell them of our God (1 Pet. 3:15)!

CHRIST IS REVEALED:

Through *Moses* as he led the people – Numbers 1:54 (John 10:14, 27)

Through *Aaron*, the high priest, who was served by the Levites – Numbers 3:6 (As a holy and royal priesthood, we serve Christ, our great High Priest – John 12:26; 1 Pet. 2:5–9; Heb. 4:14)

WEEK 7, DAY 3: **TODAY'S READING: NUMBERS 5–7**

OVERVIEW:

Laws concerning cleansing; laws concerning confession and restitution; laws concerning suspected immorality (jealousy); the princes' offerings for the dedication of the tabernacle.

HIGHLIGHTS & INSIGHTS:

The Bible tells us very specifically and distinctly that we are to "rightly [divide] the word of truth" (2 Tim. 2:15) and that, in order to make those "right" divisions, we must see ourselves as "workmen," employing one of the most difficult tasks known to man: "Study"! Through diligent study and hard work, God reveals to us the divisions He has made in His Word. In each book of the Bible, there are certain keys that help us to unlock the divisions that *God* has specifically set—what God likes to call the *right divisions*!

As we study Numbers, the key to unlocking the divisions God has set in this book is understanding that there are two very distinct generations of people to whom He refers. The first group is the generation that came up out of Egypt but, because of their unbelief, was forbidden to enter the Promised Land and died in the wilderness. The other generation grew up in the wilderness, but was permitted to enter into Canaan because they were under their parents' authority at the time of Israel's failure to trust God (Deut. 1:35–39). Quite simply, they were too young to make an intelligent decision about trusting God, and so God did not hold them accountable.

Identifying these two generations neatly divides the book of Numbers into 3 sections:

- The *Old* generation is covered in chapters 1–14.

- The *New* generation is covered in chapters 21–36.

- The chapters in between (15–20) record the period of transition during which the Old generation *died off*, and the New generation *grew up*.

Whereas the first four chapters of the book of Numbers dealt with the *outward formation* of Israel's camp, the next five chapters deal with the *inward condition* of it. God captures the central theme of this section in Numbers 5:3, saying, "that they defile not their camps, in the midst whereof I dwell." Because God was in their camp, it was to be holy—completely free from defilement! The New Testament equivalent is 2 Corinthians 6:14–7:1. Because God now dwells in us, we are to "separate" (6:17) and "cleanse ourselves from all filthiness of the flesh and spirit, perfecting holiness in the fear of God" (7:1)!

In Numbers 5, God gives the children of Israel several vital instructions.

- Lepers were to be quarantined outside of the camp. (5:1–4)

- Anything acquired through dishonesty must be confessed and recompensed. (5:5–10)

- Any suspected immorality must be tested before God. (5:11–31)

In short, God was showing them—and is picturing for us—the absolute necessity for purity, honesty, and truth.

Chapter 6 deals with God's instruction concerning the Nazarite vow. The implications are this: When a man or woman in the Old Testament wanted to be used in God's service but did not qualify because they were not a Levite or priest, they could voluntarily take the Nazarite Vow. The word *Nazarite* is a Hebrew transliteration that means "dedication by separation." The Nazarite separated himself from certain hindrances to holiness in order to be wholly devoted to the service of the Lord. Although the outward characteristics of the Old Testament Nazarite Vow no longer apply, they point to the priority God places in the New Testament on our personal surrender and consecration in order to be used to carry out His will and mission.

Chapter 7 records the free-will offering of the princes of Israel—the representative heads of each of the tribes of Israel. Several things to note here are that the gifts were totally voluntary, and although the gifts were identical, God took an enormous amount of space to specifically and separately record each one. The New Testament equivalent is the fact that "God loveth a cheerful giver" (2 Cor. 9:7) and that, though He doesn't need our treasure, He treasures when our heart of love for Him prompts us to give to Him (Matt. 6:21).

CHRIST IS REVEALED:

In the *Nazarite* who dedicated himself by separation – Numbers 6:1–8 (Jesus willingly dedicated Himself to serve the will of the Father, separating Himself from sin, even to death – John 6:38; Matt. 26:39, 42)

WEEK 7, DAY 4: **TODAY'S READING: NUMBERS 8–10**

OVERVIEW:

Consecration of the Levites; observance of the second Passover; the Lord's guiding presence in the cloud and fire; the two silver trumpets; the children of Israel leave Sinai.

HIGHLIGHTS & INSIGHTS:

As we move into Numbers 8, God unfolds for us the consecration of the Levites. God reveals that before these priests were to render their service to God, they were first to be cleansed (8:7).

There were actually three different aspects of the cleansing of the Old Testament priests that were certainly binding upon them:

1. The sprinkling of water upon them.

2. The shaving of all hair from their flesh.

3. The washing of their clothes.

These three aspects of their *physical* cleansing, however, serve to picture our *spiritual* cleansing as New Testament priests—which, as we have previously seen, is inclusive of every born-again believer in Christ! (See 1 Pet. 2:9; Rev. 1:6.) Before offering God our deeds of service, just like the Levites of Numbers 8, we too are to be cleansed! And in perfect fulfillment of the type, the New Testament describes our cleansing similarly:

1. By the sprinkling of water upon us. Hebrews 10:22 says, "Having our hearts sprinkled from an evil conscience, and our bodies washed with pure water"!

2. By the cleansing (shaving) of "all filthiness of the flesh" (2 Cor. 7:1)—those deeds of the flesh that are as much a part of us as the very hair on our body!

3. By the washing of our clothes. Ephesians 5:26 talks about Christ cleansing us by "the washing of water by the word"!

Just as the Levites' acceptance with God was on the basis of the *sin* offering and the *burnt* offering (8:8–12), so our acceptance with God is based solely on the atoning offering for sin provided by our Lord Jesus Christ (Eph. 1:6). And just as the Levites were to be presented before the Lord and completely surrendered to Him (8:13–16), we too are commanded to "present [our] bodies a living sacrifice, holy, acceptable unto God" (Rom. 12:1).

In Numbers 9, God deals with the issue of *fellowship* and *guidance*. In 9:1–14, God details the celebration of the first anniversary of the Passover, which speaks of fellowship. In 9:15–23, God explains the pillar of cloud and of fire, both of which speak of His guidance. The Passover, of course, connects to the New Testament believer in the Lord's Supper, where we, like Israel, are put in remembrance of God's work of redemption and, thus, *fellowship* through the blood of the Passover Lamb (1 Cor. 5:7). The pillar of cloud and of fire which provided *guidance* to the Old Testament saints is representative of the indwelling Spirit in the New Testament believer in Christ. Just as the children of Israel were to be totally surrendered and dependent upon God's guidance for their every move—making absolutely no plans of their own accord—so we are to be completely surrendered to the supernatural guidance of the Spirit of God in us as He directs us through the pages of His Word!

In chapter 10, Moses is told to make two trumpets. These trumpets, like the pillar of cloud and fire, were also for guidance. Whereas the cloud and fire gave guidance for the *eyes*, the trumpets provided guidance through the *ears*.

The trumpets were used for four specific purposes:

1. To be a summoning call to *assemble* the people.

2. To be a signal to *advance* the people.

3. To be a sounding blast at a time of war to *alarm* the people.

4. To be a melodious song to provide a continued *awareness* (memorial) to the people of the sacrifices of God.

The sounding of these trumpets point prophetically to:

1. The summoning call to *assemble* the church of Jesus Christ at the rapture. (1 Thess. 4:16)

2. The signal of *advance*, as our corruptible, mortal bodies put on incorruption and immortality. (1 Cor. 15:52)

3. The sounding *alarm* in Zion (Joel 2:1) as God declares war in the Tribulation Period. (Rev. 8–9)

4. The melodious song that will be ever-sounding in our ears throughout eternity as a memorial of God's glorious sacrifice on our behalf through His Son.

CHRIST IS REVEALED:

In the *Passover* – Numbers 9:2 (1 Cor. 5:7; John 1:29)

WEEK 7, DAY 5: **TODAY'S READING: NUMBERS 11–12**

OVERVIEW:
The complaint of the people; the lust of the people; the complaint of Moses; the 70 elders chosen; the plague of the quail; Aaron and Miriam speak against Moses; Miriam is stricken with leprosy; Moses prays on her behalf.

HIGHLIGHTS & INSIGHTS:
As the blessed observance of the Passover ended in chapter 9, the guiding cloud lifted off of the tabernacle in chapter 10, sending the entire camp of Israel into motion. What an exciting time it must have been as "the ark of the covenant of the Lord went before them in the three days' journey, to search out a resting place for them" (Num. 10:33), moving them ever closer to Canaan! Surely this was a time when the children of Israel were filled with praise, lifting their voices with triumphant singing and rejoicing. One would certainly think that would be the case. But sadly, chapter 11 begins, "And when the people *complained*." In fact, complaining and murmuring becomes one of Israel's favorite pastimes!

- "And when the people complained" – Num. 11:1

- "And Miriam and Aaron spake against Moses" – Num. 12:1

- "And all the children of Israel murmured against Moses and against Aaron" – Num. 14:2

- "And the men, which Moses sent to search the land … made all the congregation to murmur against him" – Num. 14:36

- "Now Korah … took men: And they rose up before Moses … and they gathered themselves together against Moses and against Aaron" – Num. 16:1–3

- "But on the morrow all the congregation of the children of Israel murmured against Moses and Aaron" – Num. 16:41

There is so much complaining in this book, some have even suggested that rather than being called the book of Numbers, it might more aptly be called, "The book of Murmurs"!

But not only did the people fall into the trap of murmuring and complaining, they also fell into the trap of lusting. It seems unthinkable, immediately following the Passover celebration—the glorious reminder of their deliverance from the *affliction* of their flesh in Egypt—that only a few days later they would be lusting for the ways their flesh was *gratified* in Egypt (Num.11:4–9)! And once again, we may need to remind ourselves of what Paul tells us in 1 Corinthians 10:6: "Now these things were our examples, to the intent we should not lust after evil things, as they also lusted." Sometimes it's easy for believers to forget that this world's system (Egypt) was the snare Satan used to hold us captive at his will (2 Tim. 2:26). Forgetting that it was that very system of evil that almost sent us to Hell, we begin to lust for the ways our flesh was gratified when we were in it. May God help us!

Note the disastrous results of the complaining and carnality of the people upon their leader. Moses himself is thrust into great discouragement and begins to voice his complaint to the Lord (11:10–15). He basically cries out, "I can't do this, God! The burden is too heavy. Just kill me!"

In the remainder of chapter 11, God answers the complaints of both Moses and the people. He gives Moses 70 elders to assist him in his work, and He gives the Jews the meat for which they lusted. In both cases, however, *they got what they wanted, but they lost what they had!* The Spirit of God anointing Moses to lead the people was divided among the 70 elders, and the meat the children of Israel lusted after was a curse that led to their death. James reminds us, "But every man is tempted, when he is drawn away of his own lust, and enticed. Then when lust hath conceived, it bringeth forth sin: and sin, when it is finished, bringeth forth death" (Jas. 1:14–15). Perhaps the key lesson here is—be careful what you ask God for!

In chapter 12, the murmuring has ascended to yet another level. Now it flows from Moses's own brother and sister—Aaron, the high priest, and Miriam, Israel's prophetess (Ex. 15:20). They state that their complaint against Moses was the Ethiopian wife he had selected, but that is only the smokescreen to mask their own jealousy and pride. Their complaint wasn't really against Moses's selection of a wife—it was against Moses's *authority*! What they really wanted was the authority of Moses's position. Verse 2 makes their motive abundantly clear. Once again, don't miss the fact that the more things change, the more they stay the same! Human nature still employs the same tactics in the twenty-first century.

Note that in his meekness (12:3), Moses doesn't seek to vindicate himself, but rather trusts God to handle the situation. God was completely able to do His job!

CHRIST IS REVEALED:

In *Moses* who "was very meek, above all the men which were upon the face of the earth" – Numbers 12:3 (Jesus said, "I am meek and lowly in heart" – Matt. 11:29)

WEEK 8, DAY 1: **TODAY'S READING: NUMBERS 13–15**

OVERVIEW:
The 12 spies sent into Canaan; their report; Moses's intercessory prayer for the children of Israel; God's pardon, but refusal to allow Israel to enter the Promised Land; laws concerning offerings, sins, and the Sabbath.

HIGHLIGHTS & INSIGHTS:
Leaving the wilderness of Sinai, the children of Israel were led northward until they reached Kadesh-Barnea, the southern tip of the land of Canaan. For the first time, they were actually able to see the land God had promised to them. Before going in to possess the land, a leader from each of the 12 tribes was chosen to spy out the land for forty days.

As the 12 spies brought back their report, there was complete agreement that Canaan "surely … floweth with milk and honey" (13:27), but ten of the spies said that overcoming the obstacles in the land was an utter impossibility. Only Joshua and Caleb said, "Let us go up at once, and possess it; for we are well able to overcome it" (13:30). As someone so aptly put it, "The 10 put the difficulty between themselves and God. The two put God between themselves and the difficulty. The 10 saw with the eye of the flesh. The two saw with the eye of the faith."

The outcome is history. Israel first refused to believe, then rebelled, even suggesting that Joshua and Caleb be stoned and that a new leader be appointed to lead them all back to Egypt. The result? 38 years of wandering in the wilderness for total of 40 years, one year for each day the spies were in Canaan (Num. 14:33-34). And what a tragedy! The entire generation of people who were age 20 and above at the time of their glorious exodus from Egypt was condemned to die in the wilderness, having never experienced God's purpose in bringing them out. They picture many (shall we go as far as to say most?) believers today who, like Israel, refuse to trust God's promise to grant them victory over their enemies (the world, the flesh, and the Devil) and refuse to trust God to grant them entrance into the fullness of life, rest, fruit, and blessing in Christ (Canaan).

As we enter into chapter 15, God begins the transitional part of the book of Numbers (chapters 15-20), which covers the 38 years of wilderness wanderings where the old generation died off. To help us understand just how much dying actually took place, Dr. Leon Wood notes:

"Figuring 1,200,000 (600,000 of both men and women) as having to die in 14,508 days (38½ years), gives 85 per day. Figuring 12 hours per day maximum for funerals, gives an average of seven funerals per hour for all 38½ years, a continuous foreboding reminder of God's punishment upon them."[1]

CHRIST IS REVEALED:
As the *Glory of God* – Numbers 14:22 (Heb. 1:3; John 1:14; 2 Cor. 4:6)

---

[1] Leon Wood, *A Survey of Israel's History* (Grand Rapids: Zondervan, 1986).

WEEK 8, DAY 2: **TODAY'S READING: NUMBERS 16–19**

OVERVIEW:

Korah leads a rebellion against Moses and Aaron; the plague of judgment sent by God; duties for the priests; the tithe offering; the sacrifice of the red heifer.

HIGHLIGHTS & INSIGHTS:

The complaints that were hurled against Moses in chapter 12 came from his own brother and sister. The uprising against him in chapter 16 comes from his own cousin, Korah, and his co-conspirators, Dathan and Abiram. The sad thing is that Korah, the ringleader of the rebellion, was able to negatively influence 250 of the leaders of Israel against Moses and Aaron.

Their accusations against Moses and Aaron, the God-ordained leaders in Israel, were that they assumed too much authority and that there were others (namely them!) who deserved an equal voice in the decisions that were made for the nation. They, no doubt, were sure that they were right, and that they were only seeking to champion the "Lord's cause" for the "good of the people." The only problem was—they were wrong. Dead wrong! In fact, their actual rebellion wasn't against the authority of Moses and Aaron—it was against the authority of the Lord Himself! Moses says to Korah, "Both thou and all thy company are gathered together against the Lord" (16:11). And when the Lord recounts this story in Numbers 26:9, He also says that, "they strove against the Lord."

It is interesting to note in this whole rebellious debacle that Moses and Aaron did not seek to defend themselves. Rather, they let God be their defense (Ps. 59:9). Moses instructs Korah and his 250 rebels to bring censers (the pots used for burning incense) to the tabernacle so that God could reveal who was right in the dispute. The object lesson was incredible. The ground opened up and swallowed Korah, Dathan, and Abiram, and, as the 250 princes offered their incense, God breathed out fire, and they also went up in smoke!

One would think that the supernatural intervention of God confirming the authority of Moses and Aaron would have certainly caused the people to willfully and joyfully submit. Rather, they murmured once again, actually blaming Moses and Aaron for killing Korah and all of his cohorts! Needless to say, God was not pleased. He instructs Moses and Aaron to back away so He could consume every last one of the murmurers. Moses (what a guy!), rather than relish in God's *judgment* upon the people, he instructs Aaron to offer *atonement* for them so that the people would be spared. Before Aaron can offer the atonement, however, 14,700 people were killed!!!

Evidently, even the events of chapter 16 weren't enough to convince the people of Aaron's authority in the priesthood. In chapter 17, God wants to settle the issue once and for all. God instructs Moses to tell each tribe to present a rod (a dead stick) to be placed in front of the Ark in the tabernacle. The rod that blossomed would indicate the one He had chosen for the priesthood. Obviously, Aaron's rod was the only one that budded. But it did more than bud; in a single day, it also blossomed and bore fruit! The other rods were still as dead as a door nail. While each of the princes took back his lifeless rod, the rod of Aaron was placed in the tabernacle before the Ark to be a constant reminder to these rebels and all of the children of Israel who the high priest of Israel actually was!

Aaron's rod, of course, is a beautiful picture of the Lord Jesus Christ. Many religious leaders and teachers have arisen throughout the course of time. They all had one thing in common: they died! Today, they are nothing but a dead stick, as it were. Only one rose from the dead! He alone is the Source and Giver of life—our Great High Priest!

CHRIST IS REVEALED:

In *Aaron's Budding Rod* – Numbers 17:1–8 (1 Cor. 15:20; Acts 17:3; 26:23)

In *Aaron and His Sons* who were responsible to bear the iniquity of the people in the sanctuary – Numbers 18:1 (Isa. 53:4–7; Titus 2:14)

In the *Red Heifer* which was to be offered as a cleansing from defilement.

- It was to be without spot or blemish. (Num. 19:2)
  (Christ was "without blemish and without spot" – 1 Pet. 1:19)

- It was to have never borne a yoke. (Num. 19:2)
  (A yoke is put on an animal to subdue its wild nature and compel subjection. Christ needed no yoke, but came saying, "Lo, I come … to do thy will, O God" – Heb. 10:7)

- It was to be red. (Num. 19:2)
  (A picture of the blood of Christ – Heb. 9:14; 1 Pet. 1:2, 19)

- It was to be slain without (outside) the camp. (Num. 19:3)
  (Christ was crucified on Golgotha, a place outside of the city of Jerusalem – John 19:17)

- Its blood was to be sprinkled seven times before the tabernacle. (Num. 19:4)
  (Seven is the number of completion and perfection in the Bible. Christ offered one complete and perfect sacrifice for sin – Heb. 10:12, 14)

WEEK 8, DAY 3: **TODAY'S READING: NUMBERS 20–24**

OVERVIEW:

Miriam's death; Moses strikes the rock twice; Edom refuses to allow Israel passage on their land; Aaron's death; the judgment of the fiery serpents; the serpent of brass; Israel defeats King Arad, the Amorites, and the Moabites; Balaam is hired to curse the Israelites; the prophecies of Balaam.

HIGHLIGHTS & INSIGHTS:

Chapter 20 marks the end of Israel's wandering in the wilderness. The death of Aaron, which takes place in this chapter, happened in the fortieth year after the children of Israel came up out of Egypt (Num. 14:34), and from this point, Israel either marched or halted, but did not wander.

It is significant that this chapter groups together three significant events: Miriam's death, Moses's sin (striking the rock twice), and Aaron's death. These three events point to the fact that neither Aaron, representative of the priesthood, nor Miriam, representative of the Prophets, nor Moses, representative of the Law, could successfully lead Israel into the land of promise and rest. The way into the Promised Land was to be led by Joshua who, as we will see in the book that bears his name, is an incredible type of the Lord Jesus Christ. (Note: *Joshua* is the Hebrew rendering of the name *Jesus* and is actually translated *Jesus* in Acts 7:45!)

The reason God was so stern with Moses about disobeying His command to speak to the rock is revealed in 1 Corinthians 10:4. That wasn't just any rock. That Rock was Christ! The Rock had already been smitten once (Ex. 17:5), and God didn't want it smitten again. Striking it again would imply that Christ's one sacrifice on the Cross wasn't sufficient to pay for man's sin. Because of Moses's defilement of the type, he was not permitted to enter the Promised Land. Husbands, take note, God does not take kindly when someone spoils the picture of His Son! You, too, are a picture of Christ in your relationship to your wife (Eph. 5:22–32). Unless your relationship with your wife is right, it will be as impossible for you to enter Canaan (the fullness of life in Christ) as it was for Moses!

Chapter 21 presents another incredible picture of Christ. The people had been bitten with the fiery serpents because of two sins: 1) They spoke against God; and 2) they spoke against Moses. Because of their sin, they were dying (vs. 5–6). In like fashion, we are sinners who have sinned against God and against our fellow man (Mark 12:30–31). We have been bitten by the fiery serpent of sin and are destined to die (Rom. 6:23a – "the wages of sin is death").

God's remedy in Israel was a serpent of brass that was to be lifted up on a pole among the people, and all who looked to it were delivered from death to life. In John 3:14–15, Jesus said, "And as Moses lifted up the serpent in the wilderness, even so must the Son of man be lifted up: That whosoever believeth in him [i.e., looks to Him in faith] should not perish, but have eternal life."

It is therefore easy to compare the physical salvation provided through the serpent of brass lifted up on the pole with the spiritual salvation provided through the Lord Jesus Christ, lifted up on the cross:

1. Their salvation was *by faith*.
   It wasn't by anything they did, the command was simply to "look and live"!

2. It was *by faith alone*.
   Israel was not saved by looking at the serpent *and* keeping the Law … or bringing a sacrifice … or promising reform. They were saved by faith alone. Likewise, our salvation is not Christ *plus* anything! If anything needs to be added to Christ, then Christ is not sufficient in Himself to provide our salvation. God forbid!

3. Their was only *one remedy*.
   Many people are convinced that "there are many roads to heaven." There was only *one remedy* in the camp of Israel, and there is only *one remedy* today! Jesus said in John 14:6, "I am the way [not *a* way] … no man cometh unto the Father, but by me." Unless a person

looks to Christ by faith, the "sting of death" (1 Cor. 15:56) is inevitable and eternal.

4. Their salvation was *immediate.*
    Just as the bitten victim in Israel received an immediate miracle when he looked to the serpent of brass, so every sinner bitten by the fiery serpent of sin receives the immediate miracle of eternal life when he looks to Christ by faith.

Chapters 22–24 record the strange story of Balaam and Balak. Balak tried to hire Balaam to curse the children of Israel, but every time he opened his mouth to do so, much to Balaam's surprise—and Balak's anger—out came blessing!

CHRIST IS REVEALED:

In the *Rock* which Moses struck – Numbers 20:8–11; Exodus 17:6 (Christ, the Rock, was struck once through His death on the cross and does not need to be struck again – 1 Cor. 10:4. Rom. 6:10 – "For in that he died, he died unto sin once.")

In the *Serpent of Brass* – Numbers 21:8–9 (John 3:14)

In the prophesied *Star* and *Scepter* – Numbers 24:17 (Heb. 1:8 – scepter; Rev. 22:16 – star)

WEEK 8, DAY 4: **TODAY'S READING: NUMBERS 25–27**

OVERVIEW:

Israel's sin of fornication; God's judgment in the plague of death; the plague halted because of the zeal of Phinehas; the second numbering (census) of Israel; the law of inheritance; Moses views the Promised Land; Moses installs Joshua as Israel's leader.

HIGHLIGHTS & INSIGHTS:

As we saw in yesterday's reading, Balak was bound and determined to get Balaam to curse Israel. Because Balaam wanted the money and honor that Balak promised him for doing so, he repeatedly tried to curse them, but God would only allow him to speak blessing.

Since Balaam couldn't curse them, he suggests a way to put the children of Israel in a situation where God Himself would curse them. God outlines Balaam's simple plan in His commentary on Numbers 25:1–8 (found in Revelation 2:14) that He calls "the doctrine of Balaam."

1. He taught Balak how to cause the children of Israel "to eat things sacrificed unto idols."

2. He taught Balak how to cause the children of Israel "to commit fornication."

Though Balaam wasn't successful in getting God to turn away from Israel, he was successful in getting *Israel* to turn away from *God.* He wickedly suggests to Balak, king of Moab, that the Moabite women make friends with the men of Israel. (Keep in mind James 4:4—"Ye adulterers and adulteresses, know ye not that the friendship of the world is enmity with God?") The friendliness of the Moabite women quickly led the Israelite men "as an ox goeth to the slaughter" (Prov. 7:22)—right into sexual immorality and idol worship. Israel's disobedience resulted in a plague of death that swept through the camp of Israel. When it was all said and done, 24,000 people had been killed (Num. 25:9)!

The hero of this whole tragedy was Phinehas, the grandson of Aaron. One Israelite was so bold in his sin and lust he actually brought a Midianite woman into Israel's camp to have a sexual relationship with her right in Moses's face, as it were. Phinehas came into the tent and thrust both of them through with a javelin while in the very act. God honors the zeal of Phinehas by turning away the plague of death before any others were killed and by giving him a "covenant of peace" and an "everlasting priesthood" (Num. 25:12–13). Phinehas gives new meaning to the phrase "Blessed are the peacemakers" (Matt. 5:9).

In chapter 26, God calls for the second numbering, or census, of the children of Israel in the book of Numbers. At this point, all of the 603,550 men included in the first census were dead, with the exception of Joshua, Caleb, and Moses, and at this point, Moses wasn't long for this world either! The total of the second census was 601,730—1820 fewer than the first census taken some 38 years before. Catch the pitifulness of Numbers 26:63–65: "These are they that were numbered by Moses and Eleazar the priest, who numbered the children of Israel in the plains of Moab by Jordan near Jericho. But among these there was not a man of them whom Moses and Aaron the priest numbered, when they numbered the children of Israel in the wilderness of Sinai. For the Lord had said of them, They shall surely die in the wilderness. And there was not left a man of them, save Caleb the son of Jephunneh, and Joshua the son of Nun."

Another significant event was to take place before Israel was to enter the Promised Land. God wanted Moses to do two things:

1. To go up to Mount Abarim so that he could view the land he had been forbidden to enter (27:12–14). Just imagine what must have been going through Moses's heart at that moment!

2. To install Joshua as the new leader (27:15–23).

Chapter 27 ends with Moses blessing Joshua and laying his hands upon him—symbolically transferring the leadership that God had entrusted to him.

CHRIST IS REVEALED:

In *Joshua*, who would lead people likened to "sheep which have no shepherd" – Numbers 27:17 (Mark 6:34; 1 Pet. 2:25)

WEEK 8, DAY 5: **TODAY'S READING: NUMBERS 28–32**

OVERVIEW:

The daily and weekly offerings; the Sabbath and monthly offerings, and the offerings to be given at the appointed feasts; God's instruction concerning vows; God's judgment upon the Midianites; the division of the booty obtained from the Midianites; the officers and captains bring an offering to the Lord; Reuben, Gad and half of the tribe of Manasseh settle east of the Jordan.

HIGHLIGHTS & INSIGHTS:

Chapters 28 and 29 deal with the subject of the Lord's offerings and are an amplification of the instructions already given in Leviticus 23. Keep in mind that all of the offerings speak of Christ and find their fulfillment in Him (Matt. 5:17). Understanding that makes Numbers 28:2 beautifully significant as God speaks of these offerings as "my bread." Christ is the one in whom the Father has found His delight and perfect satisfaction (Matt. 3:17).

In chapter 30, God talks about the seriousness of making vows to Him. He wants to make certain that His people did not take *entering* into a vow with Him lightly—or take the *breaking* of a vow lightly. Though we are not instructed to make vows, as such, as New Testament believers, wasn't our very salvation a sacred "vow" of sorts, as we recognized that our lives were not our own because of the price Christ paid to redeem us, and so we exchanged our life for His? (1 Cor. 6:19–20; Matt. 16:24)

The purpose of God's command to go to war against Midian in chapter 31 was two-fold:

1) To "avenge the children of Israel of the Midianites." (31:2)

2) To "avenge the Lord of Midian." (31:3)

And it served that two-fold purpose because the Midianites had devastated Israel, not as *enemies* in a *physical* war, but as *"friends"* in a *spiritual* war. The idol-worshipping Midianites seduced the children of Israel into committing *spiritual adultery* against the Lord and becoming involved in *physical adultery* with their women. It had resulted in the death of 24,000 Israelites (Num. 25:9)!

In this war that God designed to provide *human retaliation* and *divine retribution*, three significant things stand out:

1) The easiness of the victory.

2) The enormity of the spoil.

3) The absence of the loss of life. (Not one of the Israelites was killed!)

Keep in mind that, like Israel, we have been called to war against our *physical* enemy—the flesh (Gal. 5:17)—and against our *spiritual* enemy—the devil and his principalities and powers (Eph. 6:10-17). When we walk in obedience to the Word of God and appropriate the victory that Christ has already won, we can expect the same result as the children of Israel in Numbers 31!

In chapter 32, the tribes of Reuben and Gad approach Moses for permission to settle in a piece of property recently acquired on the east of Jordan. They had set their affection on what they could see with their physical eyes ("and when they saw" 32:1) rather than what God had in store for them in the Promised Land that required the "eyes of faith." From a human/financial standpoint, their request was very reasonable and made all the sense in the world, but spiritually, it was an act of selfishness, compromise and lack of faith. Israel's place was *inside* Canaan—not *outside*! That was the whole purpose for the Exodus—to bring them into a new land (Deut. 6:23). God wanted the entire nation to enter the land as one and for all of Israel to desire to be near the tabernacle and, thus, constantly living in His presence. We see the result of their choice in 1 Chronicles 5:18–26 and 2 Kings 15:29. It wasn't long before they bowed themselves to the gods of the people around them—and they were the first to go into captivity.

Obviously, these tribes are a graphic picture of self-indulgent, worldly Christians who foolishly set their affection on things on earth rather than on the things above (Col. 3:1–2), allowing physical or financial advantages to be their first consideration and the key factor in making the decisions of life. Like Israel, our place is in *Canaan*—not in this *world*! We are to be living in this world, but all the while, our affection must be driving us to seek the things which are above, lest we, like Reuben, Gad, and half of Manasseh, be overtaken by the world, the flesh, and the devil.

CHRIST IS REVEALED:

In the *Offerings* of the *Feast of Tabernacles* – Numbers 29:12–39 (Compare Num. 29:12 with Lev. 23:24) – John 1:14 ("The Word was made flesh, and dwelt among us." Note that the word *dwelt* is the word "tabernacle," meaning "to temporarily live in a tent.")

In *Moses*, the *Righteous Judge* of the wicked – Numbers 31:1–17 (Rev. 16:5; 19:11; 2 Thess. 1:7–9; Jude 14–15)

WEEK 9, DAY 1: **TODAY'S READING: NUMBERS 33–36**

OVERVIEW:

A summary of Israel's 40 years in the wilderness; the dividing of the land of Canaan; the inheritance of the Levites; the cities of refuge; the laws concerning female inheritance within the patriarchal tribe.

HIGHLIGHTS & INSIGHTS:

In chapter 33, God provides us with a summary of Israel's journeys from Egypt to the Jordan. Note God's stern warning in 33:55: "But if ye will not drive out the inhabitants of the land from before you; then it shall come to pass, that those which ye let remain of them shall be pricks in your eyes, and thorns in your sides, and shall vex you in the land wherein ye dwell." In the New Testament equivalent, God is picturing here the fact that living in the fullness of victory that He has designed in Christ (i.e., Canaan) is dependent upon us overcoming "every weight and the sin which doth so easily beset us" (Heb. 12:1). We must be sure we understand that any area of our flesh that we refuse to deal with will become pricks in our eyes and thorns in our sides and shall vex us in our walk with Christ!

In chapter 34, God caused the children of Israel to look ahead to the time when they would possess Canaan, as He assigned to each tribe the portion of their inheritance in the land. The Levites were also assigned their special cities, and perhaps most importantly, the cities of refuge are defined in chapter 35. We will talk further about the cities of refuge when we read the book of Joshua, but do note some beautiful pictures of Christ, to whom we "have fled for refuge to lay hold upon the hope set before us" (Heb. 6:18).

1) THEY WERE APPOINTED BY GOD, NOT MOSES.
   Moses did not choose these cities, picturing the fact that the Law (Moses) cannot save anyone. Just as these cities were appointed by God to be a shelter or refuge from judgment as an act of His grace, so Christ was appointed by God, as an act of His grace (John 3:16), to be our shelter or refuge from the judgment of sin. (John 1:29)

2) THEY WERE ANNOUNCED BY GOD IN HIS WORD.
   The six cities are specifically named in Joshua 20:7–8 and could never be changed. There were other cities that were larger and more prominent, but none of them could shelter the sinner. God has also specifically named Christ as the one and only shelter from sin, though many of the world's religions are larger or more prominent. Based on the authority of God's Word, God's Refuge, Christ, will never change! (See John 14:6; Acts 4:12.)

3) THEY WERE ACCESSIBLE TO ALL MEN.
   The six cities were arranged by God so that no tribe was very far away from the place of safety. They were all very accessible. We are told by the rabbis that there were signposts that pointed the way to the cities of refuge, and that the gates of these cities were never shut. God has made Christ accessible to all men, even children (Matt. 18:3). The Holy Spirit is given to point men to Christ (John 16:13-14), and all who come will find His gates open wide (John 6:37).

4) THE GUILTY HAD TO APPROPRIATE GOD'S PROVISION TO ESCAPE PUNISHMENT.
   It wasn't enough to know that the cities of refuge existed or even to believe that they could provide refuge from judgment. The guilty had to actually enter into the city. So, it is not enough that a sinner believe that Christ, as God, existed, or even that they believe that He is God's Refuge from the judgment of sin—the sinner must be "in Christ" (2 Cor. 5:17).

CHRIST IS REVEALED:

In the *Promised Land* – Numbers 33:50–54 (The Promised Land was filled with abundance and protection for those who took God at His Word. In John 10:10, Jesus said, "I am come that they might have life, and that they might have it more abundantly.")

In the *Cities of Refuge* – Numbers 35 (Christ is our Refuge from the judgment of God and the curse of the Law – Heb. 6:18–20)

In the *Inheritance* of the children of Israel – Numbers 36:7 (Eph. 1:10–11)

WEEK 9, DAY 2: **TODAY'S READING: DEUTERONOMY 1–4**

OVERVIEW:

Moses's history lesson: from the Ten Commandments to the spies; the wilderness; the nations avoided; the nations conquered; Joshua charged to be the next leader; the people compelled to heed God's Word.

HIGHLIGHTS & INSIGHTS:

We come now to the fifth book of the Bible, the book of Deuteronomy. *Deuteronomy* simply means "second law." But understand, that it's not **another** law that is being given in this book; it's a second *giving of the law* for a generation that had not heard the first giving of the law at Sinai. However, there is a marked difference between this giving of the law and the first. When God gave the law the first time in the book of Exodus, it was pretty much: "obey Me because I'm God—and because I said!" It was a *responsibility* that was connected to *DUTY*.

But in the book of Deuteronomy, when God gave the law the second time, it is beautifully associated with a different word: *LOVE*! For the first time, God talks about *His love* for His people and His desire for His people to *love Him*! In this book, God lets His people know that yes, He wants us to *obey* Him, but He wants us to do it, not because we feel that it is our *responsibility*, not out of a sense of *obligation* or *duty*, not out of *fear* or because of the *consequences* if we don't. He wants us to do it because of *love*! Sure, it is a *responsibility*, but it is to fulfill the *law of love*!

It should be noted that the Jews refer to the first five books of the Bible as the *Torah*, meaning "teaching, doctrine or instruction." Christians commonly refer to these same books as the *Pentateuch*, a compound Greek word that means "five books." Jesus referred to these first five books of the Old Testament in at least three ways:

1) As "the law." (Matt. 5:17–18; 7:12; 11:13; 12:5; 22:40; Luke 10:26; 16:16; John 7:19)

2) As "the law of Moses." (Luke 24:44; John 7:23)

3) As "Moses." (Luke 16:29; John 5:45–46)

It is also interesting to note that the New Testament writers quote Deuteronomy more than any Old Testament book—at least 80 times! In our Lord's temptation in the wilderness, He quoted a verse relevant to each temptation, and interestingly enough, each one was from the book of Deuteronomy! (See Matt. 4:4/Deut. 8:3; Matt. 4:7/Deut. 6:16; Matt. 4:10/Deut. 6:13.)

Comparing the last verse of the book of Numbers with the first verse of the book of Deuteronomy helps us to contextualize and summarize God's intention through both of these books. The book of Numbers is God's "commandments and judgments" given through Moses while the children of Israel were in the plains of Moab, and the book of Deuteronomy is a series of addresses Moses gave to the children of Israel as they prepared to enter into the land of promise in Canaan.

1) Moses's first address. (chapters 1–4)

2) Moses's second address. (chapters 5–26)

3) Moses's third address. (chapters 27–30)

4) Moses's parting words. (chapters 31–34)

The urgency and passion behind Moses's words in these addresses is more than apparent. He preaches as a man fully aware that his death is imminent. May we likewise preach as dying men—to dying men!

It is believed that Moses wrote the book of Deuteronomy shortly *after* delivering the addresses and shortly *before* his death (34:5) in approximately 1405 BC. Obviously, the record of Moses's death and of what took place after it in Deuteronomy 34 is a divinely inspired appendix to the book that was written by another author—most likely, his successor and longtime partner in ministry, Joshua.

Remember that the children of Israel in the Old Testament are a picture of the individual believer in the New Testament. Just as the children of Israel experienced in the books of Exodus to Deuteronomy, *after* being delivered out of the bondage of Egypt (our deliverance from bondage to sin, Satan and self, i.e., the world), *before* we can actually enter into the promised land of Canaan (the victorious Christian life—the life of fullness, fruit-bearing and abundance in Christ), there is a *wilderness* to go through! It is the part of our journey where we, like the children of Israel, must learn to submit our stubborn wills to the will of our Lord as it is revealed through His Word. None of us will enter into the life of abundance God intended our salvation to bring (John 10:10) without experiencing this absolute surrender of ourselves and our wills. It has been said that it took God approximately *forty hours* to bring the children of Israel out of Egypt, but it took approximately *forty years* to bring Egypt out of the children of Israel! (And it was only an eleven-day journey through the wilderness, Deut. 1:2!)

In Deuteronomy 3:24, Moses makes reference to God's wondrous works in Israel's Exodus as what He had only "begun" to do to show Moses and the children of Israel His "greatness" and His "mighty hand." And so it is with our exodus. Paul said in Philippians 1:6, "Being confident of this very thing, that he which hath begun a good work in you will perform it until the day of Jesus Christ!" Yes, God did a mighty work in delivering us out of Egypt (the world/sin), but He has great and mighty works He still intends to perform in our lives in bringing us into the Promised Land (the life of abundance and fullness in Christ).

Moses's words to the children of Israel in Deuteronomy 4:29 are the theme verse meant to inspire us and direct us through the *52 Weeks of Pursuit*. Obviously, this is a promise given specifically to the children of Israel, and yet, the general principle revealed in this verse is one that has application for people in every generation and in every dispensation. God has always desired that His people see Him through the revelation of His holy Word, and when our pursuit of Him is so passionate that it involves all of our heart and all of our soul, we will find Him! May that continue to be our passionate pursuit in the remaining 43 weeks of our *52 Weeks of Pursuit*!

Deuteronomy 4:30 is a very significant verse for our times. Many evangelical Christians (meaning, fundamentally sound regarding the need for and means of salvation) are now teaching that God is finished with the Jew and that the church has replaced Israel. The ramifications and dangers of this teaching are huge. One of the strongest indictments in the entire New Testament is related to this very teaching! In the letter to the church in Smyrna in Revelation 2, our Lord Jesus Christ said that those who say they are Jews when they are not (and as Gentile, church-age believers, we most definitely are not!) are "the synagogue of Satan" (v. 9). In other words, this is a satanically-inspired teaching! The most popular violator is, no doubt, the Roman Catholic Church which teaches that their first (so-called) Pope—Peter, the Apostle to the Jews—was the one given the keys to the kingdom of heaven: the literal, physical, governmental kingdom promised to the Jews (the nation of Israel—Acts 1:6).

But the teaching that the church has replaced Israel in God's program has now also made its way into many "evangelical" churches and institutions of higher learning. What usually accompanies this teaching is that there will be no rapture and, subsequently, no Tribulation and millennial kingdom. Way back in Deuteronomy 4:30–31, however, the Bible very clearly spells out something completely different:

> When thou art in tribulation, and all these things are come upon thee, even in the latter days, if thou turn to the Lord thy God, and shalt be obedient unto his voice; (For the Lord thy God is a merciful God;) he will not forsake thee, neither destroy thee, nor forget the covenant of thy fathers which he sware unto them.

In other words, once the church has been removed at the rapture, which then ushers in the Tribulation, God will fulfill His promises to the Nation of Israel! Please note that maintaining this distinction is vital to properly understand the Bible and to remain steadfast in sound doctrine.

CHRIST IS REVEALED:

As the *Righteous Judge* – Deuteronomy 1:17 (2 Tim. 4:8)

As *Deliverer* – Deuteronomy 1:30; 2:33; 3:3 (Rom. 8:21; Gal. 1:4)

As the *Faithful one* – Deuteronomy 2:9, 12, 19 (1 Cor. 10:13; 2 Thess. 3:3; 1 John 1:9)

As *Teacher* – Deuteronomy 4:14 (John 8:28)

As the *one True God* – Deuteronomy 4:35, 39 (John 14:6; Acts 4:12; Col. 2:9)

As the *Lover of Men* – Deuteronomy 4:37 (John 15:13; Titus 3:4–5)

WEEK 9, DAY 3: **TODAY'S READING: DEUTERONOMY 5–8**

OVERVIEW:

A recounting of the Ten Commandments; the greatest commandment; instructions for new homes; instruction for the new land; admonitions to remember the Lord.

HIGHLIGHTS & INSIGHTS:

In preparation for their entrance into the land of Canaan, Moses begins his second address to the people (chapter 5) by reminding them of their responsibility to *hear* the Word of God, to *learn* it, to *keep* it, and to *do* it! Though they were anticipating a *physical* journey into the land of promise and we are pursuing God on a *spiritual* journey into the land of abundance He's designed for us "in Christ," we can heed these admonitions to *hear, learn, keep* and *do* the Word of God with the same passion and fervor they must have had.

Moses then reminds the children of Israel of the importance of them taking *personally* the covenant God had made with them. He says in 5:3, "The Lord made not this covenant with our fathers, but with us, even us, who are all of us here alive this day." Moses's words to Israel are a great reminder that the covenant of grace God has made with those of us who comprise His church is a spiritual reality we must also take *personally*—making *personal application* of all of His commands and promises. The promises of the new covenant God made aren't just intended for our forefathers; they are for us!

Moses recounts to the people the infamous Ten Commandments that he had previously received. Deuteronomy 5:29 gives us a beautiful glimpse into the heart of God and His desire for His people: "O that there were such an heart in them, that they would fear me, and keep all my commandments always, that it might be well with them, and with their children for ever!" Our Lord Jesus Christ expressed this same heart and sentiment in Matthew 23:37, saying, "O Jerusalem, Jerusalem, thou that killest the prophets, and stonest them which are sent unto thee, how often would I have gathered thy children together, even as a hen gathereth her chickens under her wings, and ye would not!" May we always set our *hearts* upon the Lord: to fear Him and to *always* keep *all* of His commandments.

In chapter 6:4–5, Moses gives what Jesus declared was the "great commandment" (Matt. 22:36–40). It is simply this: based on a firm belief that the God of the Bible is the one and only God and Lord, we are to love Him with all of our heart, all of our soul, and all of our might.

Moses then instructs the people they were responsible not only to take these words personally, but also to teach them to their children (Deut. 6:6–7). We, too, have the responsibility of teaching our children the Word of God (Eph. 6:4). This does not simply mean taking them to church for someone else to teach them, though it can certainly be a blessing to have others come alongside us in this task. The responsibility to teach our children the Word of God was given solely to parents. In verse 7, Moses instructs us to "teach them *diligently*"—not flippantly or haphazardly! And it must be done in the rhythms of daily life. It should include the times when we are simply sitting with them in our house; when we're with them on our way somewhere (walking or driving); when we're putting them to bed at night; and in the morning when they wake up. It shouldn't surprise us, then, that these are the very times that the clamor of this world and the distractions of the devil have sought to take from us. Let us seek to reclaim these special times for the Lord and our children!

But it's not simply enough to *tell* our children all the right stuff about God, to *tell* them how to have a relationship with Him. These things must be *modeled* for them! Perhaps the most *important* instruction God gives to parents in this passage is also the most *overlooked*! God says to parents in verse 6, "And these words, which I command thee [parents] this day, shall be in thine heart"! Many parents teach their children, and even *diligently* teach their children, yet it ultimately doesn't work for the simple fact that what they were teaching their children wasn't, first and foremost, *in their heart*! The right words were coming out of their *lips*, but weren't being modeled through their *life*! What God intends for our children to receive from us must not only be *taught* to them—it must also be *caught* by them! My dear brothers and sisters, God's Word must be in our hearts!

In Deuteronomy 6:10-12, God warns the children of Israel (and us) of the human tendency to *forget God*. After we have reached the place God intends for us to be, He warns of the danger of becoming *comfortable and complacent* so that we forget Him and all He did to bring us to where His promises are being fulfilled in our lives.

Finally, Moses points them toward the future, warning them of the danger of making *compromises* with the enemy and of the need to instill this disdain for the enemy into our children. Parents, we must *teach* verbally and *model* practically for our children God's instruction in 2 Corinthians 6:17–18: "Wherefore come out from among them, and be ye separate, saith the Lord, and touch not the unclean thing; and I will receive you, And will be a Father unto you, and ye shall be my sons and daughters, saith the Lord Almighty."

CHRIST IS REVEALED:

As the *Everlasting Covenant* – Deuteronomy 5:2 (Heb. 13:20–21; John 3:16; 5:24; 6:47)

As *Mediator* – Deuteronomy 5:5 (1 Tim. 2:5; Heb. 8:6)

As *Well-Pleasing* – Deuteronomy 6:18 (Matt. 3:17; 17:5; Luke 3:22)

As *Called Out of Egypt* – Deuteronomy 6:21 (Matt. 2:13–15)

As *one who Will Smite the Nations* – Deuteronomy 7:2 (Rev. 19:15)

As *Redeemer* – Deuteronomy 7:8 (Rom. 3:24; Eph. 1:7; Heb. 9:12)

As *one who Will Repay Face to Face* – Deuteronomy 7:10 (Rev. 1:7)

WEEK 9, DAY 4: **TODAY'S READING: DEUTERONOMY 9–12**

OVERVIEW:

God's promises to the fathers; God's grace to the undeserving; second tablets of commandments; love and obedience; blessing and cursing; ordinances

HIGHLIGHTS & INSIGHTS:

As we move into today's reading, the big day has finally arrived! In Deuteronomy 9:1, God said, "Thou art to pass over Jordan this day." (Their actual crossing of the Jordan into the promised land won't be recorded until Joshua 3.) From the crossing of the Red Sea until this moment, the children of Israel have traveled for 14,400 days on what should have been an eleven-day journey (Deut. 1:2). The journey into the Promised Land has taken them 14,378 more days than it needed to!

And in those 14,378 unnecessary days in the wilderness, an entire generation died because of their failure to take God at His Word. And they died having never experienced the purpose God intended when He graciously delivered them from Egypt. Remember, according to Deuteronomy 6:23, the Exodus out of Egypt was not an end in itself: It was simply a means to another end. Moses told them, "And he [God] brought us out from thence [Egypt], that he might bring us in, to give us the land [Canaan] which he sware unto our fathers."

Likewise, our deliverance from the bondage of our sin—as glorious as that was and is—is not an end in itself! Just as with Israel, we were delivered *out* of our sin so that, by taking God at His Word, we could be brought *into* the life of fullness, abundance, and fruit-bearing found in Christ by faith. Paul, inspired by the Holy Spirit, recounts the story of Israel's victory in the Exodus and their failure in the wilderness, pleading with us to make sure that what happened to them after their *physical* Exodus doesn't happen to us after our *spiritual* Exodus! He writes, "Now these things were our examples" (1 Cor. 10:6), and again, five verses later, "Now all these things happened unto them for ensamples: and they are written for our admonition" (10:11). Oh, may we have ears to hear that warning—and to heed it!

Before God brings the children of Israel into the land, He warns them of still another danger. On three separate occasions in Deuteronomy 9, Moses tells them to make sure that, after coming into the land of Canaan, they didn't start thinking they had gotten there because they were just so good or righteous, because of who they were or something they had done. In 9:4 he says, "Speak not thou in thine heart … For my righteousness the Lord hath brought me in to possess this land." In 9:5 he says, "Not for thy righteousness, or for the uprightness of thine heart, dost thou go to possess their land." In 9:6, he explains it yet again: "Understand therefore, that the Lord thy God giveth thee not this good land to possess it for thy righteousness; for thou art a stiffnecked people." My brothers and sisters, according to the book of Deuteronomy, most Christians will die in the wilderness of life having never experienced God's purpose in their Exodus, and those who actually do enter the land must be on guard against the pride that creeps in and causes us to think that we are experiencing the abundant life because of who we are or something we've done. If we experience the abundant life [Canaan], it will be because of the righteousness of Christ and His matchless grace! Paul asks a beautifully pertinent question in Romans 3:27: "Where is boasting then? It is excluded. By what law? of works? Nay: but by the law of faith."

And just a few other things to have up on your radar in today's reading…

Deuteronomy 9:2–6

In our quest to live in the reality of the abundant life found in Christ, there are many Anakims (or giants) who will seek to intimidate us and defeat us. Our God, however, is a "consuming fire"—and "he shall destroy them" (9:3). God tells us that this is a principle we must understand! The battle is the Lord's, and we simply stand in the victory He has wrought.

Deuteronomy 9:5–27

Like the children of Israel, God says that, when He found us and delivered us out of our bondage, we were unrighteous (9:5), stiffnecked (9:6, 13), rebellious (9:7, 24), corrupt (9:12), sinful (9:16), wicked (9:18, 27), and stubborn (9:27). In other words, we were a mess!

Deuteronomy 10:12 and 11:13

In these two verses, once again, God reiterates and re-emphasizes the great commandment. God wants us to *love* Him, y'all!

Deuteronomy 10:18–19

Here, the Lord introduces the biblical reality of His concern for and interest in the needs of the fatherless (orphans), widows, and strangers (aliens)—and calls us to do the same! (See Jas. 1:27.)

Deuteronomy 11:18–21

The Lord reiterates the parents' responsibility to bring our children up "in the nurture and admonition of the Lord" (Eph. 6:4), to bring up "faithful children" (Tit. 1:6). We are to teach them at all times and through every possible means (Deut. 11:19–20), but again, the Lord emphasizes that this instruction cannot simply come from our minds or mouths. It must come from our hearts and our souls; it must be part of the very fabric of who we are (11:18)!

Deuteronomy 11:13–17, 22–25

The promise of blessing in the new land was dependent upon their *love* of God and their *obedience* to Him.

Deuteronomy 11:26–28

Whether we live in the midst of the Lord's *blessing* (represented in Mount Gerizim) or the Lord's *cursing* (represented in Mount Ebal)—the choice is ours. Obedience brings blessings. Disobedience brings cursing (or conflict).

Deuteronomy 12:1–32

In these verses, an important principle begins to be repeated about a place in the promised land which the Lord chose as the place for His name to dwell. (See 12:5, 11, 14, 18, 26, as well as Deut. 14:23–25; 15:20; 16:2, 6–7, 15–16.) The word *dwell* is defined in 1 Kings 8:13 as a "settled place." Perhaps we could say it this way: God was looking for some place on this sinful planet where who He is in all of His glory was able to be *established* and *at home*. What absolutely transcends human comprehension, however, is that, for those of us who comprise the church of the Lord Jesus Christ, the *place* which the Lord our God has now *chosen* as the place He intends for "His name to dwell," the place where who He is in all of His glory is able to be settled and at home—is *in us*! Paul said in 2 Corinthians 6:16, "Ye are the temple of the living God; as God hath said, I will dwell in them, and walk in them; and I will be their God, and they shall be my people." Hallelujah!

CHRIST IS REVEALED:

As the *Burnt Offering* – Deuteronomy 12:14–16 (Eph. 5:2, Heb. 10:10, 12)

WEEK 9, DAY 5: **TODAY'S READING: DEUTERONOMY 13–17**

OVERVIEW:

Warnings against following other gods; clean and unclean animals; seven-year release; bondservants; three feasts; civil judgments; kings

HIGHLIGHTS & INSIGHTS:

If you've ever wondered just how *jealous* our Lord is for the undivided *attention* of the *minds* of His people and the undivided *affection* of the *hearts* of His people, look no further than Deuteronomy 13! And if you've ever wondered just how *zealous* Satan is to divert the minds and hearts of God's people away from Him, again just look at Deuteronomy 13! This chapter lets us know that Satan will go to great lengths to counterfeit and falsify the Word of God through his own false prophets in order to move the hearts of God's people away from loving, worshipping and obeying only Him. God warns the children of Israel that this deception can arise from three main sources:

1. From someone performing signs and wonders. Historically and biblically, signs and wonders (miracles) have had a place in the purposes of God. However, in and of themselves, they have never been the ultimate test of truth (Ex. 7:11, 22; 8:7). Indeed, after the rapture of the church, 2 Thessalonians 2:9–10 explains that Satan, in the person of the Antichrist, will dazzle the world with "all power and signs and lying wonders, and with all deceivableness of unrighteousness." (Also see Rev. 12:9; 16:14.)

2. From someone using the intimacy of their relationship to draw people away from the Lord (such as a family member, a relative, or close friend).

3. From a foreign philosophy of life and/or foreign practices of worship.

And this isn't just an Old Testament phenomenon. In the middle of the first century, the Apostle Paul was concerned that the church in Colossae would be deceived by the "enticing words" or empty philosophies of men (Col 2:4–8) and that the church in Corinth might be "beguiled" by the subtlety of Satan through his "ministers" (2 Cor. 11:3, 15a). But this wasn't just a first-century phenomenon either! God's people are still vulnerable today. Satan's "ministers of righteousness" (2 Cor. 11:15b) are alive and well in the twenty-first century!

And just who are these false prophets in our world today? Who are these "ministers of Satan" who appear to be speaking for God, but in the process of their "ministry" are actually turning people to follow and serve other gods? One good place to begin looking are with those who "in the name of God" are turning people away from Him to serve the god of *money* (1 Tim. 6:10), the god of *self* (2 Tim. 3:2), the god of *pleasure* (2 Tim. 3:4) or the god of "this present evil world" (2 Tim. 4:10; Gal. 1:4)!

Deuteronomy 13 is also clear about how *not* permissive, *not* compliant and vengeful God is toward any person Satan is able to use for such purposes, as well as any person who falls prey to their deception. Moses tells them that, when they come into the Promised Land, any person who is seeking to turn people away from loving and following the one true God is to be immediately killed—whether a family member or the closest of friends (13:6–9). I'd say God is pretty serious about how He feels about the divided allegiance and affection of His people!

Even more, according to Deuteronomy 13:12–16, if there ever was a city that listened to these Satanic prophets and started serving other gods, the children of Israel were to come into that city and completely annihilate every person and every animal. They were to gather all of the contents and goods of the city into a big heap and burn all of it and the entire city too. It was to remain a ruin forever as a reminder that there is one Lord in Israel (Deut. 6:4) and "Him only shalt thou serve" (Matt. 4:10; Deut. 6:13). "Behold therefore the...severity of God" (Rom.11:22)!

In chapter 14, Moses reminds the children of Israel that, as God's chosen people, He intends for them to stand out from the other nations of the world because of their relentless surrender to personal holiness (14:2). He gives clear instruction that their worship (14:1) and dietary practices (14:3–21) were to be different (peculiar) from the rest of the world. He provided a list of clean and unclean animals and forbid them to eat any animal that had died on its own since the blood could not be removed from it. Others could eat these animals, but not the chosen, separate people of Israel. And, as they are a picture of the individual believer, we too are a chosen people who have been called to be separate and holy (Titus 2:14; 1 Pet. 2:9). There may be practices that are socially and culturally accepted but which have no place in the life of God's people.

The tithe in Deuteronomy 14:22 is the second tithe that is commanded of the people (Lev. 27:30; Num. 18:26). This tithe is a tenth of the yearly increase of their fields. It was to be brought to the place of offering that the Lord had chosen. A portion was to be eaten with rejoicing to be a reminder that everything comes from the blessing of the Lord. Notice also, at the end of this chapter, that God also established a tithe that was to be collected once every three years to create what might be called a "welfare system" to support the fatherless, the widows, and the "strangers" (foreigners) who had no land to grow food or derive an income.

Chapter 15 records added instruction regarding the "seventh year" described in Exodus 23 and Leviticus 25. Not only was the land to rest in the seventh year, but debts were to be forgiven as well! In this new theocratic nation (a nation whose supreme ruler is God), the poor and the needy were never to be taken advantage of or brought under the yoke of bondage to others. In 15:7–15, Moses lays out God's instruction concerning generosity to the poor. The Lord reminds the children of Israel of how they were in bondage in Egypt and how He had released and redeemed them. God wanted to be sure that, in the Promised Land, His treatment of Israel was the standard by which they treated others who were oppressed. And may we never forget our Lord Jesus Christ's generosity toward us when we were spiritually poor!

Chapter 15 ends with instruction concerning the consecration of the firstborn males of the herd or flock. Moses tells them that they were to be sanctified or "set apart" for the Lord. If the animal was to be offered as a sacrifice to the Lord, it had to be completely without blemish— because it is an obvious picture of our Lord Jesus Christ who was "a lamb without blemish and without spot" (1 Pet. 1:19).

In chapter 16, God commands the children of Israel to observe the Passover even after they came in to the land. Passover served as a reminder to Israel that their deliverance from the bondage of Egypt was through the blood of the Passover lamb. It is the Old Testament equivalent of the Lord's Supper, the memorial feast our Lord instituted with His disciples the night before His death. That memorial feast reminds us that our deliverance from the bondage of Egypt (sin and the world) was through the blood of the true Passover lamb, our Lord Jesus Christ (1 Cor. 5:7).

There are actually three feasts described in chapter 16. The first is the Passover, followed by seven days of the Feast of Unleavened Bread. The second is the Feast of Weeks (or the Feast of Harvest, Ex. 23), later to be known as Pentecost. A freewill offering is to be given "according as the Lord thy God hath blessed thee" (Deut. 16:10). The third feast is the Feast of Tabernacles (sometimes called the Feast of Ingathering or Feast of Booths: Ex. 23; Lev. 23; Num. 29). This, again, is a time of giving and rejoicing (16:15).

In 16:18–20, Moses provides instruction concerning the selection of judges and officers. Like God, judges were not to be a respecter of persons, nor were they to receive gifts from people. God wanted those holding these positions in Israel to be completely free to "judge righteous judgment" (John 7:24). The chapter concludes (16:21–22) with a further admonition against idolatrous worship and, specifically, taking up the pagan practices of idol worship in groves of trees. God didn't want any worldly or idolatrous practices anywhere near His altar of sacrifice and worship!

Chapter 17 gives statutes concerning the discovery and investigation of idol worship (vs. 2–7). Those who were found guilty of worshipping or serving other gods were to be put to death. Implementing the death sentence, however, required the witness of two or more witnesses, and those witnesses must be the first ones to administer the punishment. At the end of 17:7, God explains that the reason for such harsh punishment was to rid Israel of evil.

In 17:14–20 , God gives instructions for the selection and duties of a king. At this time, God alone was Israel's King, but He knew that in time to come, they would want a physical, tangible king like the other nations of the world. (This prophecy would come to pass some 400 years after being in the land!) God said He would concede to their wishes for a king, but He would choose him from among the children of Israel (no foreigners!). He also commanded that kings refuse to multiply to themselves: horses, wives, silver and gold. And to ensure that each king in Israel completely understood what God had written in His law, he was required to write his own copy of the law and read it every day of his life so that he would fear the Lord, keep His words, and do them; so his heart wouldn't be lifted up and so his days could be prolonged (17:19–20). If only Israel's kings would have heeded these admonitions! And as those who have been made kings by the Lord Jesus Christ (Rev.1:6; 5:10), we would do well to carefully consider the spirit of these instructions!

CHRIST IS REVEALED:

As the *Unblemished Sacrifice* – Deuteronomy 15:21 (1 Pet. 1:19; 2 Cor. 5:21)

As the *Passover Lamb* – Deuteronomy 16:1 (John 1:29, 36; Rev. 5:12)

As the *Righteous Judge* – Deuteronomy 16:18; 17:8 (Rev. 19:11; Rom. 14:10)

WEEK 10, DAY 1: **TODAY'S READING: DEUTERONOMY 18–22**

OVERVIEW:

Levites and priests; prophets; cities of refuge; civil statutes; warfare; unknown murders; family statutes; civil statutes; sexual sin.

HIGHLIGHTS & INSIGHTS:

As Moses continues his second address in chapter 18, he acknowledges that, when they came into the land, there would be no land inheritance for the tribe of Levi. That sounds inconsiderate, disparaging, offensive and unfair until, in verse 2, we learn that the Lord had provided an inheritance for the Levites that was a thousand times more blessed than territory on a map. He Himself was their inheritance! As we discussed in the book of Leviticus, the word *Levite* means "joined to." The Levites were joined to the Lord in a spiritual relationship that was more significant and satisfying than any kind of earthly or physical inheritance. As you consider the blessings of the Levitical priesthood, remember that they are an Old Testament picture of us! We are now of the ones who are joined to the Lord; we now comprise His "royal priesthood" (1 Pet. 2:9; Rev. 1:6; 5:10). We are the ones for whom God now intends to provide an inheritance solely in Christ, not in the things of the earth. Colossians 3:1–2 tell us, "If ye then be risen with Christ, seek those things which are above, where Christ sitteth on the right hand of God. Set your affection on things above, not on things on the earth."

Deuteronomy 18:15–19 provides one of the greatest prophecies in the entire Old Testament of our Lord Jesus Christ. God reveals to His people that another "Prophet" like Moses will come! In the Gospel of John, there were numerous times during Christ's earthly ministry when someone asked if He was "that Prophet" or declared that He was, indeed, "that Prophet." They were referring to this very prophecy in Deuteronomy 18. And in the book of Acts, both Peter (in Acts 3:22–23) and Stephen (Acts 7:48) quoted this passage in reference to Christ. Sadly, nearly every person who was aware of this prophecy missed Christ's fulfillment of it, even though it was staring them right in the face!

In 18:20–22, God declares that throughout history the prophets through whom He is actually speaking will be easy to identify. They are 100% accurate, 100% of the time!

Chapter 19 continues God's instructions about designating key cities in the new land as cities of refuge. Again, the cities of refuge are a picture of the refuge we have in Christ. In the same way the innocent manslayer would plead his case to the elders of the city, Psalm 62:8 tells us to "pour out [our] heart" to God, who is our Refuge. Hallelujah!

In 19:13, God warns for the first time about the shedding of what He calls "innocent blood." This phrase is found at least twenty times in Scripture. "Innocent blood" is a precious thing in God's sight, most obviously because of His knowledge that His only Son would one day be the ultimate example of "innocent blood" being shed.

Chapter 19 concludes with several civil statutes. God reveals that moving a landmark is actually stealing land from your neighbor. He instructs that matters of law are to be established with a minimum of two witnesses, and preferably three. This principle is repeated in the New Testament in Matthew 18:16; 2 Corinthians 13:1; 1 Timothy 5:19; and Hebrews 10:28. We would do well to apply this principle. How many times have we decided something in our own mind on the word of only one person? False lawsuits are the next civil matter that God addresses. If someone sued another person falsely for a specific amount, the false accuser would be required to pay that amount to the defendant. Wouldn't that limit a great number of lawsuits in the twenty-first century! Lastly, the commandment concerning fair and just judgments in Deuteronomy 19:21, an "eye for an eye, tooth for a tooth," is directed to the civil government, not individuals. Sadly, it was soon twisted (and often is to this day!) to provide an excuse for personal vengeance—vengeance that is always reserved by and for the Lord (Deut. 32:35; Rom. 12:19).

In chapter 20, God lets Israel know that the army that would be utilized in the Promised Land would be different than any military power in the history of the world. Before any battle, priests would address the children of Israel, reminding them that their strength as an army would come from placing their confidence in the Lord who was with them, that He was the one who would fight their enemy, and that He would grant the victory (20:4). It is the biblical principle of Zechariah 4:6, "Not by might, nor by power, but by my spirit, saith the Lord of hosts." It is also a picture of how the New Testament reveals that we are to do battle! Ephesians 6:10 says, "Finally, my brethren, be strong in the Lord, and in the power of his might."

However, even though God intended to grant this army constant victory, He wanted to be certain that they were focused and fearless! In 20:5–9, God gives four reasons that young men in Israel could be excused from military duty: 1) If they had recently purchased a new house; 2) If they had recently planted a vineyard; 3) If they had recently taken a wife; and 4) If they were just plain afraid! God wanted His army free of distractions and deserters! In the warfare we face, may we likewise be focused and fearless!

God continues His military instructions in 20:10–20. When the children of Israel approached a city to overtake it, they were first to offer the option of a peaceful surrender. The inhabitants were to be given the chance to open the gates, pay tribute, and become their servants. If the city chose not to surrender, God told them to go into it and wipe out every male—sparing the women, children, and animals—and take the spoils of the city for themselves. For the six nations listed in verse 17, however, they were to wipe out anything that moved or breathed! It would appear that these peoples and cities were of such a demonic nature and possession that the only solution was extinction.

Chapter 21 gives further instruction concerning the shedding of innocent blood. There was a ceremonial washing included in the process of being released from the guilt of shedding this innocent blood (21:6–9). Many centuries later, on the day of Pentecost in Acts 2, the Jews ask Peter what they should do because of their guilt in shedding the blood of the only innocent man who ever lived (not to mention their own Messiah). Peter's instruction utilizes the principle established in Deuteronomy 21 and includes the "ceremonial washing" of baptism as a part of their repentance for crucifying the Lord of glory (Acts 2:37–38). It is not a baptism for acquiring New Testament salvation. It is exclusively the biblical requirement for removing Israel's guilt for being the ones responsible for shedding the innocent blood of the Lord Jesus Christ on Calvary (Deut. 21:8-9).

After providing instructions for taking a wife from the captives of the new land (21:10–14), Moses then gives statutes for families. He lets Israel know that inheritances were to be divided by statute—not emotions. Next, Moses explains that stubbornness and rebelliousness in a son was an offense worthy of death! Three times in this passage, God references a stubborn and rebellious son not obeying or hearkening to the voice of his parents. Our goal in bringing up our children should be that *our* voice will control and instruct their little mind and body. Then as they mature, we must constantly shift that control and guidance to the *Lord* and His *Word*. Biblically, if they never learn to respond to the authority of *our* voice when they are children, they will not respond to the authority of *God's* voice when they are adults.

Chapter 22 gives statutes on civil and family matters—from taking care of your brother's belongings, to clothing, construction, plowing, divorce, adultery, rape and incest. Over and over again the statutes and commandments are written to purify and sanctify a land in which the holy God of the universe would dwell with His people. This had been a land of transvestites and homosexuals, a land of incest and adultery, and a land of selfishness and self-gratification. The Lord desired a pure and holy nation in a completely undefiled land. It is the Old Testament picture of the New Testament instruction given to us in 2 Corinthians 6:17–18: "Come out from among them, and be ye separate, saith the Lord, and touch not the unclean thing; and I will receive you, And will be a Father unto you, and ye shall be my sons and daughters, saith the Lord Almighty."

CHRIST IS REVEALED:

As *Prophet* – Deuteronomy 18:15 (John 5:46; Acts 3:22–23)

As *Sin Bearer* – Deuteronomy 21:22–23 (Gal. 3:13; 1 Pet. 2:24)

WEEK 10, DAY 2: **TODAY'S READING: DEUTERONOMY 23-26**

OVERVIEW:

Requirements to be in the congregation; cleanliness; civil statutes; divorce; civil statutes; firstfruits offering; charge to hear and obey.

HIGHLIGHTS & INSIGHTS:

By the time Moses finished his second address (chapters 5–26) with all of the statutes, commandments and judgments for what life was to be like in this new land God was preparing them to enter, the children of Israel must have been thinking, "Man! How are we going to keep all of this stuff straight?!" And truthfully, God had a lot of requirements, stipulations and specifications for their new lifestyle in the new land! But Moses didn't want them to miss the purpose behind all of the rigorous and meticulous details, so he concludes by revealing the real intent of God's heart (26:16–19). He tells the children of Israel that all of these instructions were given simply because God desired "to make thee high above all nations which he hath made, in praise, and in name, and in honour; and that thou mayst be an holy people unto the Lord thy God, as he hath spoken" (v. 19). How awesome is that?!

And since the children of Israel are a picture of the individual believer in the New Testament, God's heart is the same for us. 1 Peter 2:9–10 says that His intent and purpose for us is to make you and me "a chosen generation, a royal priesthood, an holy nation, a peculiar people; that ye should shew forth the praises of him who hath called you out of darkness into his marvelous light: Which in time past were not a people, but are now the people of God: which had not obtained mercy, but now have obtained mercy." The real desire of God's heart for His people has always been the same! That we might be a peculiar people because of the holy life we live in the midst of this dark world as we seek to glorify the holy name of our God!

However, one of the most blessed and marvelous differences between us and the children of Israel is that we have been made free from the *external* law of Moses, because we have been placed in Christ, who Himself fulfilled all of the stringent requirements of the Old Testament law (Matt. 5:17). And He did that so we might be free to live by the law of the Spirit who has taken up residence in us *internally*! This is one of the key truths God has revealed to us as New Testament saints:

> Romans 7:6 – "But now we are delivered from the law, that being dead wherein we were held; that we should serve in newness of spirit, and not in the oldness of the letter."

> Romans 8:1–4 – "There is therefore now no condemnation to them which are in Christ Jesus, who walk not after the flesh, but after the Spirit. For the law of the Spirit of life in Christ Jesus hath made me free from the law of sin and death. For what the law could not do, in that it was weak through the flesh, God sending his own Son in the likeness of sinful flesh, and for sin, condemned sin in the flesh: That the righteousness of the law might be fulfilled in us, who walk not after the flesh, but after the Spirit."

> Galatians 5:18 —"But if ye be led of the Spirit, ye are not under the law."

May we never be moved, as Paul feared we might, from "the simplicity that is in Christ" (2 Cor. 11:3). And may we never be moved from the simplicity of the greatest commandment: "And thou shalt love the Lord thy God with all thy heart, and with all thy soul, and with all thy mind, and with all thy strength: this is the first commandment. And the second is like, namely this, Thou shalt love thy neighbor as thyself. There is none other commandment greater than these" (Mark 12:30–31). We are not bound to serve the law of Moses. We are *free from* the law of Moses, so we can be free to *fulfill* the law of the Spirit and the law of love (Rom. 8:2; Gal. 5:13–14). Praise God for the simplicity of life in Christ!

But note in today's reading in chapter 23, that certain people were not to be admitted into the citizenship of the children of Israel. They could reside in the area, but due to impurities (mutilation, illegitimacy, ancestry, etc.) they could not join the congregation of Israel. Again, the point is, the Lord desired a pure and holy congregation of peculiar people. The simple reality was, sin had lasting consequences! Moses reveals in chapter 23 that the reason holiness, cleanliness and purity had such an important place inside the congregation of Israel—was because the holy, clean and pure presence of the Lord was in their midst! (See 2 Cor. 6:16–18)

Chapter 23 ends with the topic of vows and generosity. Vows were and are sacred to God. Vows made to God were not to be made flippantly and, once they were made, were to be kept! In Ecclesiastes 5:4–5 God lets us know that it is better not to vow a vow, than to vow a vow and not pay it. Deuteronomy 23:24–25 tells Israel that they are to be a generous people and, at the same time, be careful not to take advantage of the generosity of others.

Deuteronomy 24 is a very significant chapter because of its teaching regarding divorce. In Matthew 19, our Lord deals with the same issue. Jesus emphatically declares that divorce was not God's plan from the beginning—but it was a concession made by God "because of the hardness of your hearts" (Matt. 19:8). Note in 24:2, the woman in a divorce situation is permitted to become another man's wife, but 24:4 refers to her as being "defiled." There's no way around it, sin always has lasting consequences.

Once again, in chapter 24, God reveals His heart of compassion for the poor, the fatherless, widows, and strangers. God wanted to make sure that the rich and powerful never took advantage of them or oppressed them. He reminded them that they had been slaves in Egypt and wanted them to treat others in their affliction the way He had treated them. (The New Testament equivalent of this principle is found in Ephesians 4:31–32.) This new land and nation God was establishing was to be a nation of abundant generosity and care for others. If the children of God are to be a reflection of their Father, they (we) must be abundantly loving and generous!

Chapter 25 gives instruction for those who would serve as judges in Israel, followed by detailed specifications for the kinsman-redeemer. An actual example of this situation is found in the book of Ruth, as Ruth, a Gentile from a cursed race (the Moabites), is redeemed through the relationship she had with Boaz, her Jewish kinsman-redeemer from the city of Bethlehem. The principle of the kinsman-redeemer, here and in Ruth 3–4, is a beautiful picture of our Lord Jesus Christ who became our "kinsman" by taking on human flesh in Bethlehem so that He might "redeem" us Gentiles, part of the cursed human race, taking us to be His lawfully wedded wife! The Bible is an amazing Book!

The chapter continues with statutes for honesty in business. In that day, merchants would carry their own weights that would be placed on the scales when making transactions. Some would put a lesser weight on the scale when *buying* a certain commodity and a heavier weight when *selling* it. Practically speaking, it was a very deceptive and dishonest way of being able to "buy low and sell high." God lets them know that such practices were an "abomination" to Him (25:16). Our omniscient Lord knows of our honesty with people and deals with us accordingly.

The offering of the firstfruits in Chapter 26 was a special one-time gift offered to the Lord from the first harvest in the new land. It was to be a hallowed worship experience that included a time of remembrance, a time of rejoicing, and a time of confession. Once the Lord brought them into the Promised Land, He wanted them to recognize that they would be living in houses they did not build, eating from crops and gardens they did not plant, living in abundance from the gracious hand of the Lord!

In 26:16–19, God confirmed with the children of Israel all that had been commanded them. He had commanded that all of His statutes, commandments and judgments be kept with all of their heart and soul. The people vow that they will walk in His ways and keep His commandments. The Lord vows that they will be His peculiar people, holy to Him. And this concludes Moses's second address in Deuteronomy.

CHRIST IS REVEALED:

As the *Generous One* – Deuteronomy 24:19–21 (2 Cor. 8:9; Rom. 8:32)

As the *Kinsman Redeemer* – Deuteronomy 25:5–6 (Rom. 3:24; Col. 1:13–14)

As the *Firstfruit Offering* – Deuteronomy 26:10–11 (1 Cor. 15:20, 23)

As the *Deliverer* – Deuteronomy 26:8 (Gal. 1:3–4)

WEEK 10, DAY 3: **TODAY'S READING: DEUTERONOMY 27-30**

OVERVIEW:

The altar to be built; blessing and cursing; the new covenant; return to the Lord; the choice set before the children of Israel.

HIGHLIGHTS & INSIGHTS:

In chapter 27:1–3, Moses commands that, after crossing the Jordan River into the Promised Land, Israel was to build a memorial of stones covered with plaster upon which "all the words of this law," the Ten Commandments, would be written. (Joshua completes this in Joshua 8:30–35.) This memorial was to be set upon Mount Ebal (Deut. 27:4), the mountain associated with cursing (v. 13). God is clearly declaring that the Law can only bring a curse! Romans 3:20 tells us, "Therefore by the deeds of the law there shall no flesh be justified in his sight: for by the law is the knowledge of sin." And Galatians 3:10 says, "For as many as are of the works of the law are under the curse: for it is written, Cursed is every one that continueth not in all things which are written in the book of the law to do them."

In 27:5–7, an altar was to be built at the base of this mountain where both the burnt offering and the peace offering were to be sacrificed. Both of these Old Testament offerings find their fulfillment in the sacrifice of Christ on the cross. Galatians 3:13 tells us, "Christ hath redeemed us from the curse of the law, being made a curse for us: for it is written, Cursed is every one that hangeth on a tree." The picture here in Deuteronomy 27 is that the Law condemns every man, and the ensuing curse of his sinfulness can only be remedied by the substitutionary death of Christ. Only through Christ is the curse of sin removed, and only through Christ can a condemned sinner find peace with God! Romans 5:1–2 tells us, "Therefore being justified by faith, we have peace with God through our Lord Jesus Christ: By whom also we have access by faith into this grace wherein we stand, and rejoice in hope of the glory of God"!

In 27:11, Moses instructs that the 12 tribes were to be divided equally between two mountains: Gerizim (representing *blessing*—v. 12) and Ebal (representing *cursing*—v. 13). The valley between these two mountains forms a natural amphitheater about two miles wide providing a perfect arena for the Levites to be heard as they were commanded by God to speak to Israel (27:14), and the mountains provided a perfect illustration of God's message to Israel of their choice of *blessing* or *cursing* once they entered the land.

Next the Levites were to speak to the people, beginning each of the next twelve verses with the same word: "cursed" (27:15–26). The words *blessed, bless* or *blessing* are not to be found. Once again, the simple but profound truth God is communicating is that the Law is capable of producing only *cursing*!

In chapter 28, God describes the reality of *blessing* or *cursing* once they enter the new land. The *blessings* are laid out in 28:3–6, and God's promises for *obedience* are found in verses 7–14. God then spells out the *curses* in 28:15–19, and the promises of *disobedience* are found in verses 20–68 (that's 49 straight verses of warnings of cursing!). But God was also clear that the choice was entirely theirs. Simply put, *obedience* would bring *blessing*, and *disobedience* would bring *cursing*. If the children of Israel diligently listened to the Lord and did His commandments, the Lord would set them "on high" (28:1). The Lord would bless their homes, their work, their nation, and everything that has anything to do with their lives. But, if they did not hearken, curses would be certain to "come upon" them and "overtake" them (28:15). They would be cursed in their bodies, their work, their homes, their land, and their nation. Even the rain would be dust (28:24). In verse 30, three of the military exemptions (20:5–7) would be turned into curses. Without the Lord fighting for them, they would inevitably be conquered.

This chapter is not only a warning to Israel, but also a prophecy of their future. The blessings of the Lord that He talks about in this chapter will be seen repeatedly in the kingdom as they obey Him. The curses will likewise be seen in the conquests, the captivities, and the famines throughout the rest of the Old Testament and beyond. Jeremiah cries in the book of Lamentations as he looks out of his window and sees the people and the city destroyed as these very curses have unfolded.

Practically speaking, what are we to learn from these things?

- God does what He says He will do!
- The Lord works and moves in the physical realm of our world.
- The Lord can bring rain and stop rain.
- The Lord can physically heal.
- The Lord can cause a battle to be won.
- Our Lord does answer prayer!
- And we will all serve somebody! (28:47–48; Rom. 6:16)

Chapters 29 and 30 complete the third message from Moses. Chapter 29 begins with a reminder of the covenant God made with them in Horeb and their inability to keep it. Moses reminds them of the provision and protection of the Lord, the wrath of the Lord, and their unique relationship with Him. Once again, Moses reminds them that if they obey God they will be blessed, and if they disobey Him they will be cursed. God tells them that there are certain secret things that He had not revealed to them, but He lets them know in no uncertain terms that everything He had revealed to them, they were required to obey (29:29)!

In chapter 30, our Lord reveals that if, after living under the curse of their disobedience, Israel would return to Him and once again obey the things He had commanded through His Word, He would extend His grace and compassion to them (Ps. 111:4) and allow them to live in His blessing. This passage is not only a promise to Israel, but also a prophecy of their future. It looks forward to a time of renewal for the children of Israel in the last days when they shall return unto the Lord and obey His voice.

In 30:11–20, Moses extends the invitation to the children of Israel. The words have been plain, not hidden, or out of reach (30:11). It was all really very simple. God condenses these four chapters (Deut. 27–30) into two simple verses. The first verse is 30:15: "See, I have set before thee this day *life* and *good*, and *death* and *evil*." The choice was theirs: *life or death* and *good or evil*. Seems like it should have been the biggest no-brainer in history! The second verse is 30:19, where Moses says to the people: "I call heaven and earth to record this day against you, that I have set before you life and death, blessing and cursing: therefore choose life, that both thou and thy seed may live." Again, how hard could that decision be? But don't miss the fact that God presents that same choice to you and me today and every day for the rest of our lives (Gal.6:7–8). It really is that simple, y'all!

CHRIST IS REVEALED:

As the *Peace Offering* – Deuteronomy 27:7 (John 14:27; Rom. 5:1; Col. 1:20)

As the *Blessing of God* – Deuteronomy 28:1–2 (Eph. 1:3; 1 Pet. 1:3)

As *Life* – Deuteronomy 30:15 (John 11:25; 6:40)

WEEK 10, DAY 4: **TODAY'S READING: DEUTERONOMY 31-34**

OVERVIEW:

The transition of leadership to Joshua; the word from the Lord; the song of Moses; Moses's blessing upon the Tribes; the death of Moses; the succession of Joshua.

HIGHLIGHTS & INSIGHTS:

In Deuteronomy 31, one of the greatest men who ever lived is about to die. I can imagine what must have been going through Moses's mind and heart at this moment as he reflected on the past forty years of his life.

1. He, no doubt, had thoughts about *what could have been.*

Certainly his mind went back to that fateful five minutes when, out of frustration with God's people, he struck the Rock for a second time, rather than speaking to it as God had instructed him to do. That one impulsive fleshly choice resulted in God's decision not to use Moses to bring His people into the abundant life He had designed for them in Canaan. From a practical standpoint, let the Word of God etch this truth into our minds and hearts: God's grace, mercy, compassion and forgiveness (Ps. 86:5,15) do not negate the fact that our sin always has consequences (Gal. 6:7). And may this tragedy in Moses's life impress on our minds and hearts the necessity of always being filled with, controlled by, and walking in the Spirit—not only daily or hourly, but moment by moment and second by second! Moses's failure teaches us that the entire course and direction of our life can be altered by one moment's impulsive action or reaction of our flesh. God help us!

One day we will all stand at the Judgment Seat of Christ. We will walk back through every day of our lives from the moment we were saved until the moment we entered the Lord's presence, whether by death or by Rapture. Then we will see our lives the way our Lord Jesus Christ sees them now. When the Lord allows us to reflect upon our lives, much like Moses had the opportunity to do in today's reading, may our minds and hearts not be consumed with thoughts about *what could have been*! May we walk each day of our lives in simple obedience, in the filling and power of the Holy Spirit, so that we'll have no regrets at our final accounting at the Judgment Seat!

2. He, no doubt, had thoughts about *what actually was.*

Though Moses, no doubt, spent countless sleepless nights rehearsing the whole striking-the-rock-twice incident—wondering why God seemed to have such a knee-jerk reaction to his knee-jerk reaction—and wondering whether the punishment actually fit the crime, there's certainly none of that now. All of that was water under the bridge at this point.

God's Plan A for Moses was obviously for him to *finish well*. Finishing well in Plan A meant obeying God and being the one to lead God's people into the Promised Land. Because of Moses's failure in Numbers 20:7–13, however, God made clear to him that Plan A was an impossibility. It just wasn't going to happen.

But, in His grace, God also had a Plan B for Moses! And Plan B was, first and foremost, for Moses to forget "those things which [were] behind, and … press toward the mark for the prize of the high calling of God" (Phil. 3:13–14). In other words, not to sit around feeling sorry for himself, pouting about the failures of his past, but to begin from where he was and seek to obey God in the course God had for him in Plan B!

Perhaps, because of some kind of failure in your past, you too have missed God's Plan A for your life. So what do you do now? Well, you can do what a lot of people do: wallow around in self-pity for the rest of your life, rehearsing it all over and over in your mind, wishing you had done something different or made better decisions! But all of that rehearsing won't do a single thing to change what now is! It will only bind you to the *past*, causing you to miss the incredible opportunities God has for you in the *present* and to ensure that you will never tap into the glorious things God has designed for you in the *future*! Learn from the example of Moses—God most definitely has a Plan B for your life, and there is most definitely a way for you to *finish well* in God's Plan B!

In Deuteronomy 31, Moses sees the big picture. He knows that for him to finish well, the children of Israel didn't need to get all sentimental and preoccupied with *his death*. They were on the brink of entering into the *life* God had intended for them when He brought them out of Egypt (Deut. 6:23)! This was a time for forward thinking, jubilation, expectation and faith! Moses could have very easily played on the people's sympathies, made the whole ordeal of his death the people's focus, and failed in his responsibility to orchestrate the beautiful transfer of leadership to Joshua by making it all about him. But Moses is too much of a man of God and a man of character for that! Moses realizes that, for him to finish well in his Plan B, how he prepares the people for entering the land and how he coordinates the transition to Joshua is vital. It is apparent by Moses's attitude and demeanor that he is going to finish well. Moses's attitude toward Joshua at this moment is much like John the Baptist's attitude toward Jesus in John 3:30: "He must increase, but I must decrease." God had already made the people aware that Joshua would succeed Moses, but Moses wanted to handle this transfer with such grace and dignity that it would please the Lord and, at the same time, generate excitement and expectation in the hearts of God's people about their future with God in the land, under the leadership of Joshua.

Though today's chapters record Moses's *physical death*, they also record an even more significant death: his *death to self*! Oh, that more leaders would learn from Moses's example and use their platform of leadership to advance the work of God and magnify the glory of God. By God's grace, may we, like Moses, get the focus off of ourselves and completely on the Lord Himself and become passionate about Him receiving from our lives the glory that is due His name (Ps. 29:2; 96:8). And whether we're living God's Plan A or Plan B, may we make certain that, in every remaining moment and detail of our lives, our passion is for the work of God and the glory of God!

3. He, no doubt, had thoughts about *what would be*.

Of all people, Moses had a clear understanding of the purposes of God in the Exodus. He realized that God was desiring, not first and foremost, to rescue *the children of Israel* from their bondage in Egypt, but to rescue *His own name*! Moses understood that everything that had taken place in the preceding forty years was really about God's name being rescued from how it was being polluted on the earth. Ezekiel 20 provides incredible commentary of God's purpose and intention from the time of the Exodus to their entrance into the land. Several times in this chapter, God makes abundantly clear that the issue was *Him*—not *them* (the children of Israel). Sure, the children of Israel were most definitely the beneficiaries of the wonderful and powerful demonstration of God's deliverance, but the scripture is clear, God did what He did for His own name—not theirs! He says in Ezekiel 20:9, "But I wrought [worked] for my name's sake, that it should not be polluted before the heathen, among whom they were, in whose sight I made myself known unto them, in bringing them forth out of the land of Egypt." (God repeats this same intention in 20:14 and 20:22.)

And in Deuteronomy 31, even as Moses is hours away from drawing his last breath on this planet, he has no thought whatsoever about his own name. His preoccupation is for the name of the one by whom he was called, the only name that is worthy of glory!

The same is true for us. Though we are most definitely the beneficiaries of the work of God through Christ's death, burial and resurrection, God did what He did in delivering us out of the bondage of our sin to rescue His own name from how it was being polluted all over this sinful world! Therefore, like Moses, may we give no thought whatsoever to our own name—but to the name of the one by whom we were called, the only name on earth that is worthy of glory!

In 31:14–18, God summons both Moses and Joshua into His holy presence in the tabernacle before Moses's death to inform them that, despite all of His incredible grace upon the children of Israel, they would rebel after getting into the land. What a travesty! May we learn from their horrific mistakes.

God gives Moses inspiration in writing a song that would be used for years to come in reminding Israel of their sin. The book ends with Moses lovingly seeking to speak blessing on the tribes of Israel that were about to enter the Promised Land.

CHRIST IS REVEALED:

In *Joshua* – Deuteronomy 31:7 (John 1:17; Rom. 3:21–22; Acts 13:39)

In the *Rock* – Deuteronomy 32:4, 31 (Rom. 9:33; 1 Cor. 10:4; 1 Pet. 2:8)

WEEK 10, DAY 5: **TODAY'S READING: JOSHUA 1–5**

OVERVIEW:

The commission of Joshua; the covenant with Rahab; crossing the Jordan river into the Promised Land; the memorial of the twelve stones; the circumcision of God's people at Gilgal.

HIGHLIGHTS & INSIGHTS:

The book of Joshua is the story of how Israel crossed the Jordan River and claimed the inheritance that God had promised them. Before actually possessing the land, however, there were still many battles for them to fight, and many enemies they would need to defeat. And once again, we find that God is painting an incredible picture of the Christian life through His record of Israel's history. As we seek to take possession of our "inheritance in Canaan," we, likewise, have many battles to fight and many enemies to overcome—the world, the devil, and these bodies of flesh we all live in. 1 Thessalonians 4:4 tells us that we have been called to "possess [our] vessel in sanctification and honor." For this to happen, just like the children of Israel in the book of Joshua, we must allow our Joshua, the Lord Jesus Christ, to lead us to victory in every battle and against every enemy (Eph. 6:10; 2 Cor. 10:4–5).

Keep in mind as we develop this picture in the book of Joshua that Canaan is **not** a picture of heaven. We do not have to battle to gain our home in heaven—it is a gift (Eph. 2:8–9). Rather, Canaan represents the abundant inheritance that God has for each of us in Christ. We sometimes refer to this inheritance as "the victorious Christian life." Jesus referred to it as the abundant life (John 10:10). It is the life of fullness and fruit-bearing God designed all of us who have received Christ to possess. Practically speaking, it is when the life of Christ in all His fullness is being manifested through our bodies (2 Cor. 4:11), while at the same time, we are manifesting the "fruit of the Spirit" (Gal. 5:22–23), "fruit unto holiness" (Rom. 6:22), and the fruit of souls won to Christ (Col. 1:6).

Notice that the book of Joshua begins with the ending of a life: "Moses my servant is dead" (Josh. 1:2). Moses was the lawgiver, and the simple but poignant fact is that the law could not give life or defeat sin! Romans 7:5 says, "For when we were in the flesh, the motions of sins, which were by the law, did work in our members to bring forth fruit unto death." Moses brought the children of Israel to the edge, but Joshua (Jesus) must take them in and give them the victory! Verse 2 continues "now therefore arise." We must die to ourselves and our self-righteousness (Phil. 3:4–9) and allow God to raise us up to "walk in newness of life" on a daily basis! (Rom. 6:4, 13)

Joshua 1:8 was certainly a key challenge for how God wanted Joshua to approach His Word and has been a challenge for every child of God since it was delivered personally to Joshua! God told Joshua: "This book of the law shall not depart out of thy mouth; but thou shalt meditate therein day and night, that thou mayest observe to do according to all that is written therein: for then thou shalt make thy way prosperous, and then thou shalt have good success."

For every person God has delivered from the bondage of sin and redeemed to Himself, He intends for His Word to be a core value. Each of us has a value system, and in our value system, there are certain things at the very center—the things of life that are the *most important* to us. They are the things in our life that are our *highest priority*. The things that make us tick. They *motivate* us; they are a *passion* to us; they are *what we're really all about*!

Can you honestly say that the Word of God is one of your core values? And how would you know if it was or not? Actually, Joshua 1:8 lets us know that there are two key indicators.

1. Our core values are easily identifiable by what we *talk about*.
   Without even trying or consciously recognizing we're doing it, we talk about what's important to us! Joshua 1:8 says, "This book of the law shall not depart out of thy mouth." If the Word of God is one of our core values, it will be identifiable in the fact that we are constantly talking about it! What would those who know you best say you constantly talk about?

2. Our core values are easily identifiable by what we *think about*.
   Again, without even trying or attempting to make it happen, the reality is, we think about what's important to us. Joshua 1:8 goes on to say, "But thou shalt meditate therein day and night." Can you honestly say that the Word of God is something you constantly find yourself thinking about?

May it be evident to God, to us, and to others that the Word of God is one of our "core values!"

Chapter 2 deals with the Jewish men who were sent to spy out Jericho and their subsequent covenant with Rahab the harlot. Don't miss how Rahab's story pictures the story of everyone of us who know Christ!

1. She was a sinner. (Rom. 3:23)
    Joshua 2:1 plainly states that she was a harlot.

2. She was under condemnation. (John 3:18)
    The city had already been declared condemned by God. And just like the people of the world today, the people of the city would be destroyed whether they *felt* condemned or not!

3. She heard the Word of God. (Rom. 10:17)
    The message she heard was a convicting message of judgment that caused her to recognize that the God of Israel was the one true God and Lord! (Josh. 2:8–11; John 16:8)

4. She believed the Word. (Rom. 10:9; Eph. 2:8)
    Hebrews 11:31 states that Rahab believed and was saved by faith.

5. She sought to win others. (Mark 5:18–20)
    When a person trusts Christ, their first desire is to share Him with others, especially their own family. Rahab immediately shares her burden to see her family saved. (Josh. 2:12–13)

6. She was delivered from judgment. (1 Thess. 4:13–18, 2 Thess. 1:7–9)
    Just like Rahab in Joshua 6:22–25, we have been rescued from God's coming judgment upon this world.

7. She went to a wedding. (Matt. 1:5)
    Matthew 1:5 lets us know that Rahab married into the royal lineage of Israel. In fact, the Messiah actually came through her family line! How gracious is our God to take a harlot and make her the mother of the royal family through which Messiah came? We, too, have a wedding and a marriage feast to look forward to because of God's incredible grace! (Rev. 19:7–9,17–19)

In chapters 3 and 4, Israel follows Joshua and the Ark of the Covenant across the Jordan River. Note in Joshua 3:16, that the water that flowed down from the city of Adam stood up and was stopped by the Ark. It is a beautiful picture of the fact that the effects of Adam's sin which flowed from Adam down to us (Rom. 5:12, 17), are stopped by Jesus Christ when we "cross over the Jordan" in our lives and take possession of the life of fullness found in Christ (Rom. 6:14).

In chapter 5, all of the Jewish males were circumcised. Note that circumcision was a mark of a covenant relationship (Gen. 17:9–14) that provided *external* evidence of an *internal* reality (Deut. 10:16). A perfect and discreet description of circumcision that captures both its physical and spiritual significance is that it is "the cutting away of the flesh that reveals the source of life." Note that God refers to the covenant relationship of our salvation in Colossians 2:11 as the true circumcision. Practically speaking, if the flesh isn't cut away in our lives, we will not reproduce spiritual life!

CHRIST IS REVEALED:

Through *Joshua* – Joshua 1 (His very name means "Jehovah is salvation." He is the one who leads us to the Promised Land.)

As Rahab's *Scarlet Thread* – Joshua 2:18. (It is a type of the blood of Christ which brings about deliverance from judgment and safety from death.)

As *Captain of the Host of the Lord* – Joshua 5:14–15 (Heb. 2:10)

WEEK 11, DAY 1: **TODAY'S READING: JOSHUA 6–10**

OVERVIEW:

The conquest and destruction of Jericho; the sin of Achan; the destruction of Ai; the deception of the Gibeonites and their subsequent covenant with Israel; Joshua leads Israel in victory after victory.

HIGHLIGHTS & INSIGHTS:

As Christians, we face many Jerichos in our lives. Like the spies at Kadesh, we often want to give up at the sight of insurmountable odds (Num. 13:28–33). But Joshua chapter 6 teaches us that no wall is too high, no barrier so impenetrable, and no sin so great that our Lord Jesus Christ cannot give us the victory. Joshua 5:14 in yesterday's reading reminds us that the soldier who fights most powerfully and experiences the victories God intends is the one who bows the lowest before battle! God is picturing for us the fact that the battles we face in the Christian life are won on our *knees* and on our *faces* before the Lord (Eph. 6:10–18; 1 Pet. 5:6–8).

Note also that no man can take a city by himself. It is no small thing that Joshua had the loyal cooperation of the priests and the people and that together they overcame the enemy! The book of Hebrews commands us not to forsake assembling ourselves together, as so many in the last days are doing (The old "You don't have to go to church to be spiritual" stuff!), but to exhort one another, especially as we get closer to Christ's return (Heb. 10:25). We all need the accountability and help that our brothers and sisters in our own local church provide in order to keep our enemies defeated so we can possess the fullness of what God intends for our lives (1 Cor. 1:10). It is the only way we can live in victory (Matt. 16:18).

In chapter 7, God reveals the consequences of secret sin. Achan had secretly taken some of the spoils from Jericho in direct disobedience to God's command (Josh. 6:18–19). Because of this sin in Israel's camp, they suffered their first defeat. What's interesting is that, in Joshua 8:2, unlike the battle of Jericho where the spoils of the city were to be reserved to God alone, God now instructed the children of Israel to take the spoils from Ai unto themselves! Had Achan simply waited a few days, he would have had all the wealth he could have carried (Matt. 6:33). How much like our flesh to prematurely *take* what the Spirit is fully capable of and even planning to *provide*!

In chapter 8, Ai represents the daily battle we have against the flesh (Gal. 5:17). In 8:3, notice the wording—"So Joshua arose" and, thereby, led Israel to victory. For New Testament believers, it is only through the power of Christ's resurrection that we can conquer and defeat the enemy of our flesh! In verse 6, we are told that "they will come out after us," picturing that the members of our fleshly bodies will come out to fight against the Spirit until we receive our glorified bodies! (See Rom. 8:23; Eph. 4:30; Rom. 6:12–13; Col. 3:5.) The end of verse 9 says, "Joshua lodged that night among the people." We have this same promise in the biblical "nighttime" in which we are presently living in the church age (Rom. 13:12; 1 Thess. 5:4–9), that our Joshua, the Lord Jesus Christ, lodges with us, as it were, by His Spirit, to provide our victory over the flesh. (See Rom. 7:24–25; 8:9–14; Eph. 3:16.)

Gibeon was the next city to be taken after the victories of Israel at Jericho and Ai. Notice that the Gibeonites used deceit as their tool to avoid destruction. In chapter 9, they posed as ambassadors from a far country who wanted to be the servants of Israel. They succeeded in getting this agreement (or covenant) from the leaders of Israel before their true identity was revealed. My brothers and sisters, may we beware! Like the Gibeonites, our flesh will do everything in its power to try to make deals with us—so it can escape death!

There is also a lesson for us to learn by the timing of the ordeal with the Gibeonites. It is often after taking God at His Word, trusting Him for great spiritual victories, that the flesh's next attack will be to "work wilily" (9:4) in agreeing to be the servant of the Spirit so it doesn't have to die! We must learn that our flesh is as deceptive as Satan himself. We must never let our guard down. The only answer to the flesh is *death*! May we join Paul in saying, "I die daily"! (1 Cor. 15:31).

CHRIST IS REVEALED:

In the *Ark of the Covenant* – Joshua 6 (Like God's presence dwelt in Israel in the Ark, God's presence now dwells in us by the Spirit of Christ – 1 Cor. 6:19; Rom. 8:9)

Through *Joshua* – Joshua 8 and 10 (He is the only one who can lead us to daily victory over our flesh.)

WEEK 11, DAY 2: **TODAY'S READING: JOSHUA 11–14**

OVERVIEW:

Joshua conquers kings and cities for Israel; the land is divided by lot among the tribes; Caleb requests and obtains the mountain of Hebron from Joshua.

HIGHLIGHTS & INSIGHTS:

Word has been spreading throughout the Promised Land of this weak nomadic people that have been transformed into powerful warriors—and their omnipotent God! As we move into Joshua 11, the kings of the land have been struck with fear and are conspiring to keep them from completely overtaking their cities (11:1–5). In fact, the word *king* or *kings* is found over fifty times in today's reading! Knowing that these various kingdoms banding together might be intimidating to Joshua and his people, God reassures him that He, by His power, will slay the conspirators and grant victory to Israel just as He had done with the previous individual kings and their armies (11:6-9).

In 11:10, Joshua defeats the king who was the head of the villainous kingdoms with the sword, the same way that our Joshua, the Lord Jesus Christ, will defeat the king who is the head of the kingdom of darkness with the sword that proceeds out of His mouth (2 Thess. 2:8; Rev. 19:15, 21). And in 11:21, we find that Joshua not only utterly destroyed all of the kings and their cities, but also the giants and their cities! (The Anakims were giants.)

Have the kings from the kingdom of darkness been conspiring together against you? Are there giants that seem to be coming down out of the mountains against you? Trust in the sword of the Word of God of our Joshua! He's got this! By trusting the Word of God and the God of the Word against the enemy, in time, one by one, you will be able to list the kings and giants that have been defeated as you take possession of your possession, just as surely as Joshua's defeated foes are listed one by one in Joshua 12!

As we begin chapter 13, the Lord reminds Joshua, "Thou art old and stricken in years, and there remaineth yet very much land to be possessed." There are no doubt, many who are reading this today who feel the same way! But regardless of our age, I'm sure the Lord could speak these same words to each of us, "There remaineth yet very much land to be possessed!" May we passionately pursue possessing our possession!

In the remainder of chapter 13, God identifies the various places in the land that Joshua and the children of Israel still needed to possess. What is interesting is that, before they have actually taken physical possession of these various places, God has them divide the land as if it was already theirs (13:7). In fact, it was as good as theirs because God had given His word in verse 6, saying, "Them will I drive out from before the children of Israel." The point is, to go ahead and divide the land as the inheritance to the various tribes required faith in God and His Word. That is the pathway to victory every time!

Chapter 14 is a significant chapter. Forty-five years have passed since Joshua and Caleb and the other ten leaders spied out the land that God had promised to them. While in the land, Caleb had set his eyes and his heart on a particular piece of property. He never forgot it, and his desire for God to give it to him never waned. Even in his old age, Caleb was anxious to claim the inheritance God had promised him (14:6-9). Though he was now 85 years old, he said in 14:12, "Give me this mountain!" This was the mountain of Hebron, the same mountain that the ten spies feared because of the giants that lived there in "great and fenced" cities (14:12). Caleb received permission to go and conquer this mountain and the giants that lived there. Interestingly, the name *Hebron* means "fellowship." It is the very thing that God desires from each of us. God has promised fellowship to us, but like Caleb, we must claim the promise of God that we are "more than conquerors" in defeating the giants in our lives that seek to keep us from it (Rom. 8:37).

What mountain are you trusting the Lord to give you today? Have you possessed Hebron, the mountain of fellowship?

CHRIST IS REVEALED:

Through *Joshua* – Joshua 11–14 (As the one who conquers the kings and giants in our lives – Rom. 8:37, and as the one who gives us our inheritance – Acts 20:32; Eph. 1:11)

WEEK 11, DAY 3: **TODAY'S READING: JOSHUA 15-18**

OVERVIEW:

The land of Canaan is divided among the tribes of Israel.

HIGHLIGHTS & INSIGHTS:

In Joshua 15, Caleb, the eternally strong warrior (Josh. 14:11, a picture of God the Father), decides to reward the man who conquers and takes the city of Kirjathsepher (the "city of the Book") with his daughter, Achsah, as his wife. Othniel (whose name means "lion"), who "just happens" to be from the tribe of Judah, conquers and takes "the city of the Book" in order to obtain his bride. Achsah, whose name means "anklet," was given to Othniel as the promised reward for his accomplishments in battle. Her anklet was what distinguished her from other women. During this time period, women were covered from head to toe with clothing, making it nearly impossible to tell one from the other. Othniel's bride, however, was clearly recognizable by her walk.

Those are the details of the story, but what is all of this actually picturing in the Prophetic or Doctrinal application of Scripture?

The picture here is that God the Father gave the love-gift of the church to Christ, the Lion from the tribe of Judah, because of Christ's accomplishments in battle. Through His death, burial and resurrection, He fulfilled every prophecy in the Book of God (all three components of the gospel were all carried out precisely "according to the scriptures"—1 Cor. 15:3–4), and thereby, Christ purchased to Himself a bride. Like Achsah, Christ's bride, the church, is clearly recognizable by her walk (Rom. 6:4; Eph. 4:1, 17; 5:2, 8, 15).

The picture continues in chapter 15:18–20, as Achsah (the bride of Christ who is known by her walk) "let [her request] be made known" to her father (Phil. 4:6). She humbles herself by getting off of her donkey and pleads that her father might grant her a field. Jesus said in Matthew 13:38, "The field is the world!" But her request is not for just any field! She desires a field that would be watered by springs. Water, biblically, is a picture of the Word of God (Eph. 5:26). Her father grants her request so she can produce much fruit. As Christ's bride, we have been commissioned to take His Word to the world, that we might "bring forth fruit, and that [our] fruit should remain" (John 15:16). The Bible is an incredible Book, y'all!

There are several other observations we must make from today's reading to help us understand some of the key issues we face, as we, like Israel, seek to possess our inheritance (Acts 20:32; Eph. 1:11–14).

1. **Some of the children of Israel chose to dwell "on this side of Jordan." (Num. 32)**
   Like many believers today, they are indeed God's children and are glad of it, but that's about it. They missed the point of their exodus (Deut. 6:23). They are more interested in going to God's home when they die than in allowing God to make them His home while they live. Notice that they were the first to fall to the enemy because they settled for less than God intended for them (2 Kings 10)!

2. **Some were only "partial possessors." (Josh. 16:10)**
   They could have driven the enemies out, but chose to put them under tribute instead. In the same way, many "partial possessors" today think they can spiritualize their flesh and use it for "ministry" or some other perceived benefit rather than utterly destroying it on a daily basis.

3. **Some were conquerors and possessed all of their inheritance. (Josh. 8:26; 19:47)**
   This is what Paul was praying we might allow God to do in us in Ephesians 1:18–20 when he said, "The eyes of your understanding being enlightened; that ye may know what is the hope of his calling, and what the riches of the glory of his inheritance in the saints, And what is the exceeding greatness of his power to usward who believe, according to the working of his mighty power, Which he wrought in Christ, when he raised him from the dead, and set him at his own right hand in the heavenly places."

4. **One wanted more—Caleb. (Josh. 15)**

   In like fashion, Paul prayed in Philippians 3:10–14, "That I may know him, and the power of his resurrection, and the fellowship of his sufferings, being made conformable unto his death; If by any means I might attain unto the resurrection of the dead. Not as though I had already attained, either were already perfect: but I follow after, if that I may apprehend that for which also I am apprehended of Christ Jesus. Brethren, I count not myself to have apprehended: but this one thing I do, forgetting those things which are behind, and reaching forth unto those things which are before, I press toward the mark for the prize of the high calling of God in Christ Jesus."

In terms of dealing with your flesh and taking possession of all that God intended your salvation to be, which of the four groups listed above do you think you presently fit into?

Also in today's reading, the Scriptures provide us with several action steps for beginning the process of possessing our inheritance:

1. **"Arise!" (Josh. 18:8a)**

   In other words, get up out of your "safe place"! Sometimes we have to purposely and purposefully choose to get up out of our mediocrity and comfort in order to take possession of our possession! (Phil. 3:14)

2. **"Go for a walk!" (Josh. 18:8b)**

   "Walk" through every area of your life and allow the Lord to reveal to you areas of your life that you still haven't allowed Him to possess (Psa. 139:23–24).

3. **"Tell Joshua (Jesus) what you see!" (Josh. 18:8c–9)**

   Take what the Lord shows you about where you are in relationship with Him and pour your heart out to Him about it. Allow Him to change you and to possess all of you today. We will not live in the full possession of the spiritual inheritance God intended our salvation to provide until our Lord Jesus Christ fully possesses all of us!

CHRIST IS REVEALED:

Through *Othniel* – Joshua 15:17 (His name means "lion," and he is from the Tribe of Judah – Rev. 5:5)

As *Shiloh* – Joshua 18:1 (*Shiloh* means "peace," as in rest from war – Gen. 49:10; Matt. 11:28; Col. 3:15–16)

WEEK 11, DAY 4: **TODAY'S READING: JOSHUA 19-21**

OVERVIEW:

The remaining lots are divided among the tribes of Israel; the cities of refuge are designated; the 48 cities are given to the Levites from among the other tribes' inheritance.

HIGHLIGHTS & INSIGHTS:

In chapter 19, Simeon is given his inheritance from within the inheritance of the tribe of Judah (vs. 1, 9). This action actually fulfilled Jacob's deathbed prophecy in Genesis 49:7, when he said, "I will divide them [Simeon and Levi] in Jacob, and scatter them in Israel." This was the consequence for their over-the-top anger that led to the murder of every male in the city of Shechem because the king's son had defiled their sister, Dinah. Once again, we are reminded of the biblical principle that sin bears great consequences, even when forgiveness has been granted (Gal. 6:7–8). How many of God's people have suffered life-altering consequences because of the momentary lapse of reason caused by uncontrolled anger, wrath, or lust? Dr. Bob Jones, Sr., used to say, "Don't sacrifice the permanent on the altar of the temporary." May God help us!

In chapter 20, God appoints six cities to be a place of refuge for those who innocently killed somebody, meaning unintentionally or as the result of an accident—not a premeditated act. In the city of refuge, they were protected from the avenger of blood by the elders of the city until the death of the high priest. Upon his death, they were free.

Once again, God has painted an absolute masterpiece of His Son and the incredible refuge we have found in Him!

The Cities of Refuge:

1. They were appointed for those who were guilty of shedding innocent blood.

2. They were appointed to protect from the avenger of blood.

3. A refugee was safe as long as he stayed in the city.

4. Only the death of the high priest set them free.

5. These cities were always readily accessible to all.

6. Knowing they existed wasn't enough to protect a person. He had to flee to them.

7. One seeking refuge had to leave everything (family, friends, possessions, etc.) in order to come to the city.

8. The cities of refuge were the responsibility of the Levites. (Num. 35:6)

The Lord Jesus Christ:

1. We were all responsible for shedding Christ's innocent blood. (1 Pet. 2:24; Isa. 53:4–12)

2. By turning to Christ as our Refuge, we are protected from the true avenger of blood—God the Father. (Deut. 32:35, 43)

3. Those who have found refuge in Christ are safe and secure. (Rom. 8:31–39)

4. It is only through the death of our High Priest, the Lord Jesus Christ, that we are able to be set free indeed from the penalty of our sin. (Heb. 6:20; John 8:36)

5. Jesus is accessible to anyone, at anytime. (Rom. 10:13; 2 Pet. 3:9)

6. Just knowing what Jesus did and who He is doesn't save a person. One must flee to Him and trust Him with their life. (Eph. 1:12–13)

7. One must be willing to forsake family, friends, and possessions in order to come to Jesus. (Matt. 10:34–39; Luke 18:22)

8. As New Testament priests, it is now our responsibility to lead others to the only true Refuge—the Lord Jesus Christ. (Rev. 1:6; 2 Cor. 5:18)

CHRIST IS REVEALED:

As the *Cities of Refuge* – Joshua 20 (Ps. 46:1)

WEEK 11, DAY 5: **TODAY'S READING: JOSHUA 22-24**

OVERVIEW:

The two and a half tribes who chose their inheritance on the other side of Jordan build an altar and call it Ed; Joshua exhorts Israel's leaders; Joshua exhorts all the people of Israel and brings them to a point of decision.

HIGHLIGHTS & INSIGHTS:

We read in Numbers 32 that two and a half tribes (Reuben, Gad, and half of Manasseh) chose to live on "this side" of the Jordan River before they ever saw what God had in store for them in the land on the "other side." They are the classic biblical example of a people who willfully chose less than God's best for their lives. Sadly, many believers through the centuries have failed to learn from their tragic mistake. As the old saying goes, "If we don't learn from the mistakes of history, we are destined to repeat them!"

In chapter 22 in today's reading, Joshua allows these two and a half tribes to return to the land of their choosing. God in His grace allowed them to go because He never forces anyone to live close to Him. In reality, they were leaving the fertile land of Shiloh (the place of *peace* and *rest*) for their chosen inheritance in Gilead (which means "stony place"!). As Jesus taught us in the parable of the seed and the sower, it is impossible to bear fruit from stony ground (Matt. 13:3–9). May we learn from the example of these two and a half tribes to never settle for anything less than God's absolute best for our lives! A life of fruit bearing requires the land of our inheritance in Canaan.

On their way back to their inheritance, these two and a half tribes built an altar they called Ed (meaning "witness") as a memorial to remind their children and the other tribes in Israel that they, too, were the people of God and worshipped the God of Israel. In reality, it was an attempt to convince their children, along with the children of Israel, that they were spiritual and really loved the Lord, even though they had chosen to live away from the Ark of the Covenant and, as a result, the very presence of God with Israel.

Kids, however, aren't stupid. The children in these tribes saw through their parents' rationalizations and justifications, even while they did things that bore "witness" of their spirituality. That altar didn't witness to anything other than their parents' disobedience and compromise! I have observed through the years that children can put up with their parents' faults, frailties and failures—if they will own them! One thing kids just can't seem to withstand, however, is hypocrisy, when parents try to give the appearance of spirituality without the reality. Perhaps we should stop and ask ourselves, is there an Ed in our life? Have we built a "witness" for our kids and other believers that we are living closer to God than we actually do? In the twenty-first century, this could be going to church, praying before meals, reading the Bible, or acting interested in the things of the Lord—but without truly cultivating an intimate relationship with Him or longing to be close to His presence. Are you settling for less than God's best on "this side" of the Jordan, or are you passionately pursuing the closeness of His holy presence on the "other side?"

In chapters 23 and 24, Joshua knows he's about to die. He begins to give the children of Israel a history lesson, walking them back through God's faithfulness to them as a people from their inception as a nation. On one hand, he is passionately *pleading* with them to love God and continue to follow Him in obedience and faithfulness. On the other hand, he is passionately *warning* them of the consequences that would inevitably destroy them if they were not obedient and faithful to the Lord. If they co-mingled—if they had any connection whatsoever—with the nations they had previously destroyed, those nations would become snares and traps, scourges in their sides and thorns in their eyes. Ultimately, those nations would overtake them!

In 24:14–15, Joshua concludes his address with a time of decision. He asks the children of Israel to go all the way with the God who had delivered them from the gods their "fathers served on the other side of the flood, and in Egypt"—or to forget serving the Lord and go back and serve their false gods. Notice, God wanted His people to go one way or the other. He wanted them to be cold or hot, but not to be "lukewarm," to compromise and live somewhere in the middle (Rev. 3:15–16).

In Joshua 24:24, "The people said unto Joshua, The Lord our God will we serve, and his voice we will obey." Is that the decision of your heart today? If so, then tell your "Joshua" about it!

CHRIST IS REVEALED:

Through *Joshua* (the prophet), *Eleazar* (the priest), and *Joseph* (the king) – Joshua 24:29–33

> Note: The book of Joshua ends with three funerals: Joshua, Eleazar and Joseph. A prophet, a priest, and a king were buried right in the middle of Israel's inheritance, picturing that it is only through the death of the Lord Jesus Christ—our Prophet, Priest and King—that we have access to our inheritance in Him.

WEEK 12, DAY 1: **TODAY'S READING: JUDGES 1-4**

OVERVIEW:

Early victories and incomplete possession of the land by Israel; the forsaking of God to serve Baal and Ashtaroth; God raises up Othniel, Ehud, Shamgar, Deborah and Barak as judges to deliver Israel from the oppression of their enemies four different times.

HIGHLIGHTS & INSIGHTS:

To understand the book of Judges we must understand the last sentence in the entire book: "In those days there was no king in Israel: every man did that which was right in his own eyes." Mark those words! Not only are they the key to this book, they are also the key to human nature. Every man did that which was *right* in his own eyes—not that which was *wrong*! Unfortunately, man's idea of what is right is often the exact opposite of what God says it is (Prov. 14:12). This truth will become evident throughout the book of Judges with the recurring expression, "And the children of Israel did evil in the sight of the Lord" (2:11; 3:7, 12; 4:1; 6:1; 10:6; 13:1).

The book of Judges gives us incredible insight into how former sold-out believers can so spiral downward that they become, as Paul talked about in 2 Timothy 2:20, "vessels … unto *dishonour*." They can actually forget "that [they were] purged from [their] old sins" (2 Pet. 1:9). How unbelievably tragic! But biblically, we all have that potential. It is vital that we learn the practical spiritual lessons in the book of Judges (Rom. 15:4).

There are four keywords that summarize the repeated pattern we find in the book of Judges:

1. Commitment

2. Complacency

3. Compromise

4. Corruption

The pattern is easy to find. Judges 1 lets us know that when Israel was strong (*committed*), they put their enemies to tribute. Instead of choosing to "utterly drive them out" as God had commanded (1:28), they made them subservient (they paid taxes). Doing it this way, the children of Israel actually went from being *committed* to *complacent*! That *complacency* led to their "incomplete obedience," or their *compromise* (Judg. 1–3). And that *compromise* then led to their "complete disobedience" (Judg. 3–16), which led to their *corruption*, expressed in their utter rebellion and depraved behavior (Judg. 17–21).

Because the nation of Israel is a picture of an individual New Testament believer, the book of Judges reminds us that we must constantly be on guard to avoid this deadly downward cycle that spirals God's people away from *HIM* and His *Word*! The book of Joshua starts with an exhortation to meditate in God's Word day and night (Josh. 1:8). But in the book of Judges, the words *book*, *law*, *commandments*, *statutes*, or *judgments* do not appear even once! This downward spiral of complacency, compromise, and corruption is clearly linked to God's people *neglecting God's Word* and refusing to *obey it*. May we hear and heed this graphic spiritual warning!

There's another scary pattern that is introduced to us in today's reading (Judg. 2:7–10). It is a generational pattern that is repeated throughout the Old Testament. It happens like this:

- The First Generation

  A first-generation encounter with God means the believer didn't grow up in a Christian home and was, therefore, saved out of the clutches of Satan and his world's system. This believer *knows God* and *knows His works* (Josh. 24:14–17, 31). and lives a life of *commitment*.

- The Second Generation

   The children of a first-generation believer, however, tend to *know God* but only know *about* His works (Judg. 2:7). These believers often live lives of *compromise.*

- The Third Generation

   The children of the second generation are even further away. They do not know God and they don't even know about His works (Judg. 2:10). And this generation lives a life of *conflict.*

So much could be said about this pattern (and *should* be said!), but maybe the best take-away today is simply this: though our children and grandchildren will never experience the dramatic rescue we "first-generation Christians" had from Satan and his world's system, we must be certain that they are continuously seeing the mighty *works* of God in *our* lives and in their *own!* Judges 2:7 says it this way: "And the people served the Lord all the days of Joshua, and all the days of the elders that outlived Joshua, who had seen all the great works of the Lord, that he did for Israel." May we lead our children and grandchildren to experience first-generation encounters with our God!

Chapter 3 records a rather bizarre story. It is certainly historically accurate, but, like most of the Old Testament, was recorded in such a fashion so that it pictures New Testament truth which we can read and be admonished by (1 Cor. 10:6, 11). The story is of "a very fat man" (3:17) by the name of Eglon who was the king of Moab. He is a picture of a believer who has allowed their *flesh* to overtake them—regardless of their actual physical girth. After all, our flesh has an appetite for a whole lot more than food!

To deal with Eglon, God sends a judge by the name of Ehud to deliver Israel from the Moabites. The way Ehud overcame this "very fat man" was with a "dagger" (a sword!) that he had strategically "hidden" on his right side and that just happened to have "two edges" (Judg. 3:16–17; Heb. 4:12). Ehud thrust the sword into Eglon's belly. The passage says that "the dirt came out," and he killed him (Judg. 3:21–22).

Did you catch all of that? God, the Master Teacher and Artist, is revealing that we are to deal with ("judge") the self-consumption of our flesh which continuously seeks to rule us by "hiding" a "two-edged sword" on our right side (Psa. 119:11; Heb. 4:12) and thrusting it into the "belly" of our flesh to reveal the "dirt" in our life so that we can "mortify" it (Col. 3:5), or put it to death! What an incredible book the Bible is!

Chapter 4 records another rather bizarre story. God uses a woman named Jael to defeat a man by the named Sisera, another oppressor of Israel. Jael was initially aligned with Sisera against Israel, but God changed her heart. She got some milk, took a hammer and a nail, and killed Sisera while he was sleeping by putting the nail through his temple! Wow! Likewise, if we allow the "milk" (1 Pet. 2:2) and "hammer" (Jer. 23:29) of the Word of God to pierce our lives and renew our minds (Rom. 12:2), we, too, can "nail" our enemies (the world, the flesh and the devil) and be free from their oppression! (Isa. 22:23; Ezr. 9:8)

CHRIST IS REVEALED:

Through the *Angel of the Lord* – Judges 2:1–4

Through *Othniel* – Judges 3:1–11 (His name means "Lion from the Tribe of Judah." He delivered Israel from an oppressive enemy - Rev. 5:5)

Through *Ehud* – Judges 3:15–16 (The Judge with a two-edged sword - Heb. 4:12; Rev. 2:12)

WEEK 12, DAY 2: **TODAY'S READING: JUDGES 5-8**

OVERVIEW:

Deborah's song to the Lord; Gideon's call and deliverance of Israel from the oppression of the Midianites.

HIGHLIGHTS & INSIGHTS:

Deborah was one of the judges during this incredibly dark time in Israel's history. Chapter 5 records a song that she was inspired to write and sing on the very day that Jael put Sisera to death (Judg. 4:18–23). Though the song obviously refers to the historical events happening at that time, it is actually prophetic in nature because it will also be the song the redeemed will sing when the true King (the Lord Jesus Christ) takes His rightful throne and the king of evil (Satan) is defeated (Rev. 5:9; 14:3). The song ends (Judg. 5:31) with the Sun going forth to reign in His might with those He loves, and there is rest in the land. And Malachi 4:2 and Revelation 19:14 says that exact thing will take place in the very near future!

Chapters 6-8 deal with one of the most well-known heroes in the book of Judges, Gideon. He is called by God to be the deliverer of Israel from the Midianites. Interestingly, *Midian* means "strife" or "contention." Proverbs 13:10 teaches us that "only by pride cometh contention," and 1 Corinthians 1:10–11 and 3:1–3 lets us know that the root of "strife" and "contention" is *carnality* or fleshliness!

And the Midianites destroyed the fruit in the land, leaving the children of Israel with nothing to eat (Judg. 6:4). How ironic! Here is Israel, starving in the midst of a land flowing with milk and honey! Does that sound at all familiar? Many people who have received eternal life are defeated by their *flesh* (John 10:10a) and, therefore, are unable to eat the fruit of the *abundant life* God intended their salvation to provide (John 10:10b). Midian's (or strife's) ultimate target is the harvest! Are you starving spiritually? Are you struggling to be fruitful because of the contentious attitude of your heart and the selfish desires of your flesh? If so, pay close attention to what Gideon did to defeat the Midianites so you can employ the same principles in your life!

God chose 300 men armed with nothing more than pitchers, lamps (lanterns) and trumpets to defeat a much larger and better equipped enemy. This was God's strategy, so that when they got the victory, only God would get the glory (Judg. 7:2). It is the New Testament principle that God teaches us in 1 Corinthians 1:27–29: "But God hath chosen the foolish things of the world to confound the wise … that no flesh should glory in His presence!"

But, notice that battle plan once again. It really was very "simple" (2 Cor. 11:3). Shatter your pitcher, blow your trumpet, shine your lamp, and stand fast in your place while God defeats the enemy (Judg. 7:19–21)! Listen, this is the only way Midian (pride, strife, contention — the flesh!) can be defeated in our lives as well! We must be *broken vessels* (pitchers) for God to use (2 Tim. 2:21). We must let our *light shine* (Mat. 5:16; Phil. 2:15–16). We must use our *mouths* as a *trumpet* to proclaim the gospel to the world (Eph. 6:19). And finally, we must *stand fast* and watch God defeat the enemy with the *sword*! (Ephesians 6:10–14)

You may also want to note that Hebrews 11:32 puts Gideon at the head of the list of judges. Though he often wavered in doubt, he was still a man of faith who dared to trust the Word of God. When you realize that he was a common man (a farmer, Judg. 6:11), and not a trained warrior, you can see how wonderful his faith actually was! As "common" men and women (Mark 12:37b)—and despite our doubts, fears, and shortcomings, may we, like Gideon, dare to trust the Word of God!

CHRIST IS REVEALED:

As the *Angel of the Lord* – Judges 6:12–21

Through *Barak*, the son of Abinoam – Judges 5:12. (The name *Barak* means "glittering sword" – John 1:1, 14. The name *Abinoam* means "beautiful father." Barak, the glittering sword, was the son of a beautiful Father!)

Through *Gideon* – Judges 6–8. (The deliverer who leads Israel to a most improbable victory.)

WEEK 12, DAY 3: **TODAY'S READING: JUDGES 9-12**

OVERVIEW:

Abimelech's rise to power and his subsequent death; the oppression of the Ammonites; Jephthah's deliverance of Israel and vow to God.

HIGHLIGHTS & INSIGHTS:

Although Gideon's fame as a courageous judge of Israel is secure (Heb. 11:32), the inviolable law of sowing and reaping (Gal. 6:7–8) enters the picture in chapter 9. The seeds of rebellion and pride that we witnessed Gideon sow in 8:27–31 are already beginning to bear some pretty nasty fruit. Abimelech, Gideon's son by his concubine (8:31), is a proud, egotistical self-monger whose whole motive and purpose in life was to gain power. He is determined to set himself up as the king in the kingdom (9:1–4).

The Bible tells us that one of the chief characteristics of those living in the last days will be a love for self (2 Tim. 3:2), much like what is being revealed in Abimelech. We would do well to "examine ourselves" (2 Cor. 13:5) for areas in our lives where we might be pridefully pursuing prestige, power, and position (Mark 8:34). In other words, are we secretly striving to set ourselves up as king in our own little kingdom? We have to look honestly at the motive behind our service for Christ to determine whether it is really for Him or for ourselves. Prior to coming to Christ, we were all driven by our pride to exalt ourselves. Sadly, many have simply changed the arena in which they are seeking to exalt themselves—from the world … to the church (3 John 9). God forbid!

Gideon's sin at the end of chapter 8 also becomes a warning to parents. Many times, biblically, what the parents do in moderation, their children will typically do in excess. Gideon's minor exaltation of self in 8:27 becomes major in and through his son. Abimelech is so enamored with self that he actually murdered all of his next-of-kin—70 of his own brothers! Only Jotham escaped, and only because he hid himself! May we learn that sin is not to be trifled with! The remainder of chapter 9 chronicles more of Abimelech's ravenous selfishness and self-centeredness. But notice, God always pays his debts, and no sin goes unnoticed! By the end of the chapter, Abimelech is killed by a wise woman (Prov. 1:20–33) who had taken shelter in a strong tower (Ps. 61:3) and who dropped a rock (1 Cor. 10:4) on his big head!

In chapters 10–12, we find Israel in one of their repeated cycles of sin because they were willing to serve any god who would make them happy. They wanted their own way, their desires fulfilled, and their ego boosted—and that is a collision course for disaster! The choice to serve self is sin, and sin always leads to sorrow and death (Jam. 1:15). It becomes increasingly difficult to understand, much less tolerate, the blatant foolishness and rebellion of God's people, Israel. How could they possibly experience all of His blessings and still repeatedly turn their backs on Him? And yet, how can we, who also have been abundantly blessed by God and have seen the consequences of Israel's choices, do anything other than end our own flirting with the world, the flesh, and the devil? We must make the decision that "It is enough! I am not my own, I have been bought by the blood of God's dear Son, and by God's grace and power, sin will no longer control me!" When we cry out to God, broken by our sin, we can be sure that He will hear us and deliver us from its dominion. (See 1 John 5:14–15; Rom. 6:12–14.)

In keeping with their pattern, Israel cries out to God again (Judg. 10:10), and in keeping with His pattern, once again, God sends them a deliverer. This time it was Jephthah, another incredible picture of Jesus Christ. Jephthah was a mighty man of valor who was the son of an harlot (Judg. 11:1), was rejected by his brethren (11:2), and went to live in the land of Tob (which means "blessing, joy, beautiful, and righteous"). While he was in Tob, he gathered vain (or empty) men unto himself (11:3) and was later called home by Israel during a time of tribulation to deliver them from their oppressors. He then came back as the captain of their salvation (11:6).

And just in case you weren't connecting all of those dots, Jesus, too, was a mighty Man of Valor who was accused of being the Son of a harlot (John 8:41). He, too, was rejected by His brethren (Luke 19:14), and

He, too, went away to a place like Tob—a beautiful place of blessing, joy, and righteousness (Ps. 48:2). While He is there, He continues to gather vain or empty men and women to Himself as worshippers, and He will come back at the end of the Tribulation to deliver Israel and be the Captain of their salvation (Heb. 2:10; Rev. 19)! Again, this Book is absolutely amazing!

Though at first Jephthath was a beautiful type of Christ, like many of the Old Testament pictures of Christ, Jephthah found a way to totally get his life jacked up! He made a horrendous mistake by vowing a vow to God that resulted in him foolishly and sinfully burning his own daughter as a sacrifice—supposedly to God (Judg. 11:34–40)! Though Jephthah's mistake was certainly extreme, his mistake is very common throughout the history of God's people! Jephthah thought there was something he could do to *earn* the blessing and favor of God. He thought that by vowing his vow, he could get God on his side. But God was already on his side! No human work or any accumulation of them can ever earn God's graciously given favor (Eph. 2:8-9) or make us the recipient of more of His power (Acts 1:8). He gives it all to us *freely* (1 Cor. 2:12). May Jephthah's horrific debacle teach us this invaluable lesson!

Though this is an incredibly sad chapter in Jephthah's life (and in the Bible!), it is also a blessing. God has set His Book apart from every other book in the world because of His honesty regarding its heroes (including Noah, Abraham, Jacob, David, Solomon, and Elijah). God is a straight shooter. He simply tells it the way it is. He doesn't sugarcoat or mask anything! The Bible is a real book about real people, people just like me and you! Hallelujah!

CHRIST IS REVEALED:

As the *Strong Tower* – Judges 9:51 (Psalm 18:2; 61:3)

Through *Jephthah* – Judges 11–12

WEEK 12, DAY 4: **TODAY'S READING: JUDGES 13-17**

OVERVIEW:

The birth of Samson; the life of Samson; the death of Samson; Micah and his mother's idolatrous religion.

HIGHLIGHTS & INSIGHTS:

Chapter 13 records the birth of one of the most infamous judges in Israel's history—Samson. We could refer to Samson as "The *strongest* man who ever lived," but in reality, he was "The *weakest* man who ever lived"! From a *physical* standpoint, Samson's strength was beyond human comprehension. From a *spiritual* standpoint, however, he couldn't muster enough strength to tell his flesh, "No!" He had the power to conquer every man on earth—except himself!

It's clear from Judges 13–16 that Samson had everything in the world going for him. God had blessed him beyond measure, but tragically, he chose to serve himself, rather than serve God's purposes for his life. Instead of becoming the champion God intended for him to become, he became a selfish, self-willed, self-absorbed, self-seeking, self-gratifying, self-loving, self-monger! And God tells us in 2 Timothy 3:1–2 that the number one characteristic that makes these "last days" so incredibly "perilous," is that we, too, are "lovers of [our] own selves"! Perhaps, then, we can learn some things from Samson's life that can help us avoid his fate.

1. **Samson was the product of a *supernatural birth.***

    Judges 13:2 tells us his mother was barren and had absolutely no hope of bearing a child apart from the supernatural working of the "angel of the Lord" (an Old Testament appearance of our Lord Jesus Christ!), who appears to her in verse 3 and causes her to be able to conceive and bear Samson.

2. **Samson was privileged to be *set apart* for the Lord's service from birth.**

    Judges 13:5 says, "For the child shall be a Nazarite unto God from the womb." That's what a Nazarite was, one who was *sanctified* or *set apart* for the Lord's service (Num. 6)

3. **Samson possessed the very *power* of the Holy Spirit of God upon his life.**

    Judges 13:25 says that "the Spirit of the Lord began to move" Samson. Judges 14:5–6 says he was empowered "mightily" by the "Spirit of the Lord" to overcome a roaring lion! And Judges 15:14–16 says he was "mightily" empowered by the "Spirit of the Lord" to overcome his enemies—a thousand at one time!

4. **Samson was provided a *beginning* that was filled with unending promise and potential.**

    The last part of Judges 13:5 says, "And he shall begin to deliver Israel out of the hand of the Philistines." What Samson did with the *beginning* God gave to him was limited only by Samson's own choices, and his willingness to be surrendered to God's plans and purposes for him.

But despite all of these incredible realities and this unending potential, Samson squandered the potential glory his life could have brought to the Lord. Because of pride, self-will, selfish ambition, and an addiction to lust, he forfeited the real impact God could have used him to have. He becomes for us the classic biblical example of a wasted life!

And I'm not sure if you recognized it or not, but his story is unbelievably similar to ours! For all of us who know the Lord Jesus Christ as our Savior, we are just like Samson.

1. **We were the product of a *supernatural birth.***

    Ours was not a physical one like Samson's, but a supernatural birth that we call salvation or being "born again." Ephesians 2:12–13 says we were without hope until the the Lord Jesus Christ ("the angel of the Lord" in the Old Testament) supernaturally drew us to Himself. And 1 Peter 1:23 says that we were "born again, not of corruptible seed [physical seed/birth], but of incorruptible, by the word of God, which liveth and abideth forever."

2. We were privileged to be *set apart* for the Lord's service from our birth!

Of course, we are referring again to our spiritual birth! 1 Corinthians 6:11 tells us that when the Holy Spirit of God "washed" us and we were "justified," at that very moment, we were "sanctified" (*set apart*).

3. We possess the very *power* of the Holy Spirit of God upon our lives!

Acts 17:28 says that "in him we live, and move, and have our being." 2 Corinthians 6:16 says that *in us*, He lives and moves and has His being! And while 1 Peter 5:8 tells us that our enemy "walks about" like a "*roaring lion*," 1 John 4:4 says that we have been given the *power*, by the one who lives in us, to *overcome* him. And Romans 6:13–14 says that, through God's *power* in us, the enemy of sin no longer has dominion (or power) over us!

4. We have been provided a *beginning* that is filled with unending promise and potential.

2 Corinthians 5:17 says that anyone who is "in Christ" is a "new creature," and that "old things are passed away; behold, all things are become new." That's the *beginning* God gave to all of us! And just like Samson, what we do with the *beginning* God gives to us is limited only by our own choices and our willingness to be surrendered to His plans and purposes through us!

Like Samson, we have everything in the world going for us! Like Samson, God has blessed us beyond measure! But tragically, many who have experienced a supernatural spiritual birth, who have been set apart by that spiritual birth for the Lord's service, who have been empowered by the Holy Spirit in them, and who have been granted a brand-new beginning with unlimited potential to bring God glory actually forfeit the real impact God intends for their lives. Just like Samson, they squander their potential to glorify God. Their ultimate accounting at the Judgment Seat of Christ will reveal that they *wasted their lives!* May we learn from the negative example of Samson's life to keep ourselves off of the path of self-love and self-destruction and fulfill God's glorious purpose for our lives!

At the end of Samson's life (Judg. 16:29–31), he's buried beneath the rubble of his own self-destruction, and his brothers have to come to pull him out to even give him a decent burial. May our brothers never have to come and pull us out of the rubble of our own self-destruction! Our God is worthy of so much more!

In chapter 17, we have an incredible picture of a false religious system. It includes

- Robed priests (17:5 – an *ephod* is a priestly garment.)
- Called "father" (17:10)
- Who use idols (17:4–5 – "a graven image and a molten image")
- As aides in worship
- In their "house of gods." (17:5)

Does that sound like any false religious system you know of? This happens to be a perfect description of the false religious system that exists today called the Roman Catholic Church!

By taking this man who was younger than Micah to be his personal "priest" whom he referred to as "father" (17:10–13), he actually thought he was doing the right thing—and that the Lord would be pleased. (Compare this, however, with 17:6!) Sadly, Satan has always found a way to concoct false religious systems to put God's name on—so he can give people a false sense of security while he is damning their souls to hell. And the whole reason this happened was because Micah neglected to consult God's Word on this matter! It is the same reason the Roman Catholic Church deceives so many into thinking they are right with God—they neglect to consult God's Word on the matter! We must pray for the people trapped in this damnable false system of religion! Over a billion of the world's population are Roman Catholic.

CHRIST IS REVEALED:

Through *Samson* – Judges 13–16 (He is the son of promise who was born to be set apart for God in order to deliver Israel from her enemies.)

WEEK 12, DAY 5: **TODAY'S READING: JUDGES 18-21**

OVERVIEW:

The corruption of the Tribe of Dan; the wickedness of the Gibeonites; the division between the Tribe of Benjamin and the rest of Israel; the destruction of the Tribe of Benjamin.

HIGHLIGHTS & INSIGHTS:

As we finish the book of Judges today, it's vital that we recall where we are at this point of Israel's history. After several years of complacency (chapters 1–2), Israel entered into a long period of compromise (chapters 3–16). During that time, God's people endured seven cycles of oppression at the hands of those over whom the Lord had previously given victory. The final five chapters of the book of Judges describe the corruption that took place when they forgot God and His Word! Some of the most bizarre and horrific stories in all of Scripture appear in this final part of the book of Judges. Remember, the key to understanding this whole book is found in the last verse of the final chapter, "In those days there was no king in Israel: every man did that which was right in his own eyes."

In chapter 18, the Tribe of Dan convinces Micah's personal priest to leave with them to be the priest of the entire tribe (18:19). This was very appealing to the priest because it was a promotion, so to speak. He was so excited that he stole Micah's "ephod [priestly garment], and the teraphim [household idol], and the graven image" so he could perform his priestly duties for the Tribe of Dan (Judg. 18:20).

Micah was, of course, devastated because not only did he lose his priest, his entire religion had been stolen (Judg. 18:24). Beware of any religion that, because of its external ritualism and idolatry, can be stolen! Micah's religion couldn't resist the weapons of warfare (18:11, 16–17). When push came to shove, his priest would not stand by him, the congregation was powerless to do anything but cry out in despair with him, and its final end was nothing more than heartache and loss (18:18–26). But the beautiful reality is that you can't steal the religion of someone who has been truly born again because it's not based on *external* realities—but *internal* ones (Luke 17:21). In fact, it's not actually even a *religion*. It is an eternal *relationship* whereby the holy, omnipotent Creator-God of the universe has become our Father, and we, His sons and daughters! (2 Cor. 6:18)! And that is something that can't be *stolen* (John 10:28).

In chapter 19, a Levite sets out on a long journey to recover his unfaithful concubine. On their journey home, she is abused all night long until the dawning of the day, and she died. Although this isn't a perfect picture by any means, it is still a very sobering reminder of the fact that in the very near future, Jehovah God will come back in the morning (Mal. 4:2) after the biblical "nighttime" of the church age (Rom. 13:12; 1 Thes. 5:2,5) to look for His unfaithful wife, the Nation of Israel, who has been abused all through this biblical nighttime and has been spiritually dead to Him. Remember, in the book of Judges, there is no king in Israel, and Israel is "dead" to God. In the next book, the book of Ruth, a Jewish kinsman-redeemer takes a Gentile bride to himself, and then the Son of David (Solomon) will come back to give Israel life once again. This, too, points us to the glories that await Israel in the future!

Chapters 20 and 21 relate how Israel dealt with this despicable sin (the abusing of the concubine by the men of Gibeah). There is a division between the men of Israel and the Tribe of Benjamin over this issue though. Shockingly, Benjamin takes the side of the Gibeonites and fights against Israel. They actually wanted to defend the unthinkable wickedness of the Gibeonites! What does that tell you about the moral state of this tribe at this time? The Tribe of Benjamin was defeated by Israel in the war, and it appeared that the sin at Gibeah had been dealt with. The only problem is that history teaches us that they never truly repented and returned to their sinful ways (2 Cor. 7:10). All of chapter 21 is a counterfeit repentance that does nothing more than make them feel good about themselves for "confessing their sin." They were not, however, actually turning (repenting) from their sin by cleansing themselves "from all filthiness of the flesh and spirit, perfecting holiness in the fear of God" (2 Cor. 7:1). Like much of the confession of sin done by Christians in the twenty-first century, it is worldly sorrow which brings about worldly repentance—as opposed to "godly sorrow" that brings about godly repentance to salvation" (2 Cor. 7:8–11). We would do well to consider whether our sorrow over and repentance of sin is worldly or godly!

CHRIST IS REVEALED:

Through the *House of God* – Judges 20:18 (God's dwelling place among His people Israel. Unfortunately, this corrupt time in Israel is much like the Laodicean church period (Rev. 3:14–22) where our Lord Jesus Christ is on the outside looking in, while all the people on the inside think He's in their midst!)

As the *Levite* – Judges 19:1

WEEK 13, DAY 1: **TODAY'S READING: RUTH 1-4**

OVERVIEW:

Elimelech and Naomi and their two sons sojourn into Moab during a time of famine; Elimelech's death; the marriage of Naomi's two sons to Orpah and Ruth; the death of Naomi's sons; Naomi's decision to return to Bethlehem and Ruth's decision to go with her; Ruth goes to glean in the field of Boaz in Bethlehem; Boaz's kindness to Ruth; Naomi informs Ruth that Boaz can fulfill the role of kinsman-redeemer; Ruth approaches Boaz at the threshing floor; Boaz fulfills the role of Ruth's kinsman-redeemer, taking her to wife; Ruth gives birth to Obed, King David's grandfather.

HIGHLIGHTS & INSIGHTS:

The book of Ruth is the record of one of the greatest love stories of all time. For those of us living in the church age, it is one of the most important stories in the entire Old Testament.

Ruth was born into this world a Gentile, a member of a cursed race. She was a Moabitess, and we learn from Deuteronomy 23:3, the Moabites were a race of people cursed by God due to sin. And as the story unfolds, Ruth finds herself in a time of famine (1:1), and in the midst of this famine, one day, someone shared with her good news from a far land—that the Lord had visited His people in Bethlehem, giving them bread (1:6)! Upon hearing that good news, she left her father and mother and the gods she served in her homeland, and went to partake of the Lord's provision of bread in Bethlehem (1:15–18).

In chapters 2–3, she arrived in Bethlehem and "just happened" to go to work gleaning in the harvest field of the only man on earth who would carry out for her the Old Testament provision of the kinsman-redeemer (Lev. 25:23–28). His name was Boaz, a mighty man of wealth, a Jew, from the city of Bethlehem (2:1–2). Boaz takes one look at her in his field, falls head-over-heels in love with her (2:5), and takes her out of his harvest field to be his bride (4:9–10). "And," as the old saying goes, "they lived happily ever after."

Nice story, right? But check this out! Ruth's story is, for us, one of the most important in the entire Bible because it is actually our story! Like Ruth, we were born into a race of people that had been cursed by God due to sin (Rom. 5:12; 6:23a). We call it the "human" race. But one day, someone shared with us "good news" from a far land, that God had visited His people in Bethlehem (Luke 2:4, 7) as the Bread of Life (John 6:35) and could feed the famine sin had left in our soul. Upon hearing that "good news," ("gospel," 1 Cor. 15:1–4), we, too, left our father and mother (Matt. 10:37) and the "gods" we once served in our homeland (1 Thess. 1:9), and we became a partaker of God's provision on our behalf (Eph. 3:6).

And now, we have gone to work, gleaning in the harvest field (Matt. 13:38) of our Jewish Kinsman-Redeemer, the mighty man of wealth (the "God-man") from the city of Bethlehem, until He calls us out of His harvest field (1 Thess. 4:16) to make us His bride (Rev. 19:7; 21:9), and so shall we ever be with the Lord (1 Thess. 4:17), living happily ever after (Rev. 21:4)!

Hallelujah! The Bible is a supernatural Book, y'all!

CHRIST IS REVEALED:

Through *Boaz*, the mighty and wealthy Jewish kinsman-redeemer from the city of Bethlehem who took a Gentile bride out of his harvest field – Ruth 2–4 (Isa. 9:6; Heb. 4:15; Luke 2:4–7: Rev. 19:7; Matt. 13:38)

WEEK 13, DAY 2: **TODAY'S READING: 1 SAMUEL 1-4**

OVERVIEW:

God gives Samuel to Hannah; Hannah gives Samuel to God; Samuel gives himself to God; God gives Samuel to Israel; Eli misappropriates the tabernacle by permitting his sons to disobey; Eli misses God's message; Eli misuses the Ark of the Covenant; Samuel lives; Eli dies.

HIGHLIGHTS & INSIGHTS:

The book of 1 Samuel begins at a time when "the word of the Lord was precious" (3:1). It was precious for the same reason that gold or platinum are precious commodities today—it was incredibly rare! If the Lord were making a declaration concerning our day, He would, no doubt, repeat those very words (Amos 8:11–12).

At this point in the history of Israel, God's people were in the place He wanted them—the Promised Land—yet they hadn't actually "possessed their inheritance" or "possessed their possession" the way He had intended. God had repeatedly warned them in Deuteronomy 8 and 9 of the danger of forgetting Him after He had brought them into the land, but it becomes apparent in the book of 1 Samuel that God's warning had totally gone unheeded. It resulted in two extremely unfortunate realities:

1. God's people didn't fear Him and, therefore, didn't bring Him the honor and glory He deserved.

2. God's people weren't experiencing the life He had designed for them to enjoy in the "land that flowed with milk and honey" (Deut. 26:9).

Again, Israel is an Old Testament picture of New Testament believers who are in Christ and therefore possess *eternal life* but who aren't possessing the *abundant life* God intended their eternal life to bring them. As in the days of Samuel, many believers today (dare we say, most!) simply do not fear the Lord and, therefore, don't bring Him the glory that is due His name (Ps. 29:2; 96:8), choosing to live beneath the privilege God designed them to possess.

A bright spot in 1 and 2 Samuel, however, is Samuel himself, the one for whom these books were named. He was the first of the prophets, the last of the judges, and the man God would use to usher in Israel's earthly kings. He would faithfully serve God and His people but ultimately be rejected by the people. Though Israel rejected Samuel, God tells him not to take it personally, because it was actually Him they were rejecting (1 Sam. 8:7)! Because of their rejection of God's leadership, they sought out earthly kings to lead them. This didn't come as a shock to God, however! He prophesied they would do this very thing back in Deuteronomy 17!

The book of 1 Samuel is fast-paced and layered with historical and spiritual significance. In Chapter 1, it is out of a rather sinful and precarious marital situation that Samuel is born to Hannah and Elkanah. Hannah is actually one of Elkanah's two wives. Though polygamy had become *culturally* acceptable at this time, it certainly wasn't *biblically* acceptable! God's intention has always been and will always be *one man* and *one woman* for *one lifetime!* (See Gen. 2:24; 1 Tim. 3:2.) Because of this sinful marriage arrangement, some might refer to Samuel as illegitimate. In God's eyes, however, there are no illegitimate children! There may be illegitimate *parents*, but every child is legitimate. Every child is formed by God Himself in His mother's womb and is "fearfully and wonderfully made" (Ps. 139:13–14), and God has designed a perfect will for each of us, regardless of the marital status or immoral behavior of our parents! Samuel is a beautiful biblical example of that!

In Chapter 2, when Hannah presents back to God His gift to her, from a human standpoint, she is handing Samuel over to a priest who has long departed from God's perfect will. He is a carnal, obese old man (1 Sam. 4:18) who had allowed his own sons, who were "sons of Belial" (or Satan, 1 Sam. 2:12), to run the tabernacle. And, run it they did—right into the ground! God, however, would receive the offering of Hannah's only begotten son and use him mightily in fulfilling His purposes in the nation of Israel!

Chapter 3 tells us that Eli's "eyes began to wax dim, that he could not see." We can assume that Eli suffered from cataracts or some other condition that had caused blindness. In this case, however, this is a *physical* picture of his *spiritual* condition. And his spiritual blindness was certainly a greater travesty than his physical blindness!

God tells us in 2 Peter 1:5–9 that if, after coming to faith in Christ, we fail to give "all diligence" to add to our faith virtue, knowledge, temperance, patience, godliness, brotherly kindness, and charity, the same thing that happened to Eli *physically* will happen to us *spiritually*! We will become spiritually *blind*, not able to see "afar off," to see eternal things through the eyes of faith (2 Cor. 4:18), and ultimately, we will even forget that we have been purged from our "old sins." In other words, we will get to the place that as born-again, blood-bought, eternally-secure believers in Jesus Christ, we are living like we did when we were lost! May we be certain to heed Peter's warning!

Because of Israel's disregard for the Word of God and their subsequent disobedience (disregarding the Word of God will *always* result in disobedience to the God of the Word!), in chapter 4, the nation of Israel is annihilated in battle against the Philistines. They lost 4,000 soldiers in the first battle, 30,000 soldiers in the second battle, and their most prized possession—the Ark of the Covenant, or the presence of God in their midst! God finishes the chapter with a graphic picture of the spiritual reality of Romans 6:23a: "For the wages of sin is death." In the battle against the Philistines, Eli's two sons, Hophni and Phinehas, both died (4:11). And when Eli received word of their death and that the Ark of the Covenant was taken by the Philistines, he fell over backwards and died! And when Phinehas's pregnant wife heard that the Ark of God was captured and that both her father-in-law and her husband had died, the trauma sent her into labor. And in the process of delivering the child, she, too, died!

Just prior to her death, Phinehas's wife gave her newborn son one of the saddest names possible: Ichabod, meaning, "the glory has departed." With her final breath, she uttered these fateful words: "The glory is departed from Israel: for the ark of God is taken" (4:22). Sadly, *Ichabod* is a perfect description of many twenty-first-century churches: the glory of God's presence that is designed to be manifested through Christ's body has departed. While the people of the church gather on Sundays to celebrate the presence of Christ inside the four walls of their building, Christ stands *outside* the church knocking on the door, as it were, waiting for someone to recognize that His presence is not there and open the door to let Him in (Rev. 3:20)!

Can you hear Him knocking?

CHRIST IS REVEALED:

Through all that *Samuel* was intended to be – judge, priest, and prophet. (John 5:30; Heb. 7:26; Acts 7:37)

WEEK 13, DAY 3: **TODAY'S READING: 1 SAMUEL 5-10**

OVERVIEW:

God wreaks havoc on His enemies through the Ark of the Covenant; Samuel leads Israel in reformation and worship; Israel demands an earthly king and Saul is installed as the first earthly king of Israel.

HIGHLIGHTS & INSIGHTS:

The account of the Ark of our God in the house of Dagon (the fish god) in chapter 5 is classic. The image of the idol that the Philistines worshiped and served "fallen upon his face," having his head and hands lopped off, bowing before the presence of the one true God represented in the Ark is not only awesome—it is a preview of coming attractions! Revelation 17 and 18 is the prophecy of a time in the near future when all of the false systems of religion in the world, represented in Babylon, will come crashing down to the earth and be destroyed by the King of kings and Lord of lords!

We might think that seeing their god as a mere "stump" on the ground before the presence of the God of Israel would have brought the Philistines to their spiritual senses. Beholding the absolute powerlessness and pitifulness of their idol should inspire them to repent like the Thessalonians who "turned to God from idols to serve the living and true God" (1 Thess. 1:9). But that, obviously, did not happen! The Philistines become one of the greatest biblical examples of how "the god of this world [Satan] hath blinded the minds of them which believe not, lest the light of the glorious gospel of Christ, who is the image of God, should shine unto them" (2 Cor. 4:4). God is clear that lost people are unable to *see* the truth because they have been *blinded* by Satan! That's why some of the most intelligent and rational people can believe obvious *lies* when the *truth* clearly makes more logical sense!

Thankfully, the power of the glorious gospel of Christ is able to shine past the blinders Satan uses to keep the gospel hidden from lost people (2 Cor. 4:3–4). Romans 1:16 tells us that "it [the gospel] is the power of God unto salvation!" The power is not in our ability to communicate. It is not in our winsome personality or our ability to influence others. It is not in our ability to reason and/or debate with people. The power of God is in the simplicity of the message of the gospel (2 Cor. 11:3–4)!

As God's redeemed people, therefore, we must take advantage of every opportunity our Lord opens to us to declare the gospel to the people in our sphere of influence. Paul asked the church to pray "that God would open unto us a door of utterance" (Col. 4:3). We, too, can ask for opportunities to declare to the lost the powerful, life-changing, eternal-destiny-changing message of Christ's death, burial and resurrection. This was exactly the purpose God had for Paul (and for us): "To open their eyes [the lost], and to turn them from darkness to light, and from the power of Satan unto God, that they may receive forgiveness of sins, and inheritance among them which are sanctified by faith that is in [us]" (Acts 26:18). May God help us to faithfully proclaim the gospel of Christ!

More than just devastating the Philistine idols, however, God's awesome presence manifested through the Ark was also devastating to the people to whom it did not belong. In 1 Samuel 5:6–12, God allowed them to be struck with a miserable ailment (hemorrhoids) that affects virtually any and every activity of life. The Philistines quickly concluded that perhaps they'd be better off without the prized possession of the Israelites in their midst.

In chapter 6, they seek the counsel of their own pagan priests and demonic diviners about how to return the Ark, and they get some pretty outlandish advice. They concoct a self-styled version of a "trespass offering," which included making golden images of the hemorrhoids God had used to judge them! It is utterly amazing what people will do "in the name of God"—totally disregarding what He has clearly revealed in His Word!

In chapter 6, the Philistines returned the Ark to the children of Israel on a "new cart" (6:7). God is foreshadowing an event that will come to pass in 2 Samuel 6 because of this "new cart." And God also metes out extreme devastation upon the Philistines for the inquisitiveness that caused them to look into the Ark of the Lord: 50,070 men dropped dead (1 Sam. 6:19)!

In chapter 7, the Ark is returned to the children of Israel. They do not take it to "the house of the Lord" in Shiloh (4:3), however. For twenty years, the Ark—representing the presence and power of God—stays in the house of a man of Israel named Abinadab!

In 7:3, Samuel calls the house of Israel to repentance. The gods that he calls them to forsake, Baalim and Ashteroth, indicate the deplorable depths of sin to which God's people had plummeted. Baalim was a male god, and Ashtaroth was a female god, and the sinful behavior which Satan had devised for the worship of these "gods" was nothing short of gross debauchery!

Samuel promises Israel that in accordance with their genuine repentance, God would deliver them out of the hands of the Philistines. Israel does repent, and Samuel offers a lamb as a burnt offering to the Lord. He cries out to God for Israel, "and the Lord heard him" (7:9). The Lord answered with thunder from heaven against the Philistines, and Israel defeated them handily (7:10–12). It has been noted that Samuel accomplished more with one prayer depending on the *Spirit's* power than Samson accomplished in twenty years depending upon the power of the *flesh*! Samuel then served as a faithful prophet and judge in Israel, ministering to the people from city to city, speaking the word of the Lord and helping to settle their disputes all the days of his life (7:13–17).

Despite all the great things we learn about Samuel, however, chapter 8 reveals a place of major failure in Samuel's ministry: his own home! Evidently, Samuel had the impression, like many of God's faithful ministers through the centuries, that if he took care of the things of the Lord, the Lord would take care of the things concerning his family. And though God has called us to be a minister in His work, edifying and expanding His family (1 Cor. 15:58; 2 Cor. 5:18-19), our responsibility to the *Lord's family* does not negate or diminish the responsibility we have to our *own family*! Quite simply, our spouse and our children must be our first place of ministry!

God places such importance on the family that, in the New Testament, those holding the office of a pastor were to have "faithful children not accused of riot or unruly" (Titus 1:6) and be "one that ruleth well his own house, having his children in subjection with all gravity" (1 Tim. 3:4). God gives a similar command for fathers in general (Eph. 6:4), but in 1 Timothy 3 and Titus 1, Paul is listing the requirements for those who would provide the spiritual oversight and feeding of the family of God.

Samuel's family, however, did not meet these expectations. As Samuel came to the end of his ministry, he "made his sons judges over Israel" (8:1), but they "walked not in his ways, but turned aside after lucre, and took bribes, and perverted judgment" (8:3). The people used this decision by Samuel, and his sons' lack of godly character, as one of the justifications for demanding that Samuel install a king to rule them "like all the nations" (8:5). God reveals the disingenuousness in their request by telling Samuel that their problem wasn't really with Samuel's authority—it was with His! Yes, Samuel certainly should have made ministering to his family a greater priority, but his failure as a father was nothing more than a smokescreen the people used to get what they wanted all along: to be out from God's direct authority and to be conformed to this world (2 Sam. 8:5; Rom. 12:2).

It is interesting to note that 1 Samuel 8 records the first of Israel's three *rejections* of the triune God in Scripture:

- Israel rejects God the *Father* by choosing Saul. (1 Sam. 8:7)
- Israel rejects God the *Son* by choosing Barabbas. (Luke 23:18)
- Israel rejects God the *Holy Spirit* by refusing Stephen's message. (Acts 7:51)

Perhaps we should all ask ourselves today, "Is there any area of my life that is communicating to God that I am rejecting His authority?"

In chapters 9 and 10, God concedes to Israel's desire for a king, but clearly communicates to them what it will ultimately cost them. It is another example in Scripture where God gave the people what they wanted, but in doing so, the people lost what they had (Ps. 106:15). In this case, God gave them the king they had requested, but they lost the omniscient, omnipresent, and omnipotent kingship of the God who so loved and cared for them that they were the very "apple of His eye" (Deut. 32:10).

CHRIST IS REVEALED:

Through all that *Samuel* was intended by God to be — judge, priest, and prophet. (John 5:30; Heb. 7:26; Acts 7:37)

WEEK 13, DAY 4: **TODAY'S READING: 1 SAMUEL 11-14**

OVERVIEW:

The rise of King Saul as he obeys God; the fall of King Saul as he relies upon his own reasoning; Jonathan, Saul's son, acts in great courage.

HIGHLIGHTS & INSIGHTS:

At the end of chapter 10, Saul returned to his home town after being anointed the king of Israel. At this point, his leadership had not yet been firmly established, as word was still traveling throughout the land that he had been installed as king. In chapter 11, however, Saul gets the opportunity to establish his leadership, because Nahash, the leader of the Ammonite army, was threatening to come against Israel in Jabesh-Gilead. Saul's swift response to rally the armies of Israel and the subsequent demolition of the Ammonite army unified the nation of Israel, and the people became zealous to follow their new king and leader.

In chapter 12, Samuel takes the occasion of Israel's renewal and rededication to further establish Saul's leadership. Samuel walks the people back through his own ministry among them, as well as their history under the leadership of Moses and Aaron and several of the judges. Samuel described God's faithfulness to them as a people and a nation and how their request for an earthly king was actually a slap in God's face, as it were, since the Lord their God was their king (12:12)!

Samuel tells them that even though they had done this evil to the Lord, He was still willing to take them from where they were and bless them. In 12:14–15, he proclaims this incredibly gracious promise—and incredibly powerful warning: "If ye will fear the Lord, and serve him, and obey his voice, and not rebel against the commandment of the Lord, then shall both ye and also the king that reigneth over you continue following the Lord your God: But if ye will not obey the voice of the Lord, but rebel against the commandment of the Lord, then shall the hand of the Lord be against you, as it was against your fathers."

To prove to the people that he was in fact speaking for God and that the Lord had been offended by their request for a king, Samuel predicted that the Lord would send thunder and rain on that very day, which was during the wheat harvest—a time of the year when rain seldom, if ever, fell. When Samuel prayed, the thunder clouds rolled in, and it began to rain—striking the hearts of the people with both the fear of the Lord and of Samuel (12:18). The people owned their sin for requesting a king, and Samuel assures them of God's grace and His pleasure in them continuing to be His people, while still warning them that they needed to follow the Lord without wavering and to serve Him with all of their heart (12:21–25).

The events of 1 Samuel 13 happen two years into Saul's reign as king (13:1). And even at that early stage, we already see glimpses of "the beginning of sorrows" in the reign of Saul.

First, Saul exalts himself and his leadership by taking credit for the victory his son, Jonathan, achieved in Geba (13:1–4). Secondly, as the Philistines rallied together to fight Israel, Saul delayed in leading the attack against them, and the armies of Israel were found cowering in caves, fearful for their very lives. When Samuel didn't return when Saul expected, he took it upon himself to carry out the role of a priest in sacrificing the burnt offering. Just as he was offering the sacrifice, Samuel arrived, immediately asking him what in the world he thought he was doing! Like a little child, Saul explains to Samuel that he didn't want to have to offer the sacrifice, but since Samuel wasn't around to do it, he forced himself (v. 12) to violate his own will and conscience for the sake of the people. Yeah, right!

Samuel tells Saul that, though he had been positioned to lead Israel for the remainder of his life, because of his failure to obey the Lord, his reign in the kingdom would not continue (13:14). Samuel explained that the person God wanted to lead to His people was "a man after his own heart." Samuel's declaration was made to Saul privately, so no one in Israel knew the decision God had made, and it would be a number of years before the transition to a new king would actually be made.

In chapter 14, rather than seeking to humble himself before the Lord to become "a man after God's own heart," Saul is lifted up with pride. Watching him try to hang onto his position and power would be pitiful if it weren't so prideful. He begins to make foolish decisions in chapter 14 that result in him threatening the life of his own son. He would have killed him had he not been rescued by the people. Saul becomes foolish, fleshly, and full of himself, and he brings the nation of Israel down with him.

In the New Testament, Paul, whose original name was Saul, makes only one mention of his namesake: "And when He had removed him" (Acts 13:22). How ironic that the first king of Israel is known only for being removed so that God could fulfill His plan.

God is still seeking men and women after His own heart! We need to ask ourselves today, "Is there any area of my life where I, like Saul, am being lifted up with pride and need to humble myself before the Lord?"

Jonathan, King Saul's son, seems to have the heart of a lion (1 Sam. 14:6), but his life is caught in the web of his father's sin. Although he himself remains pure, the effects of his father's sin will ultimately end his life. There is no private sin or private life. What we do will ultimately affect those around us—most often and most severely, those we love (Num. 32:22–24)!

CHRIST IS REVEALED:

Through all that *Samuel* was intended by God to be — judge, priest, and prophet. (John 5:30; Heb. 7:26; Acts 7:37)

WEEK 13, DAY 5: **TODAY'S READING: 1 SAMUEL 15-17**

OVERVIEW:

Saul's disobedience costs him the kingdom; God chooses David to be king; David kills Goliath.

HIGHLIGHTS & INSIGHTS:

The three chapters in today's reading are some of the most dramatic in all of Scripture. God rejects a king, appoints another one out of total obscurity to replace him, and instantaneously promotes the new king-elect in the eyes of the entire nation of Israel. These events have been preached on countless times because of the clear and practical messages God is communicating through each of them.

In Chapter 15, God gives King Saul a very clear command to totally annihilate the enemy, and it looks as if Saul is going to obey Him. He gathers the troops, confidently prepares them, and courageously leads them to battle, and yet somehow, Saul finds a way to turn the victory into a defeat. After accomplishing the hard part (trusting God to grant the victory), Saul allows his flesh to control his thinking, "reinterpreting" God's command to annihilate everything related to enemy, and does something that suited and satisfied his own carnal desires. He keeps some of the spoils of battle, rationalizing that it was to offer sacrifices to God (15:15), and forever forfeits the hand of God upon his life. Samuel declares to Saul (and to us) that "to obey is better than sacrifice" (15:22), and after they separated, "Samuel came no more to see Saul until the day of his death" (15:35). May we learn from this tragic event in Saul's life to simply *do what we know*! Just do it, without *compromising* anything, without *rationalizing* anything, and without *justifying* anything! May we follow the simple counsel Mary gave to the servants at the wedding in Cana of Galilee in John 2:5: "Whatsoever he saith unto you, do it!"

With the removal of God's Holy Spirit from Saul's life, the oppression of an evil spirit quickly took His place. Ironically, the only cure for the oppression of the evil spirit was the beautiful playing of the harp by a young man named David, who, unbeknownst to Saul, was God's choice to replace him as Israel's king (16:14–19)! Note that in the Old Testament, kings would be anointed for service with the indwelling of the Holy Spirit, but unlike born-again New Testament believers, they were not "sealed with the Holy Spirit" (Eph. 1:13). They could lose the Spirit's anointing. This is why, after King David's sinful act with Bathsheba, in his confession in Psalm 51, he prays in verse 11, " take not thy Holy Spirit from me."

As the emphasis in the Scripture forever shifts from Saul to David, it is thrilling to note that at the very heart of that shift was the *heart*! While Saul was chosen based on outward appearance, David was chosen because he was a man after God's own heart! Chapter 16:7 says, "But the Lord said unto Samuel, Look not on his countenance, or on the height of his stature; because I have refused him: for the LORD seeth not as man seeth; for man looketh on the outward appearance, but the Lord looketh on the heart." It is vital to recognize just how serious our God is about the state of our "inner man" (Eph. 3:16). The word *heart* is found 765 times in the Bible and only rarely refers to our physical blood-pumping muscle!

Keeping the issue of the heart in mind, in chapter 17 we come to the familiar story of David and Goliath. While many retellings emphasize the fact that David desired to defend the name of God against the big, bad, evil Goliath who defied the God of Israel—which was certainly his primary motivation—it is also interesting to note David's other motivations. Prior to taking on the giant, David discusses the situation around the campfire. After David is told the blessings that would be given to the man who defeated Goliath, he clarified what he heard another two times (1 Sam. 17:25–30)! To further emphasize the point, David's eldest brother overhears him asking about the rewards and accuses David of having a bad heart and ulterior motives. But that is not the case. God is strongly endorsing the fact that blessings often naturally accompany exercising faith in Him and doing what is right by Him and that we need not shy away from desiring to glorify God through His blessing upon our life.

CHRIST IS REVEALED:

Through *David's Name*, which means "beloved" – 1 Samuel 16:13 (Matt. 3:17; 17:5; Mark 1:11; 9:7; Luke 3:22; 9:35)

WEEK 14, DAY 1: **TODAY'S READING: 1 SAMUEL 18-21**

OVERVIEW:

David and Jonathan become friends; David is promoted in the sight of Israel and despised in the eyes of Saul; Saul plots and attempts to kill David; David is helped by Jonathan and others to escape Saul.

HIGHLIGHTS & INSIGHTS:

In chapter 18, we are introduced to perhaps the greatest record and example of friendship the world has ever seen. Would to God that every believer had the benefit of a deep friendship like that of Jonathan and David. Note some of the key statements found in today's reading about their incredible relationship...

"The soul of Jonathan was knit with the soul of David." (18:1)

"Jonathan loved him [David] as his own soul." (18:3)

"Jonathan Saul's son delighted much in David." (19:2)

"Then said Jonathan unto David, Whatsoever thy soul desireth, I will even do it for thee." (20:4)

"And Jonathan...loved him [David] as he loved his own soul." (20:17)

It is a travesty that, because many homosexuals use these statements to justify their sinful and reprobate lifestyle (Rom. 1:24-28), we must clarify the relationship between Jonathan and David. To interpret the love shared between Jonathan and David as something romantic or sensual is as perverted as homosexuality itself and only proves the trustworthiness of Scripture because those who interpret the relationship this way are doing exactly what God described in Romans 1:25: "[They] changed the truth of God into a lie." It is unfortunate that any explanation of the perversion of Scripture is necessary, but the satanic agenda in the twenty-first century to promote this biblically reprobate lifestyle as normal and culturally acceptable requires that it be mentioned.

Chapter 18 also shows us the wisdom by which David conducted his life. Scripture mentions repeatedly this unique quality which helped elevate David into a national leader.

"And David...behaved himself wisely." (18:5)

"And David behaved himself wisely in all his ways; and the Lord was with him." (18:14)

"David behaved himself more wisely than all the servants of Saul; so that his name was much set by." (18:30)

But his wisdom was not the only reason David was rising in popularity in the kingdom. He was also viewed as a military hero (and rightfully so) for defeating the Philistine champion, Goliath! David's wisdom prompted King Saul to promote him to the position of commander over the entire military (18:5). This appointment was short-lived, however, as Saul recognized that David's character and courage were making him extremely popular throughout the entire kingdom—especially with the ladies (18:7-8). His jealousy caused Saul to fear that David would try to overthrow his kingship, and so, in a very telling sign, "Saul eyed David from that day and forward" (18:9).

The book of Numbers talks about jealousy as a "spirit" (Num. 5:14, 30), and apparently, as in Saul's case, it makes a person see things that aren't really there! The book of Proverbs also warns that "jealousy is the rage of a man" (Prov. 6:34). Interestingly, as soon as Saul opened himself up to jealousy, the Lord allowed that "evil spirit" to overtake him, and Saul makes his first attempts on David's life. David was able to dodge Saul's javelin (twice!), however, and successfully flee from his presence (18:10-11).

Saul recognized that the Lord's hand had been removed from his life—and placed on David—making him even more jealous and, therefore, fearful. Saul demoted David from the position of commander over the entire army to a captain over only 1,000 soldiers (18:12–13). Such treatment would be so devastating and humiliating to most leaders that it would cause them to react carnally. David, however, continues to conduct himself according to godly wisdom, which, ironically, makes Saul even more afraid of him. Saul's demotion actually made David more accessible to the people and they become all the more endeared to him (18:16)!

Evidently, Saul is able to step back enough to realize David's popularity and determine that it wouldn't be in his best interest to blatantly murder him. So he concocts a plan to kill him, making it look like it happened naturally in the course of battle. He promises David his oldest daughter in marriage if he will promise to continue to fight the king's battles (18:17), even though David had already been promised Saul's daughter as the reward for defeating Goliath!

Saul reneged on his promise and gave his daughter to another man, but promised David his other daughter, Michal, in exchange for the foreskins of a hundred Philistine soldiers (17:25). Saul was obviously convinced that attempting such an incredible feat would certainly result in David's death, but because the Lord's hand was on his life, David promptly delivered double the "dowry" the king requested—the foreskins of two hundred Philistine soldiers!

At the end of chapter 18, Saul is forced to face the reality that not only was the Lord's hand upon David, but the heart of his son, Jonathan, and his daughter, Michal. Rather than celebrate this obvious God-ordained reality, 1 Samuel 18:29 says, "And Saul was yet more afraid of David; and Saul became David's enemy continually." Practically, we should expect that the hand of God upon a person's life will bring out extreme reactions from other people: extreme *love* from those who are in tune with God and extreme *hatred* from those who aren't!

In chapter 20, we see David make some unwise decisions. Rather than inspiring one another to cry out in faith for the Lord's wisdom, direction and protection against Saul, David and Jonathan craft an elaborate plan of lying and scheming in order to create the protection David needed. And as the old saying goes, "It's never right to do wrong to get the chance to do right."

The lying and scheming continues into chapter 21, as David gives evidence that he is no longer trusting the "wisdom of God" but the "wisdom of men" (1 Cor. 1:5–7). In 21:1–9, David lies to Ahimelech, and in 21:10–15, he lies to Achish. This is never God's way, as James reminds us that "the wisdom that is from above is first pure" (Jam. 3:17).

Notice that this blatant deception and obvious lack of faith in God is actually coming out of the life of "the man after God's own heart!" If trusting the arm of the flesh as opposed to the power of God, and resorting to the wisdom of men after so often displaying the wisdom of God was this great of a temptation to David, we must consider a couple of questions about ourselves!

- What situations am I presently facing in which I could be tempted to scheme, lie, or deceive in order to protect myself?

- What would it look like in these potentially tempting situations to trust the wisdom of God (as David did in chapters 17–18) rather than the wisdom of men (as displayed in chapters 19–21)?

CHRIST IS REVEALED:

As the "*Friend that sticketh closer than a brother*" – 1 Samuel 18:3 (Prov. 18:24, John 15:13–16)

By *Jonathan*, who, knowing that it was God's will to make David king, stripped himself of his royal robe, promising all that he had to David – 1 Samuel 18:3–4 (Phil. 2:5–8)

WEEK 14, DAY 2: **TODAY'S READING: 1 SAMUEL 22-25**

OVERVIEW:

David is a fugitive from Saul and runs to Nob, Gath, Adullam and the wilderness; David spares Saul's life; Samuel dies; Abigail saves Nabal's life.

HIGHLIGHTS & INSIGHTS:

In chapter 22, David leaves Gath and escapes to the cave called Adullam. When word of his whereabouts spread, many down-and-outers gathered where he was. 1 Samuel 22:2 describes them as "in distress," "in debt," and "discontented." David became a captain over 400 of these men, and the number soon grew to about 600 (23:13)! As the old saying goes, "Misery loves company," and these men, David included, were certainly miserable. David cries out to the Lord in song during this time, and the songs are recorded in Psalms 54 and 142.

David is clearly concerned that if Saul kills him, he will do the same to his parents, so he arranges for the king of Moab to protect them. That was a fitting place since David's father's grandmother, Ruth, was actually a Moabitess. After securing their protection, David goes to secure his own place of protection. God sends the prophet, Gad, to specifically tell David to get himself back into the land of Judah.

When Saul gets word of what David was doing and where he was headed, he throws a little pity party for himself and accuses his own men of conspiring against him (22:7–8). He berates them for not informing him of the covenant Jonathan had made with David sometime earlier (18:3; 20:16).

Then, no doubt seeking to suck up to the enraged king, Doeg, one of Saul's key leaders, tells him that David had gone to Nob to see Ahimelech the priest who had inquired of the Lord for him and ministered to him. Saul sent for all the priests of Nob. He commands his soldiers to annihilate them, but they refused. Saul then commands Doeg to do it, and he kills sixty-five priests in cold blood. Abiathar, one of Ahimelech's sons, escapes with the ephod (an instrument through which God revealed His will at this time) and goes inform David. David tells Abiathar to stay with him, knowing that Saul would certainly seek to take his life.

In chapter 23, David hears that the Philistines were fighting against God's people in Keilah, and he inquires of the Lord whether he should fight them. God unhesitatingly tells David to go for it! David's men, however, want confirmation. God again declares that He would deliver them into their hands, and David and his men defeat them "with a great slaughter" (23:5).

When Saul hears that David and his men were shut in the gated and barred city of Keilah, Saul is so spiritually disoriented that he viewed it as his "God-given" opportunity to put an end to David's life. David asks the Lord whether he should trust the people of Keilah to protect him, but God reveals that they would give him up. David departes into the wilderness of Zish and hides out in a mountain, as Saul seeks daily to kill him (23:14).

Verses 16 –18 provide one of the most beautiful moments in this chapter. David was tired, discouraged and afraid, and God used Jonathan to encourage him. Jonathan went and found David in the wilderness "and strengthened his [David's] hand in God" (23:16). May God use each of us to strengthen the hand of those around us in God! Can you think of someone who could use that strengthening ministry from you today?

The Ziphites send word to Saul of David's whereabouts and conspire with Saul to help find him. Saul pursues David until a messenger comes to tell Saul the Philistines had invaded the land. When David hears that Saul has departed, he took refuge in strongholds in a place called Engedi (23:19–29).

In chapter 24, Saul returns with 3,000 soldiers to seek David at Engedi and "just happens" to go by himself into the very cave where David and his men were hiding. (To "cover his feet" in verse 3 meant to relieve himself.) David's men urged him to rid himself of his enemy. And with all that Saul had done, it would be hard to fault David had he taken advantage of his enemy—alone, unprotected, and literally within arm's reach! David might easily have interpreted this moment as God's plan, that this was *the day* and this was *the way* the Lord intended to deliver David from Saul's irrational and unreasonable pursuit.

And David was certainly tempted! But instead of killing Saul, he snuck up and cut off a piece of his robe. This would embarrass the king and let Saul know David could have killed him if he'd chosen to. But immediately, his conscience pricked him. David worried that he had failed the spirit of the test, and once again, David's sensitive heart pleased God. David was sensitive to the Lord's perfect will for his life. Let us examine just how sensitive we are to carrying out the perfect will of God for our lives. Even more, God used the realization that David had refused the chance to take Saul's life to appease Saul—at least for a while.

In Chapter 25, we meet Nabal, and those of us who have worked for a bona fide, biblical fool take great hope. *Nabal* means "fool," and like so many biblical characters, he certainly lived up to his name! Abigail saves her fool of a husband, and for this, God blesses her abundantly. Many would have thought themselves powerless to redirect an army like David's, but Abigail was "a woman of good understanding" (25:3) who knew when to make haste (25:18).

This passage reminds us of the biblical mandate that "Vengeance is mine; I will repay, saith the Lord" (Rom. 12:19). David had trusted God by not taking out vengeance upon Saul, but he was about to seek vengeance against Nabal. God uses Abigail's wise handling of the situation to avert David's vengeance against her husband. And within a matter of two weeks, God exercised His vengeance against Nabal, and he died! May we learn to trust God to deal with the enemies that surround us, rather than trying to deal with them ourselves in the power of the flesh!

CHRIST IS REVEALED:

Through *David's Refusal to take the kingdom by force or before God's appointed time* – 1 Samuel 24:10–13 (The Lord Jesus Christ refused to become king of Israel until God's appointed time – John 6:15)

By *Abigail's effort to make peace between David and* Nabal – 1 Samuel 25:21–28 (God was in Christ, reconciling the world to Himself – 2 Cor. 5:19)

WEEK 14, DAY 3: **TODAY'S READING: 1 SAMUEL 26-31**

OVERVIEW:

David spares Saul's life again; David lives in the land of the Philistines and defeats many enemies; Saul consults with a witch regarding going to war; David recovers his family and the families of his soldiers who are kidnapped; Saul's sons are killed in battle; Saul takes his own life.

HIGHLIGHTS & INSIGHTS:

After Nabal died at the end of chapter 25, David married his widow, Abigail. David was a man with many talents and abilities and a good heart; however, fleshly violations such as this will ultimately blossom into a snare of epic proportions in the future. When God prophesied hundreds of years earlier that Israel would want an earthly king like the other nations of the world, this was one of the key stipulations that God declared: "neither shall he [a king] multiply wives to himself" (Deut. 17:16–17). David had been anointed by Samuel for kingship in Israel (16:1–13), but before being installed as the nation's leader, he has already violated one of God's key commands.

Perhaps that same lapse in judgment led to his decision to return to the land of the Ziph, placing him in the direct path of his irrational and unpredictable enemy, Saul, once again. God in his grace caused a "deep sleep" to fall upon Saul and his band of soldiers, and by taking Saul's spear and water bottle rather than his life, David again proves to him that he did not aspire to kill him (26:7–12).

Physically, the "deep sleep" that God poured out upon Saul and his men is a picture of a *spiritual* condition. Isaiah 29:10–11 describes "the spirit of deep sleep" that causes a person's spiritual eyes to close and the Bible to become as if it were sealed to them. Biblically and practically, God pours out this spirit upon people who willfully close their eyes to the truth of God's word that has been revealed to them. In Matthew 13:15, Jesus talked about people whose "eyes they have closed; lest at anytime they should see with their eyes."

The fact is, God will give us what we communicate to Him that we really want. Pharaoh hardened his heart, and God helped him get what he wanted—God hardened Pharoah's heart. People in the last days reject the truth of God, and God will give them the lie they told him they wanted—they will believe the lie of the Antichrist (2 Thess. 2:8–12). People close their eyes to God's truth, and God will help them in the process—He will close their eyes (Isa. 29:10–11; Matt. 13:15). We must ask ourselves what it is that our lives are telling God we actually want! And is there any area in our life where we are willfully rejecting truth that has been revealed to us?

One of the most admirable qualities David possessed was how he regarded *God's* authority in his life, and thus, how he regarded *man's* authority in his life. Samuel had anointed David king while Saul still held the office. David, however, never manifested a sense of entitlement. He never sought directly or indirectly to undermine the king's authority or to stage any type of insurrection. Though God had promised to deliver Saul into David's hand, David declared on several occasions that he would "not stretch forth his hand against the Lord's anointed" (1 Sam. 24:6; 26:9, 11, 23). In other words, regardless of his own anointing, as long as God allowed the previously anointed king to sit on the throne, David wasn't going to be party to any action to remove him. David operated from biblical principles that were still to be recorded in God's word: "To every thing there is a season, and a time to every purpose under heaven" (Eccles. 3:1) and "He hath made every thing beautiful in his time." (Eccles. 3:11)

Chapter 28 is another sad chapter, both in the Bible and the life of Saul. When we first met him in 1 Samuel 9, Saul stood "higher than any of the people" (9:2; 10:23). God had set before him a future that was incredibly bright and promising. By chapter 28, however, he has "stooped" lower than any of the people (28:14). He asks a demonically-empowered witch to tell his future because God was no longer communicating with him or to him. He asks her to call Samuel from the dead, and—surprisingly enough—Samuel does appear! It even surprised the witch and, by the sound of her voice, freaked her out (28:12)! This passage, as you can imagine, has prompted many theological discussions and debates. Perhaps the simplest explanation for what happened with Samuel's appearance to Saul is that he was there, not because of the witch's power, but because God sent him to deliver a message.

The death of Saul is also the subject of considerable debate as there appears to be two contradictory accounts of how it happened. 1 Samuel 31:4–6 says that, after being wounded in battle, Saul fell on his own sword and took his own life before the enemy was able to taunt him or torture him. In 2 Samuel 1:2–10, however, the Amalekite reports to David that Saul had fallen on his own sword and, though greatly wounded, Saul was convinced that his injury wasn't going to kill him, so he asked the Amalekite to finish the job. The Amalekite tells David that he believed Saul was going to die from his self-inflicted wound, so he saw no harm in doing as Saul asked.

So, which account is right? Is this actually a contradiction in the Bible?

Let's be clear. If this is a contradiction in our Bible, we should close our Bible right now and never open it again! Then, we ought to use this *52 Weeks of Pursuit* as kindling for our next bonfire. Then we can spend as much time as it takes to find something productive that makes us happy because we're all in a lurch (1 Cor 15:32)! If this is a contradiction, then the entire Bible is a sham—a worthless piece of unreliable literary trash. It is not the word of God, merely the words of men! And it is the exact opposite of what 1 Thessalonians 2:13 says it is!

But thankfully, this is not a contradiction in the Bible—because there are none! As with these two accounts, there sometimes can be *apparent* contradictions in the Bible, but there are no *actual* contradictions! It is, in fact, the perfect, inspired, infallible, inerrant Word and words of God (Pro. 30:5–6; 1 Thes. 2:13). The *apparent* contradictions that are in the Bible can usually be unraveled by employing basic reasoning skills or by comparing Scripture with Scripture (1 Cor. 2:13). In this particular *apparent* contradiction, the answer is very simply that the story that the Amalekite told David in 2 Samuel 1 was a lie. He may have concocted the whole story to look heroic in the eyes of David or to give explanation for why he had Saul's crown and arm band. His fabrication, however, ended in his death (2 Sam. 1:15).

To summarize the book of 1 Samuel, let's take a hypothetical sheet of paper and divide into two columns. At the top of the first column, we'll write "What *not* to do." At the top of the second column, we put "What *to do*." In the first column, we would explain the lives of Eli and Saul. In the second column, we would explain the lives of Samuel and David. That is the essence of the entire book. The beautiful thing about our God is that He graciously allows us to choose the column from which we will conduct our lives!

Which should lead us to ask: If someone were to read an account of our lives over the past several years as we have done with these four men in 1 Samuel, which column would they place us in: "What *to do*" or "What *not* to do"?

CHRIST IS REVEALED:

Through the *Urim*, which was used to determine God's will – 1 Samuel 28:6 (Today Christ reveals His will through His Spirit as we read His Word. "God … hath in these last days spoken unto us by His Son" – Heb. 11:1–2)

WEEK 14, DAY 4: **TODAY'S READING: 2 SAMUEL 1-4**

OVERVIEW:

The death of Saul; David mourns the death of Saul and Jonathan; David's song of sorrow; David is crowned king of Judah; Ishbosheth is made king of Israel; Abner deserts Ishbosheth to align with David; Joab murders Abner; Ishbosheth's murder; David's execution of Ishbosheth's murderers.

HIGHLIGHTS & INSIGHTS:

The book of 2 Samuel continues the narrative of 1 Samuel, so it begins as 1 Samuel ends, with the death of Saul.

David's reaction to Saul's death gives us an incredible glimpse into the heart of this man, whom Scripture calls a "man after God's own heart" (1 Sam. 13:14; Acts 13:22). With all that Saul had done (and tried to do) to David, we would expect David to be elated, but amazingly, David genuinely grieved and lamented Saul's death (2 Sam. 1:11–12, 17). He composed a song as a beautiful memorial to Israel's first king (1:19–27) and put to death the Amalekite who claimed to have killed Saul for daring to destroy the Lord's anointed.

But now the question was, who would be Saul's successor? In 1 Samuel 16:13, God had commanded Samuel to anoint David as Israel's next king. But that had been years before, and Abner, Saul's cousin and the commander of Saul's army, was determined to keep the kingship within the family or, more accurately, under his own authority. He moves to persuade the elders of Israel to put Saul's son, Ishbosheth, on the throne.

Once again, it is incredible to watch the "man after God's own heart" operate. Having been anointed as God's chosen successor, David could have justified facing Abner in battle for his "right" to be named king. Instead, David inquired of the Lord (2 Sam. 2:1, 4), placing his life and the entire situation completely in God's hands. It is a great lesson for those of us living in the last days, who are intensely interested in our rights (Rev. 3:14, *Laodicean* means "the rights of the people") and whom the Scripture calls "lovers of their own selves" (2 Tim. 3:1–2). We are prone to self-promotion and personal advancement, rather than waiting upon God, seeking God, and trusting God.

But David demonstrates how unnecessary it is to fight for our rights. If Jehovah had indeed anointed David as king, then Jehovah would deal with his enemies and put him on the throne. Likewise, when we take self off the throne and submit patiently and confidently to Christ's Lordship, He will, in His faithfulness, carry out His will in our lives, in His way and in His time. Maybe you are facing a situation which is tempting you to promote yourself and make happen what you know is God's will. Like David, submit to God who is more than able to bring His plans to fruition.

God led David to Hebron where he was anointed king of Judah, but the other tribes of Israel refused to recognize David's kingship. Eventually, Abner and Ishbosheth had a major falling out, and Abner pledged his loyalty to David. When Joab, the captain of David's army, returned from battle and heard that David had met with Abner, he was furious! He assassinated Abner, stabbing him under the fifth rib (the perfect location to assure death). In response, David publicly condemned Abner's murder by cursing Joab and his house and by proclaiming a time of mourning for Abner, while openly mourning for Abner himself.

With Abner out of the way, Ishbosheth's position became weaker, while David's grew stronger. Baanah and Rechab realized that David's rule over Israel was inevitable and decided to impress David by killing Ishbosheth. David, however, was not impressed! David knew God would never lead men to violate His Word to enthrone His king (i.e., It's never right to do wrong to do right!) and that God was more than able to fulfill His promises without the help of murderers! David called for Baanah's and Rechab's execution, exposing their bodies to the humiliation of public display, while the head of Ishobosheth was respectfully and honorably buried in the tomb of Abner.

CHRIST IS REVEALED:

In *David's Song of Sorrow* – 2 Samuel 1:19–27 (Even though Saul had made David his enemy, David continuously loved Saul. Christ loved us, even though we had made ourselves His enemies – Rom. 5:8, 10a; Eph. 2:1, 4–5a)

In *David's Partial Reign* – 2 Samuel 2:4 (Though David had been anointed as Israel's king, he actually reigned over only a small percentage of his full kingdom, while he patiently waited for God's timing. Similarly, the Lord Jesus Christ has been anointed King over all the earth, but awaits the Father's timing to actually possess His kingdom. Only a small percentage of the world's population recognize Christ as their Lord and King, but one day soon, every knee shall bow and every tongue confess that "Jesus Christ is Lord to the glory of God the Father" – Phil. 2:10–11)

WEEK 14, DAY 5: **TODAY'S READING: 2 SAMUEL 5-8**

OVERVIEW:

David is anointed king over all of Israel; the stronghold of the Jebusites (Jerusalem) is captured by David; David brings the ark of God into Jerusalem; the Davidic Covenant; David's prayer of thanksgiving; David's victories over the Philistines, the Moabites, the Syrians, and the Edomites.

HIGHLIGHTS & INSIGHTS:

David had reigned over the tribe of Judah for seven and a half years in Hebron. In chapter 5, he is anointed king over the entire nation of Israel, and reigned for thirty-three years, making his entire reign forty years.

With the extension of his kingdom, he needed a more central location from which to rule and chose Jerusalem to be the capital city. The only problem was that the Jebusites lived in Jerusalem and Israel had not been able to capture this stronghold (Jos. 15:63; Judg. 1:21). The Jebusites were so cocky, they basically said to David, "The lame and the blind could defeat you!" But David and his men took the city, and Jerusalem became known as "the city of David"!

Like David, the Lord Jesus Christ has been anointed (*Messiah* means "anointed") of God to rule from the throne of our hearts over our entire life. We must allow Him to remove any and all strongholds that the enemy has established. 2 Corinthians 10:3–5 says, "For though we walk in the flesh, we do not war after the flesh: (For the weapons of our warfare are not carnal, but mighty through God to the pulling down of strong holds;) Casting down imaginations, and every high thing that exalteth itself against the knowledge of God, and bringing into captivity every thought to the obedience of Christ."

But in 2 Samuel 5, as soon as the stronghold was defeated and David was established in Jerusalem, their old enemy, the Philistines, show up! Until we receive our glorified body, we're never going to be "out of the woods," and one of the key times Satan will attack us is when he thinks we have been lulled by the blessing of a recent victory.

As the Philistines threatened Israel, David sought clear direction from the Lord, and victory was granted. When the Philistines attacked a second time, David didn't assume another victory, but again sought clear direction from the Lord. These are key principles for our understanding concerning spiritual warfare!

In chapter 6, David is about to do something monumental—return the ark (which represented God's presence among His people) to its rightful place! The ark was in the possession of the Philistines for twenty years, and sadly, no one seemed to miss it or desired to see it returned. Its return was an exciting and worshipful experience for all involved. The spiritual atmosphere was electric! There was a great lesson to be learned, however. God is never interested in self-styled worship, and good intentions and proper motivation mean nothing if there is not complete obedience to God's Word.

In David's zeal to see the ark returned, the method of carrying it (on a new cart) violated God's clear instructions (Num. 4:15; 7:9). When the oxen pulling the cart stumbled on Nachon's threshing floor and well-meaning Uzzah reached forth to keep the ark from falling off, just as God had warned, he was immediately zapped (2 Sam. 6:6–7)! The incident made David question whether returning the ark was what he really wanted, and for three months, it stayed at the house of Obed-edom. After seeing how the ark brought blessing to Obed-edom and his entire family, David thought it might be advantageous to return it to Jerusalem after all.

In chapter 7, God established the Davidic covenant. This key, unconditional covenant promised that David would have a child who was yet to be born who would succeed him and establish his kingdom. This son (Solomon) would build the temple instead of David, and his throne would be well established forever, even in spite of the sins he may commit. Lastly, David's house, kingdom, and throne would be established forever. David was deeply moved by God's covenant of grace, and he humbly came into

God's presence and offered the prayer of thanksgiving recorded in 7:18–29.

In chapter 8, David consolidates the kingdom by defeating the Philistines, the Moabites, the Syrians, and the Edomites in rapid succession. The key to theses conquests is found in 8:14, "And the Lord preserved David whithersoever he went."

CHRIST IS REVEALED:

Through *David, the Anointed King over Israel* – 2 Samuel 5:3 (Christ is the Lord's Anointed. *Christ* is the Greek word for the Hebrew word *Messiah*, which means "anointed one" – Ps. 2:2; John 1:41)

WEEK 15, DAY 1: **TODAY'S READING: 2 SAMUEL 9-12**

OVERVIEW:

David's kindness to Mephibosheth; the defeat of the Ammonites and Syrians; David's sin with Bathsheba; Nathan's parable and David's repentance; the death of David and Bathsheba's baby; the birth of Solomon.

HIGHLIGHTS & INSIGHTS:

In chapter 9, God gives us an incredible picture of salvation through the account of David's blessing upon Mephibosheth, Jonathan's son. Mephibosheth beautifully portrays all of us in our lost condition.

1) Mephibosheth was born into Saul's family which was rejected due to sin (1 Sam. 15:23, 26). We were born into Adam's family, which was also rejected due to sin (Rom 5:12).

2) When David sought him, Mephibosheth was in Machir, which means "sold." When God sought us, Romans 7:14 says we were "sold under sin."

3) Just as Mephibosheth was unable to walk due to a fall (2 Sam. 4:4), we, too, were unable to walk due to the Fall that crippled us spiritually. Because of it, we were unable to walk and to please God.

4) Mephibosheth lived in a land called Lodebar, meaning "no pasture" (2 Sam. 9:4–5). In our lost condition, we, too, lived in a land of famine and barrenness (the world), which provided no pasture (nothing to satisfy the hunger of our souls).

David beautifully portrays the Lord Jesus Christ in providing our salvation.

1) David made the first move (2 Sam. 9:1). As Mephibosheth was unable to make the first step toward David because of his lameness, we were also unable to make the first step in seeking the Lord (Rom. 3:10–12).

2) David extended this grace to Mephibosheth because of a covenant he had made with Jonathan (1 Sam. 20:14–17). We, too, have been extended the grace of the Lord Jesus Christ because of what Hebrews 13:20–21 calls "the everlasting covenant."

3) This was an act of David's kindness (1 Sam. 20:15). In fact, in 2 Samuel 9:3, David calls it "the kindness of God." And Titus 3:4–6 says, "But after that the kindness and love of God our Saviour toward man appeared, Not by works of righteousness which we have done, but according to his mercy he saved us, by the washing of regeneration, and renewing of the Holy Ghost; Which he shed on us abundantly through Jesus Christ our Saviour."

4) David made him a part of his own family (2 Sam. 9:11). Like all of us when we came to the Lord for salvation, Mephibosheth simply sought to be a servant, but David made him a son! "Behold what manner of love the Father hath bestowed upon us, that we should be called the sons of God" (1 John 3:1).

5) David provided for Mephibosheth's every need and exceeded his needs (2 Sam. 9:9–10). David took Mephibosheth from the place of famine to feeding him at the king's table! Likewise, the Lord Jesus Christ took us out of the barrenness of our life and met our every need (Phil. 4:19), even exceeding our every need (2 Cor. 9:8, 11).

As we move into chapter 11, we enter the darkest chapter of David's life. God's epitaph of David is found in 1 Kings 15:5: "David did that which was right in the eyes of the LORD, and turned not aside from any thing that he commanded him all the days of his life, save only in the matter of Uriah the Hittite." 2 Samuel 11 is the record of that "matter," that David first took Uriah's *wife* and then took his *life*!

So just how did "the man after God's own heart" get himself in this unbelievably sinful mess? David said in Psalm 27:4: "One thing have I desired of the Lord, that will I seek after; that I may dwell in the house of the Lord all the days of my life, to behold the beauty of the Lord, and to enquire in his temple."

That "one thing" David was seeking after was expressed three ways:

1) "That I may *dwell* in the *house* of the Lord."

2) "To *behold* the *beauty* of the Lord"

3) "To *enquire* in his *temple*."

But in 2 Samuel 11:1–4, when David commits this terrible atrocity against the Lord and Uriah, he was *dwelling* in his *own house* … not the Lord's house (11:1–2a). He was *beholding* the *beauty* of Bathsheba … not the Lord's beauty (11:2b). And he *enquired* after the *woman* … not after the Lord (11:3–4).

David's sin is great lesson about the priority of *worship*. Jesus taught us in Luke 10:42, as David confirms here in Psalm 27:4, that worship is in the "one thing" that is "needful." We could say that is the main thing! And as the old adage says, "The main thing, is to keep the main thing, the main thing!" We must constantly be aware of the depths the flesh can take us when we lose worship as the main thing in our lives.

Sadly, it takes "the man after God's own heart" over a year to own up to his sin and only when confronted by the prophet Nathan. Nathan assures David that his sin would be forgiven, but the consequences of it would follow him the remainder of his life (12:10–14). God help us to count the incredible cost of sin and the terrible atrocity of giving "great occasion to the enemies of the Lord to blaspheme" (12:14).

CHRIST IS REVEALED:

In the prophet Nathan giving *Solomon* the name *Jedidiah* – 2 Samuel 12:24–25. (Our Lord Jesus Christ is the "Beloved of the Lord" or the "Beloved of the Father." Jedidiah means "Beloved of the Lord" – See John 17:24; Matt. 3:17; 17:5; Eph. 1:6)

WEEK 15, DAY 2: **TODAY'S READING: 2 SAMUEL 13-16**

OVERVIEW:

Amnon rapes Tamar; Absalom, Tamar's brother, murders Amnon in revenge; Absalom flees to Geshur; Joab plots to have Absalom returned to Jerusalem; David restores Absalom; Absalom leads a revolt, seeking to overthrow his father; David flees in fear of his son.

HIGHLIGHTS & INSIGHTS:

In today's reading, the consequences of David's sin continue, as the Lord promised in 2 Samuel 12:11, "Behold, I will raise up evil against thee out of thine own house."

A parent can experience no greater pain than to see his own sin repeated in the lives of his children, but the principle of Galatians 6:7–8 and Proverbs 11:29 reveal that it is inevitable. In chapter 13, David's son, Amnon, commits sexual sin against his own half-sister, Tamar. When David learned of Amnon's sin, he was obviously extremely upset and angry (13:21), but he did not punish him. Leviticus 20:17 says that Amnon's punishment for raping Tamar should have been death! Most likely, David failed to exercise the proper discipline because his own sin was so fresh in everyone's mind—including his own!

Absalom, Tamar's brother, was also extremely upset, and his anger only intensified as his father did nothing—even "after two full years" (13:22–23). As a result, Absalom had Amnon killed at a family gathering and went into hiding for the next three years (13:38). After grieving Amnon's death, David longed to see Absalom, his exasperated and fugitive son.

Joab recognized that David longed to have Absalom back in Jerusalem, but he also recognized that for him to return without being punished for Amnon's murder wasn't going to be good for David's approval rating in Israel. Joab devised a clever plot (much like God did through Nathan in 2 Sam. 12:1–7) to get David to act on the situation by sending a woman to ask the king's counsel on a situation similar to the one David faced. In offering her counsel, David is caught in the web of his own moral wisdom. Backed into a corner, he must now restore, with protection, the banished, fearful, and exasperated Absalom.

David gives orders to Joab (as weak as they were) to bring Absalom back to Jerusalem, though Absalom remained unrepentant. It is a decision through which the consequences of David's sin will bear even more fruit, and once again, just as God said, would reap "evil out of his own house."

Absalom is brought back to Jerusalem, but after another "two full years," he still had not been permitted to come into his father's presence (14:28). It has now been seven years since Amnon raped Tamar and five years since Absalom has seen his father! But during those two years, while his animosity toward his father continued to grow, the hearts of the people of Israel began to be turned toward Absalom. Absalom took the favor his father extended to him and used it as the platform to launch a national rebellion. How ironic that while David schemed to spare his son's life, Absalom schemed to put his father to death. Not enough can be said about the incredible danger of "provoking your children to wrath" (Eph. 6:4; Col. 3:21). Parents, we must be extremely careful!

In chapters 15 and 16, Absalom blatantly seeks to extend his following throughout the nation, openly criticizing his father's leadership and plotting to turn the affection of the people toward himself. While David was reigning in the height of his power, the enemies within his own kingdom (who were there all along) would not dare to oppose him. Absalom's revolt, however, gave them the opportunity to resist the king's leadership and get away with it.

What Absalom's rebellion actually did for the kingdom was sift the true from the false. As difficult as it is, God says that the same thing happens in churches: "When ye come together in the church, I hear that there be divisions among you; and I partly believe it. For there must be also heresies [note that the word *heresies* is the same word that was just translated *divisions* in the previous sentence!] among you, that they which are approved may be made manifest among you" (1 Cor. 11:18–19). God not only says that it will happen in churches, but that it *must* happen! Sometimes these divisions are the only way to tell who the people in the church really are and where they stand. Remember, there is nothing new under the sun (Eccl. 1:9).

CHRIST IS REVEALED:

Through *David's restoration* of his estranged son – 2 Samuel 14:22 (2 Cor. 5:19)

Through *David* as he rebuked his followers when they wanted to execute his enemies – 2 Samuel 16:10–11 (Luke 9:54–56)

WEEK 15, DAY 3: **TODAY'S READING: 2 SAMUEL 17–20**

OVERVIEW:

Absalom chooses to follow Hushai's counsel over Ahithophel; Ahithophel commits suicide; David's army battles Absalom and his followers; Joab kills Absalom; David grieves bitterly; Joab rebukes David; the revolt of Sheba; David replaces Joab with Amasa as captain of his army; Amasa is replaced with Abishai; Joab is reinstated as captain of David's army; Sheba is killed.

HIGHLIGHTS & INSIGHTS:

Starting in chapter 17, Absalom's rebellion against his father and his wicked plot to overthrow him have reached their climax. Though God permitted his revolt as part of the consequences for David's sin regarding Bathsheba and Uriah, he also used it to purge David's kingdom and separate the loyal from the disloyal. Now the time of judgment against Absalom has finally arrived.

It is often in a crisis that our real friends are revealed. Ahithophel, David's counselor and presumed friend, was invited by Absalom to be a part of his conspiracy. Ahithophel's true nature is revealed in the repeated use of the *I* and *me* in his response in 17:1–3.

> Let me now choose out of 12,000 men, and I will arise and pursue after David this night: And I will come upon him while he is weary and weak handed, and will make him afraid … and I will smite the king only: And I will bring back all the people unto thee.

Absalom believed that Ahithophel was loyal to him, but Ahithophel's speech betrays him. The object of Ahithophel's affection was actually Ahithophel. He wanted to make certain he had a place of prominence in what appeared to be the inevitability of a new regime.

In the meantime, David sends his true friend, Hushai, to join Absalom. Having (apparently) gained both of his father's top advisors, Absalom's passion soars. He asks these two men for the best way to formalize the overthrow of his father's kingship and put an end to David once and for all. Ahithophel's plan was obviously the better of the two, but in answer to David's prayer back in 15:31, "O, Lord, I pray thee, turn the counsel of Ahithophel into foolishness," God made sure Absalom rejected his counsel. Hushai appealed to Absalom's vanity, which had been driving him for seven years, so it was his counsel Absalom followed. In the end, Absalom's vanity led to his death! As for Ahithophel, when Absalom chose Hushai's plan, it crushed his vanity, and he went out (like Judas) and took his own life. Never underestimate what people will do when they don't get their own way!

Though David had given clear instruction not to kill Absalom in the midst of the battle (18:5), Joab saw the pretty boy hanging by the locks of his hair in a tree and immediately speared him through the heart. Joab sent Cushi to inform the king of Absalom's end which sent David into deep depression and overwhelming grief. However, his grief for the one who was the source of such turmoil and revolt almost cost David his kingdom (19:1–7). The subtle lesson we learn from this is that people are not only watching and analyzing our *actions*—but also our *reactions*!

This was obviously a time of great unrest and confusion in the kingdom. David begins his trip back to Jerusalem and promises to appoint Amasa, his nephew and Absalom's general, as the captain of his army in the place of Joab, if he could turn the hearts of the people of Judah (who were extremely upset with him) to support David's return to power. Such a promise communicated only that David punished loyalty and rewarded rebellion, which wasn't actually the signal David needed to be sending amid such political unrest, instability and volatility. Amasa was successful, however, in "bow[ing] the heart of all the men of Judah" to David's side (19:14).

As chapter 20 begins, there is yet another rebellion. This time, it is a satanically influenced rebel by the name of Sheba, of the tribe of Benjamin, who was also successful in rallying a group of people against David. By this time, David certainly had to wonder, "When is all of this nonsense going to be over?"

In the process of dealing with the rebellion of Sheba, David installs Abishai as captain of the army, and Amasa is killed by Joab. Joab is then reinstated as David's general, and ultimately, Sheba is beheaded. Once again, all of the murder and bloodshed that was a result of David's sin in these chapters is a very graphic reminder to us all—"the wages of sin is death" (Rom. 6:23a)!

CHRIST IS REVEALED:

Through *Mahanaim*, a city of refuge to which David fled from Absalom – 2 Samuel 17:27 ("We … have fled for refuge to lay hold upon the hope set before us … even Jesus" – Heb. 6:18–20)

WEEK 15, DAY 4: **TODAY'S READING: 2 SAMUEL 21–24**

OVERVIEW:

God punishes Israel with a three year famine because of Saul's ill-treatment of the Gibeonites; seven members of Saul's family are put to death as retribution; victories over the Philistine giants; the last words of David; the last recorded sin of David; David builds an altar; David's sacrifice; the three-day plague.

HIGHLIGHTS & INSIGHTS:

Today's reading covers six events, which are not necessarily in chronological order. They function as an appendix to the main context of the book of 2 Samuel.

1) A major famine sent as God's judgment for Saul's treatment of the Gibeonites.

2) A series of wars with the Philistines.

3) A psalm of deliverance and praise.

4) A list of David's mighty men of valour.

5) A sinful census.

6) The severe punishment that followed the census.

Scripture doesn't specifically say what motivated David to call for the census mentioned here, but it appears that, once the nation of Israel had been re-established after Absalom's rebellion, David's heart was lifted up with pride and a desire to bask in the glory of his success. The parallel account in 1 Chronicles 21:1 says, "And Satan stood up against Israel, and provoked David to number Israel."

It is interesting to compare this great sin in David's life with his sin with Bathsheba. 2 Corinthians 7:1 commands us to "cleanse ourselves from all filthiness of the flesh and spirit." Whereas David's sin with Bathsheba is a great example of a sin of the flesh, David's numbering of the people is a great example of a sin of the spirit. Whereas his sin with Bathsheba was a sin of *passion*—done in haste; this was a sin of *pride*, done with calculation. Joab even appeals to David's conscience about defying God this way, and yet he still persisted (2 Sam. 24:3–4). The result of David's sin with Bathsheba caused great sorrow to David and the death his family members, but his sin in numbering the people resulted in the death of 70,000 men! From a human perspective, pride and rebellion do not seem quite as terrible as adultery and murder, but in David's life, they produced greater sorrow and tragedy than his sin of adultery. We must always be on guard for sins of the flesh *and* of the spirit, and we must recognize that the consequences of sin affect those we lead (family, disciples, church members, etc.) as well as ourselves.

So what practical lessons does 2 Samuel 24 teach us?

1) **We never outgrow temptation.**
   David is not a strapping youth in 2 Samuel 24. He's advanced in years, and one would think he would know better. Regardless of our age or our level of spiritual maturity, we will never be out of the reach of temptation (1 Cor. 10:12).

2) **God always gives us space to repent.**
   In this case, He gave David over nine months to "cleanse [himself] from all filthiness of the flesh and spirit" (2 Cor. 7:1; 2 Sam. 24:8). Maybe this would be a good time for each of us to ask ourselves, "Have I cleansed myself of *all* filthiness of the flesh and spirit?"

3) **Sins of the spirit are as horrific as sins of the flesh.**
   Jesus was actually more accommodating to those involved in sins of passion (the woman caught in adultery), than He was those who were persistently involved in sins of pride (the scribes and Pharisees). Though we tend to emphasize sins of the flesh, certainly, we must guard against both.

4) **Our sin always involves others.**
David's life screams to us that others are always affected by our sin. May God help us to count the horrific cost of our sin!

CHRIST IS REVEALED:

As the *one we call upon for salvation* – 2 Samuel 22:4 (Acts 4:12; Rom. 10:9, 13).

WEEK 15, DAY 5: **TODAY'S READING: 1 KINGS 1-3**

OVERVIEW:

The end of David's reign; Adonijah's attempt to take the throne; Solomon anointed and announced as king; David's final charge to Solomon; Solomon executes judgment; Solomon asks for and receives an understanding heart and discernment.

HIGHLIGHTS & INSIGHTS:

Let's begin today by looking at a few important facts about the book of 1 Kings.

- 1 Kings continues the Old Testament narrative where the book of 2 Samuel ended.

- The books of 1 and 2 Kings in our Bible appear in the Hebrew Bible as one book.

- The date of the writing of 1 Kings is approximately between 562 and 536 B.C., and though tradition has assigned its authorship to Jeremiah, it was most likely written by a Jewish captive in Babylon under the inspiration of the Holy Spirit.

- Though the books of Kings and Chronicles cover the same basic time period and content, they were written from different perspectives. The books of 1 and 2 Kings were written from a *prophetic* standpoint, and the books of 1 and 2 Chronicles were written from a *priestly* standpoint.

Whether it be in nations, corporations or churches, every transition from one leader to another has the potential to become extremely volatile. In 1 Kings 1, as a new king was about to be installed in Israel, what should have produced an exciting and new beginning filled with fresh vision and innovative ideas quickly became a powder keg as *egos* began to rise and *opinions* began to swarm like flies around raw meat. As Absalom sought to usurp the kingship from their father David, Adonijah sought to usurp the kingship from the rightful heir to the throne, their younger brother, Solomon.

It is amazing how people who should know better—in this case, Abiathar the priest; Joab, David's general; and all of the sons of the king (1:19)—actually champion the cause of someone like Adonijah. This man had an ego problem as big and as obvious as Lucifer's in Isaiah 14:13–14: "I will...I will...I will...I will...I will!" Still, people allow themselves to be won over by self-serving, self-promoting power seekers. If someone desires a leadership position, but violates God's structure of authority to get there, such antics will be only a taste of his behavior when he assumes the position! When God is orchestrating the installment of a new leader, however, there will be no violation of the principles of character, integrity, or scripture!

It is also amazing how good men in positions of leadership—in this case, David—often fail to implement a smooth succession strategy. Were it not for the boldness and tenacity of Bathsheba and Nathan the prophet, Israel might have missed God's selection for their next king: Solomon. 1 Kings 1:6 is actually astounding: "And his [Adonijah's] father [David] had not displeased him at any time in saying, Why hast thou done so?" Undisciplined children grow up to be self-seeking, self-willed, and self-indulgent adults! Adonijah is a perfect example!

As David prepares to die in chapter 2, his parting charge to his son and newly installed king was to "Man up!" (2:2). And with the kingdom in its present state, he was certainly going to need to do just that! His father had left some unfinished business that would require Solomon's immediate attention (2:5, 9) and would result in the execution of four key men in the kingdom. This, too, becomes the plight of many newly installed leaders. It often falls their lot to clean house, as it were, so that the new regime can actually be established (2:12). Those kind of bold moves for a new leader have the potential to be majorly misunderstood, but are often necessary in order for the new leader to actually lead.

In chapter 3, Solomon illustrates how a believer can love the Lord and still make major compromises that, in time, will cause that love to wane (3:3). Solomon genuinely loves the Lord, as evidenced by his request when the Lord offers to give him whatever he wanted. And yet, the connection he makes with the king of Egypt and his marriage to his daughter will become the things that ultimately lead to Solomon's demise (3:1).

Perhaps the exorbitant number of sacrifices (a thousand of them!) that Solomon offered (3:4) were an attempt to convince himself that his compromises weren't actually infringing upon his love for the Lord. Often when people over-do their spiritual responsibilities, it can be an attempt to compensate for an area or areas of clear disobedience. Perhaps we all should stop to consider the same for our lives. Though I love the Lord enough today to still be pursuing Him through His Word, is it possible that I am doing it as an attempt to overshadow compromises that I am making in my walk with the Lord? Am I violating clear commands of Scripture that, like Solomon, could in time overtake my love for the Lord? Remember the words of Samuel under the inspiration of the Holy Spirit in 1 Samuel 15:22: "Hath the Lord as great delight in burnt offerings and sacrifices, as in obeying the voice of the Lord? Behold, to obey is better than sacrifice, and to hearken than the fat of rams."

CHRIST IS REVEALED:

Through *Solomon*, the Son of David, sitting on the throne of David with his kingdom established – 1 Kings 2:12 (Luke 1:32; Mark 11:10)

WEEK 16, DAY 1: **TODAY'S READING: 1 KINGS 4-6**

OVERVIEW:

Solomon's key men; the kings of the earth come to hear Solomon; the preparation for building the Temple; the specifics in building the Temple.

HIGHLIGHTS & INSIGHTS:

It's easy to allow the material prosperity and blessing described in 1 Kings 4 to fool us. Under Solomon's leadership, the multitude of Judah and Israel were "eating and drinking, and making merry" (4:20). As wonderful as it was, however, their *financial* and *material* prosperity were not commensurate with their *spiritual* prosperity (3 John 2). There is absolutely no mention of how these abundantly blessed people were pursuing God through His word! I call this "the *curse* of God's *blessing*." We can spend so much time relishing God's blessings that we no longer have time for Him! We begin seeking the *blessing* rather than the *Bless-er* ... the *gift* rather than the *Giver* ... and the *things* of God rather than *God Himself*!

This chapter describes the kingdom of Israel at its zenith (4:21; Gen 15:18). The peace and prosperity they were experiencing was unequaled in their history (4:24–25). Its splendor will only be surpassed when the Son of David, our Lord Jesus Christ, rules and reigns from His throne in Jerusalem in His millennial kingdom!

1 Kings 4 also provides a description of the nature of Solomon's kingdom and his incredible accomplishments. First, it is unbelievably impressive! His unsurpassed wealth (vs. 22–23); the vastness of his kingdom (vs. 24–25); the governmental administration he established, the elite staff he had assembled, and the manner in which he provided for them (vs. 26–28); the wisdom and understanding that God had lavished upon him (vs. 29–31); his skill in composing songs and proverbs (vs. 32); and the grasp and insight he had concerning nature (vs. 33–34) were all beyond human comparison!

Secondly, all of those impressive characteristics provide keen insight as to the kind of wisdom for which he asked the Lord and which the Lord gave him. It wasn't *spiritual* wisdom that would give him deep insight into God and His Word, but rather a *practical* wisdom that would give him, as J. Sidlow Baxter noted, "administrative discernment, sagacious judgment, intellectual grasp, aptitude for the acquisition of knowledge, a practical wisdom in the directing of affairs."[1] We should not disdain Solomon's choice of wisdom, but we should also avoid being so enamored of his achievements that we become blind to the fact none of the description concerning Solomon in 1 Kings 4 relates to the passion of his heart for the Word of God or the God of the Word. Solomon, at least at this point, was a good man who loved the Lord, and as we will see, he will become one of the most perfect types of Christ in the entire Bible. But it is this kind of spiritual omission that will ultimately cause the "wisest man in who ever lived" to foolishly become one of the most perfect types of Antichrist in the entire Bible!

After organizing the structure of the kingdom's government, Solomon turns his attention in chapter 5 to establishing the physical structure of the King's Temple. We can begin to grasp the magnitude of the project by noting that the number of men contracted to fulfill a role in this undertaking was over 183,000! (See 2 Chron. 2:17–18.)

Chapter 6 details the dimensions, materials and actual construction of the Temple. Solomon's Temple, surprisingly wasn't actually a large structure. At 120 feet by 60 feet, its footprint was exactly double that of the tabernacle (approximately 36.6 meters by 18.3 meters). As Dr. John Kitto noted, "The importance of the Temple of Solomon, which we have been led to regard as one of the wonders of the ancient world, consisted not in its size, but in the elaborate, costly, and highly decorative character of its whole interior and furniture, and also in the number, extent, grandeur, and substantial masonry of its surrounding courts, chambers, walls and towers. Indeed, it is not too much to presume that these outer constructions, forming the massive ring in which the costly gem of the Temple was set, cost as much as the sacred building itself, immense as was the quantity of gold bestowed upon it."[2] 1 Kings 6:21 says, "So Solomon overlaid the house within with pure gold." Of course in the church age, the Lord no longer dwells in temples made with hands (Acts 7:48; 17:24) but has made our bodies His very temple (1 Cor. 6:19). May we, likewise, be "overlaid" with "pure gold" (1 Cor. 3:12).

The chapter ends in 6:38 with the statement, "So was he [Solomon] seven years in building it." Keep in mind, the number seven in the Bible is the number of completion and perfection. The Temple was *completed* in the seventh year, in accordance with God's *perfect* instruction.

CHRIST IS REVEALED:

Through *Solomon*, as the kings come before Him to seek His wisdom – 1 Kings 4:34 (Christ will one day rule the world as Israel's King in his millennial reign, and every knee will bow before Him – Phil. 2:9–11)

[1] J. Sidlow Baxter, *Explore the Book*, Grand Rapids, MI: Zondervan, 1960, p. 99.

[2] qtd. in J. Sidlow Baxter, *Explore the Book*, Grand Rapids, MI: Zondervan, 1960, p. 91.

WEEK 16, DAY 2: **TODAY'S READING: 1 KINGS 7-8**

OVERVIEW:

Building Solomon's house; the temple is furnished; the dedication of the temple.

HIGHLIGHTS & INSIGHTS:

The closing sentence of 1 Kings 6 was, "So was he [Solomon] seven years in building it [the Temple]." And what a glorious thing! God finally had a more permanent dwelling on the earth! However, the first two words of chapter 7 are very telling—"But Solomon." And at this point, Solomon joins a long list of good men in the Bible, from Adam to Noah to Abraham to David, whose testimonies were tainted by that same word.

Because, though Solomon was seven years in building *the Lord's House* (6:38), he spent *thirteen years* on his own house (7:1). It took almost twice as long to build *his own house* as it did the Lord's! And we may have to take some variables into consideration. There may not have been 183,000 workers constructing Solomon's house. And the materials used in Solomon's house may not have been prepared before they were shipped as they were with the Lord's house. But regardless, the way the Holy Spirit inspired the writing here forces us to contrast the amount of time it took to complete both houses.

And in the very next verse we're forced to make another very telling contrast. Back in 6:2 we are told the dimensions of the Temple: "the length thereof was threescore cubits, and the breadth thereof twenty cubits, and the height thereof thirty cubits." But here, in 7:2, we are told the dimensions of Solomon's house: "the length thereof was an hundred cubits, and the breadth thereof fifty cubits, and the height thereof thirty cubits." Not only did Solomon's own house take almost twice as long to build, it was also almost twice as big!

Solomon was certainly passionate about the Lord's *name* and the Lord's *house*. There was only one problem. He was twice as interested in his *own name* and his *own house*. May each of us to look at our own life and ask: "Am I any different than Solomon?" Whatever our passion for the Lord's *name*, are we more interested in our *own name*, our *own finances*, our *own house*, and our *own possessions*? Because no matter how blessed of the Lord we are, or how wise or sincere we are, or how big of a priority we think Jesus has in our life today, as long as we are in this body of flesh, we are never going to be free from the temptation to make our *own name* and our *own house* a bigger priority than the Lord's!

Chapter 7 details the specific instruction concerning the construction of the Temple. This building would become the dwelling place of God, but in the church age, Paul said we are the temple of God (1 Cor. 6:19). The New Testament is our detailed instruction for building a life that is worthy of the dwelling place of Almighty God. May we follow God's instruction concerning our spiritual temple as Solomon did for this physical temple.

At the end of chapter 7, "Solomon brought in the things which David his father had dedicated; even the silver, and the gold, and the vessels, did he put among the treasures of the house of the Lord." David made an unselfish and passionate investment of his life and resources into a Temple he knew he would never see. May we likewise unselfishly invest in the "temples" of our physical and spiritual children and grandchildren—a spiritual and moral legacy that can cause the glory of the Lord to fill them! (See 1 Kings 8.)

CHRIST IS REVEALED:

As the *Glory of God* filling His temple – 1 Kings 8:10–11 (John 1:14; Isa. 40:5; Matt. 16:27–17:2)

WEEK 16, DAY 3: **TODAY'S READING: 1 KINGS 9-11**

OVERVIEW:

God speaks to Solomon; the Queen of Sheba comes to Solomon; Solomon's kingdom increases in wealth; Solomon's heart is turned away; God's judgment upon Solomon.

HIGHLIGHTS & INSIGHTS:

Chapter 9 begins with God speaking to Solomon a second time. Twenty years have passed since their conversation in 1 Kings 3. God confirms that He wants to bless Solomon the way He blessed his father David, but also lets him know that such blessing was conditional. If Solomon walked in "integrity of heart" and in "uprightness" and kept God's statutes and judgments (9:4), he and the kingdom of Israel would be established and blessed. But if Solomon turned his back on God, no longer kept His commandments and statues, and began serving and worshipping other gods, the kingdom of Israel would be cursed. The choice seems like the biggest no-brainer in history, but today's reading reveals just how poorly Solomon chose. Before we judge Solomon too harshly, however, let's remember that God sets before each one of us a similar choice. Every day we choose whether we will sow to our flesh or sow to the Spirit (Gal. 6:7–8). May God help us to make better daily choices than Solomon ultimately made.

At this point in his story, Solomon is presented as what is perhaps the greatest type of Christ in the entire Bible. Biblically, he is identified as …

- The "prince of peace." (He was King David's son, and his name means "peace" – Isa. 9:6; 2 Sam. 12:24)

- The "beloved of the Father." (Solomon was also called Jedidiah, meaning "beloved of Jehovah" or God the Father – Matt. 3:17; 2 Sam. 12:25)

- The "son of David." (Prov. 1:1; Matt. 1:1)

- The "son of Jehovah." (1 Chron. 28:6; Luke 1:32)

- The "man of rest." (1 Chron. 22:9; Heb. 4:8–10)

- The one who sat "upon the throne of the kingdom of the Lord." (1 Chr. 28:5; Rev. 3:21)

- The one whose kingdom was a kingdom of "peace and rest." (1 Chr. 22:9; Isa. 9:7)

- The one whose kingdom was a kingdom with "no adversary" present. (1 Kings 5:4; Rev. 20:2–3)

- The one whose presence was sought by "all the earth" and "all the kings of the earth." (1 Kings 10:24; 2 Chron. 9:23; Rev. 21:24)

Unfortunately, Solomon goes from being perhaps the greatest type of *Christ* in chapter 10 to perhaps the greatest type of *Antichrist* in chapter 11! And the fact that this *could* happen to Solomon and *did* happen to Solomon should cause every one of us to sit up and take notice! Because probably none of us are more sincere and well-meaning than Solomon was. None of us have had the deck more stacked in our favor than Solomon did. And certainly, none of us have more wisdom than Solomon did, not to mention knowledge and understanding!

So what happened to Solomon?

Well, yesterday we saw that his *own house* was twice the size of *the Lord's house* and took twice as long to build. Though Solomon was obedient to his calling, there was an obvious *preoccupation* that he had with *self*. But that's certainly not all!

There was his *attraction* to *women*. 1 Kings 11:1–3 says:

> But king Solomon loved many strange women, together with the daughter of Pharaoh, women of the Moabites, Ammonites, Edomites, Zidonians, and Hittites: Of the nations concerning which

the Lord said unto the children of Israel, Ye shall not go in to them, neither shall they come in unto you: for surely they will turn away your heart after their gods: Solomon clave unto these in love. And he had seven hundred wives, princesses, and three hundred concubines: and his wives turned away his heart.

Then there was his *accumulation* of *wealth*. 1 Kings 10:14 says: "Now the weight of gold that came to Solomon in one year was six hundred threescore and six talents of gold." (Biblically, the number 6-6-6 in the Bible is always associated with the Antichrist (Rev. 13:18), what 1 John 4:3 calls the "spirit of antichrist.")

And lastly, there was his *connection* to *Egypt*. Egypt, in the Bible, is always a picture of the world and sin. God "brought out" his people from Egypt, but never wanted his people to bring out anything from there (Isa. 31:1–3; Gen. 50:24–25). In fact, in Deuteronomy 17:17, God had specifically forbidden the kings of Israel to conduct any type of business with Egypt, to multiply wives, or to accumulate gold. Solomon would have known that had he followed the instruction of Deuteronomy 17:18—to make his own copy of the law! When we distance ourselves from the Word of God, the compromises we will make will be astounding and the consequences far-reaching.

But Solomon was not the only one at risk in these areas. The truth is that Solomon was overtaken by the same four things that overtake believers to this day!

- Preoccupation of self (2 Tim. 3:2; Phil. 2:21)
- Attraction to women (Matt. 5:27–28; 2 Pet. 2:14)
- Accumulation of wealth (Col. 3:1–2; Matt. 6:19–21)
- Connection to Egypt (the world) (Jas. 4:4; 2 Cor. 6:14–18)

We must constantly be on our guard against the seductive pull of these temptations.

CHRIST IS REVEALED:

Through *Solomon* ruling in Jerusalem as the leaders of the world seek him and his wisdom – 1 Kings 10:1–6 (Phil. 2:9–11)

WEEK 16, DAY 4: **TODAY'S READING: 1 KINGS 12-15**

OVERVIEW:

Rehoboam becomes king; the kingdom is divided; Jeroboam is made king of Israel and institutes false worship; the prophet of God rebukes Jeroboam; God judges Jeroboam's house; the temple looted under Rehoboam's reign; the reigns of Abijam and Asa in Judah; the reign of Nadab and Baasha in Israel.

HIGHLIGHTS & INSIGHTS:

In chapter 12, Rehoboam, Solomon's son, becomes king after his father's death. If he rules wisely, he is in position to win the affection of the people and establish his leadership in the kingdom. But on the question of the Temple, he decides foolishly. The Temple-building project had given the nation of Israel great notoriety, but the taxes to fund it had become burdensome to the people. The old men counsel Rehoboam that if he will be a servant-leader to the people, they would follow him to the ends of the earth. The young men give him the opposite advice. They tell him that the way to establish his leadership was to be a dictator and increase the burden of their taxes. Rehoboam follows the young men.

Chapter 12, therefore, marks a key division in the book of 1 Kings—and in the kingdom. Chapters 1–11 detail the incredible forty years of Solomon's reign in the *united* kingdom in Israel. Chapters 12–22 detail the first eighty years of the *divided* kingdom, known as Israel and Judah respectively. Jeroboam becomes the king of Israel, comprised of ten of the twelve tribes, while Rehoboam is left to be the king of the two remaining tribes, Judah and Benjamin. The ten tribes become the *northern* kingdom with Samaria as its capital, while the two tribes become the *southern* kingdom, maintaining Jerusalem as its capital.

Just as Rehoboam foolishly followed the wrong counsel, Jeroboam, likewise, exercises a major lack of wisdom that seals its doom of the northern kingdom. He feared that, if the people returned to Jerusalem to participate in the annual feasts, he would begin to lose his jurisdiction over them. So to make it convenient for the people to worship, he set up one golden calf in Dan and another one in Bethel. The demonic worship in these two places included an entire blasphemous priesthood—with Jeroboam himself burning incense at the altar as if he were a priest.

Rehoboam and Jeroboam, just like many leaders throughout history, sought to lead from a position of power and pride, rather than a position of service and humility. Once a leader feels the need to protect his position or power, there is no limit to the carnal absurdities that will follow. Pray that your pastor will humbly follow Jesus's leadership style and that he will be passionate about seeking to protect Christ's glory in the church rather than his own.

The remainder of 1 Kings records the reigns of the various kings in the divided kingdom. The kings' names, the length of their reign, and Scripture's verdict concerning them are very interesting to note.

In Judah (4 kings in approximately 86 years)

1. Rehoboam (17 years)—EVIL.

2. Abijam (3 years)—EVIL.

3. Asa (41 years)—GOOD.

4. Jehosophat (25 years)—GOOD.

In ISRAEL (8 kings in approximately 86 years)

1. Jeroboam (22 years)—EVIL.

2. Nadab (2 years)—EVIL.

3. Baasha (24 years)—EVIL.

4. Elah (2 years)—EVIL.

5. Zimri (1 week)—EVIL.

6. Omri (12 years)—EVIL.

7. Ahab (22 years)—EVIL.

8. Ahaziah (2 years)—EVIL.

CHRIST IS REVEALED:

In the *Prophecy of Josiah* – 1 Kings 13:2 (Another Child shall come that shall judge the false gods and false worship of this world – 2 Thess. 1:7–10; Rev. 18:1–2, 10, 21)

WEEK 16, DAY 5: **TODAY'S READING: 1 KINGS 16-19**

OVERVIEW:

The corruption of the early kings of Israel; Elijah prophecies the drought; Elijah is fed miraculously; the widow obeys God's Word; the widow's son is raised from the dead; Elijah confronts Ahab; Elijah takes on the prophets of Baal; the Lord reveals Himself as the Lord; Elijah flees Jezebel; Elijah hears the still small voice of God; Elijah puts his mantle on Elisha.

HIGHLIGHTS & INSIGHTS:

In the northern kingdom, the pattern of Israel's kings was one of apostasy. Each one turned from God and His Word and suffered God's judgment. However, the climax of evil and carnality was reached in Ahab. 1 Kings 16:33 says, "Ahab did more to provoke the Lord God of Israel to anger than all the kings of Israel that were before him." That, my friend, is quite a statement, because the holy Lord God of Israel had been provoked a *lot*! (See 1 Kings 16:7, 13, 25–26.)

In the midst of Ahab's wicked reign, God raised up one of Israel's most powerful and well-known prophets. (In fact, he will be one of the prophets God raises back up to preach during the wicked reign of the Antichrist during the second half of the Tribulation in Rev. 11:3–6.) When God gave Elijah the words He wanted spoken, Elijah wasn't afraid of putting them out there, regardless of who the audience was!

A great case in point is 1 Kings 17:1. Elijah gets up in King Ahab's stuff and says, "As the Lord God of Israel liveth, before whom I stand, there shall not be dew nor rain these years, but according to my word" (or "until I say it will"). By the time they see each other again in 18:17, three and a half years have passed, and just like Elijah said, there hadn't been a single drop of moisture! The scene in Israel was one of crisis. There are no lakes, streams or pools of water anywhere. Not only has this led to a physical crisis, but an economic, political, moral, and spiritual crisis as well! (And note that this drought will be repeated when Elijah returns to prophesy during the Tribulation – Rev. 11:6.)

When they met again, Ahab says, "Well, if it isn't the big trouble-maker in Israel himself!" Elijah retorts, "You took the words right out of my mouth!" Elijah then nails him to the wall, declaring Ahab's guilt in refusing to follow the Word of God and leading the people of Israel to follow Baalim. Given what it about to happen, it's important to know that Baal was the sun god, or the god of fire, and his worship included all kinds of sexual perversion and debauchery.

In 18:19, Elijah calls for a showdown! He tells Ahab to gather the 450 prophets of Baal and the 400 prophets of the groves that his wife, Jezebel, has been funding. He wants all 850 of them, and all the people of Israel, to meet him at Mount Carmel to prove who the true God in Israel was, once and for all. Ahab agrees (v. 20). When they get to Mount Carmel, Elijah walks up to the platform where all 850 of Jezebel's vile prophets were assembled, looks out on all of the people of Israel, and in 18:21, he laid out God's challenge.

He basically says, "This half-Baal/half-Jehovah trash has gotta stop! You can't pick and choose what you want out of each of them, and God has had enough! If the Lord (Jehovah, the God of the Bible) is God, then adjust your lifestyle and follow Him! But, if you're so demented that you actually think that Baal is the true God—and not just your excuse for gratifying yourself sexually—then sell yourself out to him and forget Jehovah God altogether! Either way, it's time to get off of the fence. Go one way or the other!" Wow! That sounds a whole lot like the message God wants to give to the church in the twenty-first century! Oh, that God would raise up some Elijahs in these days!

When Elijah finished, the people have absolutely no response. They are halted, stuck in the middle between two contrary worlds. So in 18:23–24, Elijah says, "Okay, you 850 guys come over to this altar for Baal, and you prepare the sacrifice of a bullock. And since Baal is the so-called god of fire, don't put any fire under the sacrifice." He took the second altar for Jehovah: "I'll use this altar, the one that's broken down from lack of use, and I'll prepare the sacrifice of a bullock, and I won't put any fire under it either. Then the God who consumes the sacrifice with fire, let Him be the true God in Israel, let's all wholeheartedly follow Him, and let's put an end to all this dual worship and double-mindedness in Israel."

This time the people do have a response! They tell Elijah, "We like it! Let's go for it" (18:24).

So the 850 false prophets prepared the sacrifice and cried out to Baal for six solid hours. They threw themselves on the altar to try to get some response out of him and cut themselves so that blood was gushing out and covering the altar! At noon, Elijah mockingly says to them, "Hey fellas! Maybe your 'god' is busy talking with someone, or chasing after somebody, or on a long trip somewhere. Or maybe he's sleeping!"

Elijah then repairs the broken-down altar to Jehovah, digs a trench around it, and puts the wood underneath the bullock. But before he prays to the one true God to answer with fire, he has four barrels of water poured over the sacrifice. Then he calls for a second round of four barrels to be poured over it—and a third! By this time the water has fully engulfed the sacrifice and was laying in the trenches surrounding it.

Then, without any fanfare, drama, or religious shenanigans, Elijah prays a simple prayer. In English, the entire prayer is a grand total of sixty-three words. It takes about 16.5 seconds to pray the entire prayer! And yet, as soon as his prayer was concluded, the fire of God fell from heaven and consumed the sacrifice, along with all of the water that was in the trenches surrounding the sacrifice.

Often, when we read of a dramatic move of God like this, we assume Elijah could it pull off because he was some kind of extraordinary guy. Thankfully, God anticipated that we might pass off the power that was manifested through Elijah by skewed thinking like that. So in the New Testament, He tells us Elijah was a man who was made of the same stuff as all the rest of us, a man who faced all of the same struggles we face. In other words, he was an average, ordinary guy, but he was a guy who possessed the fire of God's presence and power on his life! James 5:17–18 says, "Elias [the Greek version of the Hebrew *Elijah*] was a man subject to like passions as we are, and he prayed earnestly that it might not rain, and it rained not on the earth by the space of three years and six months. And he prayed again, and the heaven gave rain, and the earth brought forth her fruit."

And do you remember Elijah's challenge to the people in 1 Kings 18:21? "If the Lord be God, follow him: but if Baal, then follow him." Well, they finally got it! No more double-mindedness. In fact, notice the double declaration in 18:39: *"The Lord, he is the God; the Lord, he is the God."* Hallelujah!

People in the twenty-first century ask, "Where is the Lord God of Elijah?" But God asks the people of the twenty-first century, "Where are the Elijahs of the Lord God?"

CHRIST IS REVEALED:
As the *Fire of God* consuming the sacrifice – 1 Kings 18:38 (Heb. 12:29)

WEEK 17, DAY 1: **TODAY'S READING: 1 KINGS 20–22**

OVERVIEW:

Syria attacks Israel twice; Ahab spares the Syrian king; Ahab's purchase of Naboth's vineyard; Israel and Judah unite against Syria; the death of Ahab.

HIGHLIGHTS & INSIGHTS:

Benhadad, the king of Syria, conspired with thirty-two other kings to besiege Samaria, the northern kingdom's capital city. He sent a message to King Ahab telling him that the conditions of his surrender would be all of his silver and gold and the very best of his wives and children. Unable to resist such a formidable alliance of nations, Ahab reluctantly concedes. Benhadad responds with another message declaring that his servants would enter the city to plunder Ahab's house and the houses of all of his servants (1 Kings 20:1–4).

King Ahab calls an emergency meeting with the elders of Israel who are adamant that Ahab refuse Benhadad's second demand. He does, and Benhadad is so angry that he declares that, by the time he finishes, there won't be enough of Samaria left to give his servants each a handful of its dust (20:10)! Ahab tauntingly replies that a soldier putting on his armor shouldn't boast like someone who is taking his armor off after a victory. When Benhadad receives the message while he and all of his "kingly buddies" were together partying—Ahab's taunt worked! Benhadad immediately called his soldiers to action (20:12).

Just then, a prophet comes to Ahab and tells him that despite the incredible number of soldiers in Benhadad's combined armies, the Lord would provide the victory using a relatively small Israeli army, leaving no doubt whatsoever that the Lord was the one who granted the victory (20:13).

Ahab rallies his troops. Benhadad, on the other hand, and his posse of kings were already drunk. When his soldiers informed him that the Israelite army was approaching, he foolishly orders them not to kill them, but to take them as hostages. Such a passive battle plan put his soldiers at a major disadvantage, and those who weren't killed were forced to retreat. After Ahab's victory, the prophet returned informing Ahab to go regroup himself and his troops, because Benhadad and his armies would be returning within the year (20:16–22).

Meanwhile, King Benhadad's men let their General-King know that they could defeat Israel by doing three things:

1) Fight them in the plain, not the hill country, because Israel's gods must be gods of the hills (20:23).
2) Replace the posse of kings with real military strategists (20:24).
3) Rebuild the combined armies, horses and chariots to the number they had before the devastating defeat. (20:25)

Benhadad complied with all of their counsel and demands, and several months later, he again leads the attack against Israel. From a distance, Israel looked like two small flocks of goats compared to Benhadad's armies. The prophet returned, however, to tell Ahab that God would once again show Himself mighty on their behalf—especially since they had said that Israel's God was "God of the hills, but he is not God of the valleys" (20:28). By the end of this seven-day war, the Israelite army had killed 100,000 Syrian soldiers! The Syrians sought refuge in the walled city of Aphek, but its wall fell, killing all 27,000 of the remaining soldiers (20:26-30). Go God!

Benhadad's servants approach Ahab under the guise of surrender, requesting that he spare Benhadad's life. During the encounter, Ahab says, "Oh, is *my brother* Benhadad, still alive?" The servants pick up on the whole "my brother" thing, and the result was that Ahab tells them to bring Benhadad to him. When he arrives, Benhadad promises to restore the cities that had been taken from his forefathers and to institute an urban renewal program, as it were. Then, rather than kill him as God had said, Ahab foolishly enters into an alliance with him (20:31–34).

As Ahab makes his way back home, God sends a prophet to illustrate Ahab's disobedience in not destroying Benhadad. God tells Ahab that his life will be taken for Benhadad's life (20:35–43).

Chapter 21 is the story of Naboth's vineyard where Ahab reveals himself to be nothing but a selfish, self-serving, self-seeking, spoiled brat (and those were his good qualities)! It's a sad epithet that's recorded in 21:25: "But there was none like unto Ahab, which did sell himself to work wickedness in the sight of the Lord, whom Jezebel his wife stirred up."

In response to God's sentence against Ahab and Jezebel (21:17–24), Ahab displays some semblance of actually humbling himself (21:27). If you ever wanted to know just how gracious, long-suffering, merciful and forgiving our God is, listen to the words God spoke to Elijah concerning Ahab in the last verse of this chapter: "Seest thou how Ahab humbleth himself before me? because he humbleth himself before me, I will not bring the evil in his days: but in his son's days will I bring the evil upon his house" (21:29).

In Chapter 22, Jehoshaphat, who was actually a relatively good king, makes an unholy alliance with Ahab. May it serve as an Old Testament illustration and reminder to us of the New Testament truth of 2 Corinthians 6:14-18:

> Be ye not unequally yoked together with unbelievers: for what fellowship hath righteousness with unrighteousness? and what communion hath light with darkness? And what concord hath Christ with Belial? or what part hath he that believeth with an infidel? And what agreement hath the temple of God with idols? for ye are the temple of the living God; as God hath said, I will dwell in them, and walk in them; and I will be their God, and they shall be my people. Wherefore come out from among them, and be ye separate, saith the Lord, and touch not the unclean thing; and I will receive you, And will be a Father unto you, and ye shall be my sons and daughters, saith the Lord Almighty.

CHRIST IS REVEALED:

As *Micaiah*, the prophet of the Lord, speaking whatever the Lord (Father) wants him to speak – 1 Kings 22:14 (John 3:34; 14:10).

WEEK 17, DAY 2: **TODAY'S READING: 2 KINGS 1–4**

OVERVIEW:

Ahaziah sends 102 men to their death; Elijah is taken up; Elisha is established as a prophet; Moab revolts; the miracles of Elisha.

HIGHLIGHTS & INSIGHTS:

The stubbornness and rebellion of man has no better example than Israel's King Ahaziah. He has seen and heard Elijah and the condemnation of Baal. He knows of the fire falling from heaven in judgment of Baal. But when faced with a pressing need in his life, rather than turn to the God who clearly manifested Himself as the one true God on Mount Carmel, Ahaziah still turns to Baal, the god of Ekron. Even when confronted with the truth from Elijah, he refuses to accept God's word, instead sending two captains and their respective fifty men to their deaths. How could a man be so blind? Could we ever be so blind? Yes, we could! Many times, when people (even believers) find themselves at a time of great need in their life, they don't turn to the holy and powerful God of the Bible who has proven Himself consistently and continuously for the past six thousand years. They turn rather to the "god of self" in its many forms (self-reliance, self-preservation, self-confidence, self-control, self-defense, self-determination, self-help, self-motivation, self-sufficiency, or self-will) or to the "god of money" to meet their need.

An interesting insight into the frailty of Elijah's humanness is shown in chapter 1. Even after God used him to call down fire from heaven on three separate occasions (1 Kings 18:37–39; 2 Kings 1:10, 12), the Lord still has to tell Elijah not to be afraid of the third captain sent by Ahaziah (1:15). This is the reality explained in James 5:16–18 that even though Elijah, the Prophet of Fire, tenaciously confronted kings and religious leaders with the word of the Lord, he was not a superhero. He had to deal with the same fears and weaknesses we face. God is clear that Elijah's greatness wasn't the power of his *person*, but simply the power of his *prayers*! And God's point is that, if we will be righteous men and women of fervent prayer, God's power will likewise be manifested through us.

In Chapter 2, Elisha follows and serves his leader to the end. Elisha had seen the *fire*, but what he wanted was the *Spirit*. He wasn't interested in demonstrating what Elijah demonstrated on the *outside*, he wanted what Elijah possessed on the *inside*. He understood the reality of Zechariah 4:6, that the Lord's work is "Not by might, nor by power, but by my Spirit, saith the Lord of Hosts."

In the New Testament, the Lord Jesus Christ gave us the promise of the Holy Spirit *living* and *abiding* in us in John 14–16. Paul writes that we are *sealed* with the Holy Spirit (2 Cor. 1:22; Eph. 1:13; 4:30), that we can be *filled* with the Spirit (Eph. 5:18) and manifest the *fruit* of the Spirit (Gal. 5:22–23), that we are *led* by the Spirit (Rom. 8:14), *taught* by the Spirit (1 Cor. 2:10) and *strengthened* by the Spirit (Eph. 3:16). In other words, we already have in our possession what Elisha passionately sought to receive! All we need on a daily and momentary basis is to surrender to the powerful Spirit of God that patiently waits to be released and manifested both *in* and *through* us!

Elijah is taken into heaven (2:11). Elijah's mantle is left to Elisha, and the Spirit of the Lord now works through him. The miracles will continue because Elisha will be doing the work of *God*, not the work of *Elijah*. In the last part of chapter 2, Elisha is confirmed by God in the sight of other men. Interestingly, Elisha asked that God pour out a double portion of the spirit of Elijah on him (2:9), and the number of his recorded miracles is double that of Elijah!

Chapter 3 details the deliverance of a good king (King Jehoshaphat of Judah) who gets involved with evil kings. Jehoram, Ahaziah's brother, now reigns over Israel. He put away the image of Baal, but kept the golden calf of Jeroboam (1 Kings 12:28) and reminds us of how few people offer the absolute and complete surrender the Lord requires! When Moab rebels against Israel, Jehoram calls on Jehoshaphat and the king of Edom to help. Jehoshaphat finds himself in the wrong place with the wrong people: in a desert with no water and no hope. Only then, does Jehoshaphat ask for the Lord's counsel. Elisha comes in, the Lord miraculously brings deliverance with the reflection of the sun upon water, and Israel's army defeats Moab.

Elisha miraculously helps other individuals in chapter 4. After Elisha gives a widow instruction, the Lord multiplies her only possession (a pot of oil) to pay her debts and meet her future needs (4:1–7). A woman who takes care of Elisha is given a son. When the son later dies in the field, the Lord brings him back to life through Elisha (4:8–37). A poisonous meal is purified and given to hungry men (4:38–41). Firstfruit offerings are multiplied to meet the needs of many people (4:42–44).

As Elisha's life demonstrated, the Spirit of God abiding in and controlling a person brings blessing, joy and hope to men and brings glory to God! For God's glory, then, may the power of the Holy Spirit be manifest through us, as it was through Elisha!

CHRIST IS REVEALED:

As *Judge of the Unbelievers* – 2 Kings 1 (Rev. 19:11–20:15).

As *Giver of the Spirit* – 2 Kings 2:9 (John 14:16–17).

As the *Ascended Savior* – 2 Kings 2:11 (Luke 24:51; Acts 1:9).

As the *Giver of Life* – 2 Kings 4:17 (John 6:33; 10:28; 1 John 5:11).

As the *Multiplier of Food* – 2 Kings 4:42–44 (Matt. 14:16–21; 15:32–38).

WEEK 17, DAY 3: **TODAY'S READING: 2 KINGS 5–8**

OVERVIEW:

Healing of Naaman; miracles of Elisha; a great famine and deliverance; further decline of Israel and Judah.

HIGHLIGHTS & INSIGHTS:

The healing of Naaman, the leprous Gentile, in 2 Kings 5 is one of the best-known stories of the Old Testament. Naaman was a very impressive man. He was "captain of the host of the king of Syria," a "great" and "honourable" man God had use as a "deliverer" and a "mighty man in valour" (5:1). All of the accolades mean nothing, however, because "he was a leper." None of his earthly accomplishments could overcome his dreaded and incurable disease. More than that, however, leprosy in the Bible is consistently a picture of sin. As with Naaman, none of our accomplishments or greatness can overcome the reality of our sin.

After Naaman hears of God's prophet in Israel who could heal him, he packs up his great possessions, assembles his entourage, and departs for places of power and influence. But there was no remedy there. Had Elisha not called him to his house, Naaman would have had no hope. Out of pride, Naaman initially rejected the remedy offered to him, but his ultimate obedience brought healing, and Naaman went home in peace (5:19). In the same way, the cure for our sin is always and only a gift from God (Rom. 6:23), revealed by a servant of God (Rom. 10:14). And we, too, are given peace: "Therefore being justified by faith, we have peace with God through our Lord Jesus Christ" (Rom. 5:1).

The rest of the story focuses on Elisha's servant, Gehazi. Here again, we find that haunting word that often precedes men's names in Scripture—*But.* 2 Kings 5:20 says, "But Gehazi, the servant of Elisha the man of God, said, Behold, my master hath spared Naaman this Syrian, in not receiving at his hands that which he brought: but, as the Lord liveth, I will run after him, and take somewhat of him." Naaman had offered expensive gifts for his healing (5:5), and Gehazi was quite willing to take them. After his deception and lies, however, the judgment of God came upon him. Even in the twenty-first century, the *Word* and *work* of the Lord are still being tarnished by the greed, deception and lies of some so-called servants of the Lord (5:20, 25).

In 2 Kings 6, Elisha and a young servant are in a city surrounded by bands of Syrians. Elisha had warned King Jehoram of the locations of the Syrians more than once. The Syrians had now compassed the city, terrifying the young man. Without fear, Elisha tells him, "They that be with us are more than they that be with them" (6:16). God opened the young man's eyes to the spiritual reality of the battle that Elisha had already seen. The attackers are drawn into the city, blinded, and led to the middle of Samaria. The Syrian bands are surrounded by Israel, given provisions, and sent back to Syria.

Like that young man, we must also learn to see with *spiritual* eyes and not just our *physical* ones (2 Cor. 4:18) Sadly, few Christians today have eyes to see the eternal realm though we are daily in the middle of a real, eternal, spiritual battle. Spiritual beings dwell and work in the unseen world above our heads and on the earth (Eph. 3:10; 6:12; Col. 1:16; 2:15; Rom. 8:38). Job 1 tells how they can cause physical effects on the earth and can influence people. But like Elisha's servant, we can take refuge in the fact that "greater is He that is in you than he that is in the world" (1 John 4:4). Christ has conquered our enemy in the unseen realm! Colossians 2:15 says, "And having spoiled principalities and powers, he (Christ!) made a show of them openly, triumphing over them in it."

A famine comes to the kingdom of Israel and is blamed on Elisha (2 Kings 6:25–33). As his father Ahab blamed Elijah for the troubles in Israel, King Jehoram blames Elisha. In chapter 7, however, the Lord causes the Syrians to hear the noise of a great army, and they flee, leaving behind a surplus of food and other provisions. God provides plenty for Israel, but judges the one man who rejects Elisha's prophecy in unbelief. The Lord can deal with groups and individuals simultaneously!

Chapter 8 continues with the decline of both Israel and Judah. Benhadad, the king of Syria, is murdered by Hazael. Jehoram, the son of Jehoshaphat, begins a short, but very evil reign. The chapter ends with Ahaziah, the son of Jehoram, reigning over Judah; and Joram, the son of Ahab, over Israel. As promised in 1 Kings 19:15–17, the wicked house of Ahab will soon be destroyed. God's judgment is sure.

CHRIST IS REVEALED:

As *one sent to the Gentiles* – 2 Kings 5:1–14 (Luke 4:27)

As *Healer of Leprosy* – 2 Kings 5:10 (Matt. 8:2-3; Mark 1:40–41)

As *Powerful Protector* – 2 Kings 6:16 (Luke 12:7; 1 John 4:4)

WEEK 17, DAY 4: **TODAY'S READING: 2 KINGS 9-12**

OVERVIEW:

Jehu executes judgment; Joash is spared and becomes king; Joash repairs the temple.

HIGHLIGHTS & INSIGHTS:

Two chapters in today's reading deal with Jehu, the king of Israel (9–10), and two deal with Joash, the king of Judah (11–12). Both men actually do God's work, but neither one will do it with a pure heart for God. The results will be short-lived, and because of their self-promotion, the Lord won't receive the glory that is due His name! Once again, there are many people today who do the Lord's work with the same self-aggrandizing motives and with the same results (2 Tim. 3:1–2).

Jehu was prophesied by name years earlier by Elijah (1 Kings 19:16). God intended to use this man to completely remove the lineage of the wicked Ahab. This promised avenger could have brought great glory to God by fulfilling His purpose and demonstrating to the world the incredible trustworthiness of God's promises, but he failed to do so because of his extreme cruelty and pride. Just as in the case of Jehu, God has each of us here on a specific mission. Our job is to completely embrace God's purpose for our existence and to fulfill it! Paul said in Philippians 3:12, "But I follow after, if that I may apprehend that for which also I am apprehended of Christ Jesus." In other words, the Lord Jesus had a specific purpose for his life when He took Paul into His possession, and Paul was going to do everything within his power to take that purpose into his possession. Oh, may we have the same passion as Paul!

In chapter 9, Jehu executes judgment on Joram, the king of Israel, along with Ahaziah, the king of Judah, and Jezebel, the wife of Ahab. In chapter 10, Jehu continues with his judgment upon all of the descendants of Ahab and all of the Baal worshippers in Israel. He accomplishes the tasks with intimidation (10:3–4), ruthlessness (10:14), pride (10:16) and deception (10:18–19). Jehu is rewarded for removing Baal and the house of Ahab, but because he continued the worship of the golden calf, disregarding the law of the Lord, Israel moves closer to captivity (10:32).

Chapters 11 and 12 take us to the kingdom of Judah. When Ahaziah is killed by Jehu, his mother, Athaliah ruthlessly kills all of her grandsons so that she can sit her sorry behind on the throne in Judah. Maybe you have to be a grandparent to understand the full horror of something so inhumane, but it is one of the most despicable acts in all of Scripture. The Lord hides one baby boy, Joash, from the slaughter. A faithful priest, Jehoiada, raises the boy for six years and then orchestrates his coronation as the king of Judah at the ripe old age of seven! Athaliah is removed from the throne, and Joash (also called Jehoash) becomes king.

He is a good king all of the days of Jehoiada, but "after the death of Jehoiada came the princes of Judah, and made obeisance to the king. Then the king hearkened unto them" (2 Chron. 24:17). We must be discerning with the counsel we receive and the voices we listen to! Clearly, the spiritual discernment and commitment to the Lord that Joash seemed to exercise wasn't really his own personal faith, but the faith of Jehoiada. We must do what we do because of our own personal faith and surrender to the Lordship of Christ, not because of our pastor, our parents, our discipler, our friends or our fellow church members. Sadly, the compromise of Joash led to the severe judgment of God, not only in Joash's life, but in the entire land of Judah. The effects of sin are far-reaching!

CHRIST IS REVEALED:

As the *Avenger* – 2 Kings 9:7 (Rev. 6:9)

As the *Intercessor* – 2 Kings 11:17 (1 Tim. 2:5; Rom. 8:34)

WEEK 17, DAY 5: **TODAY'S READING: 2 KINGS 13-16**

OVERVIEW:

Israel is delivered into hand of Syria; the death of Elisha; three good kings in Judah; the final kings of Israel.

HIGHLIGHTS & INSIGHTS:

In today's reading, it gets a little tricky to keep the kings of Judah and Israel straight. Both kingdoms have a king named Ahaziah, and both kingdoms have a king named Joash, whose name is sometimes spelled Jehoash. They can be identified, however, by carefully noting which kingdom they're ruling or the name of their father. For example, King Joash of Judah, the son of Ahaziah, begins his reign in chapter 12 and does that which is right in the sight of the Lord. King Joash of Israel, the son of Jehoahaz, begins his reign in chapter 13 and does that which was evil in the sight of the Lord.

Another complication is that the stories of the two kingdoms are told in parallel. It would be impossible to record everything in chronological order, however, because the history of one king often overlaps multiple kings in the other kingdom. The death of Joash, the king of Israel, is told in both 2 Kings 13:13 and 14:16 because chapter 13 is telling the story in Israel and chapter 14 is telling the story in Judah. Obviously, careful reading is required in this section!

The end of chapter 13 records an incredible example of the enduring faithfulness of our Lord. Though Israel has repeatedly worshipped Baal and the golden calves, the Lord graciously expresses His compassion on them because of His covenant with Abraham, Isaac and Jacob.

The beginning of chapter 14 gives us insight into the effect of a father on his son (or of a discipler upon a disciple). Joash started his reign well, through the influence of Jehoiada the priest. Evidently, the teaching of Jehoiada not only affected Joash, but also reached to his son Amaziah (2 Kings 14:2). He did as his father Joash had done (v. 3), and he not only knew the commandment of the Lord from the book of Deuteronomy, but he also obeyed it (v. 6).

Chapter 15 continues with two more good kings of Judah: Azariah (also called Uzziah) and Jotham. Both did what was right in the sight of the Lord as their father had done, though after much success, Uzziah's heart was lifted up to his destruction (2 Chron. 26). May we learn from his example!

Though Judah has a series of good kings, Israel spiraled downward. Though Jeroboam has outward success, he did that which was evil and could never disconnect himself from idol worship. Zachariah, Shallum, Menahem, Pekahiah and Pekah continue the evil and bring Israel near captivity. Most of these kings are murdered—one after only a one-month reign! Menahem is a ruthless and cruel leader. Pekah and his army kill 120,000 men in one day of battle. Yet, in such a dark time, Isaiah prophesies that a virgin will conceive and bear a son, Immanuel (Isa. 7:14), and Isaiah 9 is written to a people in darkness that have seen a great light.

CHRIST IS REVEALED:

As *Savior* – 2 Kings 13:5 (Luke 2:11; Acts 5:31; 13:23)

As the *Resurrection* – 2 Kings 13:21 (John 11:25)

As the *Brasen Altar* – 2 Kings 16:14 (Heb. 9:14)

WEEK 18, DAY 1: **TODAY'S READING: 2 KINGS 17–20**

OVERVIEW:

Israel is carried away; the glorious reign of Hezekiah.

HIGHLIGHTS & INSIGHTS:

In 2 Kings 17, Assyria carries Israel into exile. God had repeatedly warned Israel, through his prophets and through His righteous judgment upon other nations, but now the hammer of His judgment falls. God was "ready to forgive" and "plenteous in mercy unto all them that call" (Ps. 86:5), but in 200 years, Israel's twenty kings refused to repent and obey the word of the Lord. As 2 Kings 17:14 says, "They would not hear." Instead 17:15 tells us:

> They rejected his statutes, and his covenant that he made with their fathers, and his testimonies which he testified against them; and they followed vanity, and became vain, and went after the heathen that were round about them, concerning whom the Lord had charged them, that they should not do like them.

Scripture is clear that God's judgment comes upon our lives because we persistently follow our own stubborn will and way (Prov. 29:1).

In chapters 18–20, we meet Hezekiah, a king unlike any other in the land of Judah. Rather than trusting his own will and way, this king actually "trusted in the Lord God" (18:5). He destroyed the idols and high places; he conquered the Philistines; he resisted the Assyrians; and he fortified his city and built great water works. But his real legacy is clear: "He did that which was right in the sight of the Lord, according to all that David his father did … And the Lord was with him" (2 Kings 18:3, 7).

Hezekiah's life was not without troubles though. His faith and dependence on the Lord were severely tested. His trust in the Lord was challenged and publicly ridiculed by the messengers from Assyria who spoke scornfully about his religious reforms. But Hezekiah's immediate response was to seek God through His word and prayer. God's answer returns: "Be not afraid … I will cause him to fall" (19:6–7). When a threatening letter came from the king of Assyria, once again, Hezekiah took it to the Lord in prayer, and once again, God answers: "The king of Assyria, He shall not come into this city" (19:32). Because of Hezekiah's faithful walk and relationship with the Lord, He miraculously delivers him and the land of Judah.

In chapter 20, Hezekiah's faith is tested once again, this time through his health. Verse 6 reveals that this time of trial comes during the conflicts with the king of Assyria. His public challenges were compounded by his private health issues. Hezekiah's response was simple and consistent: he prayed (20:2).

Through the trials and life of Hezekiah, God teaches us what it looks like to walk with the Lord and to trust in Him. Note some of the Psalms that Hezekiah exemplified through his life.

- *Psalm 18:30 – As for God, his way is perfect: the word of the Lord is tried: he is a buckler to all those that trust in him.*

- *Psalm 20:7 – Some trust in chariots, and some in horses: but we will remember the name of the Lord our God.*

- *Psalm 25:2 – O my God, I trust in thee: let me not be ashamed, let not mine enemies triumph over me.*

- *Psalm 32:10 – Many sorrows shall be to the wicked: but he that trusteth in the Lord, mercy shall compass him about.*

- *Psalm 33:21 – For our heart shall rejoice in him, because we have trusted in his holy name.*

- *Psalm 44:6 – For I will not trust in my bow, neither shall my sword save me.*

- *Psalm 56:11 – In God have I put my trust: I will not be afraid what man can do unto me.*

- *Psalm 118:8 – It is better to trust in the L*ORD *than to put confidence in man.*

- *Psalm 143:8 – Cause me to hear thy lovingkindness in the morning; for in thee do I trust: cause me to know the way wherein I should walk; for I lift up my soul unto thee.*

Like Hezekiah, may our lives reflect that same kind of bold trust in our trustworthy God!

CHRIST IS REVEALED:

As *Teacher* – 2 Kings 17:27 (Mark 4:1; John 3:2)

As the *Cleanser of the Temple* – 2 Kings 18:4 (Matt. 21:12; Mark 11:15; John 2:15)

As a *Man of Prayer* – 2 Kings 19:15 (John 17; Matt. 26:39; Luke 5:16; 22:32)

WEEK 18, DAY 2: **TODAY'S READING: 2 KINGS 21-25**

OVERVIEW:

Wicked Manasseh and Amon; the last good King, Josiah; four more evil kings; the Babylonian captivity.

HIGHLIGHTS & INSIGHTS:

The righteous leadership of Hezekiah for which we were refreshingly able to rejoice in yesterday's reading is quickly replaced by the overwhelming evil of his son, Manasseh. Though we read of his later repentance in 2 Chronicles 33, Jeremiah 15:4 says that the kingdom would be removed because of the deeds of Manasseh in Jerusalem. The deeds of a leader (husband, father, teacher, pastor) have a far-reaching effect for good or for bad.

Josiah, the last good king, did that which was right in the sight of the Lord. He had chosen to do right and restore the temple before the book of the law was found. The knowledge he received from the word of God would not have been revealed to him, however, had Josiah not already chosen to do right! God reveals to us in 2 Peter 1:5-7, that virtue (choosing to do right, and doing it!) is to be added to our faith, before beginning to add knowledge. If we have not already purposed in our hearts to follow the instruction of the Lord, what need is there to accumulate more knowledge?

With the "new knowledge" received from the "newly discovered" books of the Law, Josiah humbles himself before the Lord, makes a covenant to the Lord in the presence of all the people, and begins to cleanse the temple and the land.

He is used of God to remove the idols and the high places of worship in Jerusalem. Interestingly, notice that he carries the items of sin across the brook Kidron, destroys them, and then scatters the ashes on old graves. The Lord Jesus Christ crossed the very same brook, Kidron (or, Cedron), on the way to become sin for us on the cross — where they would be buried in His grave! (Joh. 18:1)

Josiah continues his cleansing reforms — and goes to Bethel to destroy the golden calf set up by Jeroboam. The idol worship that plagued the children of Israel throughout their entire history is finally destroyed by the one who was prophesied by name. The Lord tells us concerning Josiah in 2 Kings 23:25: "And like unto him was there no king before him, that turned to the Lord with all his heart, and with all his soul, and with all his might, according to all the law of Moses; neither after him arose there any like him." It is almost unbelievable, that not until Josiah, did any king ever go up to destroy the golden calf!

After such an incredible example set by Josiah, surprisingly enough, not a single one of the final four kings follow in his footsteps. As seen in today's reading, all four of them are weak, evil kings, who are actually controlled by other foreign kings. Because of the evil of Manasseh, the Lord will not spare Judah. The leaders, the people, and the treasures that should have been dedicated to the Lord, are carried away to serve the Babylonians in captivity.

CHRIST IS REVEALED:

As the *Proclaimer of the Word* – 2 Kings 23:2 (Luke 4:16)

As the *one Promised by Name* – 1 Kings 13:2; 2 Kings 22:1 (Matt. 1:21–23; Luke 2:21)

As the *Passover* – 2 Kings 23:21 (1 Cor. 5:7; John 1:29; 1 Pet. 1:19)

As the *Innocent Blood of Jerusalem* – 2 Kings 24:4 (Matt. 27:4; Acts 13:28)

WEEK 18, DAY 3: **TODAY'S READING: 1 CHRONICLES 1-3**

OVERVIEW:

Jesus's lineage through Adam, Noah, Abraham, Israel (Jacob), Judah, and David.

HIGHLIGHTS & INSIGHTS:

At first glance, it appears that the book of 1 Chronicles is simply a repeat of 1 and 2 Samuel and that 2 Chronicles is a repeat of 1 and 2 Kings, but there are some significant differences!

- Samuel and Kings emphasize the *historical* side of things; Chronicles emphasizes the *spiritual*.

- Samuel and Kings are seen from the *human* standpoint; Chronicles is seen from the *divine* standpoint.

- Samuel and Kings are presented from the viewpoint of the *prophets*; Chronicles is presented from the viewpoint of the *priests*.

- Samuel and Kings show *man ruling*; Chronicles shows *God overruling*.

Chronicles concentrates on the reign of David and his successors and on the temple and its worship. It includes information not previously covered concerning the priests, the Levites, and the musicians, singers, and doorkeepers. It goes into detail about transporting the ark to Jerusalem and preparing to build the Temple. The northern kingdom is of little significance in Chronicles. The northern tribes are only mentioned in connection with their dealings with David's reign.

1 Chronicles opens with the longest genealogy in the entire Bible. It takes up nine solid chapters! Needless to say, this section will not qualify for the "Most Heart-Warming and Life-Changing Devotional Passage of the 52 Weeks of Pursuit" award! However, Proverbs 30:5 says, "Every word of God is pure," and every one of these words is there for a reason.

These chapters are in our Bible to provide us the historical basis of our faith. As Bruce Wilkinson said, "The opening chapters of 1 Chronicles form the skeletal framework of the entire Old Testament. They bind the Old Testament together into a unified whole, showing that it is in fact history and not merely legend or myth. From Adam to Abraham, Boaz to Benjamin, the generations are all there in their proper order to show the outworking of God's plan and purposes through the years and in the lives of men and women of faith."[1] These chapters teach us, if nothing else, that God has a plan—for the earth, the universe, Israel, and our lives!

A very basic overview of the first nine chapters of 1 Chronicles is as follows:

- The genealogy from Adam to Abraham (1:1–27)

- The genealogy from Abraham to Israel (1:28–54)

- The genealogy of the descendants of Israel (Chapters 2–8)

  * Judah (2:1–4:23)

  * Simeon (4:24–43)

  * Reuben, Gad, the half-tribe of Manasseh east of the Jordan (Chapter 5)

  * Levi (Chapter 6)

  * Issachar (7:1–5)

  * Benjamin (7:6–12)

  * Naphtali (7:13)

      *   Half-tribe of Manasseh west of the Jordan (7:14–19)

      *   Ephraim (7:20–29)

      *   Asher (7:30–40)

      *   Benjamin (Chapter 8)

- Those who returned from captivity (9:1–34)
- The genealogy of Saul (9:35–44)

CHRIST IS REVEALED:

In the *First Adam* – 1 Chronicles 1:1 (Christ is the *last* or *second Adam*. We have eternal life because the last Adam was a quickening or "life-giving" spirit – 1 Cor. 15:45, 47).

Through the genealogy of *David* – 1 Chronicles 3:1–24 (Christ, the Son of God was also called the Son of David – Matt. 1:1; Luke 3:23–38; Rom. 1:3)

[1]Bruce Wilkinson, *Your Daily Walk*, (Grand Rapids, MI: Zondervan, 1991), pg. 138.

WEEK 18, DAY 4: **TODAY'S READING: 1 CHRONICLES 4-6**

OVERVIEW:

The descendants of Solomon, Judah, Simeon, Reuben, Gad, Manasseh and Levi; temple singers and keepers appointed; the descendants of Aaron; the cities of the Levites.

HIGHLIGHTS & INSIGHTS:

As we read through what seems to be a never-ending genealogy today, rejoice in the underlying message: God doesn't view mankind as simply a mass of humanity! He is interested in each individual and knows us all by name! Hallelujah! God takes the time in these chapters to register and mention the name of every single priest and Levite, along with the family and tribe to which he belonged (Exod. 33:17).

Of particular note in chapter 4 is Jabez. God stops when He gets to his name to interject an incredible statement and about him. 1 Chronicles 4:9 says that he "was more honorable than his brethren." One of the reasons he was more honorable is not only the fact *that* he prayed, but *how* he prayed. Our Lord reveals to us in this passage that Jabez had a beautiful fourfold request, and it was of such significance that God chose to record it for us in verse 10.

1. "Oh that thou wouldest bless me indeed…"

2. "and enlarge my coast…"

3. "and that thine hand might be with me…"

4. "and that thou wouldest keep me from evil, that it may not grieve me!"

Verse 10 concludes with this monumental statement: "And God granted him that which he requested." Jabez's prayer is not held up as a model prayer, as such, but its content is well worth incorporating into our prayers! It is obvious that Jabez was a man who lived in pursuit of God and that God rewarded him for it. May God strengthen us to follow his example as we continue the *52 Weeks of Pursuit*!

CHRIST IS REVEALED:

In the *Cities of Refuge* – 1 Chronicles 6:57, 67–69 (To find protection from the avenger of blood, a person had to flee to a city of refuge. Likewise, God provided His Son, the Lord Jesus Christ, as the Refuge to whom we must flee to find protection from His judgment against sin – John 3:14–18; 10:24–30; Gal. 2:16; 3:1–14; Heb. 10:1–18; 1 John 2:2; Rev. 1:5; Heb. 6:18)

WEEK 18, DAY 5: **TODAY'S READING: 1 CHRONICLES 7-9**

OVERVIEW:

A continuation of Israel's descendants: Issachar, Benjamin, Naphtali, half-tribe of Manasseh west of the Jordan, Ephraim, Asher, Benjamin; those who returned from captivity; the genealogy of Saul.

HIGHLIGHTS & INSIGHTS:

The genealogy continues today through the remainder of the descendants of Israel. In chapter 7, however, we see an interesting phrase that is mentioned twice. 1 Chronicles 7:11 gives the number of "soldiers, fit to go out for war and battle," and 7:40 gives the number of "mighty men of valour ... that were apt to the war and to battle." Biblically, the word *apt* is also translated "prepared," "ready," and "willing." In the New Testament, believers in Jesus Christ are also called *soldiers* (2 Tim. 2:3) who are engaged in an incredible *war* or *battle* (2 Tim. 2:4; 2 Cor. 10:3). I wonder, if God were listing New Testament soldiers, the "mighty men and women of valour" who are "apt to the war and to battle," would our name be included? In Ephesians 6:10–17, that number includes only those who stand in the victory Christ has already won, having put on "the whole armor of God." Are you fit and apt for the war we call the Christian life?

Chapter 9 teaches us about God's view of service. Verse 2 says, "Now the first inhabitants that dwelt in their possessions in their cities were, the Israelites, the priests, Levites, and the Nethinims." The *Nethinims* were the "Temple servants." Their job was to do whatever needed to be done. Because of their love for the Lord, they didn't need the limelight; they were willing to work behind the scenes so that the work of the Lord could go forward.

Verse 28 says of the Levites, "And certain of them had the charge of the ministering vessels, that they should bring them in and out by tale [or count]." From an earthly standpoint, the job God entrusted to them doesn't seem that significant. Others "were appointed to oversee the vessels and all the instruments of the sanctuary, and the fine flour, and the wine, and the oil, and the frankincense, and the spices. And some of the sons of the priests made the ointment of the spices" (vs. 29–30). Once more, these responsibilities hardly seem worth mentioning. But to God, each individual fulfilling his role and completing his personal assignment was well worth mentioning because every individual was key for what He intended for the service of the tabernacle.

The New Testament teaches that God has given all of us a *ministry* to fulfill in the *church* and a *mission* to fulfill in the *world*. God calls us to faithfully carry out these assignments, however insignificant it may seem to others and even, sometimes, to us. So that we can fulfill our purpose according to His design, God has given us spiritual gifts, along with our natural talents and abilities. He has given to us our individual personality and has made us passionate about certain things. And God has orchestrated encounters with different people and various experiences in our lives. Together, these resources help us understand the specific kingdom assignment He intends for us to fulfill. But regardless of our specific ministry, we are all valuable to His kingdom. Our contribution is significant. God views our service as a sacred trust and vital to His work in and through the Body of Christ! All that He asks of us is to be faithful (1 Cor. 4:1–2).

CHRIST IS REVEALED:

In *Jerusalem* (which means "foundation of peace") – 1 Chronicles 9:3 (Christ is the only foundation of peace upon which man can stand before God – 1 Cor. 3:11; John 14:27; 2 Cor. 5:18; Eph. 2:14)

WEEK 19, DAY 1: **TODAY'S READING: 1 CHRONICLES 10-13**

OVERVIEW:

The death of Saul and his sons; David made king over Judah; Israel anoints David king; David takes Jebus (Jerusalem) as the capital city of the kingdom; David's first attempt to bring the ark into Jerusalem.

HIGHLIGHTS & INSIGHTS:

With the end of the genealogy in chapter 9, God brings us to the reign of David as Israel's king. Chapter 10 makes the transition from the reign of Saul to David by recording Saul's death. (The parallel account is found in 1 Samuel 31:1–13.) The reason for Saul's death is found in 1 Chronicles 10:13–14.

1. He was not obedient to the Word of God. (See 1 Samuel 13 and 15.)

2. He consulted a medium. (See 1 Samuel 28.)

In chapter 11, David is anointed as Israel's king in Hebron for the third and final time. (This is a classic case of "third time's the charm"!) The first anointing was done privately by Samuel (1 Sam. 16:13), and the second was done publicly as king over Judah (2 Sam. 2:4).

God gave David key responsibilities as Israel's leader in 1 Chronicles 11:2: "Thou shalt feed my people Israel, and thou shalt be ruler over my people Israel." In simple terms, God gives the same responsibilities to those He calls to provide oversight of His church: feed and lead! (See Acts 20:28; 1 Peter 5:1–3.)

The first item on David's agenda after being anointed king was to secure a capital for the kingdom. 1 Chronicles 11:4–9 explains how Jerusalem was taken, and we learn that Joab was installed as commander of David's army because of his role in removing the Jebusites from Jerusalem. Verse 10 begins a long list of the mighty men in David's army and their various accomplishments.

Chapter 11 identifies the *individuals* who were key in David's army, while chapter 12 identifies the number of mighty men from each of the *tribes*. We learn why these men were so mighty and why they were so mightily used in David's army in 12:38: "All these men of war, that could keep rank, came with a perfect heart to Hebron, to make David king over all Israel." These four qualities provide a great list for what every church should be looking for when filling positions of leadership within the church:

1. Men who understand *Spiritual Warfare* ("all these men of war" – 12:38a).

2. Men who understand *Spiritual Teamwork* ("that could keep rank" – 12:38b).

3. Men who manifest *Spiritual Maturity* ("came with a perfect heart" – 12:38c).

4. Men who manifest *Spiritual Submission to Leadership* ("to make David king over all Israel" – 12:38d).

Chapter 13 records David's first attempt to bring the ark back into his newly acquired capital, Jerusalem. The ark had been completely neglected during the reign of Saul, even though it represented God's presence with Israel. How sad that, for twenty years, nobody seemed to miss it! David, however, is zealous to see God's presence, represented in the ark, restored to its rightful place in Israel's camp. His attempt to move it is a great lesson on how doing the right thing with the right motives—but in the wrong way—will always be disastrous and, in some cases, deadly!

To move it, the ark was placed on a new cart (13:7). Apparently, David wanted it to be special because of what it represented. But the cart hit an uneven place in the road, the ark began to fall, and when well-meaning Uzza reached out to keep it from hitting the ground, he was immediately zapped—just as Numbers 4:15 said he would! God had given Israel specific instructions concerning transporting the ark so that this very thing would not happen (Exod. 25:12–14; Num. 7:9). What began as a glorious celebration ends like a funeral procession—with David very discouraged, disappointed, and even somewhat disillusioned. Remember, God says what He means and means what He says, and no amount of good intentions will override obedience to what He has specifically spoken in His Word!

CHRIST IS REVEALED:

In *David*, the anointed king – 1 Chronicles 11:3 (Christ is the "Anointed of God" who will sit on the throne of David as *King of Kings and Lord of Lords* – Rev. 19:16; Luke 1:32)

WEEK 19, DAY 2: **TODAY'S READING: 1 CHRONICLES 14-17**

OVERVIEW:

King Hiram's blessing upon David; the Philistines defeated; the ark is brought to Jerusalem; David's psalm of thanksgiving; David's desire to build the Temple; David is forbidden to build the Temple; God makes a covenant with David (the Davidic Covenant).

HIGHLIGHTS & INSIGHTS:

At the end of chapter 13, David was a discouraged, dejected, defeated, and disillusioned man. The decision to restore God's presence to its rightful place in Jerusalem had caused a great ground-swell of spiritual excitement among the people—that had come to a screeching halt with the tragic death of Uzza. Instead of returning the ark to Jerusalem, David had it stored in the house of Obededom. That's how disillusioned he had actually become. But after seeing the blessing of God upon the household of Obededom during the three months the ark was in his home (13:14), David was convinced that, regardless of the cost, having the ark in Jerusalem was non-negotiable.

Before we get to that, however, chapter 14 provides some parenthetical information to help us to understand more about David and his reign. 1 Chronicles 14:3 simply states, "And David took more wives at Jerusalem." This practice was common among ancient kings and was not only *accepted* by the people, but almost *expected* as a sign of their ruler's royalty and prestige. However, it was clearly against the law of God! It's easy to think that God was somewhat lenient about this practice, but the harvest of sorrows that David (and others kings) reaped in their families proves He was not. Once again, there are always consequences to sin! In the twenty-first century, too, the world's acceptance of sin must not influence us to violate God's holy Word or His holy calling upon our lives!

With David installed as Israel's king, the Philistines decided to come up against David's army (14:8). David spanked them like a two-year-old at Walmart, to the point that they dropped the gods they were carrying (to ensure their victory!) so they could run away faster (14:12). I certainly don't want to put my trust in any god that can be dropped like a hot potato on a field of battle or be burned!

David sought God's will before leading the troops into battle (14:10). And when the Philistines returned to do battle again, "David enquired again of God" (14:13–14). God's first go-ahead was no guarantee of a second one! We must pray about everything, asking for God's specific guidance for every decision. God did give David the go-ahead, but with a very particular battle plan to achieve the victory, a battle plan which David would not have known had he not "enquired again of God"! What clear direction from the Lord might we be forfeiting simply because we fail to ask (Jas. 4:2b)?

In chapter 15, David moves the ark into its proper place. This time, though, he did it the *biblical* way! David realized that they had received God's judgment (at Uzza's expense) because they "sought him not after the due order" (v. 13). Or, in other words, "because we didn't ask God how He wanted us to do it!" This time, David made sure that the right people were carrying the ark (15:2), that they were properly prepared for the task (15:12), and that it was being carried the right way (15:15). Once the ark was in its proper place, the priority of worship was once again restored to Israel (16:1–6). David then offered a psalm of thanks to the Lord. It is a composite of Psalm 105:1–15; Psalm 96:1–13; and Psalm 106:1, 47–48.

Chapter 17 is divided into three basic sections:

1. David's desire to build God a house. (17:1–2)

2. God's determination to build David a house. (17:3–15)

3. David's humble prayer of response. (17:16–27)

CHRIST IS REVEALED:

Through the *Exaltation and Fame of Israel's King (David)* – 1 Chronicles 14:17 (Phil. 2:9–11; Rom. 14:11)

Through *David, the Shepherd-King* – 1 Chronicles 17:7 (Matt. 1:1–2; Rom. 1:3; John 10:11; Rev. 19:16)

WEEK 19, DAY 3: **TODAY'S READING: 1 CHRONICLES 18-21**

OVERVIEW:

The extension of David's kingdom through his victories in battle; David's sin in numbering the people; God's judgment upon Israel for David's sin.

HIGHLIGHTS & INSIGHTS:

The events that God summarizes for us in chapters 18–20 took place historically *after* David was made king (chapter 12), but *before* the ark had been brought to Jerusalem (chapters 13–17). David's life in these chapters reads more like that of a World War II general than the "man after God's own heart." Here is ample proof for why God refused to allow David to build the Temple: "Thou hast shed blood abundantly, and hast made great wars: thou shalt not build an house unto my name, because thou hast shed much blood upon the earth in my sight" (1 Chron. 22:8).

Just as David multiplied *wives* for himself (14:3), 1 Chronicles 18:4 records another of David's failures to obey the laws God had laid down for Israel's kings (Deut. 17:15–17). This time he multiplied *horses*. It's obvious why God would prohibit having many wives, but the warning about horses is less clear. Apparently, it is somehow associated with the development of a spirit of pride within human leaders. David's pride will blossom in chapter 21.

In chapter 18, while David executed his wrath on his enemies (18:1–15), God's people enjoyed the execution of David's righteousness and justice (18:14).

Chapter 19 begins with a great example of the tongue-in-cheek proverb: "No good deed goes unpunished." What David fully intended to be a blessing to Hanun, king of Ammon, at the death of his father turns into a fiasco because of the new king's advisors (19:3). With so-called insight into David's motives, they advise Hanun foolishly, and the whole thing escalates into a battle that ends with the death of 47,000 soldiers (19:18–19)! It's a clear warning: We cannot always discern people's motives, and we should be careful about listening to people who think they can!

From a chronological standpoint, 1 Chronicles 20 coincides with 2 Samuel 12, when David became involved with Bathsheba. Whereas 2 Samuel records David's sin and restoration, in keeping with the rest of 1 and 2 Chronicles, the sin is not recorded here.

In chapter 21, the usually humble David is lifted up with the pride. He instructs Joab, the commander of his army, to take a census. Joab appeals to David, saying (in effect), "Listen, boss, if the motive here is to find out how many subjects are in your kingdom, let's just say that there are a whole lot of 'em, and that they all love you and are your servants! You don't need to know the number and finding out is going to lead to a bunch of problems!" David, however, had made up his mind. He was going to do what he wanted to do! And he did.

Numbering the people displeased the Lord and brought His immediate judgment upon Israel (21:7). Though David had "sinned greatly," he was quick to humble himself and own his sin (21:8). However, his sin did not just result in the death of one man, as with Uzza, but the death of 70,000 men! Though God graciously forgave David his sin, imagine how hard it would have been for the families of those 70,000 men to forgive their king. It is another tragic reminder that the consequences of sin often have devastating effects on many innocent people.

Through the "seer" (i.e., "prophet" – 1 Sam. 9:9), the Lord instructed David to acquire the threshing floor of Ornan (21:18) and build an altar there. Through the sacrifices, the judgment of God upon Israel was stayed. This threshing floor would later become the site of the Temple (2 Chron. 3:1).

CHRIST IS REVEALED:

Through the *Altar* David built so Israel might be restored to a right relationship with God – 1 Chronicles 21:18, 26 (Only through Christ can we be restored to a right relationship with God – Rom. 3:24).

WEEK 19, DAY 4: **TODAY'S READING: 1 CHRONICLES 22-25**

OVERVIEW:

David's preparation for the construction of the Temple; David's instructions and charge to Solomon; David enlisting the leaders of Israel to support Solomon in the project; the duties of the Levites; the duties assigned to the priests and to the musicians and singers.

HIGHLIGHTS & INSIGHTS:

In 1 Chronicles 21, David acquired the threshing floor of Ornan and built an altar to offer sacrifices. In chapter 22, David recognizes that the threshing floor would be the site for Temple that he had longed to build for the Lord. Though he was not permitted by the Lord to oversee its actual construction, he was given the wonderful and joyful privilege of planning and preparing for the building of it.

David realized that at Solomon's young age (he was approximately twenty at the time), he would need some help in preparing for something of this magnitude and magnificence (22:5). David said, "The house that is to be builded for the Lord must [not *should*, but *must*] be exceeding magnifical, of fame and of glory throughout all countries" (22:5). In other words, "There must not be any structure anywhere in any country on the entire planet that has the magnificence of the Lord's house!" And David continues in verse 5, "I will therefore now make preparation for it." It's as if David is saying, "I may not be able to build it, but I can certainly plan for its magnificence!" And verse 5 concludes with the statement, "So David prepared abundantly before his death."

This verse teaches us a great principle of life: We may have dreams that God never allows us to accomplish, but we may be used of the Lord to joyfully make preparations for someone else (maybe, like David, one of our children, biological or spiritual!) to accomplish that dream through their life.

In 22:6–13, David explained to Solomon his vision for building the Temple and how God had reshaped and redirected the vision to be fulfilled through his son. He walks Solomon through the Davidic Covenant, charges Solomon with the vision and responsibility for the project, and pronounces his blessing upon him. In 22:14–16, David informs Solomon of all of the materials he had already accumulated for the project, and in 22:17–19, David commands the leaders of Israel to get behind Solomon in this glorious and monumental task. The chapter ends with David's challenge and charge to Solomon and all of the leaders of Israel, "Now set your heart and your soul to seek the LORD your God; arise therefore, and build ye the sanctuary of the LORD God, to bring the ark of the covenant of the LORD, and the holy vessels of God, into the house that is to be built to the name of the LORD" (22:19).

It's hard to imagine, but in great Laodicean fashion, Solomon didn't make the Temple his first priority. He didn't even begin the project until the fourth year of his reign! During those four years, however, he began to accumulate chariots and horses, not to mention wives for himself. (See 2 Chron. 1:14; 3:1–2; 1 Kings 10:26–11:4.) As we have seen, God had clearly prohibited these things for Israel's kings in Deuteronomy 17.

In the list of David's lifetime accomplishments, something that is often overlooked are his efforts to organize the tribe of Levi for effective ministry in the Temple (chapters 23–25). Though seldom mentioned, this work was of tremendous spiritual significance!

CHRIST IS REVEALED:

Through *Solomon, the Son of David, Israel's King* – 1 Chronicles 23:1 (Luke 1:32; Matt. 21:9)

WEEK 19, DAY 5: **TODAY'S READING: 1 CHRONICLES 26-29**

OVERVIEW:

The divisions of the porters (gate keepers), the treasurers and other officers; the divisions of Israel's military; David's challenge to the leaders of Israel to the work of the Temple; David's charge to Solomon to build the Temple; David's gifts for the Temple; David's offering of praise to the Lord; the people's offering of praise of the Lord; Solomon's official installation as Israel's king; the death of David.

HIGHLIGHTS & INSIGHTS:

The major portion of chapters 26–27 is consumed with the listing of names. When reading a genealogy, or lists of names such as this, its interesting to observe the brief comments God inspired the writers of Scripture to interject. For example, 26:4–5 gives a list of Obededom's sons, but at the end of verse 5, God drops in this little statement: "for God blessed him." And that's it. But do you remember why God blessed Obededom? He sheltered the ark after the death of Uzza back in 1 Chronicles 13. He was blessed because the presence of God (represented in the ark) was manifest in his life and in his home (13:14). We, too, will be blessed like Obededom when God's presence is manifest in and through our lives and in our homes.

God also gives commentary on Obededom's sons and grandsons. 1 Chronicles 26 says, "they were mighty men of valour" (v. 6), "were strong men" (v. 7), and were "able men for strength for the service" (v. 8). Most pastors would tell you that what is lacking, but so desperately needed in the church today is *strong men*! But not men who are extroverts or intimidating. Not cocky men, dominating men, or men who are successful by the world's standards. We have been called to be strong but not in our own strength! Ephesians 6:10 commands us to "be strong in the Lord"! And his "strength is made perfect in weakness" (2 Cor. 12:9)! Real biblical strength and biblically strong men are paradoxical. Their strength is manifested through their weakness. We must be very discerning!

A search was made for "mighty men of valour" in 1 Chronicles 26:31, and "they … were found." But in Ezekiel 22:30, God says, "And I sought for a man among them, that should make up the hedge, and stand in the gap before me for the land, that I should not destroy it: but I found none"! As God is seeking mighty men (and women) of valour today, just as He did in 1 Chronicles and Ezekiel, may He find you and me!

Chapter 27 lays out the military leaders and governmental structure of the nation. The army comprised more than a quarter of a million soldiers—288,000 to be exact—with 24,000 on duty each month. It is more than apparent that this was not a rag-tag band of soldiers, but a highly organized and regimented military operation. In 28:1–8, David addresses the leaders about the building of the Temple and enlists their support of Solomon and the entire project. In verses 9 and 10, David addresses Solomon himself. In doing so, David presents a command, a promise, a warning, and an exhortation.

1) **The Command**: "Know thou the God of thy father, and serve him with a perfect heart." (28:9a)

   Note that Solomon could know *about* God from his father David, but to *know Him* would require that Solomon be acquainted with God himself! Given who Solomon's mother was (Matt. 1:6), we understand why David would tell his son, "serve [the Lord] with a perfect heart." I'm quite certain David wished he had!

2) **The Promise**: "If thou seek him, he will be found of thee." (28:9b)

   It's a reminder of the theme verse of our *52 Weeks of Pursuit*, "But if from thence thou shalt seek the Lord thy God, thou shalt find him, if thou seek him with all thy heart and with all thy soul." (Deut. 4:29)

3) **The Warning**: "But if thou forsake him, he will cast thee off for ever." (28:9c)

4) **The Exhortation**: "Take heed now; for the Lord hath chosen thee to build an house for the sanctuary: be strong and do it." (28:10)

That was David's admonition to his son concerning his commission. It fits perfectly with the commission we too have received from the Lord (Matt. 28:18–20).

Chapter 29 records of the end of David's life which ends just as it had begun. He is a humble man with an incredible heart for God. In verses 1–5, he tells the people that he not only had been setting aside money from the national budget for the great work of the Temple, but also from his own personal finances. He challenged all the people to do likewise. In response, they "offered willingly" (29:6) and "rejoiced, for that they offered willingly … to the Lord: and David the king also rejoiced with great joy" (29:9). May we also be willing to joyfully give to the Lord's work.

In 29:10–19, David blessed the Lord his God and, in verse 20, challenged the people to do the same. Note their response in verses 20–22:

> And all the congregation blessed the Lord God of their fathers, and bowed down their heads, and worshipped the Lord, and the king. And they sacrificed sacrifices unto the Lord, and offered burnt offerings unto the Lord, on the morrow after that day, even a thousand bullocks, a thousand rams, and a thousand lambs, with their drink offerings, and sacrifices in abundance for all Israel: And did eat and drink before the Lord on that day with great gladness.

Solomon is then formally installed as the new king, and 1 Chronicles ends with a brief summary of David's reign: "And he died in a good old age, full of days, riches, and honour" (29:28).

CHRIST IS REVEALED:

Through the *Temple Treasures* – 1 Chronicles 26:20–28 (In Christ "are hid all the treasures of wisdom and knowledge"– Col. 2:2–3)

WEEK 20, DAY 1: **TODAY'S READING: 2 CHRONICLES 1-4**

OVERVIEW:

Solomon's sacrifices; God's appearance to Solomon in a dream; Solomon's choice of wisdom and knowledge; Solomon's accumulation of chariots, horses, horsemen, silver, and gold; Solomon builds the Temple; the Temple furnishings.

HIGHLIGHTS & INSIGHTS:

The book of 2 Chronicles spans a whopping 427 years! For perspective, that's the equivalent of covering the high points of history since the beginning of the 17th century! The period covers nineteen kings—ten bad, seven good, and two who were good, but became bad (Solomon and Joash). As is always the case, as go the leaders, so go the people until finally the nation had so apostatized that they are carried off into captivity. The book does end, however, with a ray of hope.

In chapter 1, the reign of Solomon is established as he sets a priority on worship (v. 6). God appears to Solomon in a dream (v. 7; 1 Kings 3:5), and says, "Ask what I shall give thee." In other words, "Ask Me for anything you want, and it's as good as yours!" Solomon's humble request brought great pleasure to the Lord. Understanding the enormity of the task of leading God's people, he simply asks for the wisdom and knowledge to rule them properly. Because he wasn't selfish in asking for personal gain, God tells him, "I will give thee riches, and wealth, and honour, such as none of the kings have had that have been before thee, neither shall there any after thee have the like" (1:12). Again, I call this "the curse of God's blessing" because, quite simply, Solomon wasn't prepared spiritually to steward God's incredible material blessing upon his life.

God had made abundantly clear in Deuteronomy 17 that the kings of Israel were not to multiply to themselves silver and gold; they were not to do business with Egypt to multiply horses (or for any other reason); and they were not to multiply wives (Deut. 17:16–17). However, 2 Chronicles 1:13–17 reveals that Solomon violated all three of those commands, and 1 Kings 3:1 reveals that he violated another of God's commands by making an "affinity with Pharaoh king of Egypt, and took Pharaoh's daughter" as his wife.

Obviously, these were tragic mistakes, but make sure you don't miss seeing why they all happened! He violated these four commands because he violated another key command from Deuteronomy 17. God had commanded that a king in Israel was to write his own copy of the law. He was to make his own handwritten copy of the entire books of Genesis, Exodus, Leviticus, Numbers and Deuteronomy—forcing him to personally interact with every word of God. That was the real issue! Had the Word of God been his first priority, he would have known that God had forbidden him to involve himself in the very things he did at the outset of his reign. We must always make the Word of God our first priority, to personally interact with "every word of God"(Prov. 30:5)—in times of trial *and* in times of blessing. Perhaps, especially in times of blessing! As the old saying goes, "This Book will keep you from sin; and sin will keep you from this Book!"

In chapter 2, Solomon determines to build the Lord's house. That sounds wonderful until you realize that he included another little priority as well. He determines to have a house built for himself! There's certainly nothing wrong with that, but in light of David's strong words to Solomon about how "magnifical" (I'm totally taken by that word!) the Lord's house was to be in comparison to anything else in existence (1 Chron. 22:5), it seems inconceivable that it took almost twice as long to build Solomon's house as it did the Lord's house (7 years compared to 13 years – 1 Kings 6:38; 7:1). And if you compare the size of Solomon's house (1 Kings 7:1–12) with the size of the Lord's house (2 Chron. 3), Solomon's house is almost exactly twice as big as God's "magnifical" house! Wouldn't you have loved to hear Solomon's rationalization for that? Never underestimate the tremendous ability we have as humans to justify anything and everything we want to do. May God help us!

CHRIST IS REVEALED:

By the *Thousand Burnt Offerings* of Solomon – 2 Chronicles 1:6 (Through Christ's one offering of sin, He removed the need for the many and continual individual offerings required in the Law – Heb. 10:10–12, 14; Rom. 6:10)

WEEK 20, DAY 2: **TODAY'S READING: 2 CHRONICLES 5-8**

OVERVIEW:

The ark is brought into the Temple; the glory of the Lord fills the temple; Solomon's prayer of dedication; Solomon's sacrifices; the glory of the Lord fills the Temple again; God appears to warn Solomon.

HIGHLIGHTS & INSIGHTS:

It took 153,000 skilled workers seven years to complete it, but the Temple was now ready for the furnishings David had accumulated and dedicated for the magnificent structure he so longed to build. Once they were in place—along with the hallowed ark—Solomon led the people in offering sacrifices and heartfelt praise to God. The 120 priests playing the trumpet combined with the singers in a perfect blend ("as one" – 5:12–13). It certainly must have been an unbelievable worship experience. Even God got a little carried away! The glory of God so filled the Temple that the priests had to run for the exits (5:14)!

Don't ever forget that the Temple in the Old Testament is a picture of you and me. God no longer dwells in temples made with hands (Acts 7:48), but says, "Know ye not that your body is the temple of the Holy Ghost which is in you, which ye have of God, and ye are not your own? For ye are bought with a price: therefore glorify God in your body, and in your spirit, which are God's" (1 Cor. 6:19–20). And the glory described in 2 Chronicles 5:14 is the glory God wants to receive and manifest through each of our lives!

In chapter 6, Solomon dedicates the Temple. He addresses the people in 6:1–11, then ascends a brass scaffold and addresses the Lord Himself (vs. 12–42)! It is the longest prayer recorded in the Bible, and perhaps the most majestic and moving! It is so powerful and wonderful and spoken with such incredible sincerity that our reaction should be entirely positive. But we gotta keep it real. Solomon asks God in 6:24–25 that, if His people sin against Him but return to Him and confess His name, to please hear and forgive them. What a beautiful and humble request! The tragic thing, though, is that Solomon became an incredible sinner, but there is no biblical record of Solomon ever repenting of any of his own sins! So many who start so *strong* can end up so *overthrown*! Again, God help us (1 Cor. 10:5–6, 11).

When Solomon finishes his prayer praising and thanking God for His unequalled attributes and unfailing promises, the glory of the Lord was, again, so overpowering that the priests couldn't make their way into the Temple! And when the people saw it, "they bowed themselves with their faces to the ground upon the pavement, and worshipped, and praised the LORD, saying, For he is good; for his mercy endureth for ever" (7:3).

But even after this incredible dedication, God comes to Solomon in the night, warning that if the nation didn't remain true to Him, He would uproot them out of their wonderful homeland and destroy their magnificent Temple (7:20).

Chapter 8 jumps forward twenty years and records various accomplishments and successes in Solomon's reign. Of particular note is verse 11. Solomon wouldn't allow his wife, the daughter of Pharaoh, to live in the royal palace because, he said, the palace was holy (and he was right!). But it's a great illustration of how we deceive ourselves that we can separate our personal lives from our spiritual lives. Call it a double life or a double standard, hypocrisy or just stupidity, but our personal lives are not separate from our spiritual lives! Solomon restricted the daughter of Pharoah to a separate residence, but that did not restrict her from leading him into idolatry! (See 1 Kings 11:1–8.) Let's consider today if there is any area of our personal life that we are trying to keep separate from our spiritual life and let God's truth prevail over our self-deception.

CHRIST IS REVEALED:

Through *Solomon's Prayer* – 2 Chronicles 6:14 (Jesus is that supreme God to which Solomon was referring: "For there is one God, and one mediator between God and men, the man Christ Jesus" – 1 Tim. 2:5)

WEEK 20, DAY 3: **TODAY'S READING: 2 CHRONICLES 9-12**

OVERVIEW:

The Queen of Sheba visits Solomon; the extent of Solomon's riches and fame; Solomon's death; Rehoboam succeeds Solomon as Israel's king; Jeroboam leads a revolt of ten of the tribes; Rehoboam forsakes the law of God; God brings judgment against Rehoboam through Shishak, king of Egypt.

HIGHLIGHTS & INSIGHTS:

2 Chronicles 9 is perhaps the most glorious Old Testament picture of the Lord Jesus Christ reigning in wisdom in His millennial kingdom from His throne in Jerusalem (Phil 2:9–11)! Just as in the parallel passage in 1 Kings 10–11, however, Solomon's life does not remain a picture of the Lord Jesus Christ; instead, he becomes perhaps the greatest Old Testament picture of the Antichrist! In the midst of all of the splendor of the record of Solomon's kingdom, we find, in 2 Chronicles 9:13, the amount of gold that came to Solomon in one year: "Six hundred and threescore and six." I believe that number is 6–6–6! Also, the three-sided configuration upon which his throne was set, with six steps leading up from the front and the two sides could be written 6–6–6! (Revelation 13:18 establishes the 6–6–6 connection to the Antichrist: "Here is wisdom. Let him that hath understanding count the number of the beast (Antichrist): for it is the number of a man; and his number is Six hundred threescore and six.")

Chapter 9 ends with the death and burial of Solomon, and chapter 10 begins with the reign of his son, Rehoboam. You can summarize Rehoboam's reign by two simple little phrases. 2 Chronicles 12:1 says that when he "had strengthened himself, he forsook the law of the LORD, and all Israel with him," and 12:14 says, "And he did evil, because he prepared not his heart to seek the LORD." Rehoboam's life teaches us that we get ourselves into spiritual trouble when we begin to think that our strength is in ourselves, rather than in the Lord, in the power of His might and His Word. And Rehoboam did all of the evil, idiotic, and sinful things he did because he didn't do one simple, but monumental, thing: He "did not prepare his heart to seek the Lord." Once again, we're reminded of the purpose of the *52 Weeks of Pursuit*: "But if from thence thou shalt seek the Lord thy God, thou shalt find him, if thou seek him with all thy heart and with all thy soul" (Jer. 29:13).

Rehoboam's first decision as king was a major fiasco, as he heeded the wrong counsel. We must be careful about whose counsel we seek or take (Ps. 1:1). His harshness caused ten of the tribes to break away and form what we now refer to as the northern kingdom.

From this point on, the northern Tribes are referred to as *Israel* and the two southern Tribes as *Judah*. Jeroboham is installed as the king of Israel, while Rehoboam remains king in Judah. When you compare 1 Kings 11:28–31 with 2 Chronicles 10:15, don't miss how God is able to use the poor, idiotic, and even flat-out wrong decisions of earthly rulers to perform His will and fulfill His Word! God is big, y'all! Really big!

CHRIST IS REVEALED:

In the *Glory of Solomon's Kingdom* – 2 Chronicles 9:1–28 (Phil. 2:9–11; Rev. 20:5–6)

WEEK 20, DAY 4: **TODAY'S READING: 2 CHRONICLES 13–16**

OVERVIEW:

Abijah's battle and victory over Jeroboam, King of Israel; King Asa's reforms in Judah; his covenant with God; his pact with Benhadad, King of Syria; Asa's rebuke by Hanani; Asa's diseased feet and death.

HIGHLIGHTS & INSIGHTS:

As chapter 13 opens, God uses Abijah, the newly appointed king of Judah to discipline Jeroboam, king of Israel. In 13:4–12, Abijah appeals to Jeroboam to consider his ways and walk with God. In reply, Jeroboam's troops ambush Judah, but God fights for Judah. In the end, Israel lost a half million men (13:17). It's an extremely high price to pay for refusing to obey God! The defeat was so devastating, Jeroboam never fully recovered.

In chapter 14, Abijah dies, and his son, Asa, begins his reign. What Abijah accomplished in Judah militarily, Asa sought to do spiritually. He removed all of the foreign worship and "commanded Judah to seek the Lord God of their fathers, and to do the law and the commandment" (14:4). As a result, God blessed Judah with ten years of quiet (14:1, 5) and rest (14:6–7), and Asa had an army full of "mighty men of valour" (14:8). Judah's peace ended, however, when an Ethiopian army of one million men came against them.

> And Asa cried unto the LORD his God, and said, LORD, it is nothing with thee to help, whether with many, or with them that have no power: help us, O LORD our God; for we rest on thee, and in thy name we go against this multitude. O LORD, thou art our God; let not man prevail against thee (14:11).

Judah's smaller army was victorious because of their simple dependence and trust in the Lord (14:12–15).

In chapter 15, Azariah the prophet challenges Asa to keep up the good work of spiritual reformation in the nation. Asa responds with great enthusiasm, destroying even more idols (15:8) and decreeing that the people either seek the Lord with all of their heart and soul—or die (15:12–13). His grandmother, also the reigning queen, made an idol, and Asa crushed and burned the idol, then removed her from being queen. Sadly, following the Lord sometimes requires making tough decisions concerning members of our own families!

Chapter 16 is just sad. As Asa's wealth and power increased, his dependence on God decreased. When Baasha, king of Israel, came up against Asa, he doesn't cry out to God. Instead, he sends God's money to create an alliance with Syria. Baasha was defeated, but Asa had greatly displeased the Lord. God's prophet rebukes Asa in 16:7–9, saying, "The Lord is constantly looking for those He can bless by showing Himself strong on their behalf?" [my obvious paraphrase]. Rather than repent, Asa throws the prophet into jail (even today, when people hear God's messages, they tend to get upset with His messengers!), and his attitude didn't change. When disease struck his feet, Asa looked to man for help, not God. But "it is better to trust in the Lord than to put confidence in man" (Ps. 118:8).

Like Asa, many believers today start off wonderfully, but in the end, their spiritual feet have become diseased, and they cannot "walk in the Spirit" (Gal. 5:16) or "walk worthy of the vocation wherewith [they have been] called" (Eph. 4:1). We must be very careful as we grow older in the Lord not to allow our spiritual feet to become diseased!

CHRIST IS REVEALED:

Through the Rest God gave Judah – 2 Chronicles 14:7 (Matt. 11:29; Heb. 4:1, 8–11)

WEEK 20, DAY 5: **TODAY'S READING: 2 CHRONICLES 17–21**

OVERVIEW:

Jehoshaphat succeeds Asa; Jehoshaphat's alliance with Ahab, King of Israel; the death of Ahab; Jehoshaphat's rebuke by Jehu the seer (prophet); Jehoshaphat's national reform; Jehoshaphat's victory over the children of Moab, Ammon, and Mount Seir; the death of Jehoshaphat; the reign of Jehoshaphat's son, Jehoram; Jehoram's bitter death.

HIGHLIGHTS & INSIGHTS:

What a breath of fresh air Jehoshaphat is! He's not perfect (obviously!), but despite some stupid alliances he made with the wrong people, he was a good man and a good king. 2 Chronicles 17:3 says, "And the LORD was with Jehoshaphat, because he walked in the first ways of his father David." David is always the standard by which the kings were measured. If they followed David's example, they were blessed. If they didn't, their lives and their kingdoms ran amuck. David had his share of problems, but God was pretty taken with his heart! As the saying goes, "The heart of the matter is the matter of the heart!" Or, as God said, "keep [guard] thy heart" (Prov. 4:23).

Verses 4–9 of chapter 17 give at least five reasons the Lord was with Jehoshaphat.

1) He sought the Lord (17:4a). Don't forget that that's the goal of the *52 Weeks of Pursuit* (Jer. 29:13).

2) He walked in the commandments of the Lord (17:4b). Jesus said in John 14:15 that keeping the commandments is how we express our love for the Lord!

3) His heart was lifted up in the ways of the Lord (17:6a), instead of being lifted up, like Lucifer, toward himself!

4) He removed all of the sick ways people were worshipping Baal and Ashteroth (17:6b), along with removing all those who were practicing homosexuality (1 Kings 22:46).

5) Recognizing that the key to spiritual renewal and revival in people's lives was the power of the Word of God, he established a nationwide Bible study program for the people that was taught by princes, Levites, and priests. Who knows, maybe they even called it *52 Weeks of Pursuit* (17:7–9)!

Because of these incredible reforms in the kingdom, "the fear of the Lord fell upon all the kingdoms of the lands that were round about Judah, so that they made no war against Jehoshaphat" (17:10). As Proverbs 16:7 says, because his ways pleased the Lord, "even his enemies [were] at peace with him."

Obviously, having your enemies at peace with you is a good thing. But making alliances with them because of it is not! In 2 Chronicles 18:1, it says that Jehoshaphat "joined affinity with Ahab" — the wicked, Baal-worshipping king of Israel. Because of this alliance, Jehoshaphat joins Ahab in a battle to regain the city of Ramothgilead, which was very displeasing to the Lord and almost cost him his life! Ultimately, this alliance will lead to the marriage of Jehoshaphat's son, Jehoram, to Ahab's (and Jezebel's) daughter (21:1, 6). As is often the case, parents' compromises result in compromises in the lives of their children!

Because of Jehoshaphat's unholy alliance with Ahab, in chapter 19, God sent the prophet Jehu to rebuke him, saying: "Shouldest thou help the ungodly, and love them that hate the Lord? therefore is wrath upon thee from before the Lord" (19:2). Jehoshaphat responded well to the Lord's rebuke and moved immediately to restore justice (19:5–7) and priestly order in Jerusalem (19:8–11). Do note, however, that even though Jehoshaphat responded correctly and was forgiven, there were still consequences to his sin. The marriage of his son to Ahab and Jezebel's daughter will open the door to Baal worship in Judah and will result in the murder of every single one of his sons and grandsons except for one-year-old Joash, who was hidden by Jehoida the high priest (22:10–12). This might be a good place to say once again,

"There is always a price-tag for sin!"

Chapter 20 is one of the most practical and significant chapters thus far in our reading. There is more to talk about here than we have space to cover. Read it slowly and carefully, noting how God describes the very strange battle that takes place in this chapter. As the combined forces of Moab, Ammon, and Mount Seir plan to converge upon Jehoshaphat and the armies of Judah, God's Spirit came upon Jahaziel, a Levite, who tells the people:

- "The battle is not yours, but God's." (20:15)
- "Ye shall not need to fight in this battle." (20:17a)
- "Set yourselves, stand ye still, and see the salvation of the LORD with you." (20:17b)
- "Believe in the LORD your God, so shall ye be established." (20:20)
- "When they began to sing and to praise, the LORD set ambushments against … Ammon, Moab, and Mount Seir." (20:22)
- "The LORD … made them to rejoice over their enemies." (20:27)
- "And the fear of God was on all the kingdoms of those countries, when they had heard that the LORD fought against [their] enemies." (20:29)

These statements are so significant because they coincide perfectly with the New Testament teaching concerning the spiritual warfare you and I face daily! Just like with Jehoshaphat's battle, the battle we face is not *ours*, but *God's!* Therefore, we must "be strong in the Lord, and the power of his might" (Eph. 6:10). The battle plan for us, as for Jehoshaphat, is not for us to *fight*, but to stand in the victory Christ has already won on our behalf! (Eph. 6:11–14 repeats the word "*stand*," not fight!) And our battle, just like the battle in 2 Chronicles 20:20, is a battle where the Lord causes us to *rejoice* over our enemies by *faith* (Eph. 6:16), as we stand against the enemy, *singing* the praises of our God (Eph. 5:19).

After Jehoshaphat's death (20:35–21:1), his son Jehoram takes the throne. In his first public act, he kills all of his brothers and everyone else he thought might have the potential for usurping his authority (21:4). God judges him in many ways in chapter 21, not the least of which was afflicting him with an excruciating disease where ultimately his intestines exploded out of his body (21:18–19). Couldn't have happened to a nicer guy!

CHRIST IS REVEALED:

Through *Micaiah*, who spoke the words that God told him to speak – 2 Chronicles 18:13 (John 8:26–28; 3:34; 8:40)

WEEK 21, DAY 1: **TODAY'S READING: 2 CHRONICLES 22-26**

OVERVIEW:

The reign of Ahaziah; the usurping of the throne by Ahaziah's grandmother, Athaliah; Jehoiada's plot to put Joash on the throne; Joash becomes king and repairs the Temple; the death of Jehoiada and the demise of the nation of Judah; Amaziah reigns in Judah; the war against Edom; Israel defeats Judah; Uzziah reigns in Jerusalem; Uzziah is stricken with leprosy.

HIGHLIGHTS & INSIGHTS:

I doubt that Jehoshaphat realized how far-reaching the effects of his unnecessary alliance with Ahab would go (2 Chron. 18). In chapter 22, the reign of Ahaziah is the third generation that has been evilly affected by Jehoshaphat's "unequal yoke with an unbeliever" (2 Cor. 6:14). Ahaziah followed the counsel of his wicked mother and the counselors from the house of Ahab (22:3–4), and verse 4 says, "Wherefore he did evil in the sight of the LORD like the house of Ahab." That's quite a statement in light of the fact that 1 Kings 21:25 says, "There was none like unto Ahab, which did sell himself to work wickedness in the sight of the LORD, whom Jezebel his wife stirred up."

When Ahaziah was killed in Samaria (22:9) after only one year on the throne (22:2), his wicked and godless mother—in great Jezebellian fashion—had every one of his sons and grandsons killed so she could take the throne herself. Talk about a case of "without natural affection" (2 Tim. 3:3)! And though it was Athaliah's selfish pride that motivated this horrific act, don't discount Satan's hand working tenaciously behind the scenes to cut off the Messianic line! What Athaliah didn't realize, however, is that her sister, Jehoshabeath (the wife of Jehoiada, the priest), took Joash, the infant son of Ahaziah, and hid him so he wouldn't be killed. Clearly God's hand was also working tenaciously behind the scenes—to fulfill His promise in Genesis 3:15 and the Davidic covenant! (See 1 Chron. 17:11; 2 Sam. 7:12.)

Jehoiada kept Joash hidden until he was old enough to comprehend what had happened, at which time he began to plot Athaliah's overthrow (23:1–3). The Levites and princes were designated their assignments (23:4–7), and on a particular Sabbath, they enacted Jehoiada's plan to get Joash, the rightful heir, on the throne. When Athaliah heard the cheering and shouting in the temple, she ran in to investigate only to find her seven-year-old grandson, whom she presumed dead, crowned as the king of Judah. As any loving grandmother would do, she tore her clothes and called him a traitor (23:8–13). Sadly, those who scream the loudest are often guilty of the very things they are so enraged by! (See Romans 2:1.)

Jehoiada establishes a covenant between Jehoiada, young Joash, and the people that they would submit themselves to the Lord (23:16). To demonstrate their sincerity, the people destroyed the temple of Baal and killed Mattan, the priest of Baal, and Jehoiada reestablished God's design for worship in the Lord's Temple (23:17–19).

2 Chronicles 24:2 records that "Joash did that which was right in the sight of the Lord" but, sadly, only as long as Jehoiada was alive. Once the godly influence of Jehoiada was gone, Joash turned to idolaters for advice, resulting in the demise of the kingdom (24:15–18). God sent prophets to warn him, but rather than repent, Joash further rebelled (24:19). In the end, all of the great things Joash accomplished in the early days of his reign were undone by his wickedness in the latter part of his reign. As we have seen repeatedly in the *52 Weeks of Pursuit*, many *start* well, but few *finish* well! May we all heed God's warning: "Look to yourselves, that we lose not those things which we have wrought, but that we receive a full reward" (2 John 8).

After Joash was murdered by his servants (24:25–27), his son Amaziah became the king of Judah. 2 Chronicles 25:2 says, "And he did that which was right in the sight of the LORD, but not with a perfect heart." In other words, he did what he did "for the Lord" with an ulterior motive. In time, as it always is, that ulterior motive was revealed. After defeating the armies of an idolatrous foe, Amaziah gathered up their idols and worshipped them (25:11–14). And I love God's rebuke of him through His prophet, "Why hast thou sought after the gods of the people, which could not deliver their own people out of thine hand?" (25:15).

One of the most successful kings in Judah's history was Amaziah's sixteen-year-old son, Uzziah (26:9–14). Like so many others, however, he started strong, but ended defeated. He sought the Lord (26:5) and remained dependent upon Him "till he was strong. But when he was strong, his heart was lifted up to his destruction: for he transgressed against the LORD his God, and went into the temple of the LORD to burn incense upon the altar of incense" (26:15–16). Uzziah began to think so highly of himself, he thought God wouldn't mind if he performed a task that was only to be carried out by the priests. God did mind, however! God struck him with leprosy, and he lived the remaining years of his life an outcast from his own palace, and the Lord's (i.e., the Temple)! We must never think more highly of ourselves than we ought to think (Rom. 12:3) or that we are above the Word of God!

CHRIST IS REVEALED:

Through *Azariah the High Priest* who stood between Uzziah and the altar, because the only way to approach the Lord God of Israel was through the priests – 2 Chronicles 26:17–18 (Jesus, our great High Priest, is the only way through which any person can come to God – John 14:6; Heb. 4:14)

WEEK 21, DAY 2: **TODAY'S READING: 2 CHRONICLES 27-31**

OVERVIEW:

The reign of Jotham; the reign of Ahaz; Syria and Israel defeat Judah; the death of Ahaz; Hezekiah's reign; worship is restored in the Temple; Hezekiah destroys idolatry and paganism in Judah; the tithes and offerings of the people.

HIGHLIGHTS & INSIGHTS:

At the end of chapter 26, Uzziah was struck with leprosy because he went into the temple to burn incense. He became an outcast from the Temple and his own palace. In chapter 27, Uzziah's son, Jotham, begins to reign in Judah. He did that which as right in the sight of the Lord like his father, but without going into the Temple. Despite his personal devotion however, the people of Judah still lived "corruptly" (27:2).

When Jotham died, his son Ahaz came to the throne. To say that he didn't follow in his father's footsteps might be the understatement of the year! He was the most wicked king that Judah had yet known. He plunged the entire nation headlong into idolatry, even burning his own children as sacrifices! As a result of his wickedness, the kingdom of Judah continued to lose territory. The Edomites took over in the southeast; the Philistines occupied the cities of the southwest (28:17–18); and thousands of his people were taken as slaves into other countries. Rather than crying out to the Lord in humility and repentance, Ahaz became more wicked and trespassed against the Lord to an even greater degree (28:22). By the time he died, the Temple of the Lord was in shambles, and the entire kingdom of Judah was completely engulfed in idolatry (28:23–25).

Remarkably, Ahaz's son, Hezekiah is one of Judah's greatest kings! Four entire chapters are devoted to his reign in 2 Chronicles (29–32). For all who had a wicked father, Hezekiah's life proves that God can enable you, by His grace and power, to break that cycle of sin so you can be a holy and profitable servant of the Lord Jesus Christ!

Rather than bemoan his terrible upbringing, or allow bitterness toward his godless father (or toward God!) to rule him, when Ahaz died, Hezekiah chose to put the past behind him and made decisions in accordance with God's will and Word. To put his mode of operation into the words of Paul, "[Hezekiah forgot] those things which [were] behind, and [reaching] forth unto those things which [were] before, [he pressed] toward the mark for the prize of the high calling of God in Christ Jesus" (Phil 3:13–14)! May we follow his incredible example!

In the very first month of his reign, Hezekiah reopened and repaired the house of the Lord (chapter 29). He restored the long-neglected priority of Temple worship and reestablished the observance of the Passover (chapter 30), and he removed all idol worship and pagan practices in Judah (31:1). His obedience to God and His Word, manifest through these reforms, brought about the wonderful blessing of God. The days of Hezekiah were the greatest time since the glory days of Solomon's reign (30:26; 1 Kings 10; 2 Chron. 9). God's epitaph of him is worth striving toward: "Hezekiah … wrought that which was good and right and truth before the LORD his God. And in every work that he began in the service of the house of God, and in the law, and in the commandments, to seek his God, he did it with all his heart, and prospered" (31:20–21). May each of us, "Do thou likewise" (Luke 10:37)!

CHRIST IS REVEALED:

Through *King Hezekiah* who offered intercessory prayer for everyone in his kingdom that was seeking God – 2 Chronicles 30:18–19 (Heb. 7:25; Rom. 8:27, 34; John 17:9)

WEEK 21, DAY 3: **TODAY'S READING: 2 CHRONICLES 32-36**

OVERVIEW:

Assyria invades Judah; Hezekiah's death; Manasseh's reign; Amon's reign; Josiah's reign; the book of the Law is found; the reigns of Jehoahaz, Jehoiakim, Jehoiachin, and Zedekiah; the fall of Jerusalem; Judah is taken into Babylonian captivity; the decree of Cyrus to rebuild the Temple.

HIGHLIGHTS & INSIGHTS:

Hezekiah's positive example is further established in today's reading. His character, displayed in the incredible decisions and reforms he made during his reign, was a rare commodity in the kings of Judah and Israel. As with every king, however, God allowed him to be tested. In chapter 32, Hezekiah gets word that Sennacherib, the wicked king of Assyria, with his ferocious army "purposed to fight against Jerusalem" (32:2). When faced with similar dilemmas, so many other Jewish kings turned for help to the arm of the flesh or to pagan kings and nations. Hezekiah, however, was surrendered to the Lordship of Jehovah and displayed absolute confidence and trust in the Lord's strength for victory in the battle. When faced with the threat of Sennacherib's army, Hezekiah didn't freak out or kick into panic mode. Rather, he spoke "comfortably" (32:6) to the people of Judah:

> Be strong and courageous, be not afraid nor dismayed for the king of Assyria, nor for all the multitude that is with him: for there be more with us than with him: with him is an arm of flesh; but with us is the LORD our GOD to help us, and to fight our battles" (32:7-8a).

What faith and trust! And notice the response of the people: "And the people rested themselves upon the words of Hezekiah king of Judah" (32:8b).

Of course, this great demonstration of faith didn't cause Satan (i.e., Sennacherib) to roll over or shut up. He ran his blasphemous mouth even more. He tried to intimidate the people, saying, "All the other countries I've humiliated and obliterated thought their god was going to deliver them out of my hand, too. But you're going to end up just like them!"

Satan (i.e., Sennacherib) used every available means to seek to undermine the people's confidence in Hezekiah's leadership and Jehovah's lordship (32:9-18). They even "spake against the God of Jerusalem, as against the gods of the people of the earth, which were the work of the hands of man" (v.19). Clearly, Sennacherib was successful in defeating those gods because they were man-made gods. Now, however, he was coming against the God who made man!

Hezekiah and Isaiah join their hearts together in prayer to *that* God, and the rest is history! God turned loose an angel, and the battle was over just that quick! Verse 21 says that Sennacherib "returned with shame of face to his own land." In Asian and Middle Eastern culture, a "shamed face" is monumental—so monumental that when Sennacherib got home, his own sons slew him with their swords (32:21). And again I say, hallelujah!

In 32:24–26, Hezekiah is faced with another test, and he briefly allows his pride to cause him to sin against God. In great Romans 7 fashion, however, he immediately humbles himself before the Lord. May we follow his incredible example when our pride causes us to sin against the Lord.

After Hezekiah's death, his son Manasseh comes to the throne. He gets the prize—not only for the longest reign in Judah (55 years), but also for the most evil reign! His reign was even more wicked than that of Ahaz—if you can imagine that. The list of sins he was involved in and led the people into is nothing short of horrendous (33:3–8). In fact, God records that "Manasseh made Judah and the inhabitants of Jerusalem to err, and *to do worse than the heathen*, whom the LORD had destroyed before the children of Israel" (33:9, emphasis added).

However, after God disciplined him (33:11–12), Manasseh humbled himself and prayed to God, and God restored him. For those who think a family member, co-worker, neighbor, or friend is just too far gone to ever turn to God, let Manasseh's story give you hope and revive your prayers for them!

Josiah begins to reign in chapter 34. He was one of the greatest kings in Israel or Judah. We cannot do more than highlight his accomplishments, but he begins to seek the Lord as a young man, starting a national revival. Then he gets the Word of God in his hands and ears and he lives in full obedience to *all* that God had said (chapter 34–35)! May we, who already have the Word of God in our possession, obey like Josiah. And may God speak of us as He did of Josiah: "And like unto him was there no king before him, that turned to the Lord with all his heart, and with all his soul, and with all his might, according to all the law of Moses; neither after him arose there any like him" (2 Kings 23:25).

The last four kings of Judah—Jehoahaz, Jehoiakim, Jehoiachin, and Zedekiah—were evil, and the nation spiraled downward to its disastrous end morally, politically, and spiritually. Nebuchadnezzar, the king of Babylon, and his army finally broke through the north wall of Jerusalem, killing everyone regardless of their age (36:17). They removed all of the vessels out of the Temple, broke down the walls of the city, and burned the Temple to the ground (36:18–19). Those who weren't killed in the massacre were taken into captivity where they would remain for seventy years.

While Judah was in captivity, Babylon was conquered by Persia, which led to the history-changing proclamation of Cyrus in 36:22–23:

> Now in the first year of Cyrus king of Persia, that the word of the Lord spoken by the mouth of Jeremiah might be accomplished, the Lord stirred up the spirit of Cyrus king of Persia, that he made a proclamation throughout all his kingdom, and put it also in writing, saying, Thus saith Cyrus king of Persia, All the kingdoms of the earth hath the Lord God of heaven given me; and he hath charged me to build him an house in Jerusalem, which is in Judah. Who is there among you of all his people? The Lord his God be with him, and let him go up.

CHRIST IS REVEALED:

Through the *Messengers of God* who were rejected by His people – 2 Chronicles 36:15–16 (Isa. 53:3; John 1:11; Mark 8:31; Luke 9:22; 17:25; 20:17)

WEEK 21, DAY 4: **TODAY'S READING: EZRA 1-6**

OVERVIEW:

The decree from Cyrus; the returning Jewish families are listed; the altar and temple are rebuilt; the adversaries come against the work.

HIGHLIGHTS & INSIGHTS:

The book of Ezra divides into two sections, each based upon the leader and the time period. Chapters 1–6 are under the leadership of Zerubbabel. Chapters 7–10 are under the leadership of Ezra, about 60 years after chapter 6.

At the beginning of the book of Ezra, the children of Israel have been in captivity for seventy years. God works in the spirit of Cyrus, a pagan king, to issue a decree that the Jews may return to their homeland and rebuild their temple, fulfilling the prophecy in Jeremiah 29:10, Isaiah 44:28, and Isaiah 45:1. Because of the wording of the decree and its emphasis upon God as "the God," many have speculated that Daniel had an influence upon the king's decree or even wrote the decree on the king's behalf. Either way, the Jews retuned to their homeland, not because of Cyrus or Daniel—but because God said they would!

The Jews' captivity in Babylon was not the same kind of slavery and bondage they had endured in Egypt. They had actually functioned quite well as a people during the Babylonian captivity. That's why only a remnant of the Jews chose to return to their homeland when Cyrus issued the decree. The ones who chose to return, however, made it to the land, and once they did, immediately began the process of restoring the temple.

The restoration is led by Zerubbabel (from the king's line) and Jeshua (from the priest's line). Knowing the scope and magnitude of this great work, these two men wisely lead the people to keep God Himself the priority—as opposed to the project—by first establishing the altar. We, too, must constantly keep *worship* as our first priority, recognizing that we are always susceptible to being so caught up in the *work* of the Lord that we forget the *Lord* of the work!

The remnant begins rebuilding the temple in the second year after their return to the land (3:8), starting, of course, with the foundation. Once the foundation was completed, an interesting dichotomy appeared. The Jews who were too young to remember the glory and magnificence of Solomon's Temple were so emotionally overjoyed and jubilant that they burst forth with great shouting and praise (3:11). But the older generation, who had witnessed the previous temple, looked at the size of the foundation of this new temple and began wailing and weeping (3:12). Both responses were so dramatic that is was impossible to discern the wailing from the rejoicing (3:13)!

Having completed the foundation, the people of God begin to experience opposition to the work in chapter 4. First, their adversaries offer to join the Jews in building the Temple, but when Zerubbabel and Jeshua refuse their offer, their real motives surface. They begin to trouble the people (4:4) and even hire counselors to "frustrate their purpose" (4:5). The adversaries then appeal to the new king to make the people stop the construction, accusing them of being a "rebellious" people, constantly guilty of "sedition" and "insurrection" (4:15–19). The new king investigates their claims and comes to the same conclusion—so the work was halted.

However, Zerubbabel and Jeshua, along with the prophets, encourage the people and lead them to begin the work again—even without permission. When they are questioned, they make request to the king, and their request to continue the work is granted.

And what a beautiful picture of the restoration God intends for our lives! It begins by making sure that, like the remnant in Ezra 4, we too are being led by a King, whom we submit to as Lord to do His will, and a Priest who not only can cleanse us from all sin (1 John 1:9) but can also be "touched with the feeling of our infirmities" (Heb. 4:15). There are times when we just need to get back to the altar of God—where it is just us and God—so that the intimacy of our fellowship with Him can be restored and revived! And unlike the Jews in today's reading, we don't have to lay the foundation again. 1 Corinthians 3:11 says that Christ is our foundation, one that cannot be moved (2 Tim. 2:19). We need only to concern ourselves with how we build our temple upon that foundation (1 Cor. 3:10–15). And as we do, let's not forget that there will be adversaries (1 Cor. 16:9).

As pictured in today's reading, the first attack of the enemy will be to attempt to get us to compromise by becoming "unequally yoked" with them (4:1–2; 2 Cor. 6:14–18). If that doesn't work, the adversary will then trouble us, attempting to "frustrate our purpose," too. Many well-intentioned Christians have been knocked out of the battle simply because their purpose was frustrated. When those attacks come (and they will), we need to persevere in the work to which God has called us and appeal to our King to intervene on our behalf. We won't always know how God's plan will unfold. Our responsibility is to be faithful to our purpose and persevere in the work of the Lord! (1 Cor. 15:58)

CHRIST IS REVEALED:

Through the *Great Stones* used in building the Temple of God – Ezra 5:8 (Christ is the Stone which the builders rejected and He has become the Cornerstone of our faith – Ps. 118:22; Matt. 21:42)

WEEK 21, DAY 5: **TODAY'S READING: EZRA 7-10**

OVERVIEW:

Ezra leads a second group of Jews to return to the land; the sinful condition of the people; Ezra's prayer and confession; the people repent.

HIGHLIGHTS & INSIGHTS:

Ezra 7 begins around sixty years after the end of chapter 6. Ezra leads a second wave of Jews who had chosen to leave their captivity and return to Jerusalem. Ezra, who obviously had a good testimony before King Artaxerxes, receives a letter authorizing their return.

Note that 7:6 says he was a "ready scribe in the law of Moses." Though Ezra could not perform all of his duties while in captivity, he still had made himself ready for the time when God would use him. We should ask ourselves, "Am I preparing myself, through my relationship with God and His Word, for whatever He may want to accomplish in and through me in the future?" For whatever reason, we may not be able to accomplish God's purpose now, but we can make ourselves *ready* for when God changes our circumstances and allows it to happen.

And what did Ezra do to make himself ready? "Ezra had prepared his heart to seek the law of the Lord, and to do it, and to teach in Israel statutes and judgments" (7:10).

First, Ezra knew to *seek* the law of the Lord. Proverbs 2:4–5 says that when we're seeking God's Word as if it were silver and searching for it as we would for "hid treasures," that's when it will do its transforming work in us. Then we will understand "the fear of the Lord, and find the knowledge of God"! Are you presently preparing yourself for what God may have for you in the future by seeking the truth of His Word now?

Second, Ezra was prepared to *do* the law of the Lord. Many of us have a good handle on the *knowledge* of God's Word, but do we seek it (John 13:17)? We know we should "seek those things which are above" (Col. 3:1–2), but do we seek those things? We know we should "[submit ourselves] one to another" (Eph. 5:21), but do we actually submit? We know we should "love [our] neighbour as [ourselves]" and not "bite and devour one another" (Gal. 5:14–15), but do we do these things? We know we should be "patient" with one another and not be bitter against others, offering the same forgiveness to them that we have received from God (Jas. 5:8–9; Eph. 4:32), but do we truly forgive? There are lots of things we know, but how much do we actually put into practice?

Third, God's hand was upon Ezra (7:6, 28). This was certainly not a coincidence! God's hand was upon Ezra because Ezra was a man surrendered to His purposes. We too can have God's hand upon our lives, if we, like Ezra, willingly humble ourselves under God's hand and for His purposes (1 Pet. 5:6). Many Christians want the blessing of God's hand upon their lives, but pursue their own purposes. It doesn't work that way!

Once Ezra approaches the outskirts of Jerusalem, he learns the true condition of those who had previously returned. Though they had *physically* returned to the place God intended them to be (the Promised Land), they were not there *spiritually*. Once again, God's people had fallen prey to their own sinful flesh and were involved in the same abominations as the heathen peoples around them. The same may be true for us. Going physically to a good church, or coming daily to the *52 Weeks of Pursuit*, is no guarantee of a good spiritual condition! The battle with the flesh is a spiritual battle, not just a physical one! We can never think we've conquered our flesh or that we can coast spiritually. Remember 1 Corinthians 10:12! The moment we think we are the strongest is actually when we are the most vulnerable!

Ezra's response to the spiritual condition of God's people was absolute brokenness. His is an incredible example of the heart God intends those in positions of spiritual leadership to possess! In 9:3, Ezra testifies, "And when I heard this thing, I rent my garment and my mantle, and plucked off the hair of my head and of my beard, and sat down astonied." Ezra was so distraught, he was unable to even move a muscle; it was as if he actually had turned into a stone! In 9:5 he says, "And at the evening sacrifice I arose up from my heaviness." Sin in the lives of God's people was a weight in this godly and passionate leader's soul!

In Ezra's prayer, this leader personally identifies himself with the people of God (9:6–15). He refers throughout his prayer, not to *they*, *their* and *them*—but to *our*, *we* and *us*! Rarely do leaders today express the brokenness over sin that Ezra demonstrated in this prayer, nor the personal identification with the people they're seeking to lead. We may talk to others about it, we may think it's terrible, we may have even have expected something "like this" to happen, but rarely in Laodicea do we experience brokenness and heaviness because of it! And in our prayers, seldom, if ever, do we identify ourselves with our people because of sin in our midst. Perhaps that's also the reason we fail to see the revival Ezra was able to lead God's people to experience!

CHRIST IS REVEALED:

Through *Ezra* (a priest) making intercession for his people – Ezra 9:1–5; 10:1 (Jesus is our High Priest who "ever liveth to make intercession for them" – Heb. 7:25–27)

WEEK 22, DAY 1: **TODAY'S READING: NEHEMIAH 1-4**

OVERVIEW:

Nehemiah prays to God about Jerusalem's desolate condition; Nehemiah petitions the king for permission to rebuild the walls of Jerusalem; Nehemiah organizes the people and they begin repairing the walls; opposition to the work arises.

HIGHLIGHTS & INSIGHTS:

The book of Ezra describes the Jews' return to Jerusalem, starting in 536 BC, to rebuild the Temple and restore Temple worship. After this small revival (only a remnant of God's people returned), God sent a prayerful man named Nehemiah to Jerusalem in 445 BC to rebuild the walls of the ruined city in order to restore safety and order to the inhabitants of Jerusalem.

After hearing reports of the sad state of Jerusalem, Nehemiah began to pray even though he held a high position in the king's court (Neh. 1:11) and had no worries for himself. He could have easily justified not doing anything more. But instead of merely praying, he risked his life by petitioning the king to rebuild the walls of Jerusalem (Neh. 2:1–6). So often we pray expecting God to do all the work. Nehemiah got up from his knees, stood on his feet, and did something about the need at hand! The Lord will direct our steps (Prov. 16:9), but for Him to do that, we have to be standing and moving!

And God did more than just move the king to grant Nehemiah's request. He also worked in the king's heart to make him willing to fund the entire project! Truly our God is able to do "exceeding abundantly above all that we ask or think" (Eph. 3:20). But do recognize that, just like Nehemiah, we need to *ask* and then we need to *act*! We must, as the old saying goes, "Pray as if it all depends upon God, but work as if it all depends upon us!" God expects us to do the *possible* and trust Him for the *impossible*.

In chapter 3, God lists the names of the workers and the actual work He used them to accomplish. Each man had a specific area of responsibility. As someone said, "No man can do everything, but every man can do something." However, some of the nobles didn't do anything (3:5)! God said in 1 Corinthians 1:26 that "not many noble, are called" to do the work of God. If we ever find ourselves at a place in time where we are not involved in the work of the Lord, it may be time to examine ourselves. Perhaps we feel that we're above doing such insignificant tasks or believe we are too "noble" for such trivial work; perhaps we think of ourselves "more highly than [we] ought to think" (Rom. 12:3). Keep in mind, we are "servants of the most high God" (Dan. 3:26).

Ten gates were repaired in this chapter, and they paint an incredible picture of the Christian life:

1. **The Sheep Gate** (3:1)
   This gate speaks of Christ's sacrifice for us on the cross. It was the first gate to be repaired because, without the sacrifice of the Lamb of God, there is no salvation. The Sheep Gate had no locks or bars because the door of salvation is always open for the sinner to enter!

2. **The Fish Gate** (3:3)
   As the recipients of salvation, we have been called to be "fishers of men" (Mark 1:17).

3. **The Old Gate** (3:6)
   We are to follow the "old paths" of the Word of God that we might find "rest for [our] souls" (Jer. 6:16).

4. **The Valley Gate** (3:13)
   We are not to think more highly of ourselves than we ought to think, but lower ourselves, having an attitude of humility, just as our Lord Jesus Christ did (Phil. 2:5–9).

5. **The Dung Gate** (3:14)
   This is the gate through which the waste of the city was taken, picturing the fact that we are

to "cleanse ourselves from all filthiness of the flesh and spirit, perfecting holiness in the fear of God" (2 Cor. 7:1).

6. **The Gate of the Fountain** (3:15)
   We need to "be filled with the Spirit" (John 7:37–39; Eph. 5:18).

7. **The Water Gate** (3:26)
   This gate speaks of the Word of God (Eph. 5:26). Also, it is the seventh gate mentioned! (As we have previously seen, seven is the number of perfection or completion in the Bible.) Psalm 19:7 says that God's Word is "perfect," and it "just so happens" that this gate needed no repairs!

8. **The Horse Gate** (3:28)
   The horse is a symbol of war in the Bible. We are soldiers of Jesus Christ (Eph. 6:10–17; 2 Tim. 2:1–4).

9. **The East Gate** (3:29)
   This gate is a picture of Christ's return, that time when the "Sun of righteousness" will rise in the east with healing in His wings (Mal. 4:2).

10. **The Gate Miphkad** (3:31)
    This gate is a picture of God's judgment. The Hebrew word *miphkad* means "appointment, account, or census." One day we all have an appointment with our Lord Jesus Christ at His Judgment Seat, at which time we will give an account of the life we lived after being inhabited by His Holy Spirit (Rom. 14:10–12; 2 Cor. 5:10).

In chapter 4, the enemy appears. We can always be certain that, when God's work is being accomplished, the enemy will always come against it! The enemy will ridicule us, try to discourage us, and attempt to strike fear in us—anything to try to halt the work of the Lord through us! And chapter 4 reveals how this remnant actually overcame their enemies—through prayer (4:9). But again Nehemiah did more than pray, he also set a watch! Four times in the New Testament Jesus told us to "watch and pray" (Matt. 26:41; Mark 13:33; 14:38; Luke 21:36). May we also give diligence to both!

CHRIST IS REVEALED:

As the *King's Cupbearer* – Nehemiah 1:11 (Nehemiah served the king beverages at his table, just as Jesus drank the cup of the King's wrath for us on the cross – Luke 22:42)

Through *Nehemiah* – Nehemiah 1–3 (As Nehemiah left the king's court and his high position to go far away to build a wall of protection for God's people, Jesus left the King's court and His exalted position to build a wall of protection for us.)

As the *Sheep Gate* – Nehemiah 3:1 (Jesus is the "Lamb of God, which taketh away the sin of the world." To become one of Christ's sheep, we must enter through the door which is Christ Himself – John 1:29; 10:1, 7–10)

WEEK 22, DAY 2: **TODAY'S READING: NEHEMIAH 5-9**

OVERVIEW:

The anger of Nehemiah over wealthy Jews taking advantage of poorer Jews; the enemy attacks with deceit, slander and threats; the people who returned are numbered; the Word of God is preached to the people; the Levites cry out to God praising Him for His mercy and goodness.

HIGHLIGHTS & INSIGHTS:

Nehemiah 5 is a sad chapter. The Jews are greedily using each other for material gain, and no building takes place! The Jews were experiencing great economic hardship, not only because of the famine (Hag. 1:7–11), but also because of the taxes and tributes being inflicted upon them. To provide food and basic necessities for their families, the poorer Jews were having to mortgage their property and sell themselves into servitude to their Jewish kinsmen. God instructs and admonishes His people, both the ancient Jews and Christians today, to watch out for one another—to love, help, and care for one another. Proverbs 3:27 tells us to "withhold not good from them to whom it is due, when it is in the power of thine hand to do it." Philippians 2:4 says, "Look not every man on his own things, but every man also on the things of others."

But in Nehemiah 5, the Jews were doing the exact opposite! Rather than *pray for* each other, they *preyed upon* each other. If we aren't careful, we can become so selfish and self-serving that we end up making money on those we should be ministering to! And Nehemiah's extremely angry response to the Jews gauging one another for personal gain is the same response our Lord Jesus Christ had in His day (Mark 11:15–17)! Nehemiah very wisely put this evil and selfish practice to an end and refocused the people to the work at hand (Neh. 5:9–12).

In chapter 6 the work on the walls resumes. And it is no coincidence that, when the work restarted, the enemy also reappeared! This time, however, Sanballat and his men aim their attack against Nehemiah, the leader. Satan knows that everything rises and falls on leadership. He knows that if he can get Nehemiah to stop leading, the work of rebuilding the walls will quickly come to a complete halt. If you are in any type of leadership position (pastor, father, mother, teacher, discipler), there is a high price to pay! There is a large target on your back at which the enemy is constantly aiming. That is why we must learn to put on the whole armor of God on a daily basis (Eph. 6:10–18)!

Four times, Sanballat tries to arrange a meeting with Nehemiah "just to talk," as it were (Neh. 6:3–4). Nehemiah did not fall for this deception, however, because he was "not ignorant of [Satan's] devices" (2 Cor. 2:11). May we, likewise, learn to beware of the smiles of the enemy, for Satan is often more dangerous when he appears to be our friend than when he appears to be our enemy! May we also learn to stay focused on the task at hand. When our enemy extends an invitation, it is likely designed to redirect us, to halt the work of the Lord through us.

When his first four invitations failed to get the response Sanballat was hoping for, he sent the fifth messenger with a different strategy. He arrives with an unsealed letter filled with slanderous accusations against Nehemiah (6:5). "It is reported" (6:6) is one of the devil's chief weapons when wanting to disrupt the work and the people of God. Phrases such as "People are saying..." or "I've been hearing..." or "Did you know..." usually introduce gossip and lies. In this case, Nehemiah's life and character refuted every lie in the letter. As servants of God, we can't control what people say about us, but we can control the character and testimony we display!

As a tremendous leader of God's people, once again Nehemiah takes his problem to the Lord in prayer (6:9). And we can do with same. Had Nehemiah stopped the work to defend his reputation, the walls would never have been built! Because he gave the problem to God, the walls were completed in just fifty-two days (6:15). As a result, God was glorified, and the enemy was embarrassed (6:16). May all the work we allow the Lord to do through us end with this same incredible result!

Chapter 7 is a numbering of all the people who had returned from the exile. In Chapter 8, Ezra returned to Jerusalem to assist Nehemiah with the dedication of the walls and the sanctifying of the people. The people gathered to hear the Word of God at the "water gate" (8:1) because, biblically, water pictures the Word of God (Eph. 5:26).

Nehemiah 8:1–9 provides a description of what we might refer to as the "perfect church service!"

- The people all assembled to listen.

- The Word was exalted high.

- The preacher read and explained the Word so the people could understand it.

- The people wept at hearing the Word, which no doubt revealed their sensitivity to the working of the Spirit as He revealed areas of sinfulness in their lives!

This reading of the Word of God in chapter 8 provoked the leaders to pray to the God of the Word. All of chapter 9 is a prayer that provides a beautiful spiritual summary of the Old Testament history of the Jews. In this prayer, they praise God for His mercy to them despite their unfaithfulness to Him. May we praise Him today for the same!

CHRIST IS REVEALED:

Through *Nehemiah* – Nehemiah 5:17–19. (Nehemiah was the governor of the people, but he fed all who came to his table (Jews, nobles, and even Gentiles!) at no cost to them.)

WEEK 22, DAY 3: **TODAY'S READING: NEHEMIAH 10-13**

OVERVIEW:

The leaders who placed their seal on the covenant with God; the city of Jerusalem is populated by the Jews; the dedication of the city wall; Nehemiah condemns the people's wicked ways and reforms the abuses.

HIGHLIGHTS & INSIGHTS:

After making a "sure" covenant with God to do all things according to His Word, the leaders sealed it (Nehemiah 9:38). Chapter 10 lists the names of the leaders who entered into this covenant with God that day. I'll bet they never realized that their names would be recorded eternally in God's Word as an example for believers in every generation!

In 10:28–39, we see the people actually applying the Word in a practical way to their everyday lives. They gave evidence that they weren't just coming to the Word of God to gain *information*, but because they were desiring *transformation*! It's one thing for people to pray and sign a covenant. It is quite another for them to actually separate themselves from evil (10:28), straighten out their homes (10:28–30), honor the Sabbath (10:31), contribute to the house of God (10:32–33), and serve God with their tithes and offerings (10:34–39). Today, too many Bible conferences, Bible studies, Bible lessons, and church services end with people who feel emotionally stirred and blessed, but who never proceed to repentance, obedience, and transformation of life! Maybe this is a good time to honestly ask ourselves: Can I detect life change through what God is teaching me through the ministry of the Word in my own local church and the *52 Weeks of Pursuit*?

In chapters 11 and 12, the city of Jerusalem is populated, and its wall is dedicated. A portion of the Jews had to live in the city, for the good of the city and for the glory of God. This required faith because they had to leave their homes for an unspecified place. All of the leaders moved into Jerusalem, some of the people graciously volunteered, and the rest of the people cast lots to determine who would move. At least 10% of the people were to live in Jerusalem (11:1–2). In the end, 3,044 men actually made the move (11:3–19). If this represents 10% of the male Jews who returned from exile, it indicates just how small the returning remnant was. As Jesus taught in Matthew 7:14: "Because strait is the gate, and narrow is the way, which leadeth unto life, and few there be that find it."

Nehemiah returned to Babylon for a few years, leaving the governing of the city to his brother, Hanani (Neh. 7:2; 13:6). Hanani was "a faithful man, and feared God above many" (7:2), but when Nehemiah returned, he discovered that the people had fallen back into their old ways. Sadly, sin in the lives of God's people tends to repeat itself.

When Nehemiah returned to Jerusalem, he found that the inner rooms of the temple were being misused (13:7). The Levites were not being supported for their work in the Temple, so they had to leave the house of God to work in their fields to sustain themselves (v. 10). The sabbath day was being abused (vs. 15–22), and the Jewish men, including the priests, were taking heathen wives (vs. 23–31; Deut. 23:3–5). Nehemiah, the courageous leader, honestly confronted the people with the their sin and explained God's judgment concerning it (13:1–3, 8–9, 11). Are we judging the sin in our own lives? And are we being a good enough friend to those we love (or are leading) to confront them with their sin, that our Lord might receive the glory that is due His name through their lives?

CHRIST IS REVEALED:

As the *Wall of Jerusalem* – Nehemiah 12:27 (God is our fortress in whom we trust – Ps. 91:2)

WEEK 22, DAY 4: **TODAY'S READING: ESTHER 1-3**

OVERVIEW:

Vashti (a Gentile woman) is removed from her royal position as queen; Esther (a Jewish woman) is chosen to be the new queen; the evil plot of Haman against the whole Jewish race.

HIGHLIGHTS & INSIGHTS:

The events of Esther take place between Ezra 6 and 7. What Esther 1:3 calls the third year of Ahasuerus's reign is actually 483 BC. *Ahasuerus* is not a man's name, but the title used to refer to the supreme ruler in Persia at this time, just as a pharaoh was the supreme ruler in Egypt.

Interestingly, God's name is not found in Esther, although Jewish scribes have found the name *Jehovah* "hidden" in five different verses. It's a beautiful spiritual lesson: when it seems that God is nowhere to be found, if we look beneath the surface, we will actually find Him working behind the scenes to accomplish His purposes for our lives (Rom. 8:28)!

The book of Esther opens with the king holding a seven-day feast for all the people in his palace (1:5). After seven days of excessive drinking (1:10), Ahasuerus decides to show off Vashti, his beautiful trophy wife and queen, to all of his male friends. In her wisdom, however, and with apparent high moral values, Vashti refuses to cater to the king's selfish, carnal, and drunken request. This, of course, infuriates the male chauvinist king and his male chauvinist princes, so they decide together that the king should remove her from her exalted position and publicize her removal so that all the women in the kingdom would not follow her rebellious example, but be sure to honor their husbands (1:15–20).

After about four years, the king begins to miss his wife and regrets his rash decision to put her away (2:1). Recognizing his loneliness, his servants convince him to pick a new queen from among the beautiful women in his kingdom by holding the rough equivalent of a beauty pageant. And "it just so happens" that God had placed a Jew named Mordecai in a very important position, seated at the king's gate (2:21). Mordecai, a cousin of Esther who had brought her up after her parents died (2:7), entered her into the king's contest and ordered her not tell anyone that she was a Jew (2:10, 20). In God's sovereignty, and because of her distinct character and beauty, the king chose Esther to be his new queen and held a feast in her honor.

At the end of chapter 2, Mordecai uncovers a plot to kill the king. He notifies Esther who tells the king in Mordecai's name, and it all gets written down in the book of the chronicles of the king. While this may seem like a rather insignificant detail at the time, it ends up being the very thing that God uses to save His people from destruction.

In chapter 3 the king makes a man named Haman his chief advisor. And he just happens to despise the Jews! Haman, a picture of the flesh, is a self-seeking, self-serving, egomaniac. When Mordecai refuses to bow to him as he passes, Haman is ticked off (3:5) and offers the king the equivalent of about $25 million in silver to pass a law to exterminate all of the Jews (3:13). The money would likely come from the sale of the slain Jews' property, much like Hitler did during WWII and the Roman Catholic Church did during the Crusades. The king passed the law, and the date for their execution was set by casting lots (Est. 3:7, Prov. 16:33). In God's providence, the date was set an entire year away (3:7), providing plenty of time for God's plan to unfold through the plan of Mordecai, to halt this satanically generated plot against the Jewish people.

CHRIST IS REVEALED:

Through *King Ahasuerus* – Esther 1–2. (A day is soon coming when God will remove (rapture) the church (His Gentile bride and queen) off of this earth because of her unfaithfulness to Him and replace her with the Nation of Israel (His Jewish queen) for His 1000-year reign on earth as King.)

WEEK 22, DAY 5: **TODAY'S READING: ESTHER 4-7**

OVERVIEW:

Mordecai and the Jews mourn over the king's commandment to destroy them; Esther and Mordecai work a plan to save the Jews; Esther plans a banquet for the king at which she makes her request of him to save her people, the Jews; the king belatedly honors Mordecai for his service to him in uncovering the assassination plot; Esther accuses Haman before the king and Haman is executed.

HIGHLIGHTS & INSIGHTS:

In chapter 4, Mordecai grieves and weeps in sackcloth and ashes in the streets of the city over the decree issued by the king to destroy the Jewish race. He does this right in the king's gate where everyone could see him, without fearing the consequences or being ashamed of his God or his people. Esther, not understanding why Mordecai was expressing such extreme public emotion (and commotion!), sends a servant to find out what was wrong. Mordecai sends word back to her explaining his actions, along with a copy of the king's decree to exterminate the Jews, so she might understand just how desperate the situation actually was. Mordecai convinces Esther that she is the one that God wants to use to deliver His people, suggesting that her rise to such an exalted position in the kingdom might well have been "for such a time as this" (4:14). We must admire Esther, for she presents herself before the king as a "living sacrifice" (Rom. 12:1), knowing she could die if the king doesn't hold out the golden scepter to her.

Based on Mordecai and Esther's behavior, we would do well to ask ourselves two simple but very sobering introspective questions:

- Am I, like Mordecai, deeply concerned for those who are condemned?
- Am I, like Esther, willing to sacrifice myself to intercede on behalf of those facing inevitable judgment?

Rather than just making her request to the king concerning her people, Esther wisely extends a more formal invitation for the king and Haman to attend a special banquet that she wanted to prepare. She was clearly aware of the king's strong affinity for food and wine and decided her best chance for getting her request granted would be when the king was of a "merry heart" (Prov. 15:13, 15; 17:22). At the banquet, the king asks Esther what was on her mind and confirms his willingness to grant her petition—even if it were for half of the kingdom! Once again, rather than present such a grave and monumental request at an inappropriate or inopportune time, she chooses to invite him to yet another banquet on the following day (Ecc. 3:11).

Haman leaves Esther's first banquet feeling like he was sitting on top of the world! Not only was he the king's right-hand man, but he was the only man in the kingdom that the queen invited to her special banquet. As he walks past the king's gate after the banquet, however, he is again enraged because of Mordecai's refusal to do obeisance to him. When he gets home, he tells his wife and friends about the high of his day, the special honor of his exclusive time with the king and queen and of the low of his day, with that despicable Jew not bowing to him in the gate! They suggest that Haman build a gallows for Mordecai's terrible "insurrection," so that he can be hanged on them the next day before Esther's second banquet.

While Haman is plotting these things in his house, the king finds himself unable to sleep in his house. He commands that the recent chronicles of his kingship be read to him, and as they are, he is reminded that Mordecai foiled the recent assassination attempt against him. He also realizes that no kindness had been extended to Mordecai for his heroic deed, but cannot think of exactly how to honor him. He hears that Haman is in the court and calls him in to seek his counsel on an appropriate way for the king to bestow honor upon a very special individual.

Thinking that the king must certainly be referring to him, Haman concocts an extravagant plan to exalt himself before all the people. The king thought Haman's plan was perfect and was excited to see it enacted. What a humiliating shock it must have been to Haman when the king assigned him to personally ensure that every last detail of the plan was lavished upon "Mordecai the Jew" (6:10)! Haman was so beside himself that he immediately goes home to tell his wife and his counselors what had happened, and rather than encourage him, they basically tell him that this will prove to be something he will not be able to overcome (6:13). While they were discussing this matter, the king's chamberlains came to tell Haman that it was time for Esther's second banquet.

As the banquet begins in chapter 7, the king is very eager to hear what request Esther has in her heart and why she was being so mysterious about it. When she finally tells the king that there was a conspiracy unfolding to exterminate her and her people—the king is absolutely furious! He wants to know immediately who had devised such a heinous plan, and where he is (7:5)! And what an unbelievable surprise it is to the king when Esther points across the table and says, "The adversary and enemy is this wicked Haman" (7:6). The king orders that Haman be executed upon the very gallows that he had commanded to be built to hang Mordecai. And as the old saying goes, "It couldn't have happened to a nicer guy!"

CHRIST IS REVEALED:

Through *Esther* – Esther 5–7. Esther goes before the King to plead for the salvation of her people knowing it may cost a very high price: her own life! Jesus goes before the Father (or King) as our Advocate (1 John 2:1; Rev. 12:9–10) to plead our case for forgiveness in light of the very high price He paid to obtain it: His own life!

WEEK 23, DAY 1: **TODAY'S READING: ESTHER 8-10**

OVERVIEW:

King Ahasuerus issues another decree allowing the Jews to defend themselves and destroy their enemies; the Jews defeat and destroy their enemies; the feast of Purim is instituted to commemorate this victory; Mordecai's prosperity and promotion.

HIGHLIGHTS & INSIGHTS:

Our overview of the book of Esther has primarily been on the storyline, the *historical* application. And what an intriguing story it is! It is packed full of all of the things that make an interesting story: a villain, a hero, hatred, love, danger and romance. And while the book of Esther has been recorded with precise historical accuracy, in the *doctrinal* or *prophetic* application, this story is an incredible picture of the daily drama of the Christian life as "the flesh lusteth against the Spirit, and the Spirit against the flesh" (Gal. 5:17).

The *doctrinal* or *prophetic* application is what a verse, passage, chapter or book of the Bible is teaching us through the real-life illustrations in pictures and types. In the book of Esther:

- King Ahasuerus is a picture of the human soul, particularly our will—where *decisions* are made, *policies* are determined, and *decrees* are put into motion.

- Vashti is a picture of the fallen human spirit, representing our old, or fallen, nature.

- Esther is a picture of the human spirit revived by the Holy Spirit, representing our new nature.

- Mordecai is a picture of the Holy Spirit.

- Haman is a picture of the flesh.

With these pictures in mind, it is a monumental thing when Ahasuerus gives his ring to Haman in Esther 3:10 because whoever has possession of the king's ring has the power and control. Chapter 3 becomes, then, a perfect picture of the flesh (Haman) in control, lusting against the Spirit (Mordecai), and chapter 4 becomes a perfect picture of the Spirit (Mordecai) lusting against the flesh (Haman). (See Gal. 5:17.)

Also in chapter 4, when the flesh (Haman) is in control, the Spirit (Mordecai) is grieved. What an incredibly graphic and horribly sad glimpse of what actually takes place in "the midst of our city" (on the inside of us – Est. 4:1) when the flesh is "wearing the ring" (is in control of our lives). We "grieve" the Holy Spirit of God within us (Eph. 4:30)! What a difference it would make if we could see and hear what Esther 4:1 describes through the picture of Mordecai, as the Holy Spirit in us is wearing "sackcloth and ashes" and weeping with a "loud and bitter cry"!

In today's reading, because of the law of the Medes and Persians (8:8), the king could not cancel the decree that had been written to put the Jews to death. The only way to prevent the execution demanded by the old law was to institute and implement a new law. It is a perfect picture of what Paul revealed in Romans 8. The law of sin and death (the Old Testament) is binding and in effect. "The wages of sin" is most certainly "death" (Rom. 6:23a). There is no reversing that. The only remedy is the institution and implementation of the new law provided in and through our Lord Jesus Christ that supersedes the old law, "the law of the Spirit of life in Christ Jesus" (Rom. 8:2). Hallelujah!

In light of these incredible pictures, Esther 8:8 also pictures beautifully the New Testament teaching of the "eternal security of the believer." As pictured in the law of the Medes and Persians, once something had received the seal of the king, no man could reverse it—not even the king himself! In the New Testament, Ephesians 1:12–14 and 4:30 teach us that the moment we called on the name of the Lord Jesus Christ, trusting Him alone for our salvation, He sealed us with His own Spirit! Ephesians 1:14 calls the Spirit the "earnest" (or down payment; literally "engagement ring"), guaranteeing our complete redemption and the inheritance of eternal life. We can rejoice and rest in the fact that when the King of creation and salvation seals us with His Holy Spirit, we are secure in Him for all of eternity! (Also see Daniel 6:17.)

Esther 8:10–14 is a beautiful picture of the urgency of taking the life-and-death message of the gospel to the ends of the earth. The scribes hurriedly wrote the message and the official ambassadors quickly took the "good news" to the four corners of the kingdom. Likewise, we have become the King's ambassadors, commissioned to take the message of good news to the four corners of the globe while we still have time! And when the Jews received the message of good news—namely, that the *old* law ensuring *death* had been superseded by a *new* law ensuring *life*, it not only provided deliverance, but incredible rejoicing!

In chapter 9, the Jews avenged themselves of their enemies, trusting God to destroy them—all 75,810 of them! (There were 75,000 in 9:16; 500 in 9:6; 300 in 9:15; and the 10 sons of Haman in 9:13.)

Lastly, in chapter 9, while recognizing the historical reality of what happened in Esther's day, we can see at least six powerful New Testament principles concerning the Christian life that apply directly to believers in our day.

- **Principle #1: What I do to ensure victory *today*, is the same thing I must do to ensure victory *tomorrow*. (9:12–13)**

  The middle of verse 13 says, "Do tomorrow also according unto this day's decree." The victory in the Christian life is simply a matter of reckoning our death to self and Christ's life within us on a daily basis. (See Rom. 6:11; 2 Cor. 4:10–11; 1 Cor. 15:31.)

- **Principle #2: Even though my flesh is already dead, I must take it out daily and nail it to the cross. (9:13–14)**

  The end of verse 13 says, "And let Haman's ten sons be hanged upon the gallows." Notice that the ten sons of Haman were already dead, but they still took them out and hanged them the next day. (See Romans 6:11–15.)

- **Principle #3: In order to attain and sustain victory in my spiritual walk, my motives must be free of self interests. (9:10b, 15b, 16b)**

  Verse 10 says, "but on the spoil laid they not their hand." Verse 15 says, "but on the prey they laid not their hand." Verse 16 says, "… but they laid not their hands on the prey." (See 1 Corinthians 6:19–20.)

- **Principle #4: As I walk in the victory of the fullness and power of the Spirit, God's love will be shed abroad through me, causing me to fulfill the "one another" commands of Scripture toward my brothers and sisters and to express compassion for the poor. (9:22)**

  Galatians 5:22 says, "But the fruit of the Spirit is love." Romans 5:5 says, "The love of God is shed abroad in our hearts by the Holy Ghost which is given unto us."

  Check out the New Testament "one another" commands: John 13:34; Rom. 12:5, 10, 16; 13:8; 14:13, 19; 15:5, 7, 14; 16:16; 1 Cor. 4:6; 6:7; 11:33; 12:25; 16:20; Gal. 5:13, 15, 26; Eph. 4:2, 25, 32; 5:21; Col. 3:9, 13, 16; 1 Thess. 3:12; 4:18; 5:11; 1 Tim. 5:21; Heb. 3:13; 10:24–25; Jas. 4:11; 5:9, 16; 1 Pet. 1:22; 3:8; 4:9–10; 5:5, 14; 1 John 1:7; 3:11, 23; 4:7, 11.

  And see Galatians 2:10, "Remember the poor."

- **Principle #5: There is a memorial feast that I am to celebrate in remembrance of the day God turned my inevitable destruction into deliverance and salvation. (9:17–32)**

  See 1 Corinthians 11:23–26.

- **Principle #6: I must constantly remember that God's Spirit (Mordecai) will not override my will (King Ahasuerus), and only through yielding my will to Him will I ever experience the spiritual wealth and peace of the Spirit in the kingdom I call my life. (10:1–3)**

  See Romans 6:13–22.

CHRIST IS REVEALED:

Through *Mordecai* – Esther 10:3. (Mordecai became "next unto [the] king" after delivering God's people from sure destruction. Jesus "sat down on the right hand of God" after delivering us all from sure destruction – Heb. 10:12–14)

WEEK 23, DAY 2: **TODAY'S READING: JOB 1–6**

OVERVIEW:

Job's godly character and wealth; the dialogue between God and Satan; Satan permitted to afflict Job; the negative counsel of Job's wife; Job's three friends come to visit; the first speech of Eliphaz; Job's response.

HIGHLIGHTS & INSIGHTS:

Job is one of the most incredible men in the entire Bible. He was of such impeccable character that God Himself used Job's sacrifice, service, and surrender to get in Satan's face in Job 1. Satan responded that Job only did what he did, and was who he was, because of all of the good things God had done for him. (Basically, he accused God of buying Job's affection.) Satan told God, "Take all of your blessing away, and you'll see how worthy Job thinks You are of his worship and service" (1:11).

In 1:12, God tells Satan he may do whatever he wanted to Job, except harm Job himself. So Satan goes after Job. In one day, Job gets word that all of his oxen and donkeys were killed, along with all of the servants who kept them; that fire had fallen from the sky and burned up all the sheep, along with those who tended them; and that all of his camels had been stolen, and his servants who kept them had been murdered. In the span of a few hours, his entire fortune was lost. Then those dreadful things are overshadowed by the final news: every one of his sons and daughters had been killed in a tornado at the eldest brother's house!

How would you respond to God if all of these things befell you? Would God still be God to you? Would you still consider Him good? Would He be worthy of your followship? Would you, or could you, praise Him?

Besides raising such significant questions, these chapters also offer a few practical concepts for us to glean.

- **Concerning Satan**
  Satan is extremely powerful, but he is not all-powerful. Though he goes "to and fro in the earth … walking up and down in it" (1:7), the book of Job tells us he's actually on God's leash! He can only go as far as God permits. Everything that takes place in our lives is either *appointed* by God or *allowed* of God. Take heart!

- **Concerning Suffering**
  Suffering is not a matter of misfortune or bad luck, nor is it always God's chastisement for some sin we have refused to remove from our lives. Sometimes we suffer for doing what is right. God's own testimony of Job was that he "was perfect and upright, and one that feared God, and eschewed evil" (1:1).

- **Concerning People**
  Even well-meaning people can sometimes be used by Satan, as in the case of Job's "friends," to criticize, accuse, and condemn. They think they have everything figured out, when they actually don't know all the facts and are functioning from only human reasoning, temporal values, and half-truths.

While there are many obvious applications in the book of Job, there are others which are less easily seen. For these concepts, one of the most incredible commentaries I have ever read is *Job: Adventures in the Land of Uz!* by Jeff Adams.[1] The following are some of Pastor Adams's insights from chapter 1.

> In Job, God gives us an incredible illustration of believers in tribulation. If ever anyone qualified for enduring tribulation it was Job! Remember that the next major event on God's prophetic calendar is a seven-year period we often call the Tribulation which will fall upon this earth. Some of the prophecies in the book of Revelation are incredible and probe the limits of our

imagination. To help us understand, God has given us the story of a man named Job. More than a simple story about his trials, Job is a wonderful picture of the coming time of Tribulation and helps us to better understand the future.

As you approach the book of Job, consider the picture that is drawn. The parallels between what happened to Job and the prophecies of the coming time of Tribulation are too many to be mere coincidence.

Pastor Adams then describes some of those parallels.

The story of Job takes place in the land of Uz, exactly where the faithful remnant of Jews will be hidden during the Tribulation. Uz always has a connection with Edom in the Bible, and the famous Petra (from the Greek word for "rock") is in Edom, the refuge God has prepared for His people.

Job sits in his misery for seven days, while his friends look on speechless. In the coming Tribulation the Jews will suffer at the hands of the Antichrist for a seven-year period. The world will be powerless to help, and most will genuinely believe that they are only getting what they deserve. Don't think that World War II did away with anti-Semitism.

Actually, the Great Tribulation is the last half of the seven years, though we often apply the word Tribulation to the entire period. The first three and a half years are a time of false peace, when the Antichrist comes into power through a brilliant series of treaties that brings peace to the Middle East, and structures a disarmament (Daniel 8:11-14, 25, 9:27; Isaiah 28:18).

At midpoint of this seven-year period the Antichrist breaks his treaty with Israel and declares himself God in the reconstructed Jewish Temple. This is the abomination spoken of by Daniel (Daniel 9:27; 8:13-14; 11:31; Matthew 24:15). These last three and a half years are of world war and great destruction. The book of Revelation counts it as a period of 42 months (Revelation 11:2). Chapter divisions in the Bible were not added until several hundred years ago – and most people may not believe that God had anything to do with it – but it is interesting to notice that Job has 42 chapters.

He concludes with these thoughts:

Very few people can boast that the Devil himself has personally persecuted them, but Job could. He was the direct target of Satan. This is also a figure of what will happen to Israel in the time of Tribulation. Israel will be attacked by the very Devil.

At the end of the book of Job, Job's captivity is turned, and he receives double all that he lost. In a similar way, the captivity of Israel will be turned around after the purging of the Tribulation and will be restored to the position of blessing.

CHRIST IS REVEALED:

In the *Dialogue* between God and Satan – Job 1:6–12 (Through it we can understand the meaning of Christ's statement to Peter that Satan desired to "sift [him] as wheat" – Luke 22:31)

[1]Jeff Adams, *Job: Adventures in the Land of Uz!* Kansas City, MO: Reality Living Publishers, 1994. (Also available in Kindle format from Amazon.)

WEEK 23, DAY 3: **TODAY'S READING: JOB 7-11**

OVERVIEW:

Job continues his response to Eliphaz: Job reproaches his friends; Bildad's theory about Job's tribulation; Job's response to Bildad; Zophar's accusations against Job.

HIGHLIGHTS & INSIGHTS:

In yesterday's reading, Eliphaz was the first of Job's friends to offer his counsel (Job 3-4), and in chapter 6, Job responds. In chapter 7 today, Job continues his response. He begins (7:1) with a soul-deep cry, "If men are on the earth for a set time, surely my time is about up!" All of these tragedies have brought Job to the depths of despair. He feels there's nothing left to look forward to in life but long, empty days and sleepless nights (7:3–4). On one hand, he's afraid his life is over, and on the other hand, he's afraid that maybe it isn't!

Obviously, Job has no clue that his suffering was actually the result of how pleased God was with Job's godly character and pure heart. Facing such horrific things, Job simply assumes that, for some unknown reason, God must be displeased with him. And if we put ourselves in Job's situation, we can easily understand why he is so distraught. As Job concludes his response to Eliphaz, he readily admits that he is a sinner like everybody else, but holds tenaciously to the fact that his tribulation is not because of some secret sin in his life that he is refusing to confess.

Chapter 8 begins the counsel of Bildad, the second of Job's friends. Whereas Eliphaz at least attempted to grace his accusation that Job must be guilty of some secret sin, Bildad goes straight for Job's spiritual jugular. He tells Job that he's sick of listening to his excuses and that he's full of hot air (8:1). He even has the audacity to tell Job that his ten children must also have sinned and so had gotten from God's hand exactly what they deserved (8:4). Basically, Bildad tells Job that if he would simply pray and earnestly seek God, all of his tribulation would go away. With friends like that—who needs enemies?

Sadly, there are Bildads in every church. They are typically well-intentioned, but majorly misinformed! And, just as in Bildad's case, it is impossible to convince them of that. But even worse, as our biblical knowledge increases, we risk becoming just like Bildad. Pride can deceive us into thinking that we know why people go through what they go through, but as Job can tell us, that arrogant and judgmental attitude can be extremely hurtful. And like Bildad, we can also be very wrong!

In chapter 9, Job responds to Bildad's accusations. Though there were many things he could have said to defend himself, Job actually chose to admit the truth of Bildad's words. In fact, most of the things that Job's three friends said was actually true. They all possessed a great deal of information about God and His ways. They were simply off in their timing and their application of that truth.

Be sure to read carefully the seven *ifs* Job declares in chapter 9. They appear in 9:16–18; 9:19; 9:20a; 9:20b–26; 9:27–28; 9:29; and 9:30–35.

In chapter 10, Job sets forth a series of questions for God. Job wants to know how God could understand the sufferings of a man, since He had never been one (10:4). Obviously, Job could say that in his day. But for the last 2000 years, that complaint cannot be registered because God has since become a man. We do have a God who is "touched with the feeling of our infirmities" because He became one of us and was "in all points tempted like as we are, yet without sin" (Heb. 4:15). Therefore, Paul tells us in Hebrews 4:16, that we can "come boldly unto the throne of grace, that we may obtain mercy, and find grace to help him in time of need."

In chapter 11, Zophar, the third of Job's friends, begins to offer his so-called loving counsel. He also comes on with both feet, basically saying, "Job, I'm not going to let you get by with all of your meaningless talk and lies!" (11:2–3). Like Bildad and Eliphaz, he also tells Job that it's obvious that what he needs to do is repent, get his heart right with God, and everything would be all right.

Have you ever been an Eliphaz, Bildad, or Zophar—all up in somebody's face, thinking you knew what they needed, when what they really needed was someone to simply be a loving friend to them? Maybe there's someone you need to contact today, seeking their forgiveness for your haughty spirit and judgmental attitude.

CHRIST IS REVEALED:

Through *Job's Sorrowful Condition* – Job 7:1–6 (Christ is called "a man of sorrows, and acquainted with grief" – Isa. 53:3; Mark 15:34)

Through the *Daysman* (mediator) Job longed for – Job 9:33 (The Lord Jesus Christ is the only mediator between holy God and sinful men – 2 Tim. 2:5)

WEEK 23, DAY 4: **TODAY'S READING: JOB 12-16**

OVERVIEW:

Job's affirmation of faith in God's wisdom; Job's defense of his righteous testimony; Eliphaz's intensified accusations and condemnation; Job's complaint of God's dealing with him.

HIGHLIGHTS & INSIGHTS:

At this point, Job's three friends have all taken a turn to pound him. Job has been so overcome with grief he hasn't actually addressed the attacks they've hurled against him. That changes in chapter 12. He's had just about all of the "godly" counsel he could stand! Job tells his friends that their problem is that they have a lot of knowledge, but not a lot of wisdom and understanding. Nothing could be more descriptive of many (or even most) believers today!

In chapters 13 and 14, Job continues his answer to his critics, his self-appointed counselors. Job is finally collecting his thoughts and verbalizing them with much greater boldness as he defends the righteousness of his testimony. In 13:9–12, Job hurls some accusations of his own. He accuses his three friends of mocking God, of secretly being respecters of persons, of not fearing God, and of forgetting that they are also mortal bodies of clay that will ultimately return to ashes.

Finally, in verses 20–22 of chapter 13, Job presents God with two ultimatums:

> "Knock off the tribulation."

> "Let's talk! Either You ask me, or let me ask You, what in the world is going on!"

Since God hadn't taken away his trials, Job asks God four questions that he wants Him to answer (13:23-25).

In chapter 14, Job is still addressing God, not his human counselors. In chapter 15, however, Eliphaz throws his hat back into the ring. He begins with a series of questions for Job, along with a few carefully placed digs. Eliphaz tells Job that he has a heart problem and that it can even be detected in his eyes. He says Job's spirit is in rebellion against God, and the proof of it is in the words that he has spoken (15:12–13). May we never be so judgmental of people—especially when we don't know all of the facts and especially since we can't really know how God is working in a person's life!

As we begin chapter 16, Job begins to unload his frustration. From an historical standpoint, he is simply sharing what he is going through. From a prophetic standpoint, however, chapter 16 is one of six chapters (along with Job 30, Isaiah 50, 52, and 53, and Psalm 22) in the Old Testament that show us what was taking place in the heart and mind of the Lord Jesus Christ as He hung on the cross. In this chapter, Job is a picture of Christ, deserted by the Father and hanging on the cross in our place.

CHRIST IS REVEALED:

Through the *Smiting of Job* – Job 16:10 (Christ was also struck by His accusers – Matt. 27:29–44; John 18:22–33; Ps. 22:7–8; 109:25; Isa. 53)

Through *Job Suffering Not for his own Sin* – Job 16:17 (2 Cor. 5:21)

WEEK 23, DAY 5: **TODAY'S READING: JOB 17-21**

OVERVIEW:

The continuation of Job's defense of himself; Bildad's continued accusations; Job's response to Bildad; Zophar's accusation that Job is a wicked man; Job's response to Zophar.

HIGHLIGHTS & INSIGHTS:

In chapter 17, Job's words continue to picture prophetically what was taking place in the heart and mind of our Lord Jesus Christ on the cross. When Job says in verse 7, "Mine eye also is dim by reason of sorrow, and all my members are as a shadow," we see the Lord Jesus Christ consumed with the weight of our sin. "The innocent" in verse 8, who "shall stir up himself against the hypocrite," is obviously a reference to the Lord Jesus Christ. Job's innocence foreshadows the innocent Savior who died for the guilty.

Chapter 17 is also a great reminder of one of the great paradoxes of life: winners don't always win, and losers don't always lose. Many times the godly suffer, while the wicked prosper.

In chapter 18, Bildad again attempts to convince Job that some secret sin is the cause of his intense suffering. But God's record of Bildad's words also provides us unbelievable information about the Antichrist. In verse 5, Bildad mentions "the wicked." This is a prophetic foreshadowing of "that Wicked" (the Antichrist) Paul mentions in 2 Thessalonians 2:8. The chapter ends by looking to the coming Antichrist and to his ultimate destination in hell: "Surely such are the dwellings of the wicked, and this is the place of him that knoweth not God" (v. 21).

Chapter 19 is Job's response to Bildad's discourse. Job's words are like a triple-exposure photograph. They point to Christ's suffering on the cross, the Jew suffering in the Tribulation, and the lost man suffering in hell. All three are the objects of God's wrath (19:11–12). The three-fold imagery is further seen in 19:13–19.

- It points to *Israel* as a proverb and a by-word of reproach.

- It points to *Christ* counted as an enemy by the armies of God as He hung on the cross.

- It points to the *Lost Man* forever separated from everyone he knows and loves in hell.

Verses 25–27 of chapter 19 are the spiritual climax of the book of Job. Job's words are one of the greatest confessions of faith in the entire Bible. He declares that the Redeemer is alive and well; that He will physically be present on the earth in "the latter day," and that the believer will live in a new physical body! That's some pretty awesome theology for a guy who didn't have a single page of the Bible!

In chapter 20, it's Zophar's turn to take his shots at Job. Once again, the record of his words give us greater insight into the coming Antichrist, "that wicked." And in chapter 21, Job is utterly frustrated with his counselors. His words point to the future judgment and conquest of the Antichrist's false system by the Lord Jesus Christ.

CHRIST IS REVEALED:

As "*the Innocent*" – Job 17:8 (Christ is the innocent Savior who died for the guilty – Matt. 27:4)

Through *Job* as the one whom God's *Wrath* was presumably kindled against – Job 19:11 (2 Cor. 5:21)

As the *Redeemer* – Job 19:25 (Acts 20:28; Eph. 1:14; Rev. 5:9)

WEEK 24, DAY 1: **TODAY'S READING: JOB 22-28**

OVERVIEW:

Eliphaz's scathing accusations against Job; Job's desire to plead his case before God; Bildad's attack on Job; Job's desperate seeking for God.

HIGHLIGHTS & INSIGHTS:

In today's reading, Job's counselors and so-called friends are increasingly losing control of their emotions in their "discussion" with Job. At this point, they have twisted words and circumstances to fit their own ideas and agendas, but in chapter 22, Eliphaz blatantly says things that are not true. Colossians 3:8–9 tells us to "put off" a progression of emotions: "But now ye also put off all these; anger, wrath, malice, blasphemy, filthy communication out of your mouth. Lie not one to another, seeing that ye have put off the old man with his deeds." Job's friends certainly follow that progression. They first were angry that Job refused to confess his "secret" sin, they worked themselves through "wrath, malice, blasphemy, filthy, communication out of their mouth," and now, Eliphaz is lying.

Chapter 22 begins the third and final round of this bout between Job and his friends. They came with the intention of confronting and counseling him through his time of trial. But their so-called ministry is a poignant reminder to anyone who seeks to minister the Word of God to others. With the best possible intentions, we can be guilty of breaking people to pieces with our words, even while we think we're saying what God wants us to say. Job's friends had dotted all of their theological i's and crossed all of their doctrinal t's. They just didn't have a clue how to apply them. Their negative example should drive us to depend totally upon God's grace as we learn to listen when we counsel those in need and to ensure we actually understand the biblical meaning of the words we so easily allow to roll off our lips.

After Eliphaz delivers his scathing address in chapter 22, Job is so low that he has no where else to look but up. All he can do is desperately seek for God. In chapters 23 and 24, Job does just that. And as tough as that is, it's actually not a bad place to be in the light of Deuteronomy 29:13, the theme verse of our *52 Weeks of Pursuit*!

In chapter 25, Bildad begins his final remarks by declaring an indisputable truth, asking a leading question, and finally proposing a series of questions that form his conclusion. In response, Job fires back six questions that his friends absolutely cannot answer (chapter 26). Interestingly, Job's questions could and may be asked each of us at the Judgment Seat of Christ! After firing off these questions in 26:1–4, Job gives an unbelievable cosmological discourse that has proven to be several years ahead of modern science.

In chapters 27 and 28, we get a glimpse of Job's incredible spirit. We must ask ourselves whether we could maintain the integrity of heart that Job has. Every one of us must choose—every single day of our lives—whether or not we will offer our absolute surrender to Christ. Let us make that surrender this day.

CHRIST IS REVEALED:

Through *Job's* faithfulness to God through his suffering – Job 23:1–12 (Christ's faithfulness to the Father is seen as He prayed for the Father's will to be done – Luke 22:42)

WEEK 24, DAY 2: **TODAY'S READING: JOB 29-33**

OVERVIEW:

Job's recollection of days gone by; Job's proclamation of his righteousness and integrity; Elihu's accusations.

HIGHLIGHTS & INSIGHTS:

In chapter 29, Job is looking back, reflecting on how good life used to be. We call them the "good 'ole days." For most of us, the past wasn't really that good. Our memory is so bad, or so selective, that we just don't remember what made life difficult during those times! Job, however, really did have a better life in days gone by!

Job 29:1 reminds us that this is the continuation of a parable. Biblically, a parable is something that is used to give instruction to believers, but hide truth from the skeptic. (See Matt. 13:11.)

After remembering the past in chapter 29, Job is brought back to the reality of his present condition in chapter 30. In describing the misery of his terrible state historically, God once again paints an unbelievable picture of Christ's plight on the cross, the Jew in the Tribulation, and the lost man in hell. Note that Job 30 has the same feel as Isaiah 53, the classic Old Testament passage prophesying the details of our Lord's crucifixion.

In chapter 31, the tone changes rather abruptly. Job digs himself out of the depths of despair mentally, displaying a remarkable ability to hold tenaciously to his integrity even after being pulverized relentlessly both physically (by the devil), and psychologically (by his friends). Beginning in verse 5, Job fires off a series of questions regarding his personal testimony, each marked by the word *if*, which is found 20 times in the passage. In effect, Job is saying, "If I'm guilty of any of the things you have accused me of, I'm ready to receive God's judgment for it." Job ends his argument in 31:40, but in reality, no one won the debate. Job and his friends have simply dug into their own positions. This is a great lesson about debating spiritual matters: No one really wins. Everybody holds firm to their own convictions, but no real communication is taking place, because no one is actually listening. Each side just waits for the other side to stop talking so they can say what they want to say.

As chapter 32 begins, Job and his friends have stopped talking. But one other person has been present throughout this whole debate: Elihu. He has listened intently to all that's been said, but being younger, he's kept silent out of respect. But Job has brought him to his boiling point! He feels he must open his mouth and defend God, as it were. Like Job's three friends, he thinks he's speaking for God out of a pure heart and pure motives. And once again, you would never be able to convince him otherwise! He too is very knowledgeable—but like Job's three other friends, he also lacks wisdom and understanding. Everything Elihu says in chapter 32 and 33 is completely accurate; it is smack dab on the bull's eye. Unfortunately, the bull's eye is on the wrong target! As we have said before, we must allow the Lord to teach us through the negative example of Job's friends, lest we also demoralize, discourage, and defeat our brothers and sisters with knowledge, but no wisdom and understanding. God help us!

CHRIST IS REVEALED:

Through *Job's Compassion* for others – Job 29:15–17, 21–25 (Matt. 4:14; 15:30–39)

Through the *Ridicule* and *Affliction* which Job endured – Job 30:10–11 (Mark 15:15–20; Isa. 50:6; 53:2–5; Matt. 27:26–30; John 19:1–3)

WEEK 24, DAY 3: **TODAY'S READING: JOB 34-38**

OVERVIEW:

Elihu's continued accusations against Job; God's questions to Job.

HIGHLIGHTS & INSIGHTS:

In chapter 34, well-meaning Elihu still has a lot more to say to Job "in the name of the Lord"! He has convinced himself, and is trying to convince Job, that he has received his insight by inspiration of God. While the other three pointed to *some* secret sin as the source of Job's suffering, Elihu claims to know what the specific sin is! Hello, Holy Spirit! He says that Job hasn't really submitted himself to the sovereignty of God; he is bumping up against God's working in his life. Compare this claim with God's own words concerning Job: "There is none like him in the earth, a perfect and an upright man, one that feareth God, and escheweth evil" (1:8). So much for Elihu's insight and inspiration! We must not throw God's name on top of our own opinions and conclusions when dealing with people! We must have a chapter and verse to support our counsel and be sure that the verse means what we say it means in its context. Job's counselors show us how easily we can deceive and be deceived!

Throughout his rampage, Elihu's words are accurate. But he is operating under a false assumption. When our starting point is off base, it doesn't matter how many correct facts we use to make it sound godly— it's still just flat out wrong! Sadly, this is the problem with many discussions about spiritual matters and religion in these dark last days.

Finally, Elihu finishes what he felt he just had to say, and now he can shut his mouth. Hallelujah! All four men have had their turn debating Job. They have so worn him down that he has actually begun to question God himself. And finally, God speaks. But when He does, He actually *declares* nothing. He answers Job by asking questions Himself! He asks a series of at least 35 questions, depending on how you divide them, all of which are designed to show man, and Job in particular, that he really knows nothing about anything! The breakdown of chapter 38 is as follows:

- Questions about words without knowledge. (38:1–3)
- Questions about creation. (38:4–7)
- Questions about the waters. (38:8–11)
- Questions about the sun's light. (38:12–15)
- Questions about strange places. (38:16–21)
- Questions about the weather. (38:22–30)
- Questions about the heavens. (38:31–33)
- Questions in general. (38:34–41)

CHRIST IS REVEALED:

As the *one who watches how we live and all we do* – Job 34:21. (The Lord keeps His eyes on the righteous – 1 Pet. 3:12)

WEEK 24, DAY 4: **TODAY'S READING: JOB 39–42**

OVERVIEW:

The continuation of God's questions to Job; God's great power reviewed; Job's submission to God; Job's prayer for his friends; God's double blessing upon Job.

HIGHLIGHTS & INSIGHTS:

At the end of yesterday, God was in the middle of answering Job with a series of questions that brought all of Job's questions to a screeching halt! God's questions were about creation and appear to be totally unrelated to Job's situation, until you realize that Job had begun to focus only on his personal problems. God's questions were to help Job see the big picture—specifically, that

- His problems aren't as big as he thought! And,

- His problems aren't the center of the universe … God is!

God moves from cosmological and naturalistic questions in chapter 38 to questions about animals. From Job 38 to 41, God mentions 14 animals. Jeff Adams reminds us, "Seven is God's number of completion and it is associated with his perfect works – for example, the seven days of creation. Two is the number of witness or confirmation. We are considering a list of fourteen animals; could it be that God wants to confirm the perfection of His work to Job? Is there valuable truth to be learned from God's zoo?"[1]

Of particular interest are two animals: Behemoth (chapter 40) and Leviathan (chapter 41). Let's start with Behemoth. The word *behemoth* is not a translation of a Hebrew word, but a transliteration. In other words, the word has no English equivalent, so it cannot be translated. Instead, it was simply given an English spelling and pronunciation. While some speculate that the animal is an elephant, hippopotamus, or water ox, *behemoth* simply means "beast" or "animal." Also the word is a plural form, but all of the pronouns concerning this animal are singular. So, either God uses some really bad grammar—or there's something else going on here!

There is one other place in the Bible where a single animal is actually a composite of different animals:"the beast" in Revelation 13:1–2. In these verses, "the beast" (singular) is described as a composite of several beasts (plural): the leopard, the bear, and the lion. We know, of course, that "the beast" is the Antichrist. This, then, would indicate that Behemoth is a picture of the Antichrist. God is, in a sense, answering the question of Job's suffering by pointing him to the source! The same spiritual power that was behind Job's tribulation will be the mastermind behind the worldwide Tribulation in the very near future. None other than Satan incarnate!

Leviathan in chapter 41 is also intriguing. Scholars speculate that he is some sort of sea creature, such as a whale, a crocodile, a sea monster, or perhaps a mythological beast. Comparing Scripture with Scripture, however, reveals more about Leviathan. Psalm 74:14 says that, whatever a leviathan is, it has more than one head. Isaiah 27:1 specifically identifies leviathan as a "serpent" and a "dragon." And in Revelation 12:3, we read about a "dragon, having seven heads," who was "cast out, that old serpent, called the devil, and Satan" (v. 9). Once again, God was answering Job's questions by pointing him to the one who was responsible for his tribulation. None other than Satan himself! What a Book and what a God!

Jeff Adams provides an excellent summary of the book of Job in these eight points:

1. Some questions will never be answered in this life (if ever). God owes us no explanations.

2. Some believers suffer for no reason of their own making.

3. We are a small part of an immense spiritual war that has raged since the fall of Lucifer, a war of which we have little understanding.

4. If we do not exercise great caution and discernment, even our best intentions to minister to the suffering can be seized by the enemy and used to his advantage in this spiritual war.

5. Abundant facts about God do not necessarily qualify anyone to understand God's purposes or diagnose His workings in the life of others.

6. Our need is to know God, not just gain more information about God.

7. When baffled and overwhelmed by trials not of our own creation, we should lift up our eyes to see the big picture of God's plan for the universe. We should stand in awe of God's great power and let Him be God.

8. Finally, trials for righteousness' sake ultimately lead to new beginnings.[2]

CHRIST IS REVEALED:

Through *Job's Praying* for his friends – Job 42:10 (Christ both modeled for us and instructed us to pray for those who falsely accuse us – Luke 6:28; 23:34)

[1]Jeff Adams, *Job: Adventures in the Land of Uz!*, chapter 28

[2]Jeff Adams, *Job: Adventures in the Land of Uz!*, chapter 31

WEEK 24, DAY 5: **TODAY'S READING: PSALM 1-11**

OVERVIEW:

The contrast between the blessed man and the ungodly man; a prophecy of Christ and His request for the heathen as His inheritance; David cries out to God for help and deliverance from his enemies; the Lord's name is magnified and David wonders with amazement why God is even mindful of sinful man.

HIGHLIGHTS & INSIGHTS:

The word *psalm* means "hymn" or "praise." This Old Testament book was the national hymn book for the Israelites. The Psalms reveal the varied emotions and experiences of God's people: adoration, joy, faith, grace, mercy, suffering, and hope. In the eleven Psalms in today's reading, we see David writing about his emotions and experiences

- During his son Absalom's rebellion. (Psalms 3–6)

- During the persecution he experienced at the hands of Saul. (Psalm 7)

- During his time as a shepherd. (Psalm 8)

- During his reign as the king of Israel. (Psalms 9 and 11)

For the sake of space and time, we will focus today on Psalm 1. In this psalm, God contrasts the blessed man (vs. 1–3) and the ungodly man (vs. 4–6). The blessed man is separated from the world. He "walketh not in the counsel of the ungodly" (1:1). The Bible consistently refers to our daily lives as our *walk* (Eph. 4:1, 5:2). Our walk begins with trusting Christ for our salvation and continues with our faithful obedience to God's Word. Psalm 1 reveals that the man God blesses makes progress in His walk by three things that he is extremely careful *not* to do!

1. The blessed man does not *walk* in the *counsel* of the *ungodly*. (1:1a)
   In other words, he is very specific about who he allows to have a voice in his life!

2. The blessed man does not *stand* in the *way* of *sinners*. (1:1b)
   In other words, he is very careful about where he positions himself in the course of his daily life!

3. The blessed man does not *sit* in the *seat* of the *scornful*. (1:1c)
   In other words, he is very particular about those with whom he chooses to associate!

The blessed man is mindful of three groups of people who are negatively seeking to influence his life: the ungodly, sinners and the scornful. He also recognizes the downward spiral of their influence. We begin to walk according to their counsel, which leads to our standing or observing their way of life, and before we know it, we find ourselves sitting with them, participating in a way of life that scorns the very truth that God says in His Word is to characterize our lives!

The word "but" in Psalm 1:2 indicates an important contrast. Having identified the negative things the blessed man makes certain are not part of his life, the psalmist now identifies the positive things that *do* characterize the life of the blessed man.

1. The blessed man *delights* in the Word of God. (1:2a)
   It brings him joy, refreshment and pleasure and satisfaction because he loves it! (Ps. 119:47)

2. The blessed man *meditates* on the Word of God. (1:2b)
   All of the day and night, the Word of God completely saturates and permeates his thoughts and controls his mind. Note that *meditation* is to the *soul* what *digestion* is to the *body*. (Jer. 15:16)

3. The blessed man *plants* his life in the Word of God. (1:3)
   Delighting and meditating in the Word of God results in the development of a strong biblical root system that bears "fruit that remains" (John 15:16), causing him to continuously prosper spiritually.

And obviously, the perfect example of this blessed man is none other than our Lord Jesus Christ (John 14:6). He is the *way* (Ps 1:1), the *truth* (Ps. 1:2), and the *life* (Ps. 1:3)!

In Psalm 1:4–6, the psalmist describes the ungodly man. The first thing we learn about "the ungodly" is that they "are not so." That is, they are nothing like the blessed man. While the blessed man is like a tree that is strong, beautiful, and fruitful, the ungodly man is like chaff blown away by the wind because it has no roots. Paul used a similar metaphor to describe children who are "tossed to and fro, and carried about with every wind of doctrine" (Eph. 4:14). And Psalm 1:5 clearly teaches that there is a coming judgment prepared for the ungodly, at which they will fall on their knees (they "shall not stand") and confess that Jesus Christ is Lord (Phil. 2:10–11)!

In 1:6, the psalmist presents the two ways that are set before each of us: "the way of the righteous" and "the way of the ungodly." In Matthew 7:13–14, Jesus also talked about these two ways. Comparing the two passages (1 Cor 2:13), we learn that "the ungodly" have chosen the "broad way, that leadeth to destruction," whereas "the righteous" have chosen the "narrow way, that leadeth unto life." The ungodly takes heed to "the counsel of the ungodly," (1:1) as opposed to "all the counsel of God" (Acts 20:27), and chooses "the friendship of the world" (Jas. 4:4), rather than the friendships found in "the congregation of the righteous" (Psa. 1: 5b).

CHRIST IS REVEALED:

As the *Son* – Psalm 2:12. (We're told in Psalm 2:10–12 to "be wise now" and "kiss the Son" because "blessed are all they that put their trust in Him" – Eph. 1:12–14)

WEEK 25, DAY 1: **TODAY'S READING: PSALM 12-20**

OVERVIEW:

The preservation of God's Word; longing for deliverance; the foolishness of fools; the description of a godly man; the second coming of Christ; the power of God's Word.

HIGHLIGHTS & INSIGHTS:

Verse 1 of Psalm 12 establishes the theme and sets the context for the entire psalm: godly and faithful men are in short supply! It was true in David's day, and it is true in our day as well. However, the Lord promises He will arise and will serve justice toward the proud and blasphemous talkers in this world (vs. 2–4), along with the oppressors of the poor and needy (v. 5). The certainty of this truth is based on the certainty of God's Word. We can be at peace even in this evil world because we trust God's promises. His Word is true, and the Lord will preserve it and keep it pure forever (vs. 6–7). Hallelujah!

If you're in need of encouragement today, you may want to slow down through Psalm 13. It only has six verses, so it's a quick read, but they pack a wallop! David gets brutally honest with God in this psalm. Our God can not only handle our honesty, but actually welcomes it (Heb. 4:14–16). As David is writing and singing this song to the Lord, he is a discouraged, disappointed, and even disillusioned man. In the first two verses, he asks God four rather inflammatory questions. Each begin with the same two words: "How long?"

- *How long* wilt thou forget me, O LORD? for ever? (13:1a)

- *How long* wilt thou hide thy face from me? (13:1b)

- *How long* shall I take counsel in my soul, having sorrow in my heart daily? (13:2a)

- *How long* shall mine enemy be exalted over me? (13:2b)

Have you ever felt what the psalmist was feeling here? Have you ever opened your heart to the Lord in prayer and found your mouth crying out, "How long, O Lord?" As David works through his questions (and questioning!) of God, by the time his song is over, he's been brought into remembrance of God's mercy, His salvation, and how bountifully God had dealt with him through the years.

Like David, if we will simply and honestly pour out our hearts—and even our frustrations—to God, He will begin to bring to our minds His mercies toward us, the salvation He's provided us, and the bountiful goodness He's shown us through the years. Our circumstances may not immediately change (David's didn't!), but our attitude and outlook will change! May Psalm 13 be of great comfort to all of us today!

Psalm 14 is a description of lost man. May we keep ever-present in our hearts and minds that this psalm was descriptive of each of us before coming to Christ!

In Psalm 15, God contrasts the description of the lost man with His description of a *godly* man, someone in whom God dwells. God uses five sentences to provide a composite of this person:

1. **He possesses inward righteousness that works its way outward into daily living. (15:2)**
   This is the exact opposite of the Pharisees who had an outward righteousness, but inwardly were full of unrighteousness.

2. **He loves others as he loves himself. (15:3)**
   Interpersonal problems are caused when someone is not loving his neighbor as himself (Gal. 5:14–15).

3. **He honors those whose lives give evidence that they fear God, not those who live vile lives. (15:4a)**
   who are the people you respect and admire? Are they people who walk with God?

4. **He means what he says. (15:4b)**

Can others always trust the things that come out of your mouth? Do you keep your word even when it costs you something, or inconveniences you?

5. **He is not driven by financial gain. (15:5)**
   Is the priority of your life making money, getting ahead, or becoming well off—or is it loving God and advancing His kingdom and glory?

Psalm 16 contains an amazing prophecy concerning Christ's death and resurrection in verse 10. Peter was well aware of this prophecy, even referencing it in his sermon on the day of Pentecost in Acts 2:31!

Psalm 17 is a great place to find refuge during times of trial, particularly intense opposition. We can find solace and comfort through the outpouring of David's heart and in his absolute dependence upon God, not only to see him through, but to conform him into His image in the process (17:15; Rom. 8:29). May we learn from and follow David's example.

Understanding the *doctrinal* or *prophetic* context of Psalm 18 is vital. This psalm is an incredible prophecy about Christ's deliverance of His people, the nation of Israel. In 18:4–6, David describes the utter distress and hopelessness of the Jews during the Tribulation, while in verses 7–15, he describes the power and glory of the Day of the Lord—the Second Coming of Christ. Understanding the prophetic context of this psalm helps us "rightly divid[e]" (2 Tim. 2:15) David's obvious emphasis upon human works in 18:20–24. After the church is removed from the earth at the rapture, those who believe during the tribulation are not sealed with the Holy Spirit like we have been. As Jesus taught in Matthew 24:13, during the Tribulation, believers must "endure unto the end" (of their life or of the Tribulation Period) in order to be saved. Specifically, they must not take the infamous mark of the beast (Antichrist).

Psalm 19:1–6 corresponds to Romans 1:19–20. The creation of God most definitely shows forth His glory in countless ways. David even tells us in 19:4–6, just as Malachi did in Malachi 4:1–2, that the rising of the sun is a daily reminder and picture of the Second Coming of Christ! In 19:7–11, David refers to the Word of God by six different names: the *law* of the Lord, the *testimony* of the Lord, the *statutes* of the Lord, the *commandment* of the Lord, the *fear* of the Lord, and the *judgments* of the Lord. In these same verses, he teaches us six things that the Word of God has the power to do: to convert the soul, to make wise the simple, to to rejoice the heart, to enlighten the eyes, to endure forever, and to provide warning and reward. No wonder David admonishes us in 19:10 to desire it more than gold and to find that its sweetness to us spiritually is actually sweeter than a honeycomb is to us physically.

In Psalm 20, we see, once again, the Tribulation/Day of the Lord context throughout. Psalm 20:7 is classic, and its truth should characterize God's people in every generation: "Some trust in chariots, and some in horses: but we will remember the name of the Lord our God"! May it be true of us today and every day!

CHRIST IS REVEALED:

Through the *Rising* of the *Sun* – Psalm 19:4–6 (Picturing the "Sun of righteousness" rising in the east at His second coming – Mal. 4:2)

WEEK 25, DAY 2: **TODAY'S READING: PSALM 21-29**

OVERVIEW:

Psalms of victory (21), shame (25), innocence (26), devotion (27), hope (28) and glory (29); Psalms regarding the future sufferings (22), shepherding (23) and reign of Jesus Christ (24).

HIGHLIGHTS & INSIGHTS:

Sometimes Bible characters can almost seem larger than life. Even more so if the Bible characters were also those God used to write the Scriptures. Most of us know that we're no Moses, Ezekiel, Daniel, and Jeremiah—or Paul, Peter, and John! With all of our human frailties, weaknesses and sins, we can sometimes find it difficult to even relate to these men.

Perhaps that's why most of us find so much comfort and strength in the Psalms. In these songs, it's as if the writers pull back the curtain of their humanness. The psalms allow us to see that, though David and the others psalmists were certainly amazing men, they had the same frailties, weaknesses, and sins as we do! These men poured out their hearts, personally relating God to their real, everyday lives. They very honestly, candidly and even emotionally expressed whatever they happened to be thinking and feeling at the moment. And those thoughts and emotions could be all over the map!

In today's reading alone, David cries out to the Lord in Psalm 28, "Answer me, Lord, because if You don't, I'm going to feel like I've gone to hell!" (v. 1). In Psalm 25, he says in effect, "Lord, I know I've greatly sinned against you, but, O God, for Your name's sake, please pardon me!" (v. 11). You can easily sense his extreme desperation. But by the time we get to Psalm 29, David is sitting on top of the world again, joyfully declaring the unrivaled power, majesty, and glory of the Word of God (what David calls "the voice of the Lord").

Sometimes it's difficult to wrap our minds around the fact that this man, who some might call flighty or an emotional basket case, is the same man who killed a lion and a bear with his own hands. This is the same man who slew Goliath with a slingshot and a stone, the same valiant warrior in battle who the women of Israel boasted had killed tens of thousands of God's enemies (1 Sam. 18:7). But God wasn't concerned about David's emotions. God didn't want the man that He had chosen to rule in His stead in Israel to put on a fake smile and act like everything was okay when it wasn't. God wanted a man with a heart brave enough to slay giants and tens of thousands of mighty warriors *and* tender enough to lead Israel with a compassionate heart, like the heart of God Himself (Acts 13:22).

Because the Psalms are so personal and candid, we can easily find one (or more!) for every circumstance or emotion we encounter. Again, just in today's reading, if we need a reminder of God's wonderful care and protection in our lives, Psalm 23 offers encouragement and strength! If we are weighed down by the guilt of past sin, we can humbly pray Psalm 25 to remind us of God's amazing grace and forgiveness. If we are falsely accused, Psalm 26 can help us lift, not only our voices to the Lord, but our very souls! God included this tremendous book in Scripture to provide exactly this kind of biblical hope and encouragement. Praise the Lord!

In Psalm 22, God inspired David to write a song about the suffering of our Lord Jesus Christ on the cross a thousand years before His actual crucifixion. This Psalm cannot be about David because never did God actually forsake him (v.1), though there were times David *felt* as though God had! Never were David's bones ripped out of joint (v. 14) or was he so thirsty that his tongue actually stuck to his jaws (v. 15). Never were David's hands and feet pierced with nails (22:16). And never were David's garments stripped from him and gambled over (v. 18). In the annals of history, only one man and one event fits this precise description: our Lord Jesus Christ at His crucifixion! (See Matt. 27:35–49; John 19:23–24, 28–30.)

In the writing of Psalm 22, it's almost as if God invited David to write about the most horrific suffering and death he could imagine and then put it to music. The song includes the most hurtful and painful things in human experience: betrayal, false accusation, humiliation, physical torture, and abandonment. Then, a millennium later, it was as if God turned David's nightmare into reality, subjecting His only begotten Son to the very scenario David described. In so doing, however, God forever settled any accusations that He is ignorant of, indifferent to, or absent in our human sufferings because He endured the worst that the human imagination could contrive. Because of the cross of Christ, no human being can ever accuse God of not understanding what they're going through! (See Heb. 4:14–16; 2:9–10, 14, 17–18.)

David's mission statement of sorts is found in Psalm 27:4 and 8. David set his entire life to one goal: the passionate pursuit of God! (And that's our goal in the *52 Weeks of Pursuit*—to passionately pursue God through the pages of His Word.) David ferociously sought God in every situation and circumstance of his life. In the depths of depression, he clawed his way to the reason for God's apparent silence. At the peak of joy, he delighted in the glory and strength of his sovereign God, both in prayer and in song. In every emotional state, David cried out for God and sought Him with all of His heart! That's why David found such graphic pictures and illustrations of God in every aspect of his life. Again, in today's reading alone, David saw God as a *shepherd* (Ps. 23), a *light* (Ps. 27), a *rock* (Ps. 28) and as *thunder* (Ps. 29). Because David was seeking God, he was able to see God all around him. Like Jesus said in Luke 11:9, "Seek, and ye shall find!" And like Jeremiah said in Jer. 29:13, "But if from thence thou shalt seek the Lord thy God, thou shalt find him, if thou seek him with all thy heart and with all thy soul." Oh, may we seek Him like that!

CHRIST IS REVEALED:

Psalms 22, 23, and 24 provide a prophetic description of the person and work of Jesus Christ. Psalm 22 presents Christ as our suffering Savior (Matt. 27:46), Psalm 23 reveals Him as our risen Shepherd (John 10:11), and Psalm 24 makes us witnesses of His future triumphant return as the King of glory (Rev. 19).

WEEK 25, DAY 3: **TODAY'S READING: PSALM 30-36**

OVERVIEW:

David's adoration of God's mighty power; David's trust in God; the blessedness of God's forgiveness; the Lord hears the righteous; David's prayer for safety; the contrast of the godly and the wicked.

HIGHLIGHTS & INSIGHTS:

The historic context of Psalm 30 is established by the title: "A Psalm and Song at the dedication of the house of David." Prophetically, this psalm points to Israel's horrendous night of "weeping," followed by the "joy [that] cometh in the morning" (v. 5) when the Day of the Lord arises on this planet at the Second Coming of Christ, as He establishes His millennial kingdom. Devotionally, the psalmist reminds us to "extol" the Lord (30:1); to "sing" and "give thanks" to Him (30:4, 12); and to cry out, making "supplication" to Him (30:8).

Psalm 31 is significant for several reasons. First, it includes Christ's last words before He died on the cross: "Father, 'into thine hand I commit my spirit'" (31:5; Luke 23:46). Second, it's significant because of David's descriptions of the awesomeness of our God. He is our Righteousness (v. 1); our Strong Rock and House of Defense (v. 2); our Rock and Fortress and our Guide (v. 3); our Strength (v. 4); and the Preserver of the faithful (v. 23). Is there anything we could possibly face today that one or more of those characteristics will not address?

Depending upon what we may be facing at a particular time, it can sometimes feel, when we read the psalms, as if they were written just for us. A good example of that is Psalm 31:9–24. If you are facing what seems to be an insurmountable foe today, try using David's words in these verses as a prayer to the Lord.

Psalm 32 is a psalm of confession. Verses 1–4 show us the result of not "cleans[ing] ourselves from all filthiness of the flesh and spirit" (2 Cor. 7:1). Verse 7 reminds us of the tremendous priority the Bible places on singing in the midst of spiritual warfare (2 Chron. 20:21–23; Col. 3:16; Eph 5:19).

In Psalm 33 the psalmist praises the Lord on an instrument of ten strings (33:2). We may not be able to play a ten-stringed instrument to praise the Lord, but we can certainly *be* one! We can use our two feet to "walk worthy of the Lord unto all pleasing" (Col. 1:10) and our two hands to hold the powerful sword of God's Word to carry out the work of the Lord (Eph. 6:17; 1 Cor. 15:58). With our two eyes, we can see the needs of the people around us (1 John 3:17). We can use our two ears to hear the Word of the Lord (Jas. 1:19; Prov. 2:2). We can use our neck to bow our will in submission to Christ's Lordship (Ex. 32:9). And, with our mouths, we can praise the Lord, speak the Word of the Lord to the lost, and offer words of comfort, encouragement, and hope to believers (Ps. 34:1; Eph. 6:19; Heb. 3:13). May we all be an instrument of ten strings to praise the Lord every day!

The psalmist prayed in Psalm 33:8, "Let all the earth fear the Lord: let all the inhabitants of the world stand in awe of him." This prayer will be answered at the Second Coming of Christ when "every knee should bow ... and ... every tongue confess that Jesus Christ is Lord to the glory of God the Father" (Phil. 2:10–11; 2 Thess. 1:7–10). Psalm 33:12–22 is a great way of saying, "If God be for us, who can be against us—and if God be against us, it doesn't matter who is for us!" (Rom. 8:31).

For those living in fear today, Psalm 34:1–4 presents a sevenfold prescription for being "delivered ... from all [our] fears."

1. Bless the Lord at all times. (34:1a)

2. Allow His praise to continually be in our mouth. (34:1b)

3. Make our boast solely in the Lord. (34:2a)

4. Demonstrate a spirit of humility. (34:2b)

5. Magnify the Lord with other believers. (34:3a)

6. Exalt His name together with them. (34:3b)

7. Seek the Lord. (34:4a)

Psalm 35 is full of practical reminders. Verses 1–9 remind us of the lessons we learned about spiritual warfare from 2 Chronicles 20. The psalmist reiterates the truth that the battle is God's (35:1a; 2 Chron. 20:15); God fights on our behalf (35:1b; 2 Chron. 20:17a); and if we watch, we will see God's salvation (35:3–4; 2 Chron. 20:17b). And Psalm 35:12 reminds us that in a rational world good deeds are rewarded. In the real world, however, as they say, "no good deed goes unpunished!" Sad, but true.

Psalm 36 contrasts the wicked man (36:1–4) with the man who knows the Lord (36:5–12). As we read these verses, keep in mind that the old man (our "flesh") described in verses 1–4 is still part of us, a part we have been commanded to "put off" (Eph 4:22).

CHRIST IS REVEALED:

Through *David* as he "commits his spirit" to the Father – Psalm 31:5 (Luke 23:46)

As the *Angel of the Lord* – Psalm 34:7 (The Angel of the Lord is an Old Testament appearance of the pre-incarnate Christ.)

As the one in whom *No Bone is Broken* – Psalm 34:20 (John 19:36)

WEEK 25, DAY 4: **TODAY'S READING: PSALM 37-44**

OVERVIEW:

Instructions regarding the destiny of the wicked; David's petition during a time of trouble; the brevity and vanity of life; prayer and praise for deliverance; sickness, betrayal and responding to enemies; the soul's longing for God's presence; deliverance and hope in God; complaint about defeat and cry for help.

HIGHLIGHTS & INSIGHTS:

The book of Psalms is, obviously, a divinely inspired *hymnal*, or book of *praise*. What is often overlooked, however, is that it is also chock full of *practical counsel*; it is actually a *how-to manual*, if you will, for how to navigate spiritually through all types of difficulties, disappointments and discouragements! In today's reading alone, the Lord reveals

- How to deal with fretfulness, or anxiety. (Psalm 37)

- How to cope when our strength is failing. (Psalm 38–39)

- How to rest in God's faithfulness. (Psalm 40)

- How to respond to a friend's unfaithfulness. (Psalm 41)

- How to register a complaint when you can't see God's hand at work. (Psalm 44)

In Psalm 39:4, David prayed, "Lord, make me to know … the measure of my days." What a powerful reminder that everyone—not just senior citizens—should consider the brevity of life. It's so easy to get caught up with material and financial achievements and other temporal values (39:6) that we forget the real purpose of life. Jesus warned us of this same truth in Luke 12:15: "Take heed, and beware of covetousness: for a man's life consisteth not in the abundance of the things which he possesseth." The psalmist also reminds us that compared to eternity, our life on earth is very short, and our opportunities to fulfill God's purposes for our lives will soon be "no more" (39:13). Jesus declared a similar resolve in John 9:4: "I must work the works of Him that sent me, while it is day: the night cometh, when no man can work." Oh, may the words of Jesus and of Psalm 39 flood our hearts, and souls and minds with a passion to stay focused on God's purposes for our lives!

Psalm 41 is a *how-to manual* for praising the Lord even while bedridden (41:3). Apparently, the psalmist was suffering from a debilitating disease or injury (41:3, 5, 8). The description of someone who takes pity on the poor and needy in verses 1–3 turns into the plea of a discouraged, bedridden saint: "Lord, be merciful unto me: heal my soul" (41:4). The longer he pours out his heart, focusing his attention and energies on pleading to and praising the Lord, the more confident he becomes in God's strength in his hour of need. The song ends with a declaration of praise: "Blessed be the LORD God of Israel from everlasting, and to everlasting. Amen, and Amen" (41:13). Even when we face sickness or suffering, we can experience God's blessing like the psalmist did. Instead of complaining, we can

- Plead for God's mercy. (41:4,10)

- Praise Him for His deliverance. (41:1–2)

- Praise Him for His preservation. (41:2)

- Praise Him for His strength (41:3)

- Praise Him for His favor. (41:11) And...

- Bless the name of the Lord! (41:13)

In Psalm 42, the psalmist compares his thirst for God to that of a deer that, after running through the forest, is literally panting over the water in the brook (42:1–2). May this powerful illustration also describe the continuing thirst for God in our souls through the *52 Weeks of Pursuit*!

As in many of the psalms, Psalm 43 records the psalmist's honest thoughts and feelings about the dreadful circumstances of his life that caused him to feel cast off by the Lord (43:2) and cast down in his soul (43:5). As he poured out his heart to God, we see the Lord lift his discouragement, pouring into him strength (43:2), light (43:3a), truth (43:3b), His presence (43:3c–4a), joy (43:4b), hope (43:5b), and the "health of [his] countenance" (43:5c).

Interestingly, Psalm 44 is the reverse of Psalm 43! In verses 1–8, the psalmist pours out praise for God's faithfulness and blessing upon his people in the past. Then in verse 9, he begins his honest complaint against the Lord, lamenting the fact that he's unable to see God at work in his life or in the lives of God's people (vs. 9–14). He admits his confusion and shame (44:15–16). Despite those thoughts, however, the psalmist declares that he and the people of God will not forget God (44:17a), deal falsely with His covenant (44:17b), allow their hearts to turn back (44:18a) or let their steps stop following His way (44:18b). The psalm ends with the psalmist passionately pleading with God to awake from His sleep (44:23), to stop hiding His face from them (44:24a), to stop forgetting their affliction and oppression (44:24b)—and "for [His] mercies' sake" to help and redeem them (44:26). Something tells me that God answered the psalmist's cry!

CHRIST IS REVEALED:

As the *one who Does the Will of God* – Psalm 40:6–8 (John 4:34; Heb. 10:7–9)

WEEK 25, DAY 5: **TODAY'S READING: PSALM 45-53**

OVERVIEW:

A description of our King and the King's daughter; the psalmist's confidence in and praise of God; the deception of worldly wealth; David's prayer of confession after sinning with Bathsheba; the tendency of the tongue toward evil; the foolishness of atheism.

HIGHLIGHTS & INSIGHTS:

We have mentioned before the three layers of application in Scripture. Because these three layers are so easily identifiable in the Psalms (and so necessary to really understand them!), we will use this space today to review each application. In other words, today, rather than me giving you a fish—let's focus on you learning how to fish!

Application #1 – The Historical Application

> Obviously, the events we read about in Scripture really happened to real people like you and me at a particular time in history. Understanding the historical context is vital to proper interpretation and to make the second application of Scripture.

Application #2 – The Devotional or Inspirational (Practical) Application

> From the real events, situations and experiences of those real people in the historical application, we learn lessons that we can apply to our own lives as we face similar situations and circumstances.

Almost every Bible-believing person is acquainted with these first two layers of application. But there is a third layer that most people fail to see! And it is the third application that, like a spark plug, ignites the whole supernatural engine of the Bible, causing us to stand in awe of the Word of God and the God of the Word!

Application #3 – The Doctrinal (or Prophetic) Application

> This application identifies what an event or situation in history foreshadows or pictures prophetically. It is the real *teaching* of the passage (doctrine = teaching). We don't have time or space for a complete explanation, but the key to this application is recognizing that God uses the record of history in the Old Testament to point to the key events that will take place in the future. This is not to be confused with the "allegorical" approach to biblical interpretation (i.e., randomly choosing the "hidden" meaning of the passage with no real proof from a hermeneutical standpoint), the doctrinal application employs strict rules of Bible study to make consistent prophetic applications. Once you begin to identify this third layer of application in the Psalms, you'll almost begin to wonder what you used to think the Psalms were about!

With that quick review in place, then, let's examine these three layers of application as they relate to the Psalms.

In the Historical Application, we recognize that an event or circumstance in the life of the psalmist prompted the writing of his song. Many times the situation is even identified in the title, as in Psalm 51 in today's reading: "A psalm of David, when Nathan the prophet came unto him, after he had gone in to Bath-sheba." Clearly, knowing the historical context will help make clear the psalm's meaning and application!

From a Devotional (Practical) standpoint, the book of Psalms is full of personal application and meaning. As we face similar circumstances, the songs express how we think and feel, not only about ourselves, but about God, life, and people. The psalms can also help us adjust our attitudes, as we see the psalmists work through their emotions before the Lord.

All of the Psalms in today's reading are good candidates to apply the Doctrinal (Prophetic) Application, but Psalm 46 is perhaps the best example.

Obviously, the psalms are songs that were actually sung. The word *Selah* appears in the Psalms (71 times) to indicate a rest written into the musical score. But the word made it into the canon of God's Holy Word because God intended to use it as a key to help us identify the "prophetic" context of the passage. At his Second Coming, our Lord Jesus Christ will arrive on this planet to establish His millennial reign. That reign will be a thousand-year period of rest on this planet, specifically identified in Revelation 20:1–6, and generally identified throughout Scripture as "the day of the Lord" or as "that day." This is the same rest for the people of God talked about in Hebrews 4, and what Peter referred to as "the times of *restitution* of all things" and "the times of refreshing" in Acts 3:19–21.

Anytime we see the word *Selah*, then, we must mentally put on the brakes and throw our eyes and brain into reverse, recognizing that God just let us know what the passage is pointing to from a doctrinal or prophetic standpoint—the Second Coming or His millennial reign.

With this in mind, let's look again at Psalm 46, where there are three perfect descriptions of the millennium, each marked by the word *Selah*.

- Psalm 46:1–3
  God is our refuge and strength, a very present help in trouble. Therefore will not we fear, though the earth be removed, and though the mountains be carried into the midst of the sea; Though the waters thereof roar and be troubled, though the mountains shake with the swelling thereof. Selah.

- Psalm 46:4–7
  There is a river, the streams whereof shall make glad the city of God, the holy place of the tabernacles of the most High. God is in the midst of her; she shall not be moved: God shall help her, and that right early. The heathen raged, the kingdoms were moved: he uttered his voice, the earth melted. The Lord of hosts is with us; the God of Jacob is our refuge. Selah.

- Psalm 46:8–11
  Come, behold the works of the Lord, what desolations he hath made in the earth. He maketh wars to cease unto the end of the earth; he breaketh the bow, and cutteth the spear in sunder; he burneth the chariot in the fire. Be still, and know that I am God: I will be exalted among the heathen, I will be exalted in the earth. The Lord of hosts is with us; the God of Jacob is our refuge. Selah.

We can see the same pattern in Psalm 50:1–6 where a perfect description of the Second Coming is, once again, followed by *rest*! (*Selah* – the millennium!) You get the idea. Look for this pattern throughout today's reading to enjoy for yourself!

CHRIST IS REVEALED:

Through the word *Selah*, pointing to Christ's Second Coming and Millennial Reign – Psalm 46:3, 7, 11; 47:4; 48:8; 49:13, 15; 50:6; 52:3, 5.

WEEK 26, DAY 1: **TODAY'S READING: PSALM 54-63**

OVERVIEW:

A prayer of protection: a cry against deceitful friends; the psalmist's trust in God; David's prayer for deliverance from his enemies; David's confidence in God's promises.

HIGHLIGHTS & INSIGHTS:

Yesterday, the goal was to acquaint you with using the three layers of application to see how God uses His Word in the Psalms, instead of highlighting what He actually said. The psalms in today's reading are easily understood, so we will look at another way you can "learn how to fish" in the Psalms, rather than simply "handing you a fish."

Please allow me to borrow from the insight and teaching of Bruce Wilkinson:

> Just as the nation of Israel was divided into many different tribes, so the Psalms can be divided into many different types. As you continue your journey through this book, you'll find it helpful to be able to classify each psalm you read. A majority of the psalms fall into one of three categories:
>
> 1. **Lament Psalms** are petitions addressed directly to God by the individual or community in the context of distress. They usually include a description of the problems, a confession of trust, and a vow of praise to God, uttered with the confidence that God can and will deliver His people. (examples: Psalms 3–7, 22, 42)
>
> 2. **Thank Psalms**, offered publicly by one or more worshippers, acknowledge God's faithful actions on behalf of His people in the past, or express confidence in His promise to act in the future. (examples: Psalms 18, 27, 62)
>
> 3. **Praise Psalms** are hymns based on the word praise or hallelujah. They are joyful expressions of adoration for God's greatness, acknowledging Him as Creator, Sustainer, and Lover of His people. (examples: Psalms 113, 117, 146–150)
>
> In addition, you will encounter:
>
> 4. **Royal Psalms** are hymns describing the King, both earthly and heavenly, reigning over His kingdom. (examples: Psalms 2, 95–96)
>
> 4. **Woe Psalms** are poems expressing the psalmist's righteous indignation at God's enemies, and calling for God's swift retribution. (examples: Psalms 49, 109, 137)
>
> 5. **Acrostic Psalms** are highly stylized poems in which each new section, verse, or line begins with a successive letter of the Hebrew alphabet. (examples: Psalms 9–10, 25, 35, 119)
>
> 6. **Pilgrim Psalms** are songs sung by worshippers on the way up to Jerusalem for the yearly feasts. (examples: Psalms 120–34)
>
> 7. **Messianic Psalms** are prophetic songs describing the coming Messiah as King (Psalms 2, 24, 110), Servant (Psalms 22-23, 40, 60), and the Son of God. (Psalm 118).[1]

In today's reading, do note that many of them record the expression of David's heart and his confidence in God during some of his most difficult days: while being pursued (Psalms 54, 57, 59); having been betrayed (Psalm 55); and when he was brokenhearted (Psalm 56). Psalms 54, 60, 61 and 63 are psalms of lament—watch for the use of the phrase, "O, God."

CHRIST IS REVEALED:

As the one *who was betrayed by his "friend"* – Psalm 55:12 (Matt. 26:47–50)

As the one *who saves those who will call upon Him* – Psalm 55:16–17 (Rom. 10:13)

As the *Rock* – Psalm 61:2; 62:2, 6–7 (1 Cor. 10:4)

[1]Bruce Wilkinson, *Your Daily Walk: Vol. 1*, Grand Rapids, MI: Zondervan, 1991, 203.

WEEK 26, DAY 2: **TODAY'S READING: PSALM 64-70**

OVERVIEW:

David's prayer of deliverance from his enemies; David's confidence in God's promises; David's exhortation to praise God for His goodness; the blessings of God upon His people; God's judgment upon His enemies; David's prayer in time of trouble.

HIGHLIGHTS & INSIGHTS:

Have you ever felt like the psalmist did in Psalm 64, as if the whole world is against you? Even the "man after God's own heart" had people who continually spoke evilly of him! And don't forget, Jesus said, "Blessed are ye, when [not *if*] men shall revile you, and persecute you, and shall say all manner of evil against you falsely, for my sake" (Matt. 5:11). In fact, the closer we grow toward Christlikeness and the more we are used by Him to accomplish His work, the more we can expect it. Biblically, that's just the way it works! Jesus went on to say, however, that rather than allowing the persecution to consume or discourage us, we should "Rejoice, and be exceeding glad: for so persecuted they the prophets which were before you" (Matt. 5:12). In other words, we should rejoice that we've ascended into the ranks of all the godly people that God has used through the centuries to bring glory to Him! Because they all experienced the same exact treatment! We will not be the exception to the rule. Even Jesus Himself wasn't!

The good news, according to the psalmist, is that "what goes around, comes around." His actual wording is perhaps more articulate, "So they shall make their own tongue to fall upon themselves" (Psa. 64:8). Paul's warning was similar: "But if ye bite and devour one another, take heed that ye be not consumed one of another" (Gal. 5:15). When people use their tongue as a weapon—it will inevitably come back to rip 'em to shreds!

Don't you love how the psalmist addresses God in Psalm 65:2? "O thou that hearest prayer." If we're ever needing a reason we should pray, how about that the God who created the entire universe and is holy beyond our wildest imagination and comprehension said He'd listen! We certainly don't need too many other reasons! You may even want to take a minute right now to humbly tell God, "Thanks for listening!" The psalmist comes back to this glorious reality that the God of the universe actually hears us in Psalm 66:18–20!

The word *terrible* is found in today's reading in Psalm 65:5; 66:3; and 68:35. It is the old English equivalent of the modern word *awesome*.

In Psalm 66:4, the psalmist/God sets the context with the word "Selah" at the end of the verse: "All the earth shall worship thee, and shall sing unto thee; they shall sing to thy name. Selah!" The whole earth hasn't worshipped or sung to the Lord since Adam sinned in the Garden, and it won't until the Lord Jesus Christ has set in motion "the times of restitution of all things" (Acts 3:21) at the beginning of the millennium—indicated by *Selah*.

Psalm 66, 67 and 68 provide great insight into just how glorious the second coming of Christ and His millennial reign on the earth will actually be. Don't miss it in these psalms! It certainly gives a whole new meaning to the New World Order to which politicians from every nation are referring in these last days!

The name of God in Psalm 68:4, "JAH", is short for Jehovah (Yahweh), the "self-existing one," or the God who is "ever/always in the present." Psalm 68:18 prophesies the glorious resurrection of our Lord Jesus Christ. Paul explained the meaning of this psalm as a prophecy in Ephesians 4:8. Christ conquered death and Satan, both of which held mankind in captivity until His resurrection (Heb. 2:15).

In Psalm 69, David is literally singing the blues. He voices what we've all felt in our lives, as he sings out of a sea of troubles (69:1–2). Psalm 69:9 was historically true of David: "For the zeal of thine house hath eaten me up; and the reproaches of them that reproached thee are fallen upon me." Prophetically, John tells us in John 2:17 that the verse was fulfilled in the Lord Jesus Christ. Devotionally, we would do well to ask ourselves whether this verse is, likewise, true of us. Are we so passionately in love with our Savior, and so completely zealous for Him to be glorified, that when His name is reproached (also translated "defied" and "blasphemed") the reproach falls on us the same way it falls upon Him? In other words, when God's name is blasphemed and defied, do we feel what God feels?

CHRIST IS REVEALED:

As the one who *Led Captivity Captive* – Psalm 68:18 (Eph. 4:8)

As the one who was *Brokenhearted* and *Full of Heaviness* – Psalm 69:20 (Matt. 26:37)

As the one given *Vinegar to Drink in His Thirst* – Psalm 69:21 (Matt. 27:34; John 19:28–30)

WEEK 26, DAY 3: **TODAY'S READING: PSALM 71-77**

OVERVIEW:

David's prayer of praise and thanksgiving; David's prayer for Solomon (the "Son of David"); the mystery of the prosperity of the wicked; the rebuke of the wicked and proud; praise for God's majesty.

HIGHLIGHTS & INSIGHTS:

In Psalm 71, the psalmist refers to God by eight powerful names, and he makes each one personal by the insertion of the pronoun *my*.

1) My Strong Habitation. (71:3)

2) My Rock. (71:3)

3) My Fortress. (71:3)

4) My God. (71:4, 22)

5) My Hope. (71:5)

6) My Trust. (71:5)

7) My Strong Refuge. (71:7)

8) My Help. (71:12)

There's plenty of biblical substance in those eight names to have your own *personal* worship service. What a God we serve! May our pursuit of the Lord, like the psalmist's, cause us to really know our God by each of these titles.

As we continue our journey through life, we must always remember that the enemy is constantly seeking to shut us down and shut us up! That is, he wants to take our passion for God out of our souls and take our praise for God out of our mouths. Understanding the enemy's desire prompted the psalmist to say, "But I will hope continually, and will yet praise thee more and more" (71:14). Let's all make that our resolve today!

Psalm 72 is, in my estimation, a "psalm of psalms." It's an incredible Old Testament declaration of praise for the Lord Jesus Christ at His second coming! As the Queen of Sheba presented herself before Solomon, Israel's king, the son of David who sat enthroned in his wisdom, splendor, majesty, and glory over the entire world in 1 Kings 10, we see a picture of the splendor and glory that will be our Lord's when He finally takes up His throne in His millennial kingdom (72:10). In that day, the Lord Jesus Christ will unleash His power in judgment upon the earth (72:1–6) and will establish His authority and rule over the entire earth (72:7–9). Read and rejoice, my brothers and sisters! May this reality cause all of us to love His appearing with Paul (2 Tim. 4:8), long for His appearing with John (1 John 3:1–3), and pray for His appearing, per our Lord's instruction in Matthew 6:10.

In Psalm 73, Asaph voices what all of us have felt at one time or another: Why does it seem that the wicked prosper and the righteous get stepped on? (73:11–14). As Asaph said, sometimes it can almost get the best of you (73:2) or make you want to throw in the towel (73:16). So why does it seem that's the way it shakes out in life? Well, for the most part, because that's the way it is—in this life. What we sometimes forget, however, is that *this life* is not all there is! Asaph was reminded of that when he went "into the sanctuary of God, then understood I their end" (73:17). May God, likewise, grant us that eternal perspective today (2 Cor. 4:18).

Psalm 74 is Asaph's attempt at praying for the Kingdom to come—and quite a good one at that! May it, likewise, be the prayer of our hearts!

Psalm 75 deals with Israel and the Second Coming of Christ. In verses 2–6, the Lord Himself is speaking in the first person. How awesome is that? Also in verse 6, "promotion cometh." Here's the clue the psalmist gives us: It's not from the east, nor the west, nor from the south. So, obviously, it comes from the north! And why will it come from the north? Check out Psalm 48:2; Hebrews 12:22; Isaiah 14:13; and Ezekiel 1:4. The Bible is an amazing book!

Psalm 76 is another great description of our Lord's awesomeness, as He rises "to judgment" and descends upon the earth at His Second Coming (76:9). Can you answer the question of verse 7: "who may stand in thy sight when once thou art angry?" Let's answer with the words of the old hymn: "No, not one! No, not one!"

Psalm 77 also describes the Second Coming and millennium. Just when the nation of Israel is "in the day of [her] trouble" at Armageddon, when all the nations of the earth have converged upon her and she is crying out, "Will the Lord cast off for ever? and will he be favourable no more? Is his mercy clean gone for ever? doth his promise fail for evermore? Hath God forgotten to be gracious? hath he in anger shut up his tender mercies?" (77:7-9)—then notice the very next word: Selah! At that moment, when the only direction Israel can possibly look is up, the Lord Jesus Christ will step out of heaven riding on a white horse with the armies of heaven behind Him (Rev. 16:15–21; 19:11–19) and go ballistic upon all His enemies to establish "on earth peace, good will toward men" (Luke 2:14). Verses 16–19 of Psalm 77 describe the Second Coming, as our Lord steps out of the third heaven, descends through the deep that is above our heads (Gen. 1:6–7; Job 38:30; 41:31–32), and comes thundering into the earth's atmosphere, all the way down to the Mount of Olives (Zech. 14:4). What a day that will be! Let's pray it'll be seven years from today!

CHRIST IS REVEALED:

As the *Rock* – Psalm 71:3 (1 Cor. 10:4)

As the *Righteous Judge* – Psalm 72:2, 4 (2 Thess. 1:5–9)

As the *Speaker* – Psalm 75:2–6

WEEK 26, DAY 4: **TODAY'S READING: PSALM 78-82**

OVERVIEW:

The judgment of the Lord against disobedience; Asaph's prayer against enemies; Asaph's prayer for mercy and restoration.

HIGHLIGHTS & INSIGHTS:

Psalm 78 is just an incredible psalm that provides an abbreviated overview of Israel's history from Exodus 7 to 2 Samuel 10.

As we learned in Numbers 14:18 and Exodus 34:6–7, God warns that the iniquities of the fathers are visited all the way down to the third and fourth generations. In other words, the effects of sin are incredibly far reaching. And again, this principle is not teaching that *judgment* for a father's iniquities is visited to the third and fourth generation, but that the *propensities* toward those particular iniquities are "visited" that deep into a family line. At anytime, anyone in a family can choose to trust Christ as their Savior and, thereby, not only break the generational cycle of sin, but, by God's grace, choose to create a cycle of righteousness! Psalm 78 lets us know that the righteousnesses of the fathers are likewise visited to the third and fourth generation! Notice the four generations in 78:5–6:

> For he established a testimony in Jacob, and appointed a law in Israel, which he commanded our *fathers* [generation #1], that they should make them known to *their children* [generation #2]: that the *generation to come* [generation #3] might know them, even the children which should be born; who should arise and declare them to *their children* [generation #4]. (emphasis added)

The psalmist also gives four reasons to pass this kind of righteous heritage to our generational offspring in verses 7–8. Notice that two are positive and two are negative: "That they might set their hope in God [positive], and not forget the works of God [negative], but keep his commandments [positive]: and might not be as their fathers [negative]."

Psalm 78 also includes one of the most horrific things that God could ever do to a person—"He gave them their own desire" (v. 29). This is a collision course for disaster without exception, because what man naturally desires is always contrary to what God desires for him! Paul warned his son in the faith, Timothy, about four things we naturally desire (or "love")—our self (2 Tim. 3:2), pleasure (2 Tim. 3:4), money (1 Tim. 6:10), and "this present world" (2 Tim. 4:10). Psalm 78:29 should cause all of us to pray, "O God, please don't give me what I want!"

Psalm 78:40–41 lists five things Israel did against God after their deliverance out of Egypt.

- They "provoked" God. (Ps. 78:40a; 1 Thess. 5:19)
- They "grieved" God. (Ps. 78:40b; Eph. 4:30)
- They "turned back" from God. (Ps. 78:41a; 2 Tim. 4:10)
- They "tempted" God. (Ps. 78:41b; 1 Cor. 10:9)
- They "limited" God. (Ps. 78:41c; Heb. 4:2)

These five things were the result of the two root sins listed in verse 42: "They remembered not his hand, nor the day when he delivered them from the enemy." We get into a whole bunch of trouble when we forget ("remember not") what God did on our behalf the day He saved us ("delivered us from the enemy"), everything He did to bring us to that point (John 6:44), and all He has done since that day (Rev. 2:4–5; Rom. 1:21). Deuteronomy 6:12 says it plainly, "Then beware lest thou forget the Lord, which brought thee forth out of the land of Egypt, from the house of bondage." God help us today to remember!

Psalm 79 and 80 are simple to understand when we consider the three layers of application. Both psalms point doctrinally (prophetically) to Israel in the Tribulation, just prior to the Second Coming of Christ. The "wild beast" in Psalm 80:13 is defined in Hosea 13:8 as none other than "the beast" of Revelation 13. He is like a leopard, a bear, and a lion (Hosea 13:7–8), just as in Revelation 13:2 and Daniel 7:3–6. It's amazing what God will reveal (1 Cor. 2:10) when we compare Scripture with Scripture (1 Cor. 2:13).

In Psalm 81, the "solemn feast day" in verse 3 points to the second coming of Christ which will line up—just as did His first coming—with the Feast of Tabernacles. It's too detailed to get into here, but for a little recreation and enjoyment, check out 2 Chronicles 7:9; Nehemiah 8:18; Hosea 9:5; 12:9; Leviticus 23:34; Deuteronomy 16:13; 31:10; 2 Chronicles 8:13 and Ezra 3:4.

The context in Psalm 82 is set once again by the insertion of the word *Selah* (82:2) and by the last verse, "Arise, O God, judge the earth: for thou shalt inherit all nations" (v. 8). What an awesome God and an awesome Book!

CHRIST IS REVEALED:

As the *Shepherd* – Psalm 80:1 (John 10:11)

As the one who will *Arise to Deliver Israel out of her Trouble* – Psalm 80:7, 14, 19; 82:8 (Rev. 16:15–21; 19:19)

WEEK 26, DAY 5: **TODAY'S READING: PSALM 83-89**

OVERVIEW:

The psalmist's cry for deliverance for Israel; the blessedness of living in the midst of God's presence; David's desire to walk in truth; cry for deliverance from death; praise for God's covenant and promises.

HIGHLIGHTS & INSIGHTS:

Psalm 83 also points prophetically to the Second Coming of Christ. Asaph describes this incredible event, as do the other writers of Scripture, as a time when all of the nations of the world (83:6–8) will have converged "together with one consent … confederate against" the nation of Israel (83:5) to "cut them off from being a nation; that the name of Israel may be no more in remembrance" (83:4). At the end of the Tribulation when, humanly speaking, Israel is helpless and hopeless with nowhere to turn—at that very moment, our Lord Jesus Christ will step out of heaven and answer their prayers (83:1). The Apostle John reveals that Christ will return with such fury against Israel's enemies in that day that their blood will literally rise up to the horse's bridles in the Valley of Megiddo (Rev. 14:20). Asaph's prayer in 83:13–18 will, in fact, be answered:

> O my God, make them like a wheel; as the stubble before the wind. As the fire burneth a wood, and as the flame setteth the mountains on fire; So persecute them with thy tempest, and make them afraid with thy storm. Fill their faces with shame; that they may seek thy name, O Lord. Let them be confounded and troubled for ever; yea, let them be put to shame, and perish: That men may know that thou, whose name alone is Jehovah, art the most high over all the earth.

And when our backs are against the wall, when from a human standpoint we are helpless and hopeless with nowhere to turn, may this psalm remind us that "there is nothing too hard for the Lord" (Jer. 32:17). May it remind us that our God hears and answers prayer (Ps. 65:2). May it flood us with confidence that "in the day of [our] trouble," He can and will step in to do what could never be done in our own strength or power (Ps. 86:7). And may we remember that He's already proven that He can and will answer our prayers in this way—because that is what our Lord did on our behalf when, in our lost condition, we cried out to the Lord for our salvation (Eph. 2:11–17). At that time, Christ stepped in to do what we could have never done in our own strength or power. And again I say, hallelujah!

Just like the psalmist, though, the basis for our requests, and the driving passion of our entire lives, must be the glory of God Himself: "That men may know that thou, whose name alone is JEHOVAH (the "self-existing one"), art the most high over all the earth" (83:18).

Psalm 84 is a song of praise, again in the context of "the day of the Lord" (84:4, 8 – Selah). During the millennium, our Lord Jesus Christ will once again "tabernacle" among us (Ps. 84:1; John 1:14). And today, is the passion of the psalmist's heart for God and His glory in verse 2 also in our hearts? Can we genuinely and honestly say with the psalmist, "My soul longeth, yea, even fainteth for the courts of the Lord: my heart and my flesh crieth out for the living God" (84:2).

The last part of 84:11 is also a great promise and reminder. "The Lord will give grace and glory: no good thing will he withhold from them that walk uprightly." God most certainly withholds certain things, but contrary to Satan's lies (see Genesis 3:5), it is never because He is keeping something *good* from us. His restrictions are always to keep us from something He knows will be *bad* for us, something that will ultimately be harmful to us or destroy us. It can be difficult, in our flesh, to believe that, and the father of lies (John 8:44) is trying at every turn to convince us otherwise. In light of that, the end of Psalm 84 is very fitting, "O Lord of hosts, blessed is the man that trusteth in thee" (84:12).

The millennial context is also seen in Psalm 85. The description of that time is laid out beautifully: "Mercy and truth are met together; righteousness and peace have kissed each other" (85:10). But it is also beautiful when these realities exist in the life of a New Testament believer! Mercy with no regard for truth makes us wishy-washy, spineless, and too accommodating of unholy doctrine and unholy living in the church of the Lord Jesus Christ. On the other hand, truth with no regard for mercy makes us harsh, judgmental, and unloving. God's intention is that, like His Son (John 1:14), we have a perfect balance of both! (See Eph. 4:25; Eph. 4:15.)

Psalm 86:5 and 15 are favorites of mine. "For thou, Lord, art good, and ready to forgive; and plenteous in mercy unto all them that call upon thee ... thou, O Lord, art a God full of compassion, and gracious, longsuffering, and plenteous in mercy and truth." How we need those reminders—especially those of us who feel the need to do "penance," as it were, before we can let go of our spiritual failures and sins? Before we even come to Him, He is "ready to forgive," a fact made abundantly clear by the sacrifice of His only and beloved Son (1 John 4:9).

For those in the depths of despair today, we can find comfort and solace through the words of the psalmist in Psalm 88 as he lifts his complaint to the Lord, and then, we can allow the Lord to bring us out of despair through Psalm 89, where the psalmist expresses his confidence and praise to the Lord!

CHRIST IS REVEALED:

By the *Seed of David* – Psalm 89:3–4 (Christ was made of the seed of David according to the flesh – Matt. 1:1; Luke 3:31–32)

Mark Trotter was born and raised in Miami, Florida. He pastored First Baptist Church of New Philadelphia, Ohio, for 25 years, and served as the Teaching Pastor at Northwest Bible Church in Hilliard, Ohio, for eight years. In 2016, Mark moved his base of ministry to ONE Baptist Church in Douglasville, Georgia, following his heart's desire to wholly devote his ministry to the things for which he is passionate—namely, the reproduction of disciples/churches, and the training of pastors and leaders for ministry, both of which he does nationally and internationally. Mark and his wife, Sherry, have two grown children: Justin and his wife, Morgan, and Jacie and her husband, Justin. The Lord has also blessed Mark and Sherry with four precious grandchildren.